Are Legal Systems Converging or Diverging?

Emilie Ghio • Ricardo Perlingeiro
Editors

Are Legal Systems Converging or Diverging?

Lessons from Contemporary Crises

Springer

Editors
Emilie Ghio
University of Edinburgh
Edinburgh, UK

Ricardo Perlingeiro
Fluminense Federal University
Rio de Janeiro, Brazil

ISBN 978-3-031-38179-9 ISBN 978-3-031-38180-5 (eBook)
https://doi.org/10.1007/978-3-031-38180-5

This Springer imprint is published by the registered company Springer Nature Switzerland AG
The registered company address is: Gewerbestrasse 11, 6330 Cham, Switzerland

Paper in this product is recyclable.

Contents

Editors and Contributors

About the Editors

Emilie Ghio is a lecturer in corporate and insolvency law at the University of Edinburgh. She studied law at the University of Strasbourg in France and at University College Cork in Ireland before moving to England and, eventually, Scotland. She is an established and active corporate insolvency and rescue law scholar with an expansive domestic and international research portfolio, which includes numerous and varied publications (monographs, textbooks, peer-reviewed journal articles, conference proceedings, expert technical magazine articles). Emilie is currently working on several national and international research projects and is engaged with a wide network of UK, European, and international academics, industry representatives, and policymakers in insolvency law. She currently sits on the board of the Younger Academic Network of Insolvency Law and is the co-editor of the INSOL Europe Conference Proceedings and Yearbook.

Ricardo Perlingeiro has over three decades of experience as a Federal Court Judge in Brazil and as a professor of International Law and Public Law. He is currently a professor at Fluminense Federal University (Brazil), as well as a visiting professor at Birmingham City University (United Kingdom) and a visiting researcher at the University of Porto (Portugal). Professor Perlingeiro has published countless books and articles on the topics of international law and public law in Portuguese and other languages, such as Chinese, English, German, Italian, Russian, and Spanish. He was the Secretary-General of the Committee that developed the Model Code of International Judicial Cooperation for Ibero-America. He is a member of the International Academy of Comparative Law, International Association of Constitutional Law, International Association of Procedural Law, among other academic institutions.

List of Contributors

David Cabrelli The University of Edinburgh, Edinburgh Law School, Edinburgh, UK

Katharina Ó Cathaoir Faculty of Law, University of Copenhagen, Copenhagen, Denmark

Laura N. Coordes Arizona State University, Sandra Day O'Connor College of Law, Phoenix, AZ, USA

J. C. A. van Dam Dutch Council of State and Department of Constitutional and Administrative Law at Leiden University, Leiden, The Netherlands

Jennifer L. L. Gant University of Derby, College of Business, Law and Social Sciences, Derby, UK

Beth Gaze University of Melbourne Law School, Carlton, VIC, Australia

Emilie Ghio University of Edinburgh, Edinburgh, UK

Hannes Henke Martin-Luther-University Halle-Wittenberg, Halle (Saale), Germany

Fabiola Lathrop Gomez University of Chile, Santiago, RM, Chile

Lydia A. Nkansah Faculty of Law, Kwame Nkrumah University of Science and Technology, Kumasi, Ghana

Ricardo Perlingeiro Fluminense Federal University, Niterói, Brazil
Birmingham City University, Birmingham, UK

Antonios E. Platsas The University of the West of England, College of Business and Law, Bristol, UK

Natalia A. Voronina Institute of Migration and Inter-Ethnic Relations (Институт миграции и межнациональных отношений), An Autonomous Non-Commercial Organisation, Moscow, Russia

Luo Wenjun School of Law, Hubei University of Economics, Hubei, China

Wang Xi School of Law, Kunming University of Science and Technology, Platform for Promoting Research on Ecological Civilization and Environmental Rule of Law, Kunming, China
School of Law, Shanghai Jiao Tong University, Shanghai, China

Nuhu Yidana School of Law, SOAS University of London, London, UK

Bruno Zeller University of Western Australia, Crawley, WA, Australia

List of Abbreviations

ACAS	Advisory, Conciliation and Arbitration Service
ACFTA	African Continental Free Trade Area
AHCR	Australian Human Rights Commission
ALP	Australian Labor Party
AQR	Asset Quality Review
BGB	*Bürgerliches Gesetzbuch* (German Civil Code)
CAP	Coronavirus Alleviation Program
CEAS	Common European Asylum System
CEDAW	Convention on Elimination of Discrimination Against Women
CENELEC	European Committee for Electrotechnical Standardization
CERD	Convention on the Elimination of Racial Discrimination
CESCR	Committee on Economic, Social and Cultural Rights
CESL	Common European Sales Law
CIS	Commonwealth of Independent States
CISG	Convention on Contracts for the International Sale of Goods
CISPR	International Special Committee on Radio Interference
CJRS	Coronavirus job retention scheme
COMI	Centre of main interests
COVID-19	Coronavirus Disease 2019
CPC	Communist Party of China
CRC	Convention on the Rights of the Child
DDA	Disability Discrimination Act 1992
DCFR	Draft Common Frame of Reference
EAEU	Eurasian Economic Union
EASO	European Asylum Support Office
ECB	European Central Bank
ECE	Electronic Communication Equipment
ECHR	European Convention on Human Rights
ECtHR	European Court of Human Rights
ECOPOP	Ecology and Population

ECSC	European Coal and Steel Community
EFSF	European Financial Stability Facility
EGBGB	*Einführungsgesetz zum Bürgerlichen Gesetzbuche* (Introductory Act to the German Civil Code)
EI	Executive instruments
EIA	Environmental impact assessment
ELI	European Law Institute
EMU	European Monetary Union
EPA	Environmental Protection Agency
ESM	European Stability Mechanism
ETSI	European Telecommunication Standards Institute
EU	European Union
EUUKCA	EU-UK Trade and Cooperation Agreement
FCC	Federal Communications Commission
FDA	Food and Drugs Authority
FSB	Financial Stability Board
GALA	General Administrative Law Act
GAT	Ghana Amalgamated Trust
GCB	Ghana Commercial Bank
GDP	Gross domestic product
GFC	Great financial crisis
HCCH	Hague Conference on Private International Law
HECS	Higher Education Contribution Scheme
HGB	*Handelsgesetzbuch* (German Commercial Code)
HRA	Human Rights Act 2004
HRAQ	Queensland Human Rights Act 2019
IATA	International Air Transport Association
IC	Industry Canada
ICAO	International Civil Aviation Organization
ICC	International Chambre of Commerce
ICCPR	International Covenant on Civil and Political Rights
ICESCR	International Covenant on Economic, Social and Cultural Rights
ICT	Information Communication Technology
IDA	Infocomm Development Authority of Singapore
IEC	International Electrotechnical Commission
ILO	International Labour Organization
IMF	International Monetary Fund
IOM	International Organization on Migration
IPA	Interparliamentary Assembly
IPPEP	Interaction of Parties in the Process of Environmental Protection
LEI	Legal Entity Identifier
MiFID	Markets in Financial Instruments Directive
MSE	Micro and small enterprise
NAFTA	North American Free Trade Agreement

NATO	North Atlantic Treaty Organization
NCA	National Communication Authority
NDIS	National Disability Insurance Scheme
NGO	Non-governmental organization
NDC	New Democratic Congress
NPP	New Patriotic Party
OAS	Organization of American States
OECD	Organization for Economic Cooperation and Development
OMC	Open Method of Coordination
OSCE	Organization for Security and Cooperation in Europe
PECL	Principles of European Contract Law
PIDA	Public Interest Disclosure Act 1998
PIL	Private international law
PPTD	Proposal for a Pay Transparency Directive
RCORE	Regional Centre of Regulatory Excellence
RIVM	*Rijksinstituut voor Volksgezondheid en Milieu* (National Institute for Public Health and the Environment, The Netherlands)
SEISS	Self-Employment Income Support Scheme
SICREMI	Continuous Reporting System on International Migration in the Americas
SRM	Single Resolution Mechanism
TAG 2015	Type Approval Guidelines 2015
TCA	Trade and Cooperation Agreement
TCA	Temporary Corona Act 2020 (The Netherlands)
TEU	Treaty on the European Union
TFEU	Treaty on the Functioning of the European Union
TPWCD	Transparent and Predictable Working Conditions Directive
UN	United Nations
UNCITRAL	United Nation Commission on International Trade Law
UNHCR	United Nations High Commissioner on Refugees
UNIDROIT	United Nations International Institute for the Unification of Private Law
UK	United Kingdom
US	United States
WD	Whistleblowing Directive
WHO	World Health Organization
WTO	World Trade Organization

Introduction: Convergence and Divergence in Times of Crisis

Emilie Ghio

1 Introduction

While legal harmonisation/convergence is considered to be one of the most influential theses in the discipline of law,[1] the law of harmonisation is full of paradoxes. On the one hand, legal borrowing is commonplace, leading to a phenomenon of convergence; on the other hand, it is widely accepted that 'legal systems are not converging.'[2]

Legal convergence is not a new concept. The philosophical underpinnings of the concept, and consequently the concept of convergence itself, can be traced back to Socrates and Plato. Indeed, there is a close connection between Plato's theory of universals[3] and the concept of legal convergence itself. Beyond scholarly writings, legal history has undeniably been characterised by enormous borrowings. Examples of legal transplants date back to the Code of Hammurabi (seventeenth century BC)[4] and public law transplants have been common for centuries, especially as states in political transition have sought to emulate prestigious models as they have sought to transform their laws into those of dominant powers.[5]

As the twenty-first century unfolds, individual nations' affairs, news, and problems increasingly reach and captivate global audiences. During the last few decades, the internationalisation and transnationalisation of law have reached unprecedented

[1] Platsas (2009).
[2] Legrand (1996).
[3] Plato (1997).
[4] Watson (1974), pp. 22–24.
[5] Owen (2002).

E. Ghio (✉)
University of Edinburgh, Edinburgh, UK
e-mail: Emilie.ghio@ed.ac.uk

E. Ghio, R. Perlingeiro (eds.), *Are Legal Systems Converging or Diverging?*,
https://doi.org/10.1007/978-3-031-38180-5_1

levels. All lawyers understand that modern domestic laws are increasingly influenced by international legal developments. This situation has been exacerbated by the phenomenon of globalisation, characterised by Giddens as 'the intensification of world-wide social relations which link localities in such a way that local happenings are shaped by events occurring many miles away and vice versa.'[6] Twining, on the other hand, defined the term as 'those processes which tend to create and consolidate a unified world economy, a single ecological system, and a complex network of communications that covers the whole globe, even if it does not penetrate to every part of it.'[7] While some argue that the term 'globalisation' has been overused in recent years,[8] it nonetheless 'represents the reality that we live in at a time when the walls of sovereignty are no protection against the movement of capital, labor, information and ideas.'[9] Due to its ability to bring cultures and laws together, globalisation has facilitated legal transplants as law makers have resorted to the use foreign legal models. This can be explained by the fact that '[i]f the law is to retain its role of regulating society (be it no longer a national, but a global one), we have to find new ways of making law and enforcing this law.'[10] Therefore, it is generally believed that globalisation forces national legal orders to converge. In spite of this, wars, ideological conflicts, divergent national interests, and cultural clashes have led to some resistance to legal convergence. As a result, the legal world remains fragmented and governed by many different regimes. In various areas of law, one can still find diverging elements between different jurisdictions.

It is therefore not surprising that the over the years, scholarship debating the merits or shortcomings of legal convergence has abounded, often integrated into broader issues within the fields of legal history, comparative law, law reform, law and development, post-conflict reconstruction, transnational justice, legal theory, sociology of law, and so on.[11]

2 The Convergence/Divergence Scholarship

On the one hand, scholars have long postulated a relationship between the law and the society in which it operates so close that legal transplants, or legal convergence, ought to be virtually impossible. These claims are generally rooted in arguments of national sovereignty, path dependence, and legal cultures. Ever since the emergence of the nation-state, law-making has primarily been a task for national legislators (and/or courts). They make laws for relatively homogeneous societies that are

[6] Giddens (1990), p. 64.

[7] Twining (2000), p. 4.

[8] Platsas (2009).

[9] Higgins (1999), p. 82.

[10] Smits (2007), p. 1181.

[11] Twining (2009), p. 271.

usually characterised by a common culture. Therefore, the idea of law-making is closely tied to the notion of self-determination which promote a local process of law-making rather than the sourcing legal rules from a foreign supply. The sixteenth century French philosopher Jean Bodin defined 'sovereignty' as a 'supreme principle of citizens and subjects, unbound by the law [. . .] a perpertual, humanly unlimited, and unconditional right to make, interpret and execute law.'[12] The British philosopher Thomas Hobbes developed the concept further by associating it with the central role of the nation-state.[13] The idea of popular sovereignty gradually aligned state jurisdictions with nations as personifying the populi. Today, the term 'sovereignty' generally refers to notions of legitimacy, power, and authority, usually associated with a particular geographical territory. The issue with legal convergence, therefore, is that the notion itself clashes with this prevailing idea of law-making as closely tied to a state's sovereignty and self-determination. Laws are produced locally, rather than sourced from a foreign supply.

A second salient problem of law-making is how to deal with increasingly divergent legal cultures. Ever since the emergence of the nation-state, law-making has primarily been a task for the national legislator. They make laws for relatively homogeneous societies that are usually characterised by a common language and a common culture. Savigny highlighted the significance of the *Volksgeist* (the spirit of the people).[14] Characteristics identifiable as part of the nation-state were invoked as dimensions of national (legal) culture.

Associated with legal culture is the concept of path dependence, which means that a decision is shaped by the historical path leading to it, implying that 'what happened at an earlier point in time will affect the possible outcomes of a sequence of events occurring at a later point in time.'[15] This reinforces the idea that legal rules are embedded within a legal system and therefore, are interconnected with rules, concepts, institutions, and practices within that states. Oliver Wendell Holmes argued that 'if we want to know why a rule of law has taken its particular shape, and more or less if we want to know why it exists at all, we go for tradition.'[16] Richard Posner agreed that the law 'venerates tradition, precedent, [. . .] custom, ancient practices, ancient texts, archaic terminology [. . .] and interpretation conceived of as a method of recovering history. It is suspicious of [. . .] discontinuities.'[17]

Nationalist arguments usually suggest that the adoption of foreign law undermines national culture and national identity and goes against the path-dependent nature of law. In the words of Montesquieu, the laws of each country 'should be so adapted to the people for whom they are made, that it is more chance if those of one

[12] Sabine (1961), pp. 405–407.

[13] Hobbes (1651).

[14] Savigny (1973).

[15] Sewell Jr (1996), pp. 262–263.

[16] Wendell Holmes (1998), p. 708.

[17] Posner (2000), p. 573.

nation can suit another.'[18] Otto Kahn-Freund added that 'we cannot take for granted that rules or institutions are transplantable [. . .] [A]ny attempt to use a pattern of law outside the environment of its origin continues to entail the risk of rejection.'[19] Lawrence Friedman asserted that American law was not to be treated as 'a kingdom unto itself, not as a set of rules and concepts, not as the province of lawyers alone, but as a mirror of society. It takes nothing as historical accident, nothing as autonomous, everything as relative and molded by economy and society.'[20] Ultimately, Pierre Legrand claimed that law being an 'outgrowth of local society [. . .] embedded holistically in local culture [. . .] mak[es] reception and assimilation of foreign ideas problematic.'[21] He argued that '[c]omparison must not have a unifying, but multiplying effect [. . .] It must avoid complicity in the disregard for different ways of doing things and the ensuring exclusion of alterity.'[22] In his view, legal transplants do not work; legal rules cannot be transposed from one legal system to another and therefore, legal systems will never converge.[23]

On the other hand, studies promoting legal convergence are extensive and varied. Historically, they can be traced back to scholars such as Gabriel Tarde, Sir Henry Maine, and Max Weber. In particular, since World War II, landmark debates have abounded. First, about the reception of Roman Law in Europe, illustrated by the works of Paul Koschaker[24] and Franz Wieacker,[25] as well as the subsequent debates which these writings have produced.[26] Second, the literature has focused on legal systems imports or imposition by colonising powers.[27] These studies generally overlap with the literature on legal pluralism and that on law and development.[28] Third, focus has also been placed on voluntary receptions of foreign rules.[29] Fourth, an account of the literature on legal convergence cannot be complete without mentioning Alan Watson's transplant thesis,[30] and the subsequent discussions from Otto Kahn-Freund and Ugo Mattei for example.[31] As famously claimed by Watson, 'the transplanting of individual rules or of a large part of a legal system is extremely common [. . .] [T]ransplanting is, in fact, the most fertile source of

[18] Montesquieu (1748), Book I, Chapter 3.

[19] Kahn-Freund (1974).

[20] Friedman (1985), p. 12.

[21] Legrand (2003), p. 248.

[22] Ibid, p. 299.

[23] Legrand (1996).

[24] Koschaker (1953).

[25] Wieacker (1981, 1990).

[26] See Watson (1991); Tuori and Björklund (2018).

[27] See Burman and Harrell-Bond (1979); Chanock (1985).

[28] See Merryman (1977); Merry (1988); Whytock (2009).

[29] Örücü (1995, 1999, 2000, 2002, 2004).

[30] Watson (1974, 1976).

[31] See Watson (2000a, b, 2007); Kahn-Freund (1974); Mattei (1997).

development. Most changes in most systems are the result of borrowing.'[32] Finally, in recent years, as part of the European integration debate, there has been a considerable increase in academic and practical interest in law reform and harmonisation.[33]

3 Objective of This Book and Originality

While both camps have presented compelling arguments, rooted in varied studies of different legal fields or jurisdictions, no consensus has emerged. Therefore, the question of whether legal systems are converging or diverging remains unanswered. This book inserts itself in this intellectual odyssey of the concepts of legal convergence and legal pluralism. It contributes to the rich comparative law and legal transplants literature by examining legal convergence through the prism of contemporary crises. This book tests the validity of Konrad Zweigert and Hein Kötz's argument that 'legal systems give the same or very similar solutions, even as to detail, to the same problems of life.'[34]

It has long been argued that globalisation, and increased transnational exchanges, predispose the world toward more crises. With the growth of trade, finance, travel, and other networks, their complexity and instability have increased. According to Edward Lorenz, founder of chaos theory, a butterfly flapping its wings over Brazil could cause a tornado in Texas.[35] As the world economy becomes more integrated and complex, it too suffers from this butterfly effect. Indeed, the increase in the mobility of goods and services, as well as human mobility, have facilitated the spread of global crises.

Crises are thus relevant for the legal convergence thesis because they challenge countries' legal systems and prompt some institutional responses to tackle perceived shortcomings in the law. The crises witnessed by the world over the last two decades have highlighted two paradoxical tendencies:

(i) increased cooperation and a natural phenomenon of legal convergence as States find common solutions to common problems;[36] or
(ii) a preference for state-centric solutions, which prioritise domestic interests, a rejection of supranational standards and harmonisation efforts and a protection of domestic sovereignty, possibly leading to a phenomenon of legal disintegration.[37]

[32] Watson (1974), p. 95.
[33] Ghio (2022); Andenas and Baasch Andersen (2011); Legrand (2002).
[34] Zweigert and Kötz (1998), pp. 39–40.
[35] Lorenz (1963).
[36] Ghio et al. (2021).
[37] See Dyevre et al. (2018); Leruth et al. (2019); Sornarajah (2020).

Crises are an interesting phenomenon to study because they 'don't always go the shock doctrine path. In fact, it's possible for crises to catalyze a kind of evolutionary leap.'[38]

'It is a hard time to be alive. It's a time of concurrent crises.'[39] Indeed, in the last two decades only, the word 'crisis' has not merely become common; it is now everywhere. In the late 2000s, the world was hit by the failure of the sub-prime mortgage market. The 2008 collapse of the Lehman Brothers sent shockwaves around the world markets with the collapse of Greece in 2010, practically declaring itself bankruptcy by invoking the International Monetary Fund's intervention at the time. These events were followed by a civil war in Syria since 2011 and the political instability of Ukraine in 2014. In 2015, the European Union (EU) was hit by a severe immigration crisis and the world markets saw the collapse of the price of oil and in 2020, the United Kingdom (UK) left the EU. The world was recently hit by a global health pandemic, which resulted in over a million deaths to date. The COVID-19 pandemic forced many countries around the world to impose special measures on their populations such as self-isolation and restriction of movement and assembly, thereby directly affecting legal relationships, legal transactions, and legal systems overall.

In the last year or so alone, new crises have emerged. At the time of writing, it is too early to predict whether the world is on the brink of yet another financial crisis following the collapse of Credit Suisse in March 2023. Nonetheless, several commentators are worried about the prospects of contagion. A year prior, in February 2022, a full-scale invasion of Ukraine, targeting Ukrainian military assets and cities across the country was announced by Vladimir Putin. The Russian invasion of Ukraine shattered the rule established after World War II that borders should not be changed through force. Additionally, for the first time since the end of the Cold War, the threat of nuclear war has been revived. Over a year later, the conflict is still ongoing. The conflict has a broader impact on key cooperation issues such as arms control, cybersecurity, nuclear non-proliferation, global economic stability, energy security, as well as counterterrorism. Military operations and violence are hindering the delivery and distribution of much-needed aid, including food, and worsening the shortage of humanitarian resources globally. Financial markets have been thrown into turmoil, creating a significant uncertainty about the global economy's recovery. A rise in commodity prices has resulted in a 'costs of living' crisis around the world, increasing the risk of stagflation and social unrest. Aside from these destabilising effects, Russia's increasing isolation has also led to new strategic ties, in particular with China.

Therefore, the study of crises is more relevant than ever. After all, the word 'crisis' in Chinese is composed of two characters: 'danger' and 'opportunity'. A crisis, therefore, is an opportunity, a 'moment of truth'.[40] It is thus not surprising that

---

[38] Democracy Now (2020).

[39] Vashon-Maury Island Beachcomber (2020).

[40] Van Middelaar (2014).

Michael Reisman and Andrew Willard argues that crises should be at the heart of legal teaching and scholarship.[41] Studying the legal convergence thesis through the lens of crises provides a focus for the development of the discipline.

4 Structure of This Book

Studies in convergence or divergence have traditionally adopted:

- a purely thematic approach, *i.e.* comparatively studying whether one area of law is converging across countries;[42]
- a common law versus civil law dichotomy;[43]
- a purely theoretical or historical perspective;[44]
- a focus on international entities (especially the EU);[45]
- an interdisciplinary approach, usually mixing law, political sciences and/or economics;[46] and
- a focus on the evolution of an area of law following a specific crisis.[47]

Unlike these studies, this volume takes an international and cross-thematic approach with chapters focusing on how legal areas in selected jurisdictions have responded to crises. Therefore, its originality lies in:

(i) its truly global nature, with chapters and authors surveying jurisdictions in Africa, North and South America, Asia, Europe and Oceania;
(ii) the breath of legal areas covered, with a mix of private and public law areas; and
(iii) its focus on the evolution of these fields following varied domestic and international contemporary crises.

From Russia to Germany and from bankruptcy law to environmental law, the book examines whether, as a result of crises, policy and legal responses have adopted, copied, or implemented features, policies, principles and/or rules from other legal systems (convergence), or departed from existing legal norms or adopted policies and rules that are different from those of other countries (divergence).

[41] Reisman and Willard (1988), p. 15.

[42] Naude (2019); Siems (2008); van Niekerk (2002); Mullineux (2007); Robertson and Tilbury (2016); Goanta (2016).

[43] Mattei and Pres (2008); Nottage (2001).

[44] Legrand (1996).

[45] Fahey (2020); Martinico and Pollicino (2012); Beaumont et al. (2002).

[46] Crettez (2014); Platsas (2009); Fahey (2020).

[47] Gant (2016); Shadad (2009); Hernes (2018).

The book is structured as follows. Part 1 provides some conceptual and theoretical perspectives on core concepts which are discussed in the book. Emilie Ghio and David Cabrelli give brief definitions of key notions and terminology used throughout the volume, including 'globalisation', 'crisis', 'integration', 'disintegration' and 'harmonisation'. Antonios Platsas then explores the essence of the idea of legal convergence. It assesses the feasibility of genuine legal convergence projects by exploring, in particular, the theory of legal transplants. Finally, Jennifer Gant considers the concept of divergence, against the background of the diversity of legal cultures and path dependency. Her chapter also looks at the political and cultural perspectives which create further obstacles to sustained legal convergence. Against the background of Pierre Legrand's seminal 1990s work, she considers whether legal systems are still not convergence and explores potential reasons as to why this may be the case.

Part 2 of the book contains the first set of cross-thematic and jurisdictional case studies, exploring areas of domestic private law. Each chapter aims at determining whether the selected area in the jurisdiction analysed exhibits aspects of legal convergence and/or divergence. Laura Coordes explores the evolution of bankruptcy law in the United States; David Cabrelli discusses labour law in the United Kingdom; Nuhu Yidana and Lydia Nkansah look at consumer law in Ghana; Fabiola Lathrop looks at family law in Chile; and Hannes Henke analyses contract law in Germany.

Part 3 provides a similar structure while focusing on areas of public law. Wang Xi and Luo Wenjun discuss environmental law in China; Katharina O'Cathaoir analyses healthcare law in Denmark; Natalia Voronina provides an account of immigration law in Russia; and Beth Gaze analyses social rights in Australia.

Finally, Part 4 of the book looks at convergence and divergence in context. Emilie Ghio provides an account of the role of harmonisation in times of crisis; Ricardo Perlingeiro analyses international judicial cooperation in times of crisis and whether it leads to increased legal convergence. Bruno Zeller explores the influence of binding international instruments on domestic law in times of crisis, while Clara Van Dam discusses the role of soft law in times of crisis and whether it can truly promote legal convergence.

References

Andenas M, Baasch Andersen C (eds) (2011) Theory and practice of harmonisation. Edward Elgar Publishing, Cheltenham

Beaumont P et al (2002) Convergence and divergence in European public law. Hart Publishing, Oxford

Burman S, Harrell-Bond B (eds) (1979) The imposition of law. Academic Press, New York

Chanock M (1985) Law, custom, and social order: the colonial experience in Malawi and Zambia. Cambridge University Press, Cambridge

Crettez B (2014) Legal convergence and endogenous preferences. Int Rev Law Econ 39:20–27

Democracy Now (2020) "Coronavirus capitalism": Naomi Klein's case for transformative change amid coronavirus pandemic (19 March 2020). https://www.democracynow.org/2020/3/19/naomi_klein_coronavirus_capitalism
Dyevre A et al (2018) Uncertainty and legal disintegration: evidence from Brexit. https://papers.ssrn.com/sol3/papers.cfm?abstract_id=3276189
Fahey E (ed) (2020) Framing convergence within the global legal order. The EU and the world. Hart Publishing, Oxford
Friedman L (1985) A history of American law. Simon & Schuster, New York
Gant J (2016) Studies in convergence? Post-crisis effects on corporate rescue and the influence of social policy: the EU and the USA. Int Insolv Rev 25:72–96
Ghio E (2022) Redefining harmonisation. Lessons from EU insolvency law. Edward Elgar Publishing, Cheltenham
Ghio E et al (2021) Harmonising insolvency law in the EU: new thoughts on old ideas in the wake of the COVID-19 pandemic. Int Insolv Rev 30:427–459
Giddens A (1990) The consequences of modernity. Stanford University Press, Cambridge
Goanta C (2016) Convergence in European consumer sales law. Intersentia, Cambridge
Hernes V (2018) Cross-national convergence in times of crisis? Integration policies before, during and after the refugee crisis. West Eur Polit 41:1305–1329
Higgins R (1999) International law in a changing international system. Camb Law J 58:78–95
Hobbes T (1651) The Leviathan. Penguin, London
Kahn-Freund O (1974) On the uses and misuses of comparative law. Mod Law Rev 37:1–27
Koschaker P (1953) Europa und das römische Recht. Biederstein, Munich
Legrand P (1996) European legal systems are not converging. Int Comp Law Q 45:52–81
Legrand P (2002) On the unbearable localness of the law: academic fallacies and unseasonable observations. Eur Rev Priv Law 10:61–76
Legrand P (2003) The same and the different. In: Legrand P, Munday R (eds) Comparative legal studies: traditions and transitions. Cambridge University Press, Cambridge
Leruth B et al (2019) Exploring differentiated disintegration in a Post-Brexit European Union. J Common Mark Stud 57:1013–1030
Lorenz E (1963) Deterministic nonperiodic flow. J Atmos Sci 20:130–141
Martinico G, Pollicino O (2012) The interaction between Europe's legal systems. Judicial dialogue and the creation of supranational laws. Edward Elgar, Cheltenham
Mattei U (1997) Comparative law and economics. University of Michigan Press, Ann Arbor
Mattei U, Pres L (2008) Civil law and common law: toward convergence? In: Caldeira G et al (eds) The Oxford handbook of law and politics. Oxford University Press, Oxford, pp 267–280
Merry S (1988) Legal pluralism. Law Soc Rev 22:869–896
Merryman J (1977) Comparative law and social change. On the origins, style, decline and revival of the law and development movement. Am J Comp Law 25:457–482
Montesquieu C (1748) De L'Esprit des Lois. Barillot et fils, Paris
Mullineux A (2007) Financial sector convergence and corporate governance. J Financ Regul Compliance 15:8–19
Naude T (2019) Fragmentation versus convergence of consumer law within one legal system and across legal systems: an African perspective. J Consum Policy 43:11–33
Nottage L (2001) Comment on civil law and common law: two different paths leading to the same goal. Vic Univ Wellingt Law Rev 32:843–852
Örücü E (1995) A theoretical framework for transfrontier mobility of law. In: Jagtenberg R et al (eds) Transfrontier mobility of law. Kluwer Law International, Alphen aan den Rijn
Örücü E (1999) Critical comparative law: considering paradoxes for legal systems in transition. Kluwer, Deventer
Örücü E (2000) Turkey facing the European Union – old and new harmonies. Eur Law Rev 25:523–537

Örücü E (2002) Law as transposition. Int Comp Law Q 51:205–223
Örücü E (2004) The enigma of comparative law: variations on a theme for the 21st century. Martinus Nijhoff, Leiden
Owen J (2002) The foreign imposition of domestic institutions. Int Organ 56:375–409
Plato (1997) The Republic. Wordsworth Editions, Ware
Platsas A (2009) The idea of legal convergence and international economic law. Int J Priv Law 2: 385–399
Posner R (2000) Past-dependency, pragmatism, and critique of history in adjudication and legal scholarship. Univ Chic Law Rev 67:573–606
Reisman M, Willard A (eds) (1988) International incidents: the law that counts in world politics. Princeton University Press, Princeton
Robertson A, Tilbury M (2016) The common law of obligations. Divergence and unity. Hart Publishing, Oxford
Sabine G (1961) A history of political theory. Rinehart and Winston, New York
Savigny FC (1973) Vom Beruf unserer Zeit für Gesetzgebung und Rechtswissenschaft. In: Hattenhauer H (ed) Thibaut und Savigny: Ihre programmatischen Schrifften. F Vahlen, Munich
Sewell W Jr (1996) Three temporalities: toward an eventful sociology. In: McDonald T (ed) The historic turn in the human sciences. University of Michigan Press, Ann Arbor
Shadad H (2009) Coming together after the crisis: global convergence of private equity and hedge funds. Northwest J Int Law Bus 29:603–616
Siems M (2008) Convergence in shareholder law. Cambridge University Press, Cambridge
Smits J (2007) Law making in the European Union: on globalization and contract law in divergent legal cultures. Louisiana Law Rev 67:1181–1203
Sornarajah M (2020) Disintegration and change in the international law on foreign investment. J Int Econ Law 23:413–429
Tuori K, Björklund H (eds) (2018) Roman law and the idea of Europe. Bloomsbury Academic, London
Twining W (2000) Globalisation and legal theory. Cambridge University Press, Cambridge
Twining W (2009) General jurisprudence: understanding law from a global perspective. Cambridge University Press, Cambridge
Van Middelaar L (2014) The crises in the Eurozone and Ukraine have heralded the "return of politics" to European integration. LSE European Politics and Policy Blog (21 May 2014). https://blogs.lse.ac.uk/eurocrisispress/2014/05/21/the-crises-in-the-eurozone-and-ukraine-have-heralded-the-return-of-politics-to-european-integration/
Van Niekerk G (2002) The convergence of legal systems in Southern Africa. Comp Int Law J South Africa 35:308–318
Vashon-Maury Island Beachcomber (2020) A tipping point for humanity (4 June 2020). https://www.vashonbeachcomber.com/opinion/a-tipping-point-for-humanity/
Watson A (1974) Legal transplants: an approach to comparative law. Scottish Academic Press, Edinburgh
Watson A (1976) Legal transplants and law reform. Law Q Rev 92:79–84
Watson A (1991) Roman law and comparative law. University of Georgia Press, Athens
Watson A (2000a) Legal transplants and European private law. Ius Commune Lecture, Maastricht
Watson A (2000b) Law out of context. University of Georgia Press, Athens
Watson A (2007) Comparative law: law, reality and society. Vandeplas Publications, Lake Mary
Wendell Holmes O (1998) The path of law. Boston Univ Law Rev 78:699–716

Whytock C (2009) Legal origins, functionalism, and the future of comparative law. Brigham Young Univ Law Rev 2009:1879–1905
Wieacker F (1981) The importance of Roman law for modern western civilization and western legal thought. Boston Coll Int Comp Law Rev IV:257–281
Wieacker F (1990) Foundations of European legal culture. Am J Comp Law 38:1–29
Zweigert K, Kötz H (1998) An introduction to comparative law. Oxford University Press, Oxford

Emilie Ghio is a lecturer in Corporate and Insolvency Law at the University of Edinburgh.

Part I
Conceptual and Theoretical Perspectives

Terminology

David Cabrelli and Emilie Ghio

1 Crisis

At its simplest, a crisis is defined as 'an extremely difficult or dangerous point in a situation',[1] 'an unstable or crucial time or state of affairs in which a decisive change is impending especially with the distinct possibility of a highly undesirable outcome'[2] and 'a time of great danger, difficulty or doubt when problems must be solved or important decisions must be made.'[3] Therefore, a crisis is a situation which urgently requires actors to act because it has the potential to cause a detrimental change to the system.

In the sense that they result in actual changes in economic, political or social processes, crises are 'real.' Some people view crises as firmly established objects for research, such as when banks collapse and the economic system is threatened.[4] However, crises are also socially constructed because their outcomes are also influenced by how they are perceived. The interpretation of a crisis may under- or over-estimate its magnitude and impact and can attribute various blames to its cause.[5] This can be explained partially by the fact that the effects of a crisis affect

[1] Cambridge Dictionary (2021).

[2] Merriam-Webster Dictionary (2021).

[3] Oxford Learner's Dictionaries (2021).

[4] Calhoun and Derlugian (2011).

[5] White and Nandedkar (2021).

D. Cabrelli (✉)
The University of Edinburgh, Edinburgh Law School, Edinburgh, UK
e-mail: David.Cabrelli@ed.ac.uk

E. Ghio
University of Edinburgh, Edinburgh, UK
e-mail: Emilie.ghio@ed.ac.uk

E. Ghio, R. Perlingeiro (eds.), *Are Legal Systems Converging or Diverging?*,
https://doi.org/10.1007/978-3-031-38180-5_2

people differently. The way a crisis is 'narrated' thus matters. Positioning causation within the temporal sequencing of events that are identified as significant, as well as the use of 'agents' and 'victims', impacts the definition of the crisis event itself. Crises can be constructed out of events to serve political projects[6] or can be manipulated, as suggested by the common phrase 'never let a crisis go to waste.'[7]

Therefore, it is unsurprising that much scholarship has dwelt on the concept of 'crisis.' Crises may be divided into different camps, depending on whether they are economic, financial, fiscal or political in nature and in terms of their impact on society.[8] However, when it comes to theorising about the concept of 'crisis', a useful technique is to account for a division between cause and effect. For example, Sylvia Walby has defined a 'crisis' as 'an event that has the potential to cause a large detrimental change to the social system and in which there is lack of proportionality between cause and consequence.'[9] To that extent, an occurrence or event that is modest in nature, size or scope can generate a crisis in the sense of a long-term extreme impact. In effect, this demonstrates the non-linearity of the relationship between cause and effect.

The character of the relationship between the two factors of cause and effect has been divided into four groups. The first is the 'double movement', where after a period of crisis, the social and economic system reacts to adapt and revert to the state prevalent *ex ante.*[10] This can be contrasted with the second reaction, which entails a full-scale collapse of the social and economic system, e.g. an apocalypse or the end of a civilisation. The third possibility can be referred to in Schumpeterian terms. For example, after a spell of crisis, the system mutates and renews itself in a spirit of 'creative destruction.'[11] Finally, a crisis may precipitate a form of social and economic change that establishes a completely new direction for a system that is altogether distinguishable from its original trajectory, i.e. a turning point or point of inflection.[12] The classic theoretical account of this process at work is provided by Thomas Kuhn in terms of his description of a 'paradigm change.'[13] This entails a revolution in world-view amongst a community of scholars, policymakers or practitioners or the general public, to the extent that a once prevalent, but defective paradigm, is replaced by a new one, e.g. the transitions from communism to capitalism in certain societies in the late twentieth century and from Newtonian to quantum mechanics in the physical sciences.

---

[6]Hay (1996).

[7]Mirowski (2013).

[8]Walby (2015), pp. 2–7.

[9]Ibid, p. 14.

[10]The most famous proponent of the double movement phenomenon was Karl Polanyi: Polanyi (1944).

[11]Schumpeter (1976), pp. 82–83.

[12]Walby (2015), pp. 31–33; Gladwell (2015).

[13]Kuhn (1962).

As phenomena, crises may be internal or external in origin.[14] An internal crisis arises where all or some of the underlying social, technological, or economic conditions that have given rise to a subject have eroded or simply disappeared. Seen from that angle, the subject becomes entirely or partially irrelevant or obsolete, e.g. the various road traffic laws governing pre-automobile times. This can be contrasted sharply with an external crisis. Here, a shock independent of the subject or the environment which originally forged it, or the particular justification(s) for its existence, has an appreciable impact. Economists tend to refer to the latter as externalities, where costs are imposed on innocent third parties, operating outside the bilateral or multilateral relationship of those engaged in formal or informal arrangements.[15]

The crises studied in this book reflect precipitating events which have shaken the status quo and allowed new issues to permeate the international, regional, or local agenda, prompting policymaking and law-making practices to change. In the last decade or so, these crises have been numerous. Therefore, it is not surprising that in recent years, scholars have spoken of a kind of 'crisification' of policymaking.[16] This crisification is problematic. While during peaceful times, traditional policymaking practices rely on extensive analyses of a particular issue and extended phases of consultation with stakeholders, a process akin to thoughtful problem solving in which arguments and perspectives are considered and debated,[17] crises lead to a change in the policymaking actors, abbreviated decision-making procedures, and new narratives.

First, the pace of policymaking shifts to a logic of urgency, rather than bargaining or deliberation. Decisions must be made quickly and involve real choices with important practical consequences: 'they affect core values and interests of communities and the cost of decisions can be very high in socially, politically, economically and in human terms.'[18] As Arjen Boin and colleagues note, 'crisis decision-making situations are more likely than non-crisis situations to contain genuine dilemmas that can be resolved only through trade-off choices, or "tragic choices", where all the options open to the decision maker entail net losses.'[19]

Second, policymaking actors can change in times of crisis. In the case of the European Union (EU), while during peaceful times all institutions, as well as the Member States, are involved in policymaking and legislative initiatives, it is predominantly the European Commission that manages most of the crisis tools. It engages in the early warning task as part of the 70 or so early warning and rapid alert systems it maintains; it reports to networks of national actors outside the EU's institutional structure; and it liaises closely with the designated crisis experts in the

[14] External threats form part of disaster studies analysis: see Gilbert (1998).

[15] Coase (1988).

[16] Rhinard (2019), p. 2.

[17] Joerges and Neyer (2006).

[18] Rhinard (2019), p. 11.

[19] Boin et al. (2016), pp. 43–44.

Council to identify available options. In specific types of crises, certain kinds of experts are preferred by the European Commission[20] and the Council. For example, during the Eurozone crisis, the Council only involved epistemic communities.[21]

Therefore, the crisification of policymaking can lead to new forms of networks and special arrangements for decision-making, and can usher in new participation patterns which depart from traditional decision-making methods and actors. Special crisis procedures can shortcut politics and rely mostly on experts for crisis assessments.[22] Generally, when a crisis strikes in the EU, the Council rises in influence,[23] the Commission enjoys a boost of executive privileges,[24] new organisations emerge[25] and the European Parliament takes a back seat.[26]

The issue with the crisification of policymaking is that citizens around the world increasingly:

> reject the texts handed down for their approval by political elites and so the texts are then converted into legally binding instruments through means that carefully avoid those voters [. . .] So deepens the lack of understanding; so grows popular resentment to an authoritarian sense of "we know best".[27]

2 Globalisation

Globalisation is a phenomenon associated with the free trade initiatives promulgated by the World Trade Organisation ('WTO') over the past forty years. It involves the facilitation of economic integration amongst national state governments on a worldwide scale. These free trade policies have come hand in hand with the liberalisation of international flows of finance and the promotion of international investment and mobile capital. For example, the advancement of policies and law reforms that preserve positive incentives for inward investment into states are encouraged, such as the removal of controls on foreign exchange, low budget deficits maintained by national state governments, the paring down of rigid state social policies and labour laws and the introduction of low tax rates.[28] The general idea is that investment in commercial opportunities will be secured where manufacturing, production and distribution of goods and services are positioned in, and sourced from, jurisdictions where costs are lower and/or minimised, with an emphasis on improving the design, quality and standards of such products and services, as well as new technologies.

[20] Gronvall (2001).

[21] Kamkhaji and Radaelli (2017).

[22] Boin et al. (2013).

[23] Rhinard (2019), p. 627.

[24] Boin et al. (2016).

[25] Bickerton et al. (2014).

[26] Ripoll-Servent (2017).

[27] Weatherill (2016), p. 418.

[28] Davies (2004), pp. 160–161.

Globalisation has had many discontents. Resentment about the excessive power that it confers on international markets are at the heart of these anxieties, with the attendant negative effects on environmental standards, employment/unemployment, income inequality and distribution and economic growth.[29] Some ascribe the public backlash to a populist form of nationalism, with national domestic politics framed around the reshoring of jobs that have been lost through international outsourcing to competitors overseas.[30] However, others cite the steady rise of international judicialisation and legalization as the source of the discontent. Some members of the public have been convinced that the promulgation of international legal norms based on the dissemination of the rule of law are misguided insofar as they prevent their concerns about immigration to be addressed. In this vein, international human rights standards that are designed to constrain the executive power of state governments are cited as generating public concern.[31]

Globalisation and integration are also two phenomena that are inextricably linked. For example, while where there is globalisation, there will be an element of integration, the opposite is not necessarily true to the extent that there is the potential for integration without globalisation, e.g. where two states operating in a particular locality decide to bring their economic, fiscal, monetary, social and foreign policies—and the attendant laws—closer together.

3 Integration

> The action or process of combining two or more things in an effective way.[32]
>
> To form, coordinate, or blend into a functioning or unified whole.[33]

The term 'integration' refers to a process in which the quality of relations among autonomous social units (kinship groups, tribes, cities, trade unions, trade associations, political parties, etc.) changes in such a way that their autonomy is eroded and they become part of a larger aggregate. The concept of international integration also refers to the adoption of policies by different countries as if they were a single political unit. Modern global integration refers to the processes whereby functions are delegated to a new central authority, whose decisions are recognised as legitimate by the constituent parts of the global society.

Global integration is not a new phenomenon. Even ancient civilizations exchanged goods and communicated with each other. However, trade, capital, money, direct investment, technology, people, information, and ideas have all

[29] Obstfeld (2021), p. 691; Bonifai et al. (2022), p. 4.

[30] Goldstein (2022), p. 9; Mansfield and Pevehouse (2022), pp. 3–6.

[31] Voeten (2022), pp. 2–4.

[32] The Cambridge Dictionary.

[33] Merriam-Webster Dictionary.

contributed to rapid growth in international integration over the last several decades. In political sciences, the term is typically used to describe such changes among more or less sovereign political units, and in international relations, it describes cumulatively changing relations among states that result in them accepting some new central authority as a result. As the world's economies have become more closely woven together, it has become more difficult for states to effectively pursue key policy objectives, like dealing with economic recession, financial crisis, environmental problems, or health pandemics, without coordinating their actions with other states or supranational and international organisations.

There are different processes which are particularly relevant to integration. The first one is interaction. Surely, there cannot be global integration without global interaction. Global interaction is at its highest due to technological advancements in the communication and transportation sectors, which have 'shrunk' the world and made it possible for interaction to occur with relative speed and economy. The second key process of global integration is interpenetration. The contemporary international system is highly interdependent, leading to the interpenetration of norms, values and objectives. One of the most visible manifestations of interpenetration is the operation of regional international organisations with supranational authority, such as the EU internal market, where interpenetration has led to a process of deep economic integration.

4 Disintegration

After decades of international integration, the world is witnessing an unprecedented backlash against international institutions. Increasing trade-offs between international cooperation,[34] democracy, and national sovereignty have prompted popular demands to slow, and even reverse, globalisation and integration. Brexit in the United Kingdom (UK) in 2016 is perhaps the most prominent example of 'mass-based disintegration'.[35] The largest withdrawal negotiations ever seen within a supranational entity were triggered by this direct democratic vote. Although highly disruptive and unusual, Brexit is not unique. In recent years, voters have used popular referenda to reject international agreements in several countries. For example, the ECOPOP's referendum in 2014 called for the termination of any international treaty limiting Switzerland's integration powers. Similarly, former United States (US) president Trump has also fulfilled key campaign promises by withdrawing from the Paris Climate Accord and renegotiating NAFTA. There is nothing new about the scepticism expressed about international cooperation,[36] however its vehemence has increased in recent years.

[34]Rodrik (2011).

[35]Walter (2020).

[36]Hobolt and de Vries (2016); Kuo and Naoi (2015).

These disintegration initiatives have far-reaching implications far beyond their countries of origin. In the first place, the disintegration process is determined by the response of remaining member states to unilateral changes or terminations made by one member. Furthermore, mass-based disintegration bids can also encourage disintegrative tendencies in other countries, resulting in considerable political contagion. Eurosceptics across Europe, from France's Marine Le Pen to the People's Party-Our Slovakia, called for similar referenda after the Brexit referendum vote. The leaders of Italy's Five-Star Movement and Spain's Podemos also praised Greece's 2015 referendum-based bailout bid, raising fears that similar demands may be made in other Eurozone crisis countries. On a similar note, across the Atlantic, former Republican presidential candidate Donald Trump tweeted that British voters 'took their country back, just as we will take America back.'[37] While referenda aiming at international disintegration remain relatively rare, they have nonetheless become much more frequent and dominant in recent years.

By weakening the benefits of international cooperation and emboldening integration-sceptics elsewhere, disintegration processes pose considerable risks of political contagion. In 2016, The Economist warned that the 'politics of anger' may lead to an unravelling of globalisation and the prosperity it had created.[38] Academics and international institutions[39] have also noted that disintegration is becoming more popular, posing a challenge to the liberal order and international institutions more broadly.[40]

Disintegration leads to the loss of existing cooperation gains. It reintroduces the barriers to cooperation and integration that international and supranational institutions had worked to remove, which makes it costly both economically and in terms of efficiency. Global supply networks will be disrupted if disintegration results in the reintroduction of trade barriers. It is also likely to be more difficult to coordinate policies and to collaborate on an international scale.

5 Harmonisation & Convergence

The terms 'harmonisation' and 'convergence' have often been used interchangeably to describe the same process or outcome. However, it is a misconception that they can be equated with each other. Instead, 'convergence' as an idea is best understood as a facet of 'harmonisation', rather than the same thing. It is a description of a movement whereby separate things with differing attributes, features or traits end up becoming similar over a period of time.

[37] Tweet from 24 June 2016.

[38] The Economist, 2 July 2016.

[39] Hobolt (2016); Blyth (2016).

[40] Ikenberry (2018); Rodrik (2017).

In the context of the law, convergence may occur in respect of particular laws, a particular legal subject or taxonomy (such as competition law, intellectual property law, etc) or an entire legal system, when benchmarked against an identifiable standard. However, what distinguishes convergence from harmonisation are the various triggers for these phenomena. The harmonisation of laws or legal systems tends to be top-down, where an agenda for legal symmetry is pursued consciously by supranational bodies—such as the European Union, the OECD, the International Labour Organisation, etc.[41] In such a case, the relevant entity either imposes an obligation on their member states to promulgate similar laws in order to align standards across the supranational bloc, or puts pressure on them to harmonise in order to secure particular goals, such as economic efficiency, globalisation of products and services or some other objective.[42] This can be set apart from convergence, where the push factors towards its emergence are informal, spontaneous and bottom-up, following no preordained plan or agenda.[43] For example, regulatory competition, globalisation, and the promulgation of transnational standard form contracts[44] have made important contributions towards the convergence of laws across jurisdictions, especially in the areas of commercial and corporate law.[45] The same can be said in respect of the movement towards sharing best practice amongst national states, as well as international bodies. Thus, both the emulation and borrowing of laws across jurisdictions are fundamental characteristics of convergence: as new problems emerge and different nation states seek and land upon the same or similar solutions.[46]

It is crucial to stress that different forms of convergence may take place. Here, we can draw a distinction between 'formal' and 'functional' convergence.[47] In the case of formal convergence, the outward appearance and shape of the resulting law is either the same or comparable across jurisdictions. This is in contrast to functional convergence, where the legal effects or consequences of the legal convergence are the same or very similar in more than one country. However, where it differs from formal convergence is in the extent to which it is entirely possible that completely different formal, black-letter laws are reformed to achieve the requisite change and outcome. Ronald Gilson illustrates this point by emphasising how divergent states have promulgated laws designed to enable the removal of senior management, but have not uniformly reformed their black letter corporate laws to do so.[48] As such, here, there is a functional alignment of laws, but not formal convergence, to the extent that some jurisdictions have adopted informal means of policing management

[41] Antokolskaia (2006), pp. 21–23.

[42] Lohse (2011), p. 291.

[43] Platsas (2017), p. 17.

[44] For example, by UNCITRAL.

[45] Siems (2018), pp. 228–230.

[46] Nelken (2002), pp. 26–27.

[47] Gilson (2004), pp. 132–137; Gilson (2001), pp. 332–336.

[48] Gilson (2004), pp. 137–140; Gilson (2001), pp. 337–339.

or adapted other formal areas of laws (as opposed to their company laws) to achieve the same impact.

Another important distinction must be drawn between forms of harmonisation or convergence that are either 'negative' or 'positive' in character. Obviously, we must evoke some external yardstick against which we are able to say whether harmonising measures are negative or positive. And in the context of labour law, the appropriate benchmark is to enquire whether the end-product of the harmonisation drive is *less or more* socially protective of employees and workers.[49] Seen from that perspective, if the national laws of different jurisdictions contemporaneously coalesce around a deregulatory downwards agenda for labour law reform, one can refer to this as an illustration of *negative* formal or functional harmonisation or convergence. Likewise, where a supranational organisation enjoins its member states to introduce reforms that pare down the volume, depth, breadth or enforcement of its employment laws. In contrast, where one is dealing with positive harmonisation, the ultimate effect is for the relevant laws to increase the level of social protection, i.e. an upwards effect on either the volume, depth or breadth of labour laws, or the heightening of measures designed to facilitate their enforcement. In such a case, one can talk intelligently about policies centred on *positive* formal or functional harmonisation or convergence.

6 Legal Transplant

This is a term that is closely associated with the concepts of formal and functional convergence and divergence and refers to the idea that a legal rule or system of law can be lifted and moved quite easily "... from one country to another, or from one people to another".[50] The main proponent of this theory was Alan Watson who rejected the notion that the success (or otherwise) of the importation of laws from a particular jurisdiction to another will depend on the cultural niceties, social underpinnings and broader contextual differences of the host state. The terminology used in legal scholarship may also refer to legal borrowing or reception of laws, but these terms are broadly interchangeable with the concept of a "legal transplant". Commentators who are sceptical of Watson's approach include the "contextualists" and the "culturalists". Contextualists challenge the notion of legal transplants for the reason that law is not some autonomous agent, but largely dependent on the social, economic and political context and cultural norms and conventions of the host state.[51] As for the culturalists, their position is even more extreme, since they argue that it is a nonsense to talk meaningfully about a "legal transplant". Instead, in their view, legal transplants are impossible, on the basis that the laws or legal

---

[49] See the discussion in Barnard and Deakin (2002).

[50] Watson (1993), p. 21.

[51] See Kahn-Freund (1974), p. 27 and Friedman (2001), p. 95.

systems that are borrowed by the host state are changed so comprehensively by the context that they become so far removed from the original source as to be unrecognisable.[52]

References

Antokolskaia (2006) Harmonisation of family law in Europe: a historical perspective. Intersentia, Antwerp

Barnard C, Deakin S (2002) 'Negative' and 'positive' harmonisation of labor law in the European Union. Columbia J Eur Union Law 8:389–413

Bickerton C et al (2014) The new intergovernmentalism: European integration in the Post-Maastricht Era. J Common Mark Stud 53:703–722

Blyth M (2016) After the Brits have gone and the trumpets have sounded: turning a drama into a crisis that will not go to waste. Intereconomics 51:324–331

Boin A et al (2013) The European Union as crisis manager: problems and prospects. Cambridge University Press, Cambridge

Boin A et al (2016) The politics of crisis management. Cambridge University Press, Cambridge

Bonifai N et al (2022) Globalization and nationalism: contending forces in world politics. Int Stud Rev 24:1–7

Calhoun C, Derlugian G (eds) (2011) Business as usual: the roots of the global financial metldown (possible futures). New York University Press, New York

Coase R (1988) The firm, the market, and the law. University of Chicago Press, Chicago

Davies D (2004) Death of a labour lawyer? In: Conaghan et al (eds) Labour law in an era of globalization. Oxford University Press, Oxford, pp 159–173

Friedman L (2001) Some comments on Cotterrell and legal transplant. In: Nelken D, Feest J (eds) Adapting legal cultures. Hart Publishing, Oxford, pp 93–99

Gilbert C (1998) Studying disaster. In: Quarantelli E (ed) What is a disaster? Perspectives on the question. Routledge, New York, pp 3–12

Gilson R (2001) Globalizing corporate governance: convergence of form or function? Am J Comp Law 49:329–357

Gilson R (2004) Globalizing corporate governance: convergence of form or function. In: Gordon J, Roe M (eds) Convergence and persistence in corporate governance. Cambridge University Press, Cambridge, pp 128–158

Gladwell M (2015) The tipping point. Abacus, London

Goldstein J (2022) Wither the trade regime? Int Stud Rev 24:1–10

Gronvall J (2001) Mad cow disease: the role of experts and European crisis management. In: Rosenthal U et al (eds) Managing crises: threats, dilemmas, opportunities. Charles C. Thomas, Springfield, pp 155–174

Hay C (1996) Narrating crisis: the discursive construction of the "winter of discontent". Sociology 30:253–277

Hobolt S (2016) The Brexit vote: a divided nation, a divided continent. J Eur Public Policy 23:1–19

Hobolt S, de Vries C (2016) Public support for European integration. Annu Rev Polit Sci 19:413–432

Ikenberry J (2018) The end of liberal international order? Int Aff 94:7–23

Joerges C, Neyer J (2006) Deliberative supranationalism revisited. European University Institute Law Working Paper No. 2006/20

Kahn-Freund O (1974) On uses and misuses of comparative law. Mod Law Rev 37:1–27

---

[52] Legrand (2001), p. 57.

Kamkhaji J, Radaelli C (2017) Crisis, learning and policy change in the European Union. J Eur Public Policy 27:714–734
Kuhn T (1962) The structures of scientific revolutions. University of Chicago Press, Chicago
Kuo J, Naoi M (2015) Individual attitudes. In: Lisa M (ed) The Oxford handbook of the political economy of international trade. Oxford University Press, Oxford, pp 99–181
Legrand P (2001) What "legal transplants"? In: Nelken D, Feest J (eds) Adapting legal cultures. Hart Publishing, Oxford, pp 55–69
Lohse E (2011) The meaning of harmonisation in the context of European Union law – a process in need of definition. In: Andenas M, Andersen CB (eds) Theory and practice of harmonisation. Edward Elgar Publishing, Cheltenham, pp 282–313
Mansfield E, Pevehouse J (2022) Nationalism, populism, and trade agreements. Int Stud Rev 24:1–15
Mirowski P (2013) Never let a serious crisis go to waste: how neoliberalism survived the financial meltdown. Verso, London
Nelken D (2002) Legal transplants and beyond: of disciplines and metaphors. In: Harding A, Örücü E (eds) Comparative law in the 21st century. Kluwer Law International, London, pp 19–34
Obstfeld M (2021) The global capital market reconsidered. Oxf Rev Econ Policy 37:690–706
Platsas A (2017) The harmonisation of national legal systems. Strategic models and factors. Edward Elgar Publishing, Cheltenham
Polanyi K (1944) The great transformation: the political and economic origins of our time. Farrar & Rinehart, New York
Rhinard M (2019) The crisification of policy-making in the European Union. J Common Mark Stud 55:616–633
Ripoll-Servent A (2017) The European Parliament. Parlgrave Macmillan, Houndsmill
Rodrik D (2011) The globalization paradox: democracy and the future of the world economy. W.W. Norton & Company, New York
Rodrik D (2017) Straight talk on trade: ideas for a sane world economy. Princeton University Press, Princeton
Schumpeter J (1976) Capitalism, socialism and democracy. Routledge, New York
Siems M (2018) Comparative law, 2nd edn. Cambridge University Press, Cambridge
The Economist, 'The politics of anger' (2 July 2016). https://www.economist.com/leaders/2016/07/02/the-politics-of-anger
Voeten E (2022) Is the public backlash against globalization a backlash against legalization and judicialization? Int Stud Rev 24:1–17
Walby S (2015) Crisis. Polity, Cambridge
Walter S (2020) The mass politics of international disintegrationrance. CIS Working Paper No. 105. https://ethz.ch/content/dam/ethz/special-interest/gess/cis/cis-dam/CIS_2020/WP%20105%20Walter.pdf
Watson A (1993) Legal transplant: an approach to comparative law. University of Georgia Press, Athens
Weatherill S (2016) Law and values in the European Union. Oxford University Press, Oxford
White I, Nandedkar G (2021) The housing crisis as an ideological artefact: analysing how political discourse defines, diagnoses, and responds. Hous Stud 36:213–234

David Cabrelli is a professor of labour law at the University of Edinburgh, Scotland, United Kingdom.

Emilie Ghio is a lecturer in Corporate and Insolvency law at the University of Edinburgh, Scotland, United Kingdom.

The Concept of Legal Convergence

Antonios E. Platsas

1 The Concept of Legal Convergence

Legal convergence is about the coming together of legal systems.[1] Convergence of the kind can be achieved at the regional level and at the world level,[2] whereas one's thesis in the area would also make allowance for the possibility of both top-down and bottom-up approaches.[3] The concept of convergence can also relate to the processes of harmonisation (minimum harmonisation but also maximum harmonisation of legal standards),[4] approximation and uniformisation of legal standards.[5]

Ideally, such a phenomenon, when and where it occurs, has to materialise in a gradual fashion.[6] This is an idea that ought to normally apply in areas of law that are not culturally defined *stricto sensu.* Areas of cultural significance to the legal system, e.g. family law or criminal law, may still be wholly or close-to-wholly regulated by the legal system itself. At other times, culturally neutral areas of law may or may not be the subject matter of convergence. Corporate laws tend to be one's typical example here as an area of law which is rather culturally neutral but still one that would be open to convergence of approaches or harmonisation of solutions. Equally, relatively culturally neutral areas of law would not necessarily be priority areas for convergence as would be the areas of trade standards, technological standards and

[1] Markesinis (2000); van Hoecke (2000), p. 9.

[2] Platsas (2017), p. 245.

[3] Ibid.

[4] Weatherill (2020), p. 266.

[5] Platsas (2017), p. 7.

[6] Markesinis (1994).

A. E. Platsas (✉)
The University of the West of England, College of Business and Law, Bristol, UK
e-mail: Antonios.Platsas@uwe.ac.uk

E. Ghio, R. Perlingeiro (eds.), *Are Legal Systems Converging or Diverging?*,
https://doi.org/10.1007/978-3-031-38180-5_3

other economic law standards. One could, of course, argue that technological standards are still culturally neutral standards in themselves. However, even if this is the case, one notes here the fact that the practical benefit of harmonisation of technological standards through legal means by far exceeds their rather neutral essence in legal cultural terms, in which case convergence of such standards tends to be close-to-essential. So too, the legal harmonisation of such standards ought not to act as a hindrance of future technological advancements to the benefit of humanity. In any case, one notes that the concept of legal convergence would be mainly concerned with such areas as trade, technology, human rights and, to a certain extent, social rights.

Furthermore, the modern legal convergence thesis ought to carefully tread between the ideal of legal assimilation of systems and flexibility. Thus, the convergence thesis tends to be a rather multifaceted, multimodal and flexible thesis; and flexible it must be for a universe of demoi is contemplated in such a thesis. Legal systems ought to strive to come together but not always and not necessarily. Indeed, even where the convergence exercise is necessary, a certain space for organic growth of national law, around previously agreed standards, could be afforded to the legal systems participating in a circle of convergence.

Moreover, the convergence thesis makes additional allowance for accepting uniform statutory standards, especially where these would be essential for the expediency of trade in the face of a globalised world. The same could be said in relation to the creation of human rights norms but, when it comes to human rights application, one would speak here of more of an *approximation* of human rights standards in practical terms, especially considering that a certain minimum margin of appreciation could be afforded to national legal systems and authorities.

As an epistemic concept, the concept of legal convergence finds itself at the concurrence of humanism, cosmopolitanism, ecumenism, economic utility, efficiency, effectiveness, practicality, technological cooperation and political integration. There lies the leading character of the concept of legal convergence; in the fact that it aims to regulate, or even deregulate, a number of aspects of human activity to the benefit of countries, systems, citizens and corporate actors. A final point is that the vigour of the modern legal convergence thesis lies also in the fact that this is a largely technocratic exercise that would have to be democratically legitimised by the participants in a given legal convergence circle.

2 The Leading Character of the Convergence Thesis in the Discipline of Law

The legal convergence thesis is the leading thesis in the modern discipline of law. Methodologically, it is regulated by such disciplines as law, philosophy, political science and economics. Substantially, there does not seem to be any other theoretical concept or idea currently that has so many and wide-ranging connotations for so many different areas in so many legal systems. Indeed, the concept of legal convergence has significant connotations not just on the legal substance and procedure of systems but also on more subtle aspects of legal life, e.g. law's educational models around the world.

Law as a *techne* and as an *episteme* is otherwise in the process of re-aligning itself to the epistemic singularity of other disciplines, such singularity characterising the overwhelming majority of disciplines nowadays.[7] Law, traditionally a subject for the nation in the era of modernity, has certainly matured to the point that legal harmonisation projects are nowadays part and parcel of major global developments. The world, of course, does not necessarily need more law; however, the world needs more harmonised laws.

Beyond this, convergence can take the form of co-evolution of national and supranational legal solutions, reflexive efforts of harmonisation and it can also be the result of regulatory competition and dissemination of the more effective and/or efficient legal standards. The legal convergence thesis is a thesis that makes sense for countries, economies, lawyers and individuals. A yearning for simplicity is what effectively forms the practical rationale of the convergence thesis,[8] our world's architecture of international cooperation being rather complex and opaque,[9] even if the phenomenon of globalisation promotes more unified and interconnected legal and economics patterns.

3 Formal Convergence vs Functional Convergence

Prior to fully engaging with the precise epistemic co-ordinates of the concept of legal convergence, it would be important to discuss and assess a rather significant distinction in the modern convergence thesis, the one that provides for formal and functional modes of convergence. A formal mode of legal convergence is effectively one that presupposes structured efforts of legal co-ordination amongst different legal systems, normally under established patterns of international law, regional law and so on. A functional mode of legal convergence, on the other hand, is a pattern of convergence that can come about without the interference of such structured efforts whatsoever. Furthermore, a formal mode of legal convergence may fundamentally be a mode of convergence that enables convergence of form(s), structures, overall characteristics and the related in the area of legal normative matter. The functional mode of legal convergence, on the other hand, relates to the legal convergence of substantives beyond form; it is about whether or not legal institutions, legal norms, operations and frameworks of different legal systems effectively converge in their substantives, even though, as stated, there may not be any interference or input from

[7] Zweigert and Kötz (1998), p. 15.
[8] Merryman (1981), pp. 364–365.
[9] See de Witte (2014), p. 464.

formal convergence patterns. Either way, it should be noted here that convergence is about whether the very legal mentalities[10] of different legal systems have converged in points or areas of legal substance, procedure and practice. Convergence then is not just about epistemological substrata but about epistemological substrata and actual perceptions of such.[11] In effect, the confluence of epistemological substrata and the same or similar perceptions thereof, amongst recipient systems of convergent law, lead to genuine legal convergence. It is then and only then that convergence is practically achieved. Moreover, it has also been argued that formal convergence equates doctrinal convergence[12] but this approach would clearly be open to academic debate.

The author posits that, whilst formal convergence *may* relate to convergence of legal doctrine, the two should not be taken to be synonyms to one another. Legal doctrine is one thing. Legal form that may or may not pinpoint at doctrine is quite another. Also, ideally, one could expect that legal convergence is reached both at a formal and at a functional level (hybrid legal convergence thesis). In this respect, one is reminded here that, by reason of the fact that harmonised instruments of law, 'like transplants, tend to focus principally on the "formal" institutions of the law',[13] it would be quite important that both the forces of written/formal elements and unwritten/informal elements in convergent legal systems are combined.[14] In any case, occasionally, a formal/doctrinal model of legal convergence under classic international law will be necessitated. At other times, however, one ought to allow market and/or social forces, or, indeed, any other legitimate forces within legal systems e.g. political forces, to enable legal convergence at a functional level. For instance, in the area of corporate governance one could have, as one already has, functional convergence of approaches without the interference of national legislators.[15] This, then would, in principle, be a voluntary legal exercise.[16] Of course, law is still a predominantly doctrinal and a rather formal subject in so many of its theoretical and practical manifestations. As such, whereas one clearly observes the potential benefits of functional convergence, the importance of formal convergence should not be underestimated.

In the area of functional convergence, the classic example in the bibliography is the one that has been advocated by such scholars as Gilson in relation to the functional convergence of the systems of corporate governance in Germany, the United States and Japan.[17] Coffee has also persuasively argued, in a similar vein, a

[10] Legrand (1996), p. 60.

[11] Cf. Legrand (1996), p. 60.

[12] Micheler (2009), p. i.

[13] Arvind (2010), p. 79.

[14] Arvind (2010), p. 78.

[15] Cf. Coffee (1999), p. 650.

[16] Coffee (1999), p. 650.

[17] Gilson (2000), p. 11; Gilson (2001), p. 337; Gilson (2010), p. 137.

thesis which resembles Gilson's thesis.[18] The thesis would be that, even though the degree of formal convergence between comparable systems could be effectively absent, the degree of functional convergence between such systems may have materialised and could be relatively significant. Kerr's 1960 leading economics thesis, which still stands as the economics engine of the modern legal convergence thesis, as we will be seen further below, has advocated and proved that the industrialisation of a number of countries, falling in the developing and the developed world, effectively led to their convergence of cultures. This being the case, the more formalist legal scholars of us ought to take heed. Indeed, the forces of globalisation and, by extension, the forces of spontaneous and/or functional convergence could certainly outpace the more formal types of legal convergence, especially the ones that materialise on a top-down basis or the ones that require time-consuming political compromises and so on. So too, it may sometimes be more likely for legal convergence to occur through the so-called contagion effect of legal solutions,[19] or, more interestingly, by leaving the markets to have the main role in such an exercise. Markets can be wild and, when wholly left to their own devices, perilous, but markets that lead to functional convergence amongst different systems may actually stand as one of the better examples of markets. As such, the materialisation of legal convergence, based on economic and social forces, can result in more in-depth forms of legal convergence, especially in the approximation of economic and social laws. This latter model stands for a liberal legal functional model, which compares well with the more centralised, largely Westphalian, formal model. Furthermore, such scholars as Legrand would consider that the legal convergence which one observes amongst European Union (EU) legal systems is one which is merely functional and superficial (irreducibility of differences between different legal mentalities thesis),[20] otherwise a rather pessimistic thesis, for if we accepted such a thesis, one would have to take it for granted that legal convergence e.g. in the EU could never and will never occur. Finally, for one's analytical purposes, the convergence theorist ought to remind and be reminded here that three years only from Legrand's sceptical but, otherwise, largely frivolous thesis, 11 European States fully aligned their monetary legal frameworks, thereby creating the single currency, the Euro. On the 1st of January 2023, the Euro reached a membership of 20 European States, the Euro being not only a catalyst to European legal convergence, but also, by far, one of the best illustrations of hybrid (formal and functional) legal convergence examples to date in the world. There are already European legal systems that have adopted the single currency without participating in any formal legal co-ordination efforts to it.

[18] E.g. Coffee (1999).

[19] The Delaware effect, when it comes to US corporate laws, and the Californian effect, when it comes to US environmental laws, would be the classic examples here, i.e. when it comes to other US States taking legal standards of certain US States in certain areas into account.

[20] Legrand (1996), pp. 62, 63, 64, 74–78, 79, 81.

4 Epistemic Co-Ordinates

4.1 Ideological Co-Ordinates: From Philosophy to Law

The Platonic One forms the ideological core of the concept of legal convergence. The concept of convergence is directly linked to Plato's idea of universals. Elsewhere in the bibliography, such an idea would be cited as the one-over-many principle.[21] Plato always believed in the superior character of the whole over the particular by otherwise recognising the importance of both. So did his best student, Aristotle, even if he would have modified the platonic forms thesis by concluding that things are the result of both forms *and* matter.[22] Aristotle went further than Plato by pinpointing also that such notions as natural law are immutable and have the same validity from nation to nation like fire burning in the same way in Greece and Persia.[23] A rather similar point on the universal character of the law of nature was also made later by Cicero.[24] In any case, the point that Plato made as to the superior character of a singularity over a plurality has been maintained by Aristotle, as the superior character of the whole over the parts has been clearly advocated in the latter's *Metaphysics*.[25] Elsewhere, Aristotle is adamant that theoretical subjects, as in theoretical disciplines, are confined to universals.[26]

This forms a very interesting thesis, in that law, as a largely theoretical discipline, ought to have been following this tendency. However, one notes here that law, conventionally ever since 1648, has been more of a specific domestic-oriented matter than a subject that would seek universals in a similar way the convergence thesis would. As such, relevant legal universals tended to be confined within nations mostly. One law would govern the whole State. The State would thus succumb to one central law which the State's subjects would have to follow. As such, law tended to be rather provincial and centralised. Consequently, law as an *episteme* and as a fact of life tended, in partial disagreement with Platonic-Aristotelian doctrine, to pursue universals but that would be something that would predominantly be the case *within* the nation State at least between 1648 and 1945. Of course, international law pre-existed the two world wars. Nonetheless, regional and world legal convergence were practically very limited, if non-existent.

There is otherwise something unique about the idea of universals that Plato advocated in the first place. He claimed that it is habitual in human nature to actually posit a single form for each plurality of things to which we give the same name.[27]

---

[21] E.g. González-Varela (2020).

[22] Aristotle, *Metaphysics*, 8.1045a. All references to ancient texts are taken from such texts as these would be found in the Perseus Digital Library of Tufts University, unless otherwise stated.

[23] Aristotle, *Nicomachean Ethics*, 5.7.

[24] Cicero, *De Republica*, 3.22.33.

[25] Aristotle, *Metaphysics*, 1.981.

[26] Devereux (1986), p. 484 citing Aristotle's *Nicomachean Ethics*.

[27] Plato, *Republic*, 596a.

Thus, an oak, a chestnut, a maple, a linden and a pine are all different types of trees participating, however, in the form of 'treeness'. The United States (US) legal system, the United Kingdom (UK) legal system, the Brazilian legal system, the Japanese legal system and the Greek legal system are all different legal systems while participating, however, in the form of legal 'systemness', and so on. Plato put his idea of postulation of universals into action, when he explored what makes something beautiful. For him, a thing is beautiful simply because it participates in the form, the idea, or however one would name such quality as beauty.[28]

One cannot neglect, of course, from their analysis the fact that legal systems come, or tend to come, with a degree of variation, which is the result of cultural influences and predispositions. However, much of this variation is related to ideas that are now on the retreat, e.g. the nation State or centralised and unitary forms of statehood and so on and so forth. For us in law, the Platonic One has wide-ranging implications however. It actually enables us to proceed with the approximation of legal systems, thereby creating social, political, legal and economic conditions for fairer, more cosmopolitan and more unified societies. This process, normally a gradual one,[29] must meet the approval of the citizens who would be the main beneficiaries of convergent legal projects (correspondence to the democratic ideal principle). Thus, the superior character of the modern legal convergence thesis is found in the fact that this is not a merely technocratic exercise, but a technocratic exercise that has to come in agreement with the ideal of democracy.

4.2 Economics Co-Ordinates: From Economics to Law

The modern idea of legal convergence has had a lot to learn from modern economics, the *locus classicus* in the area being *Industrialism and Industrial Man.*[30] In this seminal work, which was published in the early 1960s, the authors compared the labour economics of a multiplicity of countries, concluding that the global convergence of cultures is the outcome of industrialisation processes.

Moreover, one notes here that nowadays legal convergence promotes the convergence of economies (and vice versa). Using the EU as an example, it seems that the degree of economic convergence in Europe, through the enactment of hundreds of harmonising legal instruments over the decades is now greater than that of otherwise unitary federal States such as the United States (US). Of course, for the EU to reach such a level of economic convergence, it had to create the right legal frameworks in the first place. For instance, Article 114 TFEU is in itself a powerful provision that creates a whole legal framework for the stronger approximation of laws as between the EU's Member States and their legal centre, the EU itself as an

[28] Plato, *Phaedo*, 100c–d.

[29] Markesinis (1994).

[30] Kerr et al. (1960).

organisation. In any case, so wide-ranging has been economic convergence in Europe, through the implementation of liberal economics regulations ever since the 1950s and the 1960s to date (i.e. in the area of freedom of capital, persons, services and goods), that the degree of economic approximation in the EU Member States seems to be greater now than in the US, otherwise a unitary federal nation for more than 240 years.[31]

However, unlike the US, the citizens of the EU do not, as of yet, practically use the freedom of movement of persons for the purposes of settling in another EU Member State as much as the Americans would, when it comes to them settling in another US state. At this point, it should also be remembered that the first President of the European Central Bank (ECB), Wim Duisenberg, has referred to the Euro, Europe's single currency, as a catalyst for legal convergence in Europe.[32] Europe, of course, has no President (as in a single political figure), no central government, no parliament that would enjoy legislative initiative the way a parliament of a sovereign EU Member State would enjoy; it has a little approved, impersonal, remote and largely broken technocratic bureaucracy that the people of Europe do not necessarily always support, understand, respect or trust. Duisenberg was right though: convergence is about such tangible things as the Euro that result in further legal convergence (not about abstract matter that would relate to persons or officials). The Euro, the single currency, is, therefore, a key driving engine of future legal initiatives in Europe.

One could additionally argue here that if one takes away the Four Freedoms from EU law, there would not be much left in EU law. These freedoms, together with the Euro, form much of the core of European legal convergence initiatives and policies. These Four Freedoms; the single currency; indeed, the European Convention on Human Rights (ECHR) effectively act as the six legal convergence engines of modern Europe.

Moreover, from the economics point of view, a convergence circle could also be the result of regulatory competition.[33] However, the convergence theorist notes here the greater space for regulatory competition as between the United States themselves than between the EU's Member States.[34] In all probability, this seems to be a historical-legal reaction of the Europeans to the traditional legal divergence and competition between European States with the advent of the Westphalian paradigm.

---

[31] Head and Mayer (2021), pp. 44–45.

[32] Duisenberg (2000).

[33] See e.g. Deakin (2006), pp. 71–95.

[34] Cf. Armour (2005).

4.3 Political Co-Ordinates: Political Will, Peace and Co-Operation

Whereas economic prosperity and respect for the (economic or otherwise) well-being of the citizen are the two main goals of most convergent legal projects, it is politics that practically sets the precise agenda with regard to ongoing and future harmonising legal projects. The political vision was always there though. In this respect, it should be remembered that one of France's greatest writers, Victor Hugo, already spoke, in the mid-nineteenth century, of '[a] day [that] will come when the only fields of battle will be markets opening up to trade and minds opening up to ideas.'[35] Despite two world wars that have actually started in Europe, Hugo's call is still most relevant to the Europeans and the rest of the citizens of the world.

What was missing, however, was the political will one would readily observe in Europe after the end of the Second World War. Additionally, the convergence of legal systems ought to eventually ensure the convergence of political and economic systems. Of course, the convergence of economic systems and political systems may precede the convergence of legal systems but, in the long run, all these three elements (legal, political and economic) are communicating vessels. It is therefore of significance that political, economic and legal systems dance on the same tune or, at least, a similar tune of expectations.

For all intents and purposes, the magnificence of the legal convergence thesis lies in the creation of common rules, which eventually create the guarantees for long lasting peace and prosperity. Europe, the historical mother of world wars, stands as the leading example in this respect ever since the 1950s. Since then, the Europeans have made the commencement of another world war in Europe not just unthinkable but also virtually impossible by initially imposing stringent legal measures on themselves for limiting the production of coal and steel.[36] So too, without a doubt, it is Europe as a legal space that stands at the forefront of the modern convergence thesis. Here is why: the majority of European States comply with three mechanisms of legal convergence: international law, EU law and ECHR law.[37] Such a phenomenon is now also somewhat emulated in the Americas and Africa.[38] However, the depth, the extent and the array of convergent instruments and mechanisms that simultaneously operate in Europe clearly places the particular continent in a unique position. Of course, 'Europe means different things to different people, [something] which suggest[s] that it has different overlapping territorial, political, cultural, and ideological connotations'.[39] Nonetheless, the point remains: Europe, despite institutional failures, democratic deficits, cultural differences and legal delays in its

[35] As cited in Head and Mayer (2021), p. 23.

[36] Head and Mayer (2021), p. 23.

[37] E.g. see generally de Witte (2014), pp. 445–464 and in particular pp. 445–446.

[38] See e.g. Hirsch (2021), pp. 1–27 for the recent proposals in Africa when it comes to the free movement of African people in the African continent.

[39] Lähdesmäki et al. (2021), p. 183.

convergence agenda and its political integration, is still the continent that sets the world standards in the area.

Equally, the failures of Europe's functionaries in the political integration and legal convergence of things ought to be a call for reform; not a call for the rise of political and legal nationalisms or a call for the retreat of the legal convergence thesis. This being the case, the question in Europe is not whether there should be convergence of the legal systems which this continent comprises. The question is whether and how more and deeper legal convergence between European legal systems should occur in the future.

A final point, in the area of the political coordinates of the convergence thesis, that would have to be made here, would be in relation to the emulation of solutions from other political systems. Of course, one does not speak here of blindly transplanted solutions from elsewhere in a neo-colonialist fashion. Rather, one speaks of conscious political choices made by certain countries that wish to follow the standards (political, legal and otherwise) of other countries. This can occur in a co-ordinated fashion from a given political centre—the narratives of EU integration would be the classic example here—or in a more spontaneous fashion and on a more piecemeal basis. In law, the latter approach has been called 'legal contagion'[40] effectively. Thus, on the basis that political will exists, it is possible for one legal system to borrow solutions from another legal system without the interference of a supranational or intergovernmental organisation.

5 The Legacy and the Anathema of the Westphalian Paradigm

As mentioned earlier, the legal convergence thesis runs counter the Westphalian paradigm. Traditionally, such a paradigm would, of course, have defined the totality of the world's modern legal systems, at least up until the end of the Second World War. Law was and, to a large extent, still is, in many parts of the world, the toy of the nation State. Law's magnificence otherwise lies in the fact that it mechanises political will. Nevertheless, such a will would normally emanate, at least in the case of democratic States, from the demos. However, one would also certainly be able to argue that this would be about a rather introvert and narrow perception of democracy.

Democracy, in its ideal perception, is not a provincial system of governance, even though it can be. Democracy, in its ideal perception, is about a cosmopolitan image of the world. It is about responsible, enlightened, pro-active citizens. It is about political extroversion and economic openness. Without a doubt, however, the rise and rise of nationalisms all over the world has been fuelled by the Westphalian paradigm, which has used law as its enforcing arm. Law has, thus, largely

[40] E.g. Farran (2020), p. 31.

surrendered and succumbed in the past to the Sirens of nationalism that haunted most of the nation States since 1648. The absurdity of divergence of laws, or to use German terminology, the reduction of the subject of law into a provincial discipline, a *Landesjurisprudenz*, has prevailed. Indeed, the Westphalian paradigm came with one of the greatest epistemic paradoxes in the theoretical disciplines; national lawyers would strive to bring uniformity within their own systems but would neglect to perceive their discipline as a largely unified discipline due to a rather distorted perception of the nation or due to a loosely defined type of domestic legal culturalism.

If the creation of modern States teaches us one thing, it is the fact that nations are largely artificial entities. Perhaps a common language, perhaps the same religion for many within a State, perhaps certain shared customs are what make a 'nation' but this is where the nation ends. All else revolves around the ecumene. Accordingly, one cannot simply put all of one's epistemic legal hopes on the nation. So too, even the staunchest of nationalists cannot just escape the fact that in the world of globalisation, the majority of legal systems seem to strive for similar standards unless, of course, a legal system can attest to the fact that its legal standards are clearly advantageous, as in the case of the Delaware effect and the California effect in the US in the areas of corporate and environmental regulation respectively.

The Westphalian paradigm unfortunately persists. The more-than-apparent lack of co-ordination of the world's legal systems and governments in the pandemic, ever since the beginning of 2020, has been yet another clear-cut example of the fact that national legal systems and governments cannot, on their own, deal with world problems. Local problems are best dealt at the local level. Regional problems are best dealt at the regional level. World problems are best dealt at the world level.

If logic teaches us one thing, it is that the deployment of the right resources must occur at the right time, in the right fashion and at the right place. For instance, in Europe, almost every single national government has been coming up with its own approach as to the dealing of the pandemic; at a point, vaccination nationalism prevailed and, of course, what looks like the developed world secluded initially Africa and certain parts of Asia from precious vaccinations, which the scientific community otherwise managed to create at neck breaking speed. In the case of the handling of the pandemic around the world, it would seem that both science and the convergence thesis have been somewhat betrayed by little political corner shops called nation States.

6 Flexibility at the Heart of the Modern Legal Convergence Thesis

A superior thesis is a thesis that makes space for certain flexibility. Of course, not all theses are capable of such a degree of flexibility, yet it would seem that the legal convergence thesis is. Flexibility is about sovereign States having the final say as to whether or not they would participate in legal convergence circles. Flexibility is about such States being able to enter, remain or leave a legal convergence circle, this being a matter for their demos to decide. Flexibility is also about opt-ins and opt-outs. Yet it can also be about national sovereignty being partially limited, because a sovereign country could decide to do so for its own benefit and the benefit of a legal union or alliance, or even for a common goal. Flexibility could also be about subsidiarity, a principle that has had to grow and mature in the modern EU.[41] It would also be about proportionality in the actions of supranational and intergovernmental organisations.[42] Finally, it would be about the democratic legitimisation of such a thesis altogether, the world's cosmopolitan demoi being the ultimate arbiters of whether they would wish to proceed further, deeper and for longer within a given legal convergence circle.

There is nothing inherently wrong with the idea that like-minded nations and, by extension, like-minded legal systems can proceed together by creating their own limited circles of legal convergence. They could certainly do so beyond the bureaucracies of intergovernmental and supranational institutions, especially if this would accelerate the process of legal convergence.[43] For those who would observe such an idea with scepticism, one would be reminded of the fact that much of international law is to this day about the self-determination and the sovereignty of States. As such, the convergence theorist would not object to the power of sovereign and independent States to proceed in accordance with the legitimate wishes of their electorates, when it comes to legal convergence projects, even if this would be about limited circles of legal convergence initially. Thereafter, after a legal convergence circle would have been formed, others could still join such a circle and so on.[44] It should also be possible to depart from such a legal convergence circle based on the will of the people and so on.

On the other hand, the idea of regional convergence is not always one that comes with ideal results. However, such a type of convergence would still be a first step in the area, since regional convergence could make away with national legal variation and unnecessary legal divergences within the same region. Furthermore, global models of legal convergence might be readily defeated by regional models of legal convergence. However, taking the global trade system as our example here, we ought to note that, in the absence of global legal approaches in such a system, 'international rulemaking will become fragmented amid a mix of bilateral and regional trade agreements, WTO plurilaterals, unilateral actions, and non-market measures.'[45] As such, regional systems of legal convergence may be the way

[41] The leading provision of EU law on subsidiarity would be Article 5(3) TEU. See also the TFEU Protocol No2 on the Application of the Principles of Subsidiarity and Proportionality.

[42] The leading provision of EU law on proportionality would be Article 5(4) TEU. See also the TFEU Protocol No2 on the Application of the Principles of Subsidiarity and Proportionality.

[43] Reinsch and Caporal (2021), p. 13.

[44] Ibid., p. 14.

[45] Ibid., p. 13.

forward on many occasions, but, equally, global legal convergence should be actively pursued in areas of global importance such as world trade rules and the international architecture of markets.

7 Legal Convergence as Organic Growth

Ideally, a circle of legal convergence should make allowance for further future integration of political matters and harmonisation of legal solutions. The idea of convergence and all that it comes with can most certainly flourish as an organic reality in the world's legal systems. One contemplates here the creation of positivist convergent legal standards, such standards allowing further convergence in an evolving fashion. In an exercise of legal convergence, legal transplants can be allowed to domestically mature further.[46]

First, one should, of course, identify and create relevant legal patterns, templates or blueprints; second, one should allow convergent law to flourish further in an organic fashion within legal systems, especially after the point of legal convergence would have been reached. Devereux, referring to the Eleatic Stranger, has been quite illuminating on this; thus,

> Laws are by their very nature defective in that there is a discrepancy between their simplicity and fixity and the complexity and variability in that to which they apply. The Stranger goes on to argue that the wise ruler should be free to change laws in response to changing conditions, and should be allowed to tailor his judgments to particular situations even if this goes against the precise formulation of the law.[47]

Here one would be reminded that the modern legal convergence thesis presupposes a plurality of demoi. It is demos, in its widest perception, that ought to be the maker of legal convergence projects. Thus, one's approach here ought to be quite expansive. A modern demos is not merely made out of people or citizens. It is made out of the aforementioned and all the economic actors that such a demos comes with in practical terms. This is a demos that embraces citizens, corporations and all other actors that would nowadays constitute such. Beyond this, one's perception of legal convergence ought to be one that comes in agreement with the democratic ideal. Thus, legal harmonisation projects ought to be democratically legitimised at relatively frequent points of time. The greater the penetration of convergent projects into the demos' legal system, the greater the degree of democratic legitimisation one would expect for such projects and vice versa. Legitimisation here could occur directly or indirectly and one ought to readily admit that the modern demos ought to include corporate actors too, as voices that represent the markets, countries and citizens. Quintessentially, however, the democratic legitimisation should first and foremost be decided by the citizens and so on.

[46] On the two main schools of legal transplants, see Foster (2002), pp. 58–60.

[47] Devereux (1986), p. 501 citing Plato, *Statesman*, 294a-c, 294d-295b, 295c-e, 296d-297b.

It is in European human rights law that one observes one of the better examples of organic growth in existing circles of legal convergence. For instance, European human rights judges have declared some time ago in *Tyrer v United Kingdom*[48] that the ECHR has to be seen as a living organism; one that would have to be interpreted in the light of present-day conditions and circumstances. The approach established by the European judges in the late 1970s has had wide-ranging implications in the expansion of the scope of the Convention. Accordingly, such an approach would clearly make allowance for the organic growth of the ECHR itself within Europe's domestic legal systems, which have otherwise ratified the letter of the Convention. Thus, the ECHR is, in Darwinian terms, an evolving convergent legal creature. Perhaps one could observe its living legal instrument doctrine as a counterweight to the otherwise powerful doctrine of margin of appreciation it also comes with, the latter being a doctrine which allows certain leeway to European legal systems in the application of certain of the ECHR provisions. Crucially, however, the interaction of these two mechanisms (living instrument doctrine and margin of appreciation doctrine) effectively amounts to a state of affairs that promotes the continuous (re)calibration of the scope of the Convention by the European Court of Human Rights (ECtHR), even if there would be no 'one size fits all' approach.[49]

To conclude, convergent instruments such as the Convention allow for a certain organic growth of the convergent jurisprudence they come with, even though this would ultimately be down to the ECtHR judges to adjust. In any case, the Convention's expansion to the sphere of civil *and* social rights[50] allows us to consider it as a particularly interesting instrument which promotes organic legal growth of its convergent remit over time.

8 Technocratic for the People: A Technocratic Exercise Subject to the Democratic Ideal

Furthermore, one must be reminiscent of the point that the demos in the developed world is nowadays powerful. It is the driving engine of modern society. It defines the law. It creates the law through representatives. It regulates the whole being of the State, for the State is ultimately the conception and the design of the demos. So too, the picture of the world that each State represents is to a considerable extent the perception of its demos. A multiplicity of demoi is contemplated in our thesis.

In such a universe, technocratic exercises on the idea of convergence are filtered through the demos, for the demos is the body that legitimises such an exercise. This is a legal universe of enlightened demoi, whose citizens perceive themselves, are and act as responsible world citizens. These are citizens respectful of both locality and

---

[48] App no 5856/72 (ECtHR, 25 April 1978), Series A, No 26 (1979–80) 2 EHRR 1.

[49] Ita and Hicks (2021), p. 74.

[50] E.g. Leijten (2017).

globality. They form cosmopolitan republics that are the soul and the driving engine of world legal, social and economic standards. Equally, the organic growth of the law is something one can contemplate, especially when the convergence exercise is not about uniformity but about increased legal similarity (i.e. approximation). A little bit like the organic growth of flora around human-made, posited axes, the legal convergence ideal can create centralised legal axes upon and around which domestic solutions can organically grow and flourish, especially where such variation would not actually defeat the purpose of legal convergence. The legal core would thus remain the same but slightly different solutions could grow around harmonised legal standards. At other times, of course, identical legal solutions would have to be the case. International law is abundant with such uniform examples, as is EU law.

One should be absolutely clear also about the fact that, after a certain point, i.e. after the exercise of legal convergence would have been legitimised by way of democratic will, the exercise would have to be a rather technocratic one in itself. Here one notes not only the complexities of creating convergent/harmonised law[51] but also the fact that the implementation of the convergent norm must be one that will be catered for by experts. For instance, one would have to mention in this respect the fact that legal harmonisation without harmonised implementation of convergent law cannot occur and that implementation and transposition matters would have to be carefully considered. Thus, one ought to distinguish between formal and substantive implementation matters in the sphere of convergence, in addition to identifying between externalities-to-the-legal-system and internalities-to-the-legal-system which could and, where possible, should be taken into account in the same matters.[52]

9 Conclusion

Our world's cosmopolitan republics must continue to further the cause of the legal convergence thesis because the promotion of such a thesis comes with considerable practical utility. Consequently, such a drive towards an ever more convergent world in legal terms is not about an abstract academic exercise. It is about practical benefit from the legal, political and economic point of view. The legal Academy should also promote this thesis to an even greater extent for the bettering not just of the discipline of law but also, most importantly, for the bettering of the lives of billions of people around the world. Economically closer, we can achieve more. Legally united, we will succeed. Politically divided, we shall fall. Of course, a sovereign national legal system would, by definition, be free to proceed on its own, under the free-rider principle.

---

[51] Markesinis (2004), p. xi.

[52] Platsas (2017).

Nonetheless, such an exercise should not be reduced to a sort of blind and drunken type of freedom, a distorted perception of freedom for the sake of divergence, resembling a nationalist legal chimera that cannot simply be accepted in the face of an ever more globalised and interconnected world. In fact, such an approach would not be about the pursuit of genuine political freedom. It would be about negation. Legal systems that proceed unilaterally in the world of globalisation are effectively in danger of becoming marginalised.

Let us also be absolutely clear about this: even if international organisations and their bureaucrats may have failed the idea of legal convergence in the past,[53] one must ensure that the idea of harmonisation of legal systems is salvaged. Consequently, one could reform the institutions that claim that convergence is at the centre of their operations; not the idea itself. The concept of legal convergence does not stand for some sort of a broken theory in the minds of those who live apart from the citizen, when it is actually the citizen that effectively benefits the most from such a noble cosmopolitan idea. The convergence thesis is a concrete thesis, which allows for flexibility and certain organic legal growth based on the democratic ideal.

Reverting to the point of the failures of bureaucracies, the occasional failures and the democratic deficits within European institutions, for instance, should not halt the idea of legal convergence in Europe. The failures of bureaucrats, in a largely democratic Europe and in an increasingly democratic world, ought not to be used against the idea of legal convergence. Of course, the convergence thesis can become even clearer and more concrete in the future.[54] However, the point to be reiterated here is that it is not the idea that is problematic; it is those who do not properly implement the idea that seem to be the main cause of concern. Reform would be key then.

Finally, the autopoietic essence of the convergence thesis leading to organic legal growth must not be overlooked and should be further strengthened in the future. In any case, one ought to remain faithful to what seems to be for many decades now the leading idea in the discipline of law: the convergence thesis.

References

Aristotle, Metaphysics, 1.981a, 8.1045a (Perseus Digital Library of Tufts University)
Aristotle, Nicomachean Ethics, 5.7 (Perseus Digital Library of Tufts University)
Armour J (2005) Who should make corporate law? EC Legislation versus Regulatory Competition. ECGI Working Paper Series in Law: Law Working Paper No. 54/2005
Arvind TT (2010) The 'transplant effect' in harmonization. Int Comp Law Q 59:65–88

[53] E.g. Head and Mayer (2021), p. 24 citing Alesina A, Perotti R (2004) The European Union: A Politically Incorrect View. Journal of Economic Perspectives 18: 27–48.

[54] E.g. for a recent discussion on certain terminological aspects of the legal harmonisation concept in the context of EU law and cross-border insolvency law, see Ghio (2020), p. 578.

Cicero, De Republica, 3.22.33 (De Republica, De Legibus, trans. Keyes CW, Loeb Classical Library (1928; reprint, 1970)
Coffee JC (1999) The future as history: the prospects for global convergence in corporate governance and its implications. Northwest Univ Law Rev 93:641–707
de Witte B (2014) The European Union's place among the international cooperation venues of its Member States. ZaöRV 74:445–464
Deakin S (2006) Is regulatory competition the future for European integration? Swedish Econ Policy Rev 13:71–95
Devereux DT (1986) Particular and universal in Aristotle's conception of practical knowledge. Rev Metaphys 39:483–504
Duisenberg WF (2000) The Euro as a catalyst for legal convergence in Europe. https://www.ecb.europa.eu/press/key/date/2000/html/sp000917.en.html
Farran S (2020) Legislating for customary land tenure: a comparative query. In: Donlan SP, Mair J (eds) Comparative law: mixes, movements and metaphors. Routledge, London, New York, pp 31–46
Foster N (2002) Transmigration and transferability of commercial law in a globalised world. In: Harding A, Örücü E (eds) Comparative law in the 21st century. Kluwer Law International, The Hague, pp 55–73
Ghio E (2020) International legal cooperation and the principle of harmonisation: lessons from cross-border insolvency. Revista Juris Poiesis 23:576–581
Gilson RJ (2000) Globalizing corporate governance: convergence of form or function. Columbia Law School, The Center for Law and Economic Studies Working Paper No. 174; Stanford Law School, John M. Olin Program in Law and Economics Working Paper No. 192: 1–34
Gilson RJ (2001) Globalizing corporate governance: convergence of form or function. Am J Comp Law 49:329–357
Gilson RJ (2010) Globalizing corporate governance: convergence of form or function. In: Gordon JN, Roe MJ (eds) Convergence and persistence in corporate governance. Cambridge University Press, pp 128–158
González-Varela JE (2020) The one over many principle of Republic 596a. Apeiron 53:339–361
Head K, Mayer T (2021) The United States of Europe. J Econ Perspect 35:23–48
Hirsch A (2021) A strategic consideration of the African Union free movement of persons protocol and other initiatives towards the freer movement of people in Africa (Working Paper). South African Institute of International Affairs, pp 1–27
Ita R, Hicks D (2021) Beyond expansion or restriction? Models of interaction between the living instrument and margin of appreciation doctrines and the scope of the ECHR. Int Hum Rights Law Rev 10:40–74
Kerr C, Dunlop JT, Harbison F, Myers CA (1960) Industrialism and industrial man. Harvard University Press, Cambridge
Lähdesmäki T, Mäkinen K, Čeginskas VLA, Kaasik-Krogerus S (2021) Conclusions: Europe's lived space. In: Lähdesmäki T, Mäkinen K, Čeginskas VLA, Kaasik-Krogerus S (eds) Europe from below: notions of Europe and the European among participants in EU cultural initiatives. Brill, Leiden, Boston, pp 183–205
Legrand P (1996) European legal systems are not converging. Int Comp Law Q 45:52–81
Leijten I (2017) Core socio-economic rights and the European Court of Human Rights. Cambridge University Press, Cambridge
Markesinis BS (1994) The gradual convergence. Clarendon Press, Oxford
Markesinis BS (2000) The Clifford chance millennium lectures: the coming together of the common law and the civil law. Hart Publishing, Oxford
Markesinis BS (2004) Comparative law in the courtroom and classroom: the story of the last thirty-five years. Hart Publishing, Oxford, Portland
Merryman JH (1981) On the convergence (and divergence) of the civil law and the common law. Stanford J Int Law 17:357–388
Micheler E (2009) Property in securities: a comparative study. Cambridge University Press

Plato, Phaedo, 100c–d (Perseus Digital Library of Tufts University)
Plato, Republic, 596a (Perseus Digital Library of Tufts University)
Platsas AE (2017) The harmonisation of national legal systems: strategic models and factors. Edward Elgar, Cheltenham
Reinsch W, Caporal J (2021) A renewed global trade system. In: Goodman MP, Miller S (eds) Toward a new global trade framework. Center for Strategic and International Studies (CSIS), pp 12–19
van Hoecke M (2000) The harmonisation of private law in Europe: some misunderstandings. In: van Hoecke M, Ost F (eds) The harmonisation of European private law. Hart Publishing, Oxford/Portland, pp 1–20
Weatherill S (2020) The fundamental question of minimum or maximum harmonisation. In: Garben S, Govaere I (eds) The Internal Market 2.0. Hart Publishing, Oxford, pp 261–284
Zweigert K, Kötz H (1998) An introduction to comparative law, 3rd edn. Oxford University Press, Oxford

Antonios E. Platsas is a Senior Lecturer in Law at the University of the West of England, Bristol, United Kingdom.

Resisting Legal Convergence

Jennifer L. L. Gant

1 Introduction

Legal convergence has been a concept of interest since ancient philosophers were discussing hypotheticals about the implications of shadows on a cave wall and extolling the virtues of the demos in the Athenian Forum. As noted by Antonios Platsas in the preceding chapter, convergence itself can be connected conceptually to the superiority of the singular as posited by both Plato and Aristotle, though espousing different underlying principles. Connection, coordination, and cooperation have become of particular import following the rise of the global economy in order to facilitate business across borders and to maximise the economic benefits of international trade.[1] Similarly, organisations such as the International Labour Organisation, Human Rights Commission and the United Nations (UN) seek to achieve greater harmony in the area of social justice and human rights as do treaties such as the European Convention on Human Rights (ECHR). With all of these promoting factors, full/total convergence of legal systems is as yet still out of reach.

Human society is split between the competing needs to achieve social conformity to be accepted by peers and society and the desire for difference, individuality and freedom. This cultural conundrum is one of the many reasons why true convergence remains so difficult to achieve in a democratic society. If this is transposed to the national and international level and viewed through the lens of history, it becomes obvious that these competing needs are insidious within legal culture and can be observed in the waves of liberalism to nationalism and conservatism that can be traced through the historic power struggle between the left and the right the world

[1] Gant (2015).

J. L. L. Gant (✉)
University of Derby, College of Business, Law and Social Sciences, Derby, England, UK
e-mail: j.gant@derby.ac.uk

E. Ghio, R. Perlingeiro (eds.), *Are Legal Systems Converging or Diverging?*,
https://doi.org/10.1007/978-3-031-38180-5_4

over. Although the optimist would see a continual progress toward a freer, more unified global society, the likely reality is that liberalism and conservatism come in waves over time. Where national conservatism prevails, global convergence becomes more difficult. This historical paradigm is particular acute within the European Union (EU) project over the last 30 years.

Modern discussions around comparative law and the convergence thesis have evolved since the rise in their popularity in the 1990s, becoming more complicated and intertwined with the challenge of balancing the benefits of harmonisation with the desire for nation states to maintain sovereignty and individuality. In 1996, Pierre Legrand famously wrote that European Legal Systems are Not Converging,[2] bucking the trend of the convergence thesis at the time promoted by academics and authors like René de Groot,[3] H Patrick Glenn,[4] and Basil Markensis[5] with the support of Konrad Zweigert and Hein Kötz,[6] who viewed convergence from the lens of comparative law. In the early 1990s, de Groot wrote that 'it is likely that the legal systems of the European States will form one great legal family with uniform or strongly similar rules in many areas.'[7] Glenn, writing in 1993, concurred that European legal systems would likely enjoy '*un rapprochement de plus en plus constant*' and that the *ius commune* would continue to accelerate this legal unification.[8] Finally, Markensis noted in 1994 that there is 'no doubt convergence is taking place' including a convergence of private law solutions, sources of law, procedural matters, drafting techniques, and 'a growing rapprochement in judicial views.'[9]

While it cannot be denied that there has been a growing trend towards encouraging harmonisation and convergence, particularly within the European project since the creation of the European Coal and Steel Community (ECSC) in 1951, the political will and subsequent policy underpinning this progress has evolved in perhaps surprising ways. This chapter examines the practical approach to convergence and harmonisation goals in the modern day and the real challenges that prevent a true aligning of legal principles and systems. First, the definition of convergence is queried in line with the conflicting theses of convergence proponents and detractors such as Legrand. Secondly, the fundamental challenges to true convergence are discussed with modern day examples of how these issues

---

[2] Legrand (1996).

[3] Professor emeritus of Maastricht University in Comparative Law and Private International Law with books and articles published on nationality law, comparative law, private international law, legal translation and the protection of regional and minority languages.

[4] Peter M Laing Professor at the Faculty of Law at McGill University specialized in comparative law, private international law, and civil procedure.

[5] Sir Basil Markesinis QC, LLD, DCL, FBA is a Greek-British barrister and legal scholar currently holding the position of Jamail Regents Professor at the University of Texas, Austin.

[6] See Zweigert and Kotz (1998).

[7] De Groot (1992).

[8] Glenn (1993), p. 567.

[9] Markensis (1994).

materialise. The impact of these challenges on policy and legislative direction in the EU and globally are presented in Sects. 4 and 5 respectively.

2 Defining Convergence

Most developed countries encounter similar social and economic problems that need to be resolved through some level of regulation. While the problems are often similar, the solutions and their underpinning principles as well as the scope of control exercised by government institutions are not often exactly the same. Whereas the global economy has encouraged some natural aligning of legal rules to ensure the efficient interaction of international markets and commerce, this tends to be done only as far as is necessary to improve national social or economic outcomes. Even if the rules then appear to be the same, this does not necessarily indicate a convergence of legal systems from first principles. As opined by Legrand, 'neither rules nor concepts reveal as much about a legal system as appears to be assumed. Rules, for example, are ephemeral and inevitably contingent. They are brittle.'[10]

What, then, is meant by convergence? Platsas suggests that convergence can occur through centralised (top-down) or decentralised (bottom-up) phenomena. 'Indeed, in its ideal form, the concept of legal convergence can either be an organic self-perfecting, self-evolving reality or a constantly updated centrally designed project.' Defining it as a concept, however, is less easily done.

On the surface, convergence may be the result of approximation, harmonisation and uniformization of legal standards between different legal systems.[11] It could also be considered the closer alignment of legal functions, which do not necessarily mean similar standards or rules. From the perspective of a comparative law methodology, 'the legal system of every society faces essentially the same problems and solves those problems by quite different means though very often with similar results.'[12] Thus from a comparative law perspective, one must compare legal *function* rather than legal *standards* in order to determine true convergence. The difficulty here is that when one views another legal system, the perspective is inevitably coloured by the concepts of one's own familiar legal system, thus it must be the problem itself that is under the magnifying glass rather than the rules.[13] As noted by Legrand, 'rules are pernicious to the extent that they present but the surface image of a legal system.'[14] One must go deeper to understand the underlying principles of a jurisdiction's legal system in order to find true common ground.

---

[10] Legrand (1996), p. 55.

[11] Platsas (2017), p. 245.

[12] Zweigert and Kotz (1998), p. 34.

[13] Ibid, p. 35.

[14] Legrand (1996), p. 56.

Going deeper requires a certain understanding of the legal culture that underpins the objectives of rulemaking in a jurisdiction. One of the greatest challenges to full convergence is the retention of certain vital aspects of a jurisdiction's legal culture that influence the policies informing legislation. These legal cultural characteristics are path dependent in nature and therefore traditionally difficult influences from which to deviate,[15] which will be discussed further below. The impulse to protect national individualism and sovereignty is quite clear when one examines the approach to aligning measures on the EU and global levels, also discussed below.

For the purpose of this chapter, the deeper concept of convergence is considered, which includes not just the approximation of rules between jurisdictions, but also the legal culture and principles that underpin the objectives and function of those rules. It is in the manifestation of a jurisdiction's fundamental point of reference in the approach and function of legal rules that reflects not just the legal culture of a jurisdiction, but also the challenges that the differences in legal culture actually present to convergence and harmonisation at a fundamental level.

3 Challenges to True Convergence

3.1 Legal Culture and Path Dependency

Legrand defines legal culture in the context of convergence as 'frameworks of intangibles within which interpretive communities operate and which have normative force for these communities.'[16] Despite its slightly impenetrable prose, this statement indicates the importance of the human perspective on the application and interpretation of legal rules, bringing in the judicial dimension. This inevitably includes the transcendent nature of 'collective mental programmes...that have formed not on account of the fact that we live on this planet or because of our uniqueness, but as a function of the community to which we belong'.[17] Culture is inextricably linked to a jurisdiction's history influencing the nature of legal rules and path dependent in its resistance to change.

'Rules are not the whole of law'[18] and, as described by Richard Posner, law is one of the most historically oriented, backward looking and path dependent of the professions, venerating tradition, precedent, custom, ancient practices and texts wisdom and an interpretative method that is inextricably linked to its history.[19] The historical dependence of law is self-evident in the operation of precedent in the common law and interpretative tools in civil systems as well as the entire influence of

---

[15] See Hathaway (2000); Bell (2012).

[16] Legrand (1996), p. 56.

[17] Ibid.

[18] Ibid, p. 58.

[19] Posner (2000).

constitutional law throughout the world. The way in which law develops over time is equally as influenced by history and the direction that certain rules have taken over time, creating a certain trajectory (or path) that tends to be quite difficult to dislodge or redirect, for the purpose of convergence for example.[20] Legrand explains that in relation to the conception of law as a discrete subsystem of rules within a society operating independently:

> [i]t has to be understood that the "legal" cannot be analytically separated from the 'non-legal' reality of society because the two worlds are inextricably linked. More accurately, law is a social sub-system. In other words, the "legal" can never be perceived on its own terms; to penetrate the "legal" one must appreciate the "social" that underpins it, otherwise the "legal" literally does not make sense.[21]

Further, in order to truly assess the fundamental possibility of true convergence and indeed its actual progress over time, '[o]ne has to reach beyond a synecdochic view of the law, that is, one must refute a view of the law where the part (the rules and concepts) is allowed to stand for the whole.'[22] With this thought in mind, and taking the EU project as an example, it is relevant to consider how legal culture and the peaks and troughs of conservatism and liberalism within it have influenced the integration policy of the EU over time. This example is a microcosm of the difficulties facing convergence on a global scale. In fact, given EU Member States' much closer connection, it is not surprising that global legal convergence is even further away from a future reality.

3.2 *The EU Integration Project*

Pierre Legrand rather prophetically pronounced that in eschewing the aforementioned 'synecdochic view' of the law and if one then reflects on the case of the EU,

> [...] one will have to accept that the possibility of European integration becomes as problematic as the idea of integration of European societies itself. Indeed, to integrate a group of "legal cultures" does not appear any more feasible than would the integration of different world-views privileged by a wide range of societies.[23]

While the modern concept of European integration is much older than the EU project, there have been many phases in the policy position toward integration, which has not always progressed in a straight line towards a closer union. In 1946, Winston Churchill called for a kind of united states in Europe, with a moral imperative to do right instead of wrong, rather than espousing any economic, political or social harmonisation, clearly in reaction to the great upheavals of the

[20] Gant (2015), p. 4.

[21] Legrand (1996), p. 58.

[22] Ibid, p. 60.

[23] Ibid.

first half of the twentieth century.[24] The modern push toward substantive European integration began with a specific industrial market integration with the ECSC created in 1952. Arguably, the peak of economic and social integration was achieved in the late 1990s when a Labour government in the UK erased years of conservative resistance to European integrative efforts by accepting the Social Chapter of the Maastricht Treaty. This heralded a shift throughout the EU that eased the policy of integration toward a much more cohesive and consensual convergence in not just economic, but also political and social policies and regulations throughout the European Union.[25] This shift was, however, relatively short-lived.

At the turn of the millennium, the Lisbon Strategy[26] declared that the EU was to become the most competitive and dynamic knowledge-based economy in the world, capable of sustainable economic growth, with more and better jobs, and greater social cohesion. This declaration clearly went beyond the market-making underpinning of the original Treaties and it introduced the Open Method of Coordination (OMC) as a means of spreading best practice and achieving greater convergence by helping Member States to develop their own policies in line with EU goals.[27] However, this process required a high degree of cooperation a requirement summarily defeated because of the protective measures taken individually by Member States and countries across the world as a result of the financial crisis of 2007.[28]

It is perhaps at the darkest times that the truth becomes most clear. The financial crisis revealed that the lofty targets of the Lisbon Strategy and the cooperative tools of the OMC were highly unlikely to achieve the integration sought. It became clear that in the face of recession and sovereign debt, Member States would be less concerned with adhering to soft law intentions than to protecting national economies and employment. There was a fundamental lack of commitment to the Lisbon Strategy which meant the whole policy fell flat with very little change as a result.

The Lisbon Strategy can be contrasted with the EU 2020 Strategy which introduced priorities of smart, sustainable, and inclusive growth—far less ambitious aims than that of the Lisbon Strategy and, perhaps, more realistic in reading the sign of the times. Interestingly, it seems that even the EU had its doubts about the likelihood of such voluntary convergence promoted throughout the 1990s and early 2000s, given that it introduced a concept of 'differentiated integration' with the Maastricht Treaty in 1992. This concept, discussed further below, has been criticised as 'undermining the cohesiveness and unity of the Community order'[29] but it has arguably saved the whole EU Project by providing a flexible framework within which Member States can both flex their sovereignty while meeting certain minimum standards in

[24] Davies (1997), pp. 1065–1066.

[25] Gant (2017), pp. 135–136.

[26] Council Recommendation of 19 June 2000 on the broad guidelines of the economic policies of the Member States and the Community, O.J. L 210 (2000).

[27] Barnard (2006), pp. 26–27.

[28] Gant (2017), p. 136.

[29] Craig and de Burca (2015), p. 3.

important economic and social regulatory areas across the board.[30] While this flexible framework may give hope to the proponents of further convergence and/or harmonisation, there remains a high level of disappointing evidence that these lofty ambitions may as yet be out of reach, at least for the time being.

3.3 *Is 'Nationalism in Retreat?' Hardly*

There are many words that refer to a closer alignment of law, culture and policy: harmonisation, convergence, integration, among others. All of these activities of the drawing together of different jurisdictions into a more cohesive and unified community are dependent upon 'a closeness of legal principles as well as economic and social policies' of those jurisdictions. It has been acknowledged in EU Policy and global efforts in activities towards convergence or harmonisation that a 'one-size-fits-all' approach will not capture the buy-in required to create an effective and aligned global legal community.[31] It is necessary to cater to the legal and social cultures of the jurisdictions subject to the attempted convergence in order to achieve cooperation toward those ends.

The level of closeness of convergence that can be achieved is dependent upon a certain closeness of fundamental legal principles as well as the economic and social policies of the community of jurisdictions. The resistance to changing path dependent cultural characteristics intrinsic to those jurisdictions, such as those fundamental legal principles, economic and social policy, is a key obstacle to obtaining the cooperation needed to achieve closer convergence.[32] While some of these key differences could be attributed to differences in the legal origins of a jurisdiction's legal system[33]—civil or common among others—there are also irreducible differences in legal mentality derived from essentially different stages if political, social, and legal processes toward a common concept of liberal democracy. These differences tend to be path dependent in nature and may vary considerably among jurisdictions. Given their ingrained nature, they are tremendously difficult to change without specific and at times extensive changes to legal institutions, which may also have constitutional implications.[34] These difficulties continue to be evident today in a number of examples.

One of the most significant examples of the failure or ultimate resistance to convergence in the last decade, particularly for Europe, is Brexit, commencing with the referendum in the UK in 2016. Britain's membership in the EU has had a

[30] Lynch Fannon et al. (2022), p. 33.

[31] Lynch Fannon et al. (2022), p. 251.

[32] Ibid.

[33] On the concept of legal origins, see for example: Armour et al. (2008, 2009); Ahlering and Deakin (2007).

[34] Lynch Fannon et al. (2022), p. 275.

significant influence on the direction of UK law since 1973 and has arguably pushed it into a more socially liberal and protective regulatory framework than it might naturally have adopted.[35] This demonstrates the power of a 'top-down' regulatory approach espoused by aspects of EU legislative policy as well as the dangers it presents to the fragility of nationalist sentiments when it is perceived as going too far. Arguments of the Leave campaign centred on immigration and national autonomy and against the supremacy of EU law over British law. However, the Leave campaign also favoured maintaining access to the single European market, an arguably naïve and even arrogant notion under the circumstances, while reducing the flow of immigrants from Eastern Europe.[36] Thus, Brexit was a direct reaction of the conservative elements in the UK to the push by the EU toward closer convergence and harmonisation, despite the fact that EU policy had long since adopted the concept of differentiated integration (discussed below) to account for the conservative resistance to change.

The COVID-19 pandemic of 2020-21 also provides evidence that while legal systems encountered similar economic problems, they did not come together to solve them collectively in a necessarily convergent fashion, despite the fact that the pandemic presented an opportunity to do so. The will is simply not there in the face of crisis. However, there was natural 'bottom-up' convergence in some areas, such as the temporary and sometimes long-term legislative reactions to the looming business failures that many small and medium sized enterprises faced as a result of pandemic lockdowns. For example, the growing number of business failures led many jurisdictions to introduce new mechanisms in insolvency and restructuring frameworks, while a number of changes were also made to certain tried and tested measures dealing with corporate financial distress in a number of jurisdictions. However, the approaches varied from taking a 'less is more' approach, streamlining their frameworks, while others only adjusted frameworks temporarily and still others made sweeping reforms to their systems.[37] This variance in approach certainly demonstrates different priorities in different jurisdictions, which indicates a perhaps deeper level of difference that will continue to prevent closer convergence.

Responses to COVID-19 globally were also quite different, providing a glimpse into the differing priorities of jurisdictions, along a significant spectrum of reactions. Lockdowns and restrictions differed from taking an incredibly restrictive approach requiring long quarantines and economically disastrous shutdowns of businesses, to suggestions about masks and exhortations to wash hands and reduce the spread. Differences existed throughout Europe as well, with the UK taking down its requirements at a much earlier stage to revive economic activity than many other more liberal leaning countries. Compare that with the significant restrictions in China, for example, and it becomes clear that fundamental priorities (money versus

[35] Gant (2020), p. 61.

[36] Arnorsson and Zoega (2018), p. 303.

[37] Ghio et al. (2021), pp. 438–439.

humans) still differ significantly throughout the world, which indicates certain fundamental obstacles to an eventual global community of convergent legal systems.

There are also indications of fundamental differences that will continue to inhibit closer convergence within the EU itself. Many Eastern European Member States have encountered challenges to integrating into the EU due to some fundamental differences in legal culture. Many of these differences are connected to the adjustment to a post-communism approach to justice and administration, which was required to meet the EU entry criteria. Although the EU created mechanisms to assist Member States such as Romania and Bulgaria to address shortcomings,[38] other Eastern European countries such as Poland, Hungary, and the Czech Republic have seen increased tensions as mostly right-leaning political parties tested their autonomy against EU governance.[39] Conservative right political muscle-flexing is not limited to newer Eastern European EU Member States.

The rise of Donald Trump and conservative elements throughout the world in the last decade has a lot to answer for. In the American context, Trumpism has been referred to 'a period of protectionism, isolationism mingled with militaristic bluster, scepticism toward environmental and other regulation [and] antipathy toward immigrants and people of colour generally'.[40] Trumpism is a reactionary opposition to progressive gains by those seeking to restore the *status quo*[41] and clearly contrary to any movements toward convergent themes in the global legal system. Despite the election of a Democrat moderate candidate in Joe Biden in 2020, the backlash has arguably continued to increase, demonstrating nationalist and isolationist tendencies that militate against any direct efforts towards a globalisation of legal systems. Trumpism and the attitudes that it represents are not isolated to the United States either.

Within the EU, there is also a growing voice for Euroscepticism and the promotion of policies associated with the European conservative political tradition. Since 2015, Poland's right wing ruling party, Law and Justice, has led the Warsaw Summit's efforts to persuade the western international community 'to develop a common, robust response to what it sees as Russian President Vladimir Putin's neo-imperialist destabilisation of central and eastern Europe.'[42] Membership of this group included the UK conservative party (prior to Brexit), Hungarian Prime Minister Viktor Orbán, and the French National Rally leader and recent presidential candidate (and nearly president), Marine le Pen.[43] All of these leaders and their

[38] European Commission (2006) Cooperation and verification mechanism for Bulgaria and Romania, https://ec.europa.eu/info/policies/justice-and-fundamental-rights/upholding-rule-law/rule-law/assistance-bulgaria-and-romania-under-cvm/cooperation-and-verification-mechanism-bulgaria-and-romania_en.

[39] Lynch Fannon et al. (2022), p. 273.

[40] Lieberman et al. (2019).

[41] Murib (2020), p. 296.

[42] Szczerbiak (2022).

[43] Ibid.

parties favour returning the EU to its 'original role as a looser alliance of economically cooperating sovereign member states with a more consensual decision-making process' but many also tend to have pro-Russian sympathies, which is quite contrary to the aims of the Polish Law and Justice party in convening the Summit. However, with the departure of the British Conservatives, the mainstream centre right strength within the Warsaw Summit has diminished, meaning that stronger ties must be built with the remaining radical right Eurosceptic parties despite their pro-Russian sympathies. This shift does not bode well for further convergence at EU level given that the right-leaning parties throughout Europe seem to keep gaining ground.

Finally, the unthinkable has also happened. Whereas Platsas observed that 'the Europeans have made the commencement of another world war in Europe not just unthinkable but virtually impossible',[44] the recent conflagration in the Ukraine calls this into rather uncomfortable doubt. While the whole world may not be fighting on the ground, many nations have provided aid, imposed sanctions on Russia, accepted Ukrainian refugees, and spoken out against the action. The activities of Putin are reminiscent of the Soviet era of propaganda control and misinformation and even reflects the totalitarian ideals of Nazi Germany with 'one people, one state, and one leader' despite directing that accusation at Ukraine itself. The reaction may be a result of the traumatic experience of the collapse of the Soviet Union and seeks to revive its past glory.[45] Regardless of the rationale, it signals the growing trend toward nationalism, particularly given the sympathies of many non-Western countries about the conflict. Many of the emerging markets in the world either support the Russian invasion or are neutral about it. In addition, some countries depend on Russian arms and fuel while still others feel 'a misplaced nostalgia for Soviet largesse' and see much of the West as decadent, self-serving, and hypocritical.[46] The lack of will to present a true concerted front against Putin's actions in the Ukraine only highlights the lack of cohesion within the current world order and as noted by The Economist:

> If Russia is allowed to prevail in the Ukraine, bullying, lying and manipulation will further penetrate trade, treaties, and international law – the whole panoply of arrangements that are so easily taken for granted but which keep the world turning.[47]

Nationalism is noticeably retrenching despite the rhetoric of the liberal left, and it seems that the world is even more fractured than it was following World War II and even prior to the collapse of the Soviet Union. Achieving convergence of legal systems for the benefit of all must take into account these issues as well as the seemingly cyclical shifts towards liberalism and conservatism in order to eventually succeed. Policies around convergence, harmonisation, and integration must remain

[44] Platsas section 3.3.

[45] Marayev and Guz (2022).

[46] The War in the Ukraine: Get off the Fence, The Economist 16th-22nd April 2022.

[47] Ibid.

flexible, which will inevitably slow progress toward a more closely aligned legal order, but without that deliberation the lofty aims will remain unachievable.

4 Solutions to Convergence Resistance

4.1 EU Solutions to Breaking Path Dependency: Differentiated Integration

The EU has long taken a fairly flexible approach to harmonisation and convergence due to the different legal cultures to which it must cater to achieve its ends. The policy came to be known as 'differentiated integration' and essentially refers to flexibility in the EU approach to further integration (convergence). The Treaty of Amsterdam 'legitimated mechanisms for different degrees of integration and cooperation between groups of states.'[48] It introduced articles on closer cooperation (rather than substantive harmonisation), which demonstrated that differentiated integration should be considered EU policy around harmonisation activities even prior to the turn of the millennium (1999).[49] The Lisbon Treaty then presented a clear policy move away from hierarchical governance, instead emphasising a preference for directives over regulations because as legislative instruments, directives allow greater discretion in implementation. Further, there has been a preference for framework directives over prescriptive directives.[50] The EU policy utilising a differentiated integration approach to legislation demonstrates an understanding that to achieve effective convergence in the EU, it cannot be forced because of fundamental differences in legal culture as well as resistance to too much perceived interference with national sovereignty.

There is also a general lack of will when it comes to voluntarily converging along a legislative theme. In 2014, for example, the EU attempted to nudge Member States towards the introduction of similar rules around resolving business failure. This took the form of a soft law instrument, the Recommendation on a New Approach to Business Failure.[51] The objectives of this Recommendation were to (1) contribute to the smooth functioning of the internal market by enabling the restructuring of viable businesses; (2) enhance the survival prospects of firms in financial difficulty; and (3) minimise investment decisions being made on the basis of national insolvency laws.[52] Although these goals are mutually beneficial, there was little legislative

---

[48] Craig and de Burca (2015), p. 15.

[49] Lynch Fannon et al. (2022), pp. 33–34.

[50] See European Commission (2010).

[51] Commission Recommendation of 12 March 2014 on a new approach to business failure and insolvency, O.J. L 74 (2014).

[52] European Commission, Commission Recommendation of 12 March 2014 on a new approach to business failure and insolvency (Text with EEA relevance) (2014/135/EU), p. 1.

action among the Member States following the issue of the Recommendation, which was revealed following an evaluation of the impact of the Recommendation by the DG Justice & Consumers of the European Commission in 2015. As a result, an Experts Group was convened to draft a Directive[53] which would essentially accomplish the same result, but through a more powerful legislative instrument that would require implementation into Member State legal systems.

The form that the Directive eventually took when it was published in 2019 was a fairly loose framework with multiple options and derogations available to cater to the broad preferences of different Member States. The result looks more like an exhortation to introduce preventive restructuring mechanisms that can be used by businesses in financial distress across the Member States, rather than a true harmonisation instrument. The flexibility in implementation is particularly noticeable in some of the more controversial provisions, which demonstrates how difficult it is to achieve any real harmonisation of legal areas that are conceptually complex and associated with debates around the policy goals and values that underpin them.[54]

Preventive restructuring in the EU is but one example of the (adverse) impact a differentiated integration approach has had on achieving real legal convergence. It allows for such great latitude that it is arguable that such loosely drafted legislative instruments aim, predominantly, to ensure that certain tools with similar functions are available to entities in every Member State, rather than achieving true substantive harmonisation. While there is nothing wrong with that, it does not necessarily progress the harmonisation agenda toward a truly integrated legal community. However, the approach does allow legislation to be passed and implemented that might otherwise never make it through early negotiation phases due to the differences to legal culture and socioeconomic policies that prevent a closer alignment.

4.2 *Global Convergence: Model Laws and Legislative Guides*

Efforts toward aligning certain aspects of global legal systems also take a flexible approach to encouraging cooperation between different jurisdictions. The UN Commission on International Trade Law (UNCITRAL) provides a number of examples that prove this point. In its Model Law on Cross-Border Insolvency for example,[55] the aim is to set standards rather than full convergence of substantive law. The Model Law aims to promote the modification of domestic laws with a view to enhancing predictability in a cross-border commercial context.

[53]Directive (EU) 2019/1023 of the European Parliament and of the Council of 20 June 2019 on preventive restructuring frameworks, on discharge of debt and disqualifications, and on measures to increase the efficiency of procedures concerning restructuring, insolvency and discharge of debt, and amending Directive (EU) 2017/1132 O.J. L 172.

[54]Lynch Fannon et al. (2022), p. 194.

[55]UNCITRAL Model Law on Cross-Border Insolvency (1997).

Most of UNCITRAL's legislative instruments adopt an approach that encourages coordination and cooperation between states rather than substantive harmonisation. For example, the Model Law on Cross-Border Insolvency is aimed at providing effective mechanisms for dealing with cases of cross border insolvency without requiring changes to the substance of domestic insolvency law frameworks. This is an example of a rather successful attempt to draw aspects of legal systems into a coordinated community, but without forcing convergence of substantive law. UNCITRAL is also known for the production of Legislative Guides. For example, the Legislative Guide on Insolvency Law provides a comprehensive statement of the key objectives and principles that should be reflected in a State's insolvency laws by providing a reference tool for national authorities and legislative bodies when preparing new laws or reforming old ones.[56]

Recent developments within the UNCITRAL Working Group V on Insolvency Law have seen discussions around the development of more prescriptive models, such as the Legislative Recommendations on Insolvency of Micro- and Small Enterprises.[57] This document sets out some rather specific parameters of what a restructuring framework for micro and small enterprises (MSE) should look like. Although this, and other legislative instruments, are purely soft law in nature, the work of UNCITRAL and other international organisations, such as the World Bank and the International Monetary Fund (IMF), have slowly been creeping in their mission to encourage cooperation in commercial settings across-borders towards recommendations that look more like substantive harmonisation.

Finally, in observing the negotiations around instruments such as the Recommendations for MSEs within the UNCITRAL chambers, it is clear that there remain certain fundamental differences that, regardless of a common goal, will always require compromise. These differences often pertain to the difference between well developed economies and legal systems that have evolved to cater to complex commercial transactions against emerging or developing economies, which do not have the infrastructure to support highly complex legal devices. In addition, there are also clear disagreements stemming from sovereignty and different views on the same topic preventing a meeting of the minds. As a result, legislative instruments and model laws have had to remain broad and flexible so that they can be utilised by a higher number of jurisdictions, allowing for individual legal cultures to continue to assert themselves in the way that such laws are drafted on a national level.

---

[56] UNCITRAL Legislative Guide on Insolvency Law (2019).

[57] UNCITRAL Legislative Recommendations on Insolvency of Micro- and Small Enterprises (2021).

5 Conclusion

While legal systems all tend to encounter similar problems and often come up with solutions that look the same, if one looks behind the curtain the operative principles that inform legislative design are often quite different. In terms of natural convergence—'an organic self-perfecting, self-evolving reality'—whether such a thing is occurring must be an analysis that takes into account more than just what the rules seem to do—their form and function, but must also consider the underlying legal principles and the legal culture that informs the aims of legislation. The path dependent nature of legal cultural characteristics has a significant influence on the purposes and principles that underlie regulation in individual jurisdictions. These characteristics influence the means and methods that legal regulation will take as well as the relative ease with which they can be changed to align to a supranational standard. In order for global convergence to be achieved, irrespective of whether or not that is a desirable goal in itself, a true parity of principles and culture must first be attained.

There are significant challenges to any forced convergence as well. Although there are many arguments that could be made that advocate for increased legal convergence, such as the avoidance of self-interested forum shopping (where relevant) and the creation of a better and more level field of competition, at least in the commercial law area, a forced convergence in our current (largely) liberal democracies would cause an upheaval that the current world order would not be able to support. It would also be potentially detrimental to legal systems that are not as developed as 'convergence of standards to a median level [...] between national systems at different stages of economic development would remove an individual comparative advantage' from those states with more flexible legal regimes that attract users.[58] As described above, even where convergent themes are encouraged, legislative devices that require implementation are likely needed to ensure that such proposals are implemented at all. As noted by Legrand:

> the analysis of European legal integration at the level of posited law suggesting a convergence of legal systems is misleading. Indeed, if one foregoes a surface examination at the level of rules and concepts to conduct a deep examination in terms of legal *mentalites*, one must come to the conclusion that legal systems, despite the adjacence within the European community, have not been converging, are not converging, and will not be converging. It is a mistake to suggest otherwise.[59]

Indeed, if one considers those deeper elements of the law, it is difficult to disagree with Legrand's original hypothesis.

There are certainly benefits to convergence, as noted by Platsas, 'the creation of common rules [...] eventually create[s] the guarantees for long lasting peace and prosperity.'[60] However, if one examines the world as it has developed in the last ten

[58] Gant (2014), p. 77.

[59] Legrand (1996), p. 61.

[60] Platsas section 3.3.

years or so, it is not necessarily true that the 'nation state or centralised and unitary forms of statehood' are ideas that are in retreat.[61] Rather, conservatism and isolationism have resurged in recent years. As such, an immediate and further alignment of legal systems is hardly imminent. Rather, with the rise of Trumpism, separatist activities such as Brexit, and the currently ongoing war in the Ukraine, as well as the close call in the French elections for electing a far-right candidate, it seems the world is currently on a downward trend away from liberalism. If further convergence is to be encouraged and achieved, these differences must inevitably be taken into account in the policies that underpin European and global efforts in this direction, which may eventually lead to a globally aligned legal system, but it will not be any time soon.

References

Ahlering B, Deakin S (2007) Labor regulation, corporate governance, and legal origin: a case of institutional complementarity? Law Soc Rev 41:865–908

Armour J et al (2008) Shareholder protection and stock market development: an empirical test of the legal origins hypothesis. J Empir Leg Stud 6:343–380

Armour J et al (2009) How do legal rules evolve? Evidence from Cross-Country comparison of shareholder, creditor, and worker protection. Am J Comp Law 57:579–629

Arnorsson A, Zoega G (2018) On the causes of Brexit. Eur J Polit Econ 55:301–323

Barnard C (2006) EU employment law, 3rd edn. OUP, Oxford

Bell J (2012) Path dependence and legal development. Tulane Law Rev 87:787–810

Craig P, de Burca G (2015) EU law text cases and materials, 6th edn. OUP, Oxford

Davies N (1997) Europe: a history. Pimlico, London

De Groot G-R (1992) European education in the 21st century. In: De Witte B, Forder C (eds) The common law of Europe and the future of education. Kluwer Law International, Devender, pp 7–29

Gant J (2014) Social policy and insolvency: struggles towards convergence. NIBLeJ 2:49–80

Gant J (2015) Path dependent obstacles to cross-border insolvency: a social Darwinian perspective. NIBLeJ 3:101–134

Gant J (2017) Balancing the protection of business and employment in insolvency: an Anglo-French perspective. Eleven International Publishing, The Hague

Gant J (2020) Britain and Brexit: a forecast of the future of employment protection during corporate insolvency. Int Insolv Rev 29:61–82

Ghio et al (2021) Harmonising insolvency law in the EU: new thoughts on old ideas in the wake of the COVID-19 pandemic. Int Insolv Rev 30:427–459

Glenn H (1993) La Civilisation de la Common Law. Rev Int Dr Comp 45:559–575

Hathaway O (2000) Path dependence in the law: the course and pattern of legal change in a common law system. Iowa Law Rev 86:601–665

Legrand P (1996) European legal systems are not converging. Int Comp Law Q 45:52–81

Lieberman R et al (2019) The Trump Presidency and American democracy: a historical and comparative analysis. Perspect Polit 17:470–479

Lynch Fannon I et al (2022) Corporate recovery in an integrated Europe: harmonisation, coordination and judicial cooperation. Edward Elgar, Cheltenham

[61] Platsas section 3.1.

Marayev V, Guz J (2022) Rashism or Why Russians are the New Nazi, VoxUkraine. https://voxukraine.org/en/rashism-or-why-russians-are-the-new-nazi/
Markensis B (ed) (1994) The gradual convergence: foreign ideas, foreign influences, and English law on the eve of the 21st century. Clarendon Press, Oxford
Murib Z (2020) Backlash, intersectionality, and Trumpism. Signs: J Women Cult Soc 45:295–302
Platsas A (2017) The harmonisation of national legal systems: strategic models and factors. Edward Elgar, Cheltenham
Posner R (2000) Past-dependency, pragmatism, and critique of history in adjudication and legal scholarship. Univ Chic Law Rev 67:573–606
Szczerbiak A (2022) Why is Poland's ruling party building closer links with right-wing Eurosceptic groups?, EUROPP. https://blogs.lse.ac.uk/europpblog/2022/01/06/why-is-polands-ruling-party-building-closer-links-with-right-wing-eurosceptic-groups/
The War in the Ukraine: Get off the Fence, The Economist 16th-22nd April 2022
UNCITRAL (1997) UNCITRAL Model Law on Cross-Border Insolvency
UNCITRAL (2019) UNCITRAL Legislative Guide on Insolvency Law
Zweigert K, Kotz K (1998) An introduction to comparative law, translated by Tony Weir, 3rd edn. Oxford University Press, Oxford

Jennifer L. L. Gant is a senior lecturer in law in the College of Business, Law and Social Sciences at the University of Derby, United Kingdom.

Part II
Thematic and Jurisdictional Case Studies 1: Private Law

Bankruptcy Law in the United States

Laura N. Coordes

1 Introduction

In today's global economy, borders are no barrier to financial distress. When a crisis has a global impact, one might expect legal convergence to ensue, as similar issues arise in different countries. For the United States (US) bankruptcy system, however, convergence with the insolvency laws and norms of other, foreign countries appears to be something of an afterthought. The US bankruptcy system, and particularly chapter 11 of the US Bankruptcy Code, continues to attract both foreign and domestic debtors seeking to reorganise during times of financial difficulty. Although the structure of US bankruptcy law provides some tools for convergence with the Model Law on Cross-Border Insolvency, notably in the form of chapter 15 of the Bankruptcy Code, it appears unlikely that US substantive law will adapt to better align with foreign law in response to global financial challenges. Indeed, given the wide availability of US bankruptcy procedures to foreign debtors, coupled with a desire to maintain its position as the 'gold standard' for corporate reorganisations,[1] US bankruptcy law is likely to continue playing a dominant role in resolving the financial distress of debtors around the globe.

Before assessing the impact of financial crises on bankruptcy law in the US, it is important to define the terms used in the assessment. This chapter uses the term 'convergence' to describe a bottom-up process of creating legal similarity. Laws 'converge' by exhibiting the same governing principles or even by becoming identical. By contrast, this chapter uses the term 'harmonisation' to describe a top-down process of creating legal similarity. Harmonisation can occur through

[1] Casey and Macey (2021), p. 468.

L. N. Coordes (✉)
Arizona State University, Sandra Day O'Connor College of Law, Phoenix, AZ, USA
e-mail: laura.coordes@asu.edu

E. Ghio, R. Perlingeiro (eds.), *Are Legal Systems Converging or Diverging?*,
https://doi.org/10.1007/978-3-031-38180-5_5

the imposition of supranational standards, as has been seen in many cases in the European Union (EU). The concentration of foreign cases and issues being litigated in US bankruptcy court would appear to be creating legal similarity at first blush, in the sense that large debtors, both foreign and domestic, are turning to US bankruptcy court for their restructuring needs. However, US law does not appear to be substantively converging with the bankruptcy and insolvency laws of other countries, in part due to this same concentration of cases. Indeed, although US bankruptcy law did change in response to the COVID-19 global pandemic and the crises stemming from it, there was no indication that these changes were made as part of an effort to better align with non-US insolvency laws or legal standards.

The US have seen elements of both convergence and divergence in recent trends occurring with respect to cross-border bankruptcies. Although US substantive law is not converging with that of other nations, foreign debtors—those domiciled outside of the US—frequently choose to file for chapter 11 bankruptcy (a main proceeding) in the US, instead of commencing proceedings in their home jurisdiction and filing for ancillary, chapter 15 proceedings in the US. Thus, there is a trend toward practice convergence, where US law dominates global restructuring practice, even if there is not yet substantive convergence or harmonisation of bankruptcy laws across the globe.

When foreign entities choose chapter 11 over chapter 15, they are choosing a US-centric outcome instead of one that more directly involves their home jurisdiction's courts and legal system. In some cases, this is necessary or preferable. For example, if the debtor's primary creditors are all located within the United States, a choice of a US forum for resolving insolvency issues would seem to make the most sense. Yet, a foreign debtor's choice to restructure under US chapter 11 may also stifle the development of the law in their home jurisdiction. Courts in a foreign debtor's home jurisdiction may not have the chance to grapple with important issues if the debtor is bringing those issues solely to a US court. Although a chapter 11 bankruptcy case is centralised in a sophisticated forum that is convenient for US-based creditors, foreign courts do not get to address the issues that arise, so the foreign law, as applied to the restructuring of complex entities, may not develop or be used much. Furthermore, if restructuring proceedings are concentrated in the US, courts do not get used to cooperating with each other, and cooperative principles may not develop.

A second trend that has been occurring involves companies choosing to file for chapter 15 (ancillary) bankruptcy to achieve objectives that have little to do with resolving financial distress. Because the US has a relatively lax good faith standard when it comes to cross-border cases,[2] foreign debtors can use the chapter 15 process to obtain litigation advantages they would not otherwise possess when filing solely

[2] For example, the Ninth Circuit Bankruptcy Appellate Panel recently held that, as long as chapter 15's recognition requirements are met, a bad faith filing is not a basis for denying recognition of a foreign main proceeding. Samba v. International Petroleum Products & Additives Co (In re Black Gold SARL), 635 BR 517 (9th Cir BAP 2022).

in their home jurisdiction. The choice of a US forum to achieve these litigation objectives highlights the divergences in the laws of other countries. This has the effect of making chapter 15 a litigation tool in addition to a restructuring process. Once again, there are benefits and drawbacks to this use. Although using chapter 15 to aid the debtor in litigation may also aid the debtor's reorganisation, US courts may be authorising litigation or procedures that are outside the scope of what the debtor's home country would permit. US bankruptcy law permits this outcome. However, from the perspective of global cooperation, the US would appear to be taking on a greater role in foreign proceedings, meaning, once again, that the law in foreign jurisdictions may be under-developed or even ignored.

Put simply, if the US remains an attractive forum for debtors to file for bankruptcy, it is unclear how much drive there will be for bankruptcy law to be harmonised across the globe. This is particularly true in large bankruptcy cases.

This chapter proceeds as follows. Section 2 introduces the reader to the relevant bankruptcy and insolvency-related laws[3] that form this chapter's focus. Section 3 explores the trend of foreign debtors filing for chapter 11, while Sect. 4 discusses the use of chapter 15 as a litigation tool. Section 5 provides some concluding thoughts on the role of global convergence in bankruptcy law from a US perspective.

2 Background

There are three laws relevant to this chapter's discussion: the United Nations Commission on International Trade Law (UNCITRAL) Model Law on Cross-Border Insolvency (the 'Model Law'), and chapters 11 and 15 of the United States Bankruptcy Code (the 'Bankruptcy Code' or 'Code').

The Model Law was developed in 1997 by UNCITRAL to harmonise the administration of cases involving parties from different countries.[4] Harmonisation under the Model Law was intended to occur through cooperation and coordination among different jurisdictions.[5] To achieve this, the Model Law is concerned with cooperation rather than the development of uniform laws.[6] The drafters of the Model Law recognised that it was unlikely, and perhaps even undesirable, for all

[3] This chapter uses the term 'bankruptcy' to describe the legal process in the United States for addressing insolvency and financial distress. By contrast, it uses the term 'insolvency' in two ways: (i) to identify a state of economic distress where an entity is unable to pay debts upon maturity (e.g., an 'insolvent debtor') and (ii) when referring to foreign and model laws designated as insolvency laws (e.g., an insolvency proceeding in the United Kingdom, the Model Law on Cross-Border Insolvency).

[4] Chapter 15 of the U.S. Bankruptcy Code: Ancillary and Cross-Border Cases, Cong Res Serv (2006), p. 8.

[5] UNCITRAL Model Law on Cross-Border Insolvency (1997), UN Commission on Int'l Trade L (1997).

[6] Ibid.

jurisdictions to adopt the same set of insolvency or bankruptcy laws. Thus, rather than attempting to create a uniform substantive law, the Model Law instead provides procedures to allow different countries to work together while recognising that the laws of one country will continue to differ from those of the next.[7]

However, even these procedures may differ from country to country. As the corresponding Legislative Guide notes, it 'does not provide a single set of model solutions to address the issues central to an effective and efficient insolvency law but assists the reader to evaluate different approaches available and to choose the one most suitable in the national or local context.'[8] In this way, the Model Law recognises and supports differences among nations and eschews any requirement of identical implementation of the law. At the same time, the Legislative Guide's recommended legislative principles indicate that the pull of harmonisation is strong.[9]

The US implemented the Model Law through chapter 15 of the Bankruptcy Code. Chapter 15 allows a foreign representative of a debtor to file a case in the United States that is ancillary to a primary insolvency proceeding brought in another jurisdiction, typically the debtor's home country or centre of main interests.[10] When the US bankruptcy court 'recognises' the foreign proceeding, it grants the foreign representative access to US courts and, depending on the relief requested, access to US bankruptcy tools and procedures.[11] Chapter 15 is a domestic US law, so it has no effect on other countries' laws. Nor does chapter 15 substantively conform US bankruptcy law with the laws of other jurisdictions. Instead, chapter 15, consistent with the aims of the Model Law, allows a US bankruptcy proceeding to complement and assist proceedings taking place outside US borders.

In contrast to chapter 15, chapter 11 of the Bankruptcy Code does not explicitly contemplate cross-border proceedings. Chapter 11 is the 'reorganisation' chapter of the Bankruptcy Code and likely, one of the best-known restructuring processes in the world. Many other countries have looked to chapter 11 as a basis for their own laws.[12] Chapter 11 has existed in its current form, more or less, since 1978.[13] Consequently, there is well-developed precedent in US courts on many chapter 11 issues, making the chapter 11 process appealing for many entities, domestic and foreign alike, particularly if their restructurings pose complex structural or logistical challenges. US courts have extensive experience dealing with large, complex entities, and, as will be discussed in more detail below, if chapter 11 is available to a potential debtor, it is often a good choice.

---

[7]Ibid.

[8]UNCITRAL Legislative Guide on Insolvency Law, Parts One and Two (2004), p. 2.

[9]Ibid.

[10]Chapter 15 – Bankruptcy Basics, U.S. Courts, https://www.uscourts.gov.

[11]Ibid.

[12]Warren and Westbrook (2009), p. 604 note that 'the world has turned to Chapter 11 as a model to create value for a business's creditors, workers, investors, and communities' but also observe that 'American-style reorganisation has been widely disparaged.'

[13]Warren and Westbrook (2009), p. 613.

With this background in mind, the remainder of the chapter will explore the use of both chapter 11 and chapter 15 to address financial distress and how this use can create opportunities for both convergence and divergence, particularly in times of crisis.

3 Use of Chapter 11 by Foreign Debtors

As the previous section indicated, chapter 11 is US domestic law and was not explicitly designed with foreign debtors or cross-border cases in mind. Thus, there are no explicit provisions in chapter 11 calling for inter-jurisdictional cooperation, because, unlike chapter 15, chapter 11 was not designed to be used in conjunction with foreign proceedings. Despite this, foreign debtors can and have filed for chapter 11, and some have even attempted to use the chapter 11 process in conjunction with bankruptcy and insolvency proceedings in other jurisdictions.

Recent studies have concluded that the COVID-19 pandemic corresponded with an increase in chapter 11 filings in 2020, particularly for large businesses.[14] Indeed, the pandemic 'triggered a spike in large corporate bankruptcy filings not seen since the global financial crisis' of 2008.[15] Although it is unclear whether large corporate filings will continue to trend upward, it seems reasonable to conclude that the health crisis brought on by the pandemic contributed to financial instability in businesses across the globe. It is therefore worth studying how businesses, both foreign and domestic, have used and continue to use US chapter 11 in response to crises leading to financial instability.

3.1 Nortel

One of the most salient examples of US chapter 11 being used in coordination with foreign proceedings is the *Nortel* case. The debtor, Nortel, filed for bankruptcy simultaneously in Canada, the US, and the United Kingdom (UK) in order to liquidate its global businesses.[16] Years of litigation followed, as Nortel businesses around the globe fought over who would get the money.[17] In 2014, courts in the US and Canada jointly conducted a 21-day[18] cross-border trial, and approximately two years later, the Ontario Superior Court and the US Bankruptcy Court for the District

[14] Martos-Vila and Shi (2022).

[15] Schwartz et al. (2021).

[16] McKiernan (2017).

[17] Hals (2017).

[18] McKiernan (2017).

of Delaware jointly approved a settlement for the distribution of assets to creditors.[19] Over $7 billion was finally distributed after years of litigation in multiple fora.[20]

Although Nortel's liquidation—and litigation—woes were ultimately resolved, commentators believed that the lack of coherent cross-border procedures contributed to the length of the case.[21] As one lawyer involved in the case remarked, '[i]f we knew what system we were following, rather than filing in three countries and spending two years fighting over the process, that would have made things much more efficient and the legal fees would have been more constrained.'[22]

Indeed, Nortel's liquidation was one of the most expensive cases on record: global fees for professionals involved in the case totalled nearly $1.9 billion.[23] Taking nearly 3000 days to complete, the case is one of the longest in the history of US chapter 11 bankruptcy.[24]

The Nortel case illustrates that courts can work together across borders to achieve a successful result. However, it also illustrates the inefficiencies that can arise when doing so and the need for more convergence on the procedures to be followed and the principles that should govern.

3.2 *Easy Eligibility*

Why might a debtor such as Nortel, which was headquartered in Canada, or any debtor with headquarters or substantial business outside of the US, nevertheless choose to file for chapter 11 in the US? Put differently, why would a foreign debtor want to subject itself to US bankruptcy court?

One answer lies in the ease of qualifying for chapter 11 bankruptcy. Under the Bankruptcy Code, a chapter 11 case may be filed by 'a person that resides or has a domicile, a place of business, or property in the United States.'[25] Having 'property' in the US is a particularly easy requirement to satisfy—something as simple as a bank account in the US will suffice.[26] Thus, if a foreign entity has any assets in the US—even intangible assets—it can qualify for US domestic bankruptcy law.[27] Further, because bankruptcy is an *in rem* proceeding, once a US bankruptcy case

---

[19] Ibid.

[20] Hals (2017).

[21] McKiernan (2017) notes in particular the lack of agreement on 'how to compel witnesses and collect evidence' in a cross-border insolvency.

[22] McKiernan (2017) quotes Ken Rosenberg, a partner at Paliare Roland Rosenberg Rothstein LLP, which acted for the Canadian Creditors' Committee in the case.

[23] Hals (2017).

[24] Ibid.

[25] 11 U.S.C. §109(a) (2010).

[26] Couwenberg and Lubben (2015), pp. 719–720.

[27] Ibid., p. 720.

is filed, the US bankruptcy court has jurisdiction over the bankruptcy estate, which consists of all of the debtor's property, 'wherever located.'[28]

Practically speaking, many debtors—and their creditors—may want a bankruptcy case to proceed in the US. Many large creditors are financial institutions with ties to New York and other US financial centres. Even if the debtor itself is not located in the US, if its creditors have a significant US presence or substantial US ties, the creditors may be happy to have the case proceed in the US—and the bankruptcy court should easily be able to enforce domestic Bankruptcy Code provisions against those creditors.[29] In addition, Couwenberg and Lubben have observed that most foreign debtors filing for US bankruptcy are part of a multi-jurisdictional corporate group, the owners of mobile assets, or both.[30] Because of the global nature of these companies and assets, their restructurings must be enforceable across borders.[31] Since most large creditors are linked to the United States in some way, a US bankruptcy court will often have the ability to provide the necessary cross-border enforcement.[32]

Parties to a bankruptcy case may also seek a US bankruptcy because of the advantages—real or perceived—that a US bankruptcy proceeding provides compared to one in the debtor's home jurisdiction. Because US bankruptcy law is well developed and equipped to address many complex issues, a debtor can often receive a more comprehensive restructuring in the US.[33] An entity with a complex capital structure may pose difficulties if it attempts to restructure in a jurisdiction without the necessary legal framework to do so.[34] Indeed, Dietderich has observed that a foreign debtor most often chooses chapter 11 when its home country's restructuring laws are 'suboptimal' for the outcome it is seeking.[35] Even if the jurisdiction has the requisite legal framework, the US bankruptcy process may be more efficient because of the experience of the judges and the accumulated legal precedent.[36] Finally, US bankruptcy judges, unlike their counterparts in some other jurisdictions, are specialists rather than generalists.[37]

Even though a foreign court may have the ability to cooperate and coordinate with a court in the US, having one court and one proceeding is often much simpler

[28] Ibid., p. 720.

[29] Ibid., p. 720.

[30] Ibid., p. 723.

[31] Ibid., p. 740.

[32] Ibid., p. 741.

[33] Couwenberg and Lubben (2015), p. 741.

[34] Couwenberg and Lubben (2015), pp. 744–745 note that the use of prepackaged cases ensures that the American reorganisation case will proceed much quicker than in almost any other forum.

[35] Dietderich (2021), p. 28.

[36] Couwenberg and Lubben (2015), pp. 744–745. Dietderich (2021), p. 62 explains that chapter 11's predictability appeals to international creditors.

[37] Couwenberg and Lubben (2015), pp. 742–743.

than engaging in coordination.[38] Given the advantages that the US offers as a forum, it is not surprising that foreign debtors, if they are eligible, would choose a US court and a US proceeding exclusively—and indeed, this is what happens in many cases.

3.3 Chapter 11 Stands Alone

Couwenberg and Lubben have studied the phenomenon of foreign debtors using domestic US bankruptcy law and have concluded that, by and large, foreign debtors use the Bankruptcy Code in a way that is 'diametrically opposed' to most of the current thinking on cross-border insolvency.[39] Specifically, they observe foreign debtors using US bankruptcy law to impose a global discharge on assets, without the cooperation of non-US jurisdictions.[40] This type of 'lone wolf' chapter 11 is in tension with the Model Law's efforts to facilitate cross-border coordination and cooperation among different jurisdictions.[41] Because it is so easy to file for chapter 11, and so easy for US courts to enforce the decisions that are made in a bankruptcy case, US bankruptcy law is able to succeed in reorganising foreign debtors without assistance from other jurisdictions—including the debtor's home jurisdiction.[42]

If it is so easy for foreign debtors to use US bankruptcy law to achieve their reorganisation outcomes, the need for cooperation and convergence, and the development of global principles, diminishes. When a sole proceeding is located far away from where the debtor is based, there is no reason for laws to converge or courts to work together. If a debtor's restructuring is concentrated in the US, there is little chance for the law to develop elsewhere.

At the same time, as the *Nortel* case demonstrates, it is possible, and perhaps even preferable, for a chapter 11 case to work in conjunction with insolvency proceedings in other jurisdictions. Further, not all foreign debtors choose chapter 11 to the exclusion of their home country's proceedings. For example, US courts have coordinated chapter 11 proceedings with Companies' Creditors Arrangement Act proceedings in Canadian courts.[43] More generally, Couwenberg and Lubben have observed that successful coordinated cases tend to occur between similar legal systems and where a common language governs all the proceedings.[44]

Unlike in a chapter 15 case, where comity is paramount, chapter 11 does not explicitly require courts to consider comity or even to coordinate with foreign

---

[38] Ibid., p. 722.

[39] Ibid., p. 721.

[40] Ibid., p. 721.

[41] Ibid., p. 721.

[42] Ibid., p. 722.

[43] Couwenberg and Lubben (2015), p. 723 cite Quebecor as an example of successful coordination between U.S. and Canadian courts.

[44] Couwenberg and Lubben (2015), p. 723.

courts.[45] Of course, this does not mean that US courts will not observe comity or defer to the interests of foreign courts and foreign laws, even in chapter 11 cases.[46] Although there may not be the same extent of coordination as seen in a chapter 15 case, Dietderich explains that foreign debtors are unlikely to use US bankruptcy law as a way to cheat creditors or otherwise curtail their rights, largely because many of those creditors may be based in the US.[47] Further, even if not mandated, it is often practically beneficial for US courts to observe comity and to coordinate. If they do so, a debtor's use of chapter 11 may work to the benefit of all parties.[48]

3.4 Other Examples and Pushback

Since 2013, hundreds of foreign businesses have filed for domestic US bankruptcy proceedings.[49] In 2020, the year the COVID-19 pandemic first took hold, about a dozen large foreign entities filed for bankruptcy in the US, with the US remaining 'the premier destination for the biggest, most complicated restructuring cases.'[50] As one lawyer put it, '[i]f you can satisfy jurisdictional requirements, you'd be crazy not to file in the United States.'[51] Indeed, it appears that in times of crisis, many large foreign debtors have flocked to US bankruptcy court.

Recent examples of foreign debtors filing or exploring US chapter 11 proceedings include Minera del Norte, a subsidiary of Altos Hornos de Mexico;[52] Grupo Posada SAB de V, a hotel operator with ties to 185 properties in Mexico, and which filed a prepackaged bankruptcy in the US;[53] and Alto Maipo, a Chilean company that filed for chapter 11 in Delaware in November of 2021.[54]

However, not everyone is happy about this trend, and some companies have faced backlash in their home jurisdictions when they file bankruptcy in the US. In June of 2021, Grupo Famsa, a Mexican company, filed for bankruptcy in New York.[55] However, after the filing, Mexico's banking regulator revoked the license of one of the company's units, and the company subsequently moved the case to Mexico.[56]

---

[45] Dietderich (2021), p. 28.

[46] Ibid., p. 61.

[47] Ibid., p. 62.

[48] Ibid., p. 62.

[49] Church and Hill (2021).

[50] Ibid.

[51] Church and Hill (2021) quote Eric Snyder, chairman of the bankruptcy practice at Wilk Auslander, a law firm.

[52] Gonzalez (2021).

[53] Hill and Villamil (2021).

[54] Wong (2021).

[55] Church and Hill (2021).

[56] Ibid.

This regulatory backlash illustrates a disadvantage to so-called global forum shopping: it can be costly and expensive to file in one location only to determine it is not worth the backlash at home and later move the case.

The bankruptcy of Latam Airlines Group SA provides another recent example of tension that can arise when a foreign debtor files a domestic chapter 11 case. Like many airlines, Latam was affected by the travel bans and stay-at-home orders in the early days of the COVID-19 global crisis, and it chose to file US chapter 11 bankruptcy although it is based in Chile.[57] Latam's proposed bankruptcy plan has the effect of leaving the company's local creditors with significantly less than creditors holding overseas bonds.[58] Local creditors have threatened to sue and are complaining that Latam should have filed for protection in Chile, rather than in New York.[59] These creditors perceive that local courts would have treated local creditors better.[60] Because the airline is set to emerge in a comparatively stronger position than it has been in recent years, local creditors feel that they deserve more and that a New York bankruptcy court is not sufficiently protective of their needs.[61]

In summary, it is quite easy for a foreign entity to become a debtor in a US chapter 11 case. When a non-US debtor chooses to commence a chapter 11 case, it is choosing US domestic law over a cooperative, cross-border proceeding. Practically speaking, it is possible, and even likely, that a chapter 11 case may involve coordination with a foreign court and deference to foreign principles. However, there is no well-developed playbook for a cross-border chapter 11 case, and a US-centric case may discourage the development of the law in foreign jurisdictions. At the same time, there are of course many foreign debtors that will not qualify for a domestic chapter 11 case, even under the Bankruptcy Code's very permissive rules. And if more debtors face repercussions in their home jurisdictions when they file a US bankruptcy case, as in the case of Grupo Famsa, it is possible that with time, entities may choose to file their bankruptcy cases in their home jurisdictions instead of in the US. As the next part of this chapter will discuss, even when a foreign debtor does not choose chapter 11, it may still be able to access US courts through an ancillary, chapter 15 proceeding.

---

57 Scurria and Saeedy (2021).

58 Thomson (2022) notes that, '[t]he proposals for local and international bondholders are diametrically different.'

59 Thomson (2022).

60 Ibid.

61 Ibid.

4 Chapter 15 as a Litigation Tool

The COVID-19 pandemic spurred various crises throughout the world, and financial crises were no exception. As governments put restrictions into place on movement and activities, many companies saw their revenue streams decline and turned to restructuring or liquidation proceedings as a result.[62] By one estimate, chapter 15 cases filed on behalf of foreign businesses doubled during 2020.[63]

4.1 Chapter 15's Cooperative Features

In contrast to chapter 11, chapter 15 of the Bankruptcy Code does provide explicit mechanisms that mandate cooperation across borders. For example, §1525 of the Code states that US courts must cooperate with foreign courts and foreign representatives 'to the maximum extent possible.'[64] Debtors and trustees must similarly cooperate with foreign courts and foreign representatives by any appropriate means.[65] Thus, chapter 15's provisions explicitly promote cooperation and comity across borders, consistent with the harmonising purpose of the Model Law.

The purpose of a chapter 15 is also different from that of a chapter 11. Because chapter 15 cases are ancillary to another proceeding, they are designed to be used to further the goals of the foreign main proceeding.[66] In other words, unlike chapter 11, chapter 15 is not designed to stand alone.

In furtherance of chapter 15's cooperative goals, it is relatively easy for a foreign representative to gain 'recognition' in US bankruptcy court of the foreign proceeding.[67] This is true whether the foreign proceeding is a 'foreign main proceeding,' which is a proceeding pending in the debtor's centre of main interests (COMI), or a 'foreign non-main proceeding,' one pending outside the US but also outside the debtor's COMI.[68] Chapter 15 is designed to promote convergence by providing a set of principles for courts to use in order to align proceedings in the US with those taking place elsewhere.

As an example of how easy it is to grant recognition in a chapter 15 case, consider the case law in the US surrounding whether a bankruptcy court may grant foreign main recognition if the debtor has no residence, domicile, place of business, or property in the United States.[69] In 2013, the Second Circuit Court of Appeals, in *In*

62 Cheok (2020).

63 Ball et al. (2021).

64 11 U.S.C. §1525 (2005).

65 11 U.S.C. §1526(a) (2005).

66 Shuster and Loveland (2021), p. 50.

67 Markell (2021).

68 Ibid.

69 Rochelle (2021a, b).

re Barnet, answered this question in the negative.[70] In *Barnet*, Australian corporate liquidators sought foreign main recognition of a proceeding under chapter 15, even though the debtor did not satisfy the requirements of §109 of the Bankruptcy Code for eligibility under chapter 11. The bankruptcy court granted recognition, but the Second Circuit reversed, holding that §109 applied to chapter 15 cases and, therefore, recognition could not be granted.[71]

Barnet, however, is decidedly in the minority. In a case predating chapter 15, *In re Goerg*, the Eleventh Circuit held that a foreign representative could conduct ancillary proceedings in the US with respect to a foreign debtor, even though the debtor did not qualify under §109 of the Code.[72] Further, *Barnet* has been heavily criticised by academics and 'emasculated' by many bankruptcy courts.[73] Notably, even though she was reversed by the Second Circuit, the bankruptcy judge in *Barnet* did grant recognition on remand, finding that a retainer given to US counsel for the foreign representatives, along with claims in the US, satisfied §109's eligibility requirements.[74] Other bankruptcy courts have followed suit, granting recognition on the same or similar rationales.[75]

These rationales rely on the principle that the bankruptcy court grants recognition to the foreign proceeding rather than to the debtor itself; thus, provisions in the Bankruptcy Code about debtor eligibility for domestic US bankruptcy law, such as §109, are simply irrelevant.[76] The slew of decisions granting recognition to debtors with little to no connection to the US underscores chapter 15's cooperative purpose and the extent to which the US in particular is willing to be a supportive forum for ancillary administration of cases outside of its borders.

Other aspects of chapter 15 law and practice also encourage cooperation and convergence. For example, there is nationwide authority for granting recognition to foreign plans in chapter 15 cases, even if the relief granted differs from what is available under US law.[77]

[70] In re Barnet, 737 F.3d 238 (2d Cir. 2013).

[71] In re Barnet, 737 F.3d 238 (2d Cir. 2013).

[72] In re Goerg, 844 F.2d 1562 (11th Cir. 1988).

[73] Rochelle (2021a, b).

[74] Ibid.

[75] Ibid.

[76] Ibid.

[77] Magalhaes (2021), p. 53 cites *In re Condor Flugdienst GmbH* as an example of a court recognising that relief granted in a foreign ruling need not be identical to that available under U.S. law.

4.2 Examples of Bootstrapping Litigation

Even though chapter 15 provides more explicit tools for harmonisation and cooperation across borders, it is still possible for parties to a chapter 15 case to use the protection granted to them strategically and for the purpose of gaining a litigation advantage rather than directly facilitating a restructuring. For example, parties have used—or attempted to use—chapter 15 recognition to bootstrap US court jurisdiction.

Several recent examples shed light on this practice. In *In re Sibaham Ltd.*, a group of plaintiffs attempted to commence a class action adversary proceeding against a U.K. debtor in US court.[78] The Bankruptcy Court for the Western District of North Carolina had granted recognition of the U.K. foreign proceeding, and the plaintiffs tried to use the chapter 15 recognition order as a basis for US jurisdiction for the class action.[79] However, the bankruptcy court dismissed the attempt, holding that the UK debtor and its creditors would be prejudiced if the plaintiffs proceeded with a class action in the US rather than in the UK, where the debtor's main insolvency proceeding was pending.[80]

Likewise, in *In re Marconi PLC*, the US District Court for the Southern District of New York held that a statutory predecessor to chapter 15 does not permit domestic creditors to file an adversary proceeding in an ancillary proceeding in order to establish claims against a foreign debtor.[81] The court reasoned that the entire purpose of the statute was to centralise proceedings in one court—in this case, the foreign court.[82]

A creditor again came under fire for asking a US court to declare that certain funds belonged to it in *JP Morgan Chase Bank v. Altos Hornos de Mexico, S.A. de C. V.*[83] When the debtor, a Mexican company, asked the US court to defer to the Mexican court, the district court (and later the Second Circuit, on appeal), granted the debtor's request, with the Second Circuit specifically holding that 'US courts should ordinarily decline to adjudicate creditor claims that are the subject of a foreign bankruptcy proceeding.'[84]

It is not always the case that efforts to attain US jurisdiction over issues arising in a foreign case fail, however. In *In re British American Ins. Co. Ltd.*, the Bankruptcy Court for the Southern District of Florida held that a foreign debtor with a pending insolvency proceeding in Saint Vincent and the Grenadines had standing to bring a

[78] In re Sibaham Limited, Case No. 19-31537, 2020 WL 2731870 (Bankr. W.D.N.C. May 4, 2020).

[79] *Sibaham*, 2020 WL 2731870, p. *1.

[80] *Sibaham*, 2020 WL 2731870, p. *2.

[81] In re Marconi PLC, 363 B.R. 361 (S.D.N.Y. 2007).

[82] *Marconi*, 363 B.R. at 365.

[83] JP Morgan Chase Bank v. Altos Hornos de Mexico, S.A. de C.V., 412 F.3d 418, 419 (2d Cir. 2005).

[84] Ibid.

claim against its former directors for breach of fiduciary duty in US court.[85] Indeed, the court found that US bankruptcy law had given the debtor the power to file the action in the US, and thus, specific authorisation from the court to file the case was not necessary.[86] In this instance, it may have helped that the entity seeking to bring litigation in the US was the debtor, rather than a creditor.[87]

In yet another recent case, filing a chapter 15 as a 'litigation tactic' did not bar a court from granting foreign main recognition.[88] In *In re Culligan*, a New York bankruptcy judge granted foreign main recognition even though the purpose of the chapter 15 filing was to enjoin a shareholders' suit pending in New York. In allowing the ancillary case to proceed, the court's decision contrasted sharply with chapter 11 practice. Chapter 11 cases can be dismissed if the bankruptcy filing is nothing more than a litigation tactic.[89]

The plaintiffs in *Culligan* argued that the chapter 15 filing was done in bad faith to bar prosecution of the lawsuit in New York.[90] However, the judge found that the foreign representatives had met all of the requirements for foreign main recognition and that the court has 'limited discretion to deny recognition except when it would be manifestly contrary to the public policy of the United States.'[91] Indeed, *Culligan* is not an outlier: other courts have routinely found that bad faith or litigation tactics are not a bar to recognition in a chapter 15 case, even though the same tactics would have resulted in the dismissal of a chapter 11 case.[92] The permissiveness of chapter 15 thus allows substantial room for comity and cooperation, even as it also allows parties—namely, the debtor and its foreign representatives—to use the process to accomplish litigation goals that are themselves ancillary to the debtor's restructuring.

Another possibly concerning use of chapter 15 is when that chapter is used to transfer litigation from one US court to another. In *Firefighters' Retirement System v. Citgo Group Ltd.*, the Fifth Circuit held that a state court action by a group of pension funds was sufficiently related to the Cayman Islands debtor's chapter 15 case, such that a hearing in federal, rather than state, court was required.[93] In other words, using chapter 15, the defendants were able to transfer the case from

---

[85] In re British American Ins. Co. Ltd., 488 B.R. 205 (Bankr. S.D. Fla. 2013).

[86] *British American*, 488 B.R. at 235, held that plaintiffs could pursue the claim under §1509(f).

[87] Shuster and Loveland (2021) observe that 'U.S. courts are more likely to allow standalone actions filed by the foreign representatives for a chapter 15 foreign debtor than to allow stand-alone actions filed *against* a chapter 15 foreign debtor.' (Emphasis in original).

[88] In re Culligan Ltd., Case No. 20-12192, 2021 WL 2787926 (Bankr. S.D.N.Y. July 2, 2021).

[89] For example, Gavant et al. (2021) discuss the dismissal of the National Rifle Association's bankruptcy case for lack of a good faith filing.

[90] In re Culligan Ltd., Case No. 20-12192, 2021 WL 2787926 (Bankr. S.D.N.Y. July 2, 2021).

[91] Ibid.

[92] Magalhaes (2021), p. 24.

[93] Firefighters' Retirement System v. Citco Group Ltd., 796 F.3d 520 (5th Cir. 2015).

state to federal court. This was true even though the debtor had not filed for chapter 15 until after the attempted removal of the litigation to district court.[94]

More recently, a New York bankruptcy judge held that chapter 15 permits pre-litigation discovery.[95] Section 1521(a)(4) of the Bankruptcy Code authorises discovery 'concerning the debtor's assets, affairs, rights, obligations or liabilities.'[96] In *In re Comair*, the Bankruptcy Court for the Southern District of New York held that debtor Comair's foreign representatives were entitled to pre-litigation discovery against Boeing Company in Comair's chapter 15 proceeding so that they could investigate potential causes of action Comair may have had against Boeing.[97] This was true even though Comair's foreign proceeding, in South Africa, had been substantially consummated.[98]

The court held that the requested discovery was in the interests of comity because it facilitated the foreign representative's duty under South African law to investigate Comair's affairs.[99] However, Comair had not commenced litigation against Boeing, and its plan of rescue was not conditioned on any claims Comair may have had in this litigation.[100] Nevertheless, the court held that the pre-litigation discovery was necessary for the protection of Comair's assets because those assets included contingent interests, such as potential causes of action.[101] Although Boeing contended that Comair's foreign representative was using bankruptcy as a way to gain an advantage in litigation outside of bankruptcy, the court disagreed, finding that the foreign representative needed discovery to comply with his statutory obligations under South African law.[102]

The *Comair* decision is a recent, salient example of the way in which bankruptcy courts in chapter 15 can assist foreign representatives, even after the foreign proceeding is substantially consummated, and as long as the foreign proceeding has not terminated.[103] Notably, the court did not address whether the discovery the foreign representative sought was permissible under South African law.[104] Although the court did not seem to believe that this mattered, if relief is contrary to US or foreign public policy, it is unclear whether comity would or should support it.[105]

In summary, chapter 15's commitment to comity and cooperation appears to be a double-edged sword. To be deferential to foreign debtors and foreign proceedings,

[94] *Firefighters*, 796 F.3d at 523.

[95] Rochelle (2021a, b).

[96] 11 U.S.C. §1521(a)(4) (2010).

[97] Berkovich et al. (2021).

[98] Ibid.

[99] Ibid.

[100] Ibid.

[101] Ibid.

[102] Ibid.

[103] Ibid.

[104] Ibid.

[105] Ibid.

US courts have occasionally allowed parties to centre litigation in the US and to use chapter 15 for a purpose that is not primarily about the administration of cross-border assets, but instead is about gaining a litigation advantage. However, when the debtor is the entity asking for relief, the line between using chapter 15 for a restructuring purpose and using it for a litigation purpose is blurred.

5 Concluding Thoughts

The practice in the United States around chapter 11 and chapter 15 shows that convergence is a nuanced concept. The continued use by foreign debtors of US bankruptcy law and practice in times of financial crisis threatens to stifle the development and convergence of global bankruptcy and insolvency law and policy. Of course, as other jurisdictions further develop and refine their own laws, it is possible that the US will not remain the preferred forum for large multinational enterprises to restructure.[106] Indeed, numerous countries across the globe updated their insolvency laws in response to the crises created by COVID-19.[107] On the other hand, if major creditors continue to be based in the US, chapters 11 and 15 may always be attractive options, even for foreign debtors.

In short, when large entities are faced with financial crisis, they tend to turn to the US for bankruptcy relief, in one form or another. This chapter has shown that use of US bankruptcy law by foreign debtors tends to result in a US-centric restructuring process, which may discourage the harmonisation of global bankruptcy and insolvency law. At the same time, the ability and willingness of US courts to work collaboratively and cooperatively with foreign courts, including in a chapter 11 bankruptcy, may be the key to establishing overarching cooperative principles. The more US courts must interact with and cooperate with foreign courts, particularly in response to financial crises around the globe, the more apparent the need will be for procedures to converge and harmonise.

References

Ball C et al (2021) Chapter 15 update: US bankruptcy court refuses to enforce order approving Indonesian debt restructuring plan due to third-party releases. JDSupra. https://www.jdsupra.com/legalnews/chapter-15-update-u-s-bankruptcy-court-3393563/

Berkovich R, Hoehne D, Zhang J (2021) Clearing a runway to litigating claims: the principle of comity and pre-litigation discovery in chapter 15 cases. Weil Restructuring. https://restructuring.weil.com/chapter-15/clearing-a-runway-to-litigating-claims-the-principle-of-

[106] Markell (2021) mentions other jurisdictions as possibly being attractive to U.S. debtors.

[107] DLA Piper (2020).

comity-and-pre-litigation-discovery-in-chapter-15-cases/?utm_source=newsletter&utm_medium=email&utm_campaign=December-27-2021
Casey M, Macey J (2021) Bankruptcy shopping: domestic venue races and global forum wars. Emory Bankr Dev J 37:463–507
Cheok M (2020) Media firm technicolor cites pandemic in chapter 15 filing. Bloomberg Law
Church S, Hill J (2021) Bankruptcy-friendly US extends lead as haven of foreign filers. Bloomberg Law
Couwenberg O, Lubben S (2015) Corporate bankruptcy tourists. Bus Law 70:719–746
COVID-19: An international guide to changes in insolvency law (2020) DLA Piper. https://www.dlapiper.com/en/us/insights/publications/2020/03/coronavirus-what-european-governments-are-doing-to-support-businesses/
Dietderich A (2021) 'Confessions' of a forum-shopper, Part II: debtors without borders. Am Bankr Inst J 40:28, 60–62
Gavant A, Kim Y, Scott S (2021) NRA bankruptcy dismissed for lack of good faith in filing. Mayer Brown. https://www.mayerbrown.com/en/perspectives-events/blogs/2021/05/nra-bankruptcy-dismissed-for-lack-of-good-faith-in-filing
Gonzalez C (2021) AHMSA says Minera del Norte Unit exploring chapter 11 filing. Bloomberg Law
Hals T (2017) Nortel cleared to end bankruptcy, distribute $7 billion to creditors. Reuters. https://www.reuters.com/article/us-nortelnetworks-bankruptcy/nortel-cleared-to-end-bankruptcy-distribute-7-billion-to-creditors-idUSKBN1582TO
Hill J, Villamil J (2021) Mexican Hotelier Posadas eyes quick bankruptcy to secure rebound. Bloomberg Law
Magalhaes J (2021) Chapter 15 revisited: unpacking more concepts from recent cases. Am Bankr Inst J 40:24–25, 53–54
Markell B (2021) Domestic entities as chapter 15 debtors: a possibility? Bankr L Letter No 7, vol 41, pp 1–20
Martos-Vila M, Shi Z (2022) Bankruptcy filings during and after the COVID-19 recession. Bus Law Today. https://businesslawtoday.org/2022/03/bankruptcy-filings-during-after-covid-19-recession/
McKiernan M (2017) Focus: what can be learned from Nortel case? Law Times. https://www.lawtimesnews.com/news/legal-analysis/focus-what-can-be-learned-from-nortel-case/262474
Rochelle B (2021a) Chapter 15 permits discovery to lay groundwork for a lawsuit, New York Judge Says. Rochelle's Daily Wire. https://www.abi.org/newsroom/daily-wire/chapter-15-permits-discovery-to-lay-groundwork-for-a-lawsuit-new-york-judge-says
Rochelle B (2021b) Eleventh circuit predicted to split with the second circuit on foreign recognition. Rochelle's Daily Wire. https://www.abi.org/newsroom/daily-wire/eleventh-circuit-predicted-to-split-with-the-second-circuit-on-foreign
Schwartz A, Doyle JB, Yavorsky N, Chen X (2021) Trends in large corporate bankruptcy and financial distress (Midyear 2021 Update): bankruptcy filings. Nat Law Rev. https://www.natlawreview.com/article/trends-large-corporate-bankruptcy-and-financial-distress-midyear-2021-update
Scurria A, Saeedy A (2021) Latam Airlines nears chapter 11 deal with creditors amid rival's merger push. Wal. St J. https://www.wsj.com/articles/latam-airlines-nears-chapter-11-deal-with-creditors-amid-rivals-merger-push-11637785046
Shuster G, Loveland B (2021) Keeping chapter 15 ancillary. Am Bankr Inst J 40:32–33, 50

Thomson E (2022) Latam Bondholders losing 80% cry foul over those who'll get par. Bloomberg. https://www.bloomberg.com/news/articles/2022-01-13/latam-bondholders-losing-80-cry-foul-over-those-who-ll-get-par
Warren E, Westbrook JL (2009) The success of chapter 11: a challenge to critics. Mich Law Rev 107:603–642
Wong F (2021) Chile's Alto Maipo files for chapter 11 in Delaware Court (1). Bloomberg Law

Laura N. Coordes is a professor at Arizona State University's Sandra Day O'Connor College of Law, United States.

Labour Law in the United Kingdom

David Cabrelli

1 Introduction

As well as the numerous external crises which have afflicted all post-industrial democracies over the past two decades, labour law has been exposed to an overlapping series of internal shockwaves, during which its legal and political foundations have been severely tested. These can be attributed to events (occurring over the same period) which can be characterised in terms of a deepening sense of industrial, political and technological change.[1] These sundry crises, internal and external, have placed labour law in all countries under a great deal of strain. This has witnessed, at least rhetorically, the emergence of various new paradigms of labour law and labour market regulation, with the potential for one or several of these to emerge as vectors of convergence across Western jurisdictions, while contemporaneously and somewhat paradoxically providing a degree of scope for radical divergence and regulatory competition. Labour law in the United Kingdom (UK) has shown evidence of both tendencies during this period of moments of crisis.

Those two decades were bookended by two symbolic constitutional moments of convergence of labour law norms and models in Europe, both inspired, in very different ways, by the UK. At the start of the century, a new paradigm of European Social Citizenship emerged, based on equal treatment and non-discrimination, responding to the political crisis of the rise of the far right and expansion of the European Union (EU). This new framework built partly on existing models of EU law and shared European traditions, but in many ways was based upon the advanced model of non-discrimination law in the UK at the time. This, in turn, became the

[1] This sense of perennial crisis has been documented by labour law scholars: see Ewing (1988); Hyde (2011).

D. Cabrelli (✉)
The University of Edinburgh, Edinburgh Law School, Edinburgh, UK
e-mail: David.Cabrelli@ed.ac.uk

E. Ghio, R. Perlingeiro (eds.), *Are Legal Systems Converging or Diverging?*,
https://doi.org/10.1007/978-3-031-38180-5_6

basis of a great deal of piecemeal change within UK labour law, culminating in the Equality Act 2010 in the UK, and equal treatment as a central tenet of labour law across Europe. This example is instructive because it demonstrates how a symbolic response to a perceived political crisis can emerge as a legal model of convergence in the right circumstances. Two decades later, Brexit precipitated a similar constitutional response from the EU Commission and EU Member States, which resulted in the Social Pillar, a statement of core social values, and mostly related to labour law. This was a measure designed to give both a common direction to a renewed European project, but also to head off any pending contagion of the Brexit-malaise.[2] Of course, the irony was, that this time, the UK was not a party to this new project of convergence.

Other crises—of *an economic, political and clinical nature* that afflicted the UK and EU—that have occurred during recent years can be studied to examine the convergence thesis. Three significant crises of different types show elements of convergence, with surface-level similarities masking significant differences in legal approach in other respects. The great financial crisis of 2008 ('GFC') was an *economic crisis* that led to a well-known period of 'austerity'.[3] The policy response was not limited to the reining in of public expenditure, since labour rights were perceived as both a cost and a barrier to economic regeneration. During this period, the UK labour law system witnessed the erection of a significant set of checks on the meaningful enforcement of labour law rights.[4] This aligned closely with other legal systems, in which the need for a labour market without 'rigidities' was prioritised. While this period has largely therefore been understood as a period *lacking* in convergence within social policy and labour rights, in many ways the deregulatory instincts of the British regulator can be seen as a form of negative functional *harmonisation*, albeit with idiosyncratic characteristics.

The second crisis of note was *political in character*, namely the radical change provoked by the decision of the UK to exit the European Union, which took effect on 31 January 2020. The scope for legislative or policy divergence between the approaches adopted by the UK and the EU in relation to labour market regulation has naturally increased since then. The primary justification for this premise is that many labour rights conferred on workers in the UK have EU directives as their source. Seen from this perspective, as the EU adds to the social policy acquis post-Brexit, the greater the scope for the labour laws in both jurisdictions to drift apart from each other.[5] Likewise, in the circumstances where the UK affords itself the

---

[2] See the European Pillar of Social Rights, proclaimed in 2017, proclamation-pillar_en.pdf (europa.eu) and the European Pillar of Social Rights Action Plan, EUROPEAN PILLAR; SOCIAL RIGHTS; ACTION PLAN (europa.eu).

[3] See Blyth (2013).

[4] For evidence generally supporting the claim that enforcement has been marginalised, see Dickens (2012); Barmes (2016); Busby and McDermont (2012, 2020).

[5] For a discussion of the areas where the EU has expanded the labour law and social policy acquis, see Sect. 3 below: e.g. the Whistleblowing Directive and the proposed EU Pay Transparency Directive.

opportunity to strip away or dilute certain EU-derived employment rights through legislative repeal. Yet, as this chapter will show, it is still too early to claim that has happened and a large measure of formal and functional harmonisation or convergence continues in practice, albeit with the potential in the future for functional and formal divergence.

In the final external crisis of note—which was at once *medical, clinical and social*—the COVID-19 crisis saw labour market interventions on an unprecedented scale by legislators and governments. After many years of convergence concentrating on flexible labour markets, most legal systems coalesced around measures designed to inhibit or prevent job losses, which is a paradigmatic instance of harmonisation in a time of crisis, albeit absent harmonising measures at a supranational level. However, while the UK Job Retention Scheme superficially represented an instance of this same approach, a closer analysis of the legal mechanisms used to achieve this outcome are revealing: whereas in other jurisdictions, the approach involved altering the rights and obligations of employers by changing, at least temporarily, the core duties and powers imposed and conferred by the employment relationship, the UK approach did not seek to modify the managerial prerogative within the employment contract. This illustrates policy convergence without deep legal *formal* harmonisation.

The main objective of this chapter is to probe the main crisis-related generators of flux in UK employment law since the age of austerity, as benchmarked against the policy and legal responses of other jurisdictions in the EU to the same crises. For example, what this chapter illustrates is that although UK Employment Law formally diverged from Spain, Portugal, Greece and Italy as regards the legal and policy responses taken towards the GFC, this amounted to negative functional harmonisation in practice, resulting in comparatively similar solutions. As for the crisis generated by Brexit, so far, what we see is UK and EU Employment Law failing to formally diverge as much as one might have expected in respect of labour and social protections. Instead, the picture is more complicated, amounting to a mixture of formal and functional harmonisation to date. Finally, turning to the Covid-19 crisis, a comparison between the approaches to the reform of Employment Laws that were adopted by the UK and European jurisdictions such as Germany, Luxembourg, Spain, the Netherlands and Italy, reveals variety in form, but a large deal of consistency in function, i.e. positive functional harmonisation.

The chapter is structured as follows: first, Sect. 2 turns to briefly examine the concept of 'crisis' and the distinction between external and internal crises and formal and non-formal convergence. To that extent, this part of the chapter is primarily definitional. Section 3 moves on to identify the various surface-level instances of post-crisis formal divergence in labour law, alongside those where formal convergence and/or functional convergence was prioritised. In Sect. 4, the discussion turns to carefully theorise about the preceding findings in Sect. 3, and makes a series of claims based on that analysis. Section 5 concludes.

2 A Taxonomy of Crises, Harmonisation and Convergence

The diverse range of crises addressed in this chapter are each external in nature and origin. Consistent with the definition adumbrated in chapter 'Terminology' of this book, this can be referred to as a situation where a shock independent of a particular subject or the environment which originally forged it, or the particular justification (s) for its or their existence, has an appreciable social, cultural or economic impact. Transposed to the subject of labour law, the three crises under review in this chapter—namely the economic crisis of the GFC, the British-specific political crisis of Brexit and the health, medical and social crisis that was the COVID-19 pandemic (and the accompanying government-mandated 'lockdowns')—undoubtedly satisfy that definition.

An additional question that is also prescient is whether the responses of various legislatures to the aforementioned crises were characteristic of top-down harmonisation or bottom-up convergence, or were entirely asymmetrical, when benchmarked against each other. For example, if the comparison of the differing legal responses to a crisis illustrates that they were symmetrical of their own accord, or as a result of a prescription by a supranational body (such as the EU), then that would strongly suggest top-down harmonisation of the relevant labour laws.[6] This can be contrasted with bottom-up convergence where the employment laws introduced to address the relevant crisis are consistent with each other, notwithstanding any absence of a widespread cross-jurisdictional consensus in terms of some shared blueprint for action.[7] Finally, a third potential outcome is diversity in the relevant legal responses pursued by the range of countries under review. In that case, each of the laws differ, with no evidence of any shared best practice on how to deal legally with the crisis in question.

The enquiry in this chapter also probes the nature of any harmonisation or convergence that may be detected as a result of the comparative research. Where the comparison shows that there is convergence or harmonisation in the laws prescribed to combat a crisis, their content and scope may be identical or similar. In such a case, it is common to refer to this phenomenon as formal convergence or harmonisation.[8] This differs from functional harmonisation or convergence, where the outward shape of the laws differ, sometimes radically, but the end outcome or result is the same or similar. In this way, this discourse centres around the similarity or diversity of the black-letter laws passed to deal with a crisis, as well as their end consequences.[9] Finally, the chapter also reflects on the extent to which any harmonisation or convergence of labour laws is positive or negative.[10] This refers

---

[6] See Antokolskaia (2006), pp. 21–23; Lohse (2011), p. 291.

[7] Nelken (2002), pp. 26–27.

[8] See Gilson (2004), pp. 132–137; Gilson (2001), pp. 332–336; La Porta et al. (2000), p. 20.

[9] See Gordon (2004), pp. 137–140; Gilson (2001), pp. 337–339; Clarke (2016), pp. 25–26; Gordon (2018), pp. 29–34.

[10] See the discussion in Barnard and Deakin (2002).

to the extent to which the legal response is deregulatory in nature, or in contrast, more protective of workers. Having established these basic definitional points, we now turn to compare the effect of the GFC on labour laws in the UK, Spain, Portugal, Greece and Italy.

3 From GFC-Inspired Austerity Measures to COVID-19-Related Profligacy via Brexit

3.1 The GFC

The GFC was an *economic crisis* that precipitated the introduction of a variety of regressive policies that were given the singular badge of 'austerity'. What they had in common was a sharp reduction in Government spending on public services and the introduction of measures designed to boost economic regeneration and productivity. These policies had serious consequences for many areas of law, such as social security law. Labour law was not immune from this onslaught. Part of the austerity agenda involved the implicit acceptance that labour rights were a burden on commercial businesses, imposing costs on trading, which would stifle the necessary economic recovery.[11] However, while recognising this perspective and its logical end point—that the perceived adverse effects of employment protection needed to be addressed—somewhat paradoxically, the British Government made very little attempt to dilute or strip away pre-existing employment protections. Instead, despite covert attempts to identify areas where signature employment protections could be cut back,[12] and some very limited employment law reforms,[13] much less overt measures were employed to marginalise employment rights.

At this stage in the discussion, it is salutary to distinguish between techniques and outcomes. For example, rather than take the direct line of promulgating deregulatory measures that would slash away at employment rights, the British Government adopted a more indirect technique to reflect its policy outlook. Nevertheless, the

[11] This is a common criticism of labour laws. See the following literature: Edmans et al. (2014); Bradley et al. (2014); Avdagic (2015); Deakin et al. (2014a, b).

[12] See the Beecroft Report for the UK Coalition Government: The Beecroft Report, https://assets.publishing.service.gov.uk/government/uploads/system/uploads/attachment_data/file/31583/12-825-report-on-employment-law-beecroft.pdf.

[13] Principally restricted to minor reforms centred around protections for transferring workers when the business of their employer is sold or transferred, and increasing the qualifying period from one to two years for unfair dismissal claims and the consultation periods on planned collective redundancies: see the Unfair Dismissal and Statement of Reasons for Dismissal (Variation of Qualifying Period) Order 2012 (SI 2012/989), Article 3(2) of the Trade Union and Labour Relations (Consolidation) Act 1992 (Amendment) Order 2013 (SI 2013/763) and the Collective Redundancies and Transfer of Undertakings (Protection of Employment) (Amendment) Regulations 2014 (SI 2014/16).

same outcome was reached in terms of curbing employees' enjoyment of employment rights. That is to say that it made the *enforcement* of labour rights much more challenging than it had hitherto been prior to the GFC.[14] The primary contributor to this state of affairs was the introduction of employment tribunal fees by a piece of secondary legislation,[15] which made it prohibitively expensive for employees to have their dispute resolved by an employment tribunal.[16] This involved two fee levels, with the highest enjoining an employee claimant to pay a fee of £250 to present a complaint to an employment tribunal and an additional fee of £950 for a full tribunal hearing.[17] As for appeals from the employment tribunal to the Employment Appeal Tribunal, the fee for presenting the claim was £400 and £1200 for a hearing. An additional illustration of the sorts of measures implemented that compromised the enforcement of employment rights included the power conferred on employment tribunals to order employee claimants to pay deposits of up to £1000 at a preliminary hearing, as a condition of progressing their complaint.[18]

Other reforms designed to inhibit the capacity of employment rights and laws to inspire for the want of proper enforcement, specifically targeted the resolution of disputes in the employment tribunal system. This was designed to make employment tribunal enforcement of employment rights much less attractive. For example, sections 18A and 18B were inserted into the Employment Tribunals Act 1996 to introduce a pre-employment tribunal claim procedure.[19] These statutory provisions mandated that prospective employee claimants were obliged to supply particular information about their intended employment tribunal complaint to a conciliation officer employed by a body known as ACAS.[20] The objective of this process was to incentivise the claimant and their employer to reach a settlement in a timely fashion.[21] The chink in its armour is that so long as the employee claimant serves the requisite notification upon ACAS, he/she is under no duty to submit the dispute

[14]For the distinction between enforcement of, and compliance with, labour laws, see Davidov (2021), pp. 118–119; Davidov and Eshet (forthcoming, 2022), pp. 1–3.

[15]The Employment Tribunals and the Employment Appeal Tribunal Fees Order 2013 (SI 2013/1893). See the discussion in Davidov (2021), pp. 118–119.

[16]See the research by Adams and Prassl (2017).

[17]This included unfair dismissal, discrimination, and equal pay claims.

[18]The Employment Tribunals (Constitution and Rules of Procedure) Regulations 2013 (SI 2013/1237) rules 39 and 53.

[19]See Mangan (2013), pp. 413–414.

[20]ACAS is an organisation that is autonomous from the UK Government. It has a statutory duty to promote the improvement of industrial relations, part of which entails the provision of conciliation and arbitration services in respect of the resolution of individual and collective disputes between employers and their employees and/or trade unions: Section 209(1) of TULRCA and for commentary, see Dickens (2012).

[21]Section 18A(3) of the ETA. The prescribed period is one calendar month in terms of para 6 of Schedule 1 to the Employment Tribunals (Early Conciliation: Exemptions and Rules of Procedure) Regulations 2014 (SI 2014/254).

to conciliation under the auspices of an ACAS conciliation officer.[22] Once the conciliation officer issues a prescribed certificate to the claimant employee to the effect that it is not possible for the parties to conclude a settlement, the claimant is then entitled to present a complaint to an employment tribunal.[23]

Of course, there are limits on the extent to which national law-making authorities (such as a legislature) can downgrade the enforcement of employment laws. For there is a fine line between legitimate reforms that curtail the enforcement of employment laws—for example, in the interests of preventing and deterring frivolous, scandalous, vexatious or weak cases which simply clog up the justice system—and those which fall on the wrong side of the boundary insofar as they represent a breach of the common law right to access to justice. In the academic scholarship, flat fee systems (such as those introduced in respect of employment tribunals) tend to be cast as 'highly imperfect' and 'blunt instrument[s]'.[24] This academic sentiment was given explicit judicial expression in the decision of the UK Supreme Court in *R (on the application of UNISON) v Lord Chancellor*.[25] Here, the question was whether the headline austerity-driven employment law reforms that had imposed employment tribunal fees on employees were lawful. In a judgment uncharacteristically replete with pyrotechnics, Lord Reed ruled that the subordinate legislation providing for the fees ought to be quashed. His Lordship found that there was a real risk that the flat fees would have such an effect on public behaviour that would-be employment claimants would effectively be deterred from securing access to justice. There was no requirement to meet a higher threshold of 'complete impossibility', i.e. that the condition of paying the fees rendered it completely impossible for potential employee claimants to enforce their employment rights. In terms of the statistical evidence, Lord Reed was satisfied that the flat fees were unaffordable inasmuch as they could not reasonably be afforded by everyone, thus making (i) it futile to bring a claim and (ii) the employment rights 'nugatory' in effect.[26]

This British employment policy agenda of checking employees' enjoyment of employment rights by restricting access to their enforcement—which formed part of the broader austerity approach—had a deep chilling effect on the practice of employment law. Statistics presented to the UK Supreme Court in *R (on the application of UNISON) v Lord Chancellor* illustrated how the number of claims accepted by employment tribunals had dropped by around 66–70% since the introduction of the flat fees in July 2013.[27] This represented a 'dramatic and persistent fall'.[28]

---

[22] Hepple (2013), p. 218.

[23] Section 18A(4) and 18A(8) of the ETA. For a trenchant critique of this pre-claim conciliation procedure, see Renton (2012), pp. 139–140.

[24] Wilmot-Smith (2019).

[25] [2020] AC 869.

[26] [2020] AC 869, 904F-H and 906D-E per Lord Reed.

[27] [2020] AC 869, 889G-890D per Lord Reed. See also the statistics discussed in Adams and Prassl (2017), pp. 416–420.

[28] [2020] AC 869, 890B per Lord Reed.

The preceding narrative illustrates the degree to which the post-GFC austerity policy of the UK Government did not give rise to any kind of formal modification of employment laws or rights. Instead, a negative impact in terms of access to statutory employment rights was prioritised. As an indirect means of securing or achieving the desired policy prescription of austerity and marginalising employment rights, it can be contrasted with the character of the deregulatory labour law reforms imposed by European Union institutions on some member states in response to the GFC. Marshall has charted the extent to which various European institutions such as the European Central Bank ('ECB'), the European Commission and the International Monetary Fund ('IMF') demanded that sovereign national member states cut back on their employment rights as a condition of receiving financial aid.[29] Marshall gave this phenomenon the moniker of a 'labour market crisis', which followed on from the initial shock of the GFC and the secondary sovereign debt and public deficit complications. For example, when confronted by a GFC-precipitated sovereign debt and public finance crisis, the ECB offered Italy monetary relief. However, this was only in return for structural labour market reforms, including the upending of the existing regime of collective wage bargaining that takes place between unions and employers' associations at the national level, to permit plant-level negotiations, as well as the liberalisation of the rules governing the hiring and dismissal of employees. Likewise, in the cases of Greece, Portugal and Spain, in return for financial assistance, the ECB, IMF and European Commission insisted that democratic and industrial relations processes be bypassed in order to reform labour laws in a deregulatory manner. Some examples included a reduction in statutory notice periods in Greek employment law, the sponsorship of collective bargaining at the enterprise level in Greek, Italian and Spanish labour law, and prescribing drops in severance pay in respect of dismissals under Spanish employment law. In this regard, Italy, Spain, Greece and Portugal were not alone.[30] The OECD also noted a 'clear tendency' during the period 2008–2013 for many jurisdictions to pare down 'the strictness of employment protection [...] mostly focussed on regulations governing individual and collective dismissals.'[31]

Questions here must be raised as to the position of the UK in a comparative perspective. In simplistic terms, the approach of the UK can be cast as formally divergent in terms of the legal reforms adopted by other countries in the face of the GFC. As noted above, Spain, Portugal, Greece and Italy directly modified their labour laws along similar lines, in a conscious programme of negative formal harmonisation. To that extent, as regards the position of the UK vis-à-vis these countries, it might seem straightforward to depict the trend as one that was far removed from convergence, i.e. formal divergence. However, that would be wide

[29]Marshall (2014).

[30]In effect, each of these overhauls of employment law amounted to a form of internal devaluation of the Greek, Italian, Spanish and Portuguese economies to incentivise investment to the extent that external devaluation of the Euro as a currency was impossible.

[31]OECD (2013), p. 67.

of the mark, since the position is more complex. For example, insofar as the aforementioned European jurisdictions formally harmonised their employment laws (to some extent) in response to the GFC and the UK instead marginalised employment rights (as a manifestation of the more expansive austerity agenda) via a more subtle law reform programme of enforcement limitation centred around deterring access to employment protection, there is much substance in the claim that the overall comparative picture is one of negative *functional* harmonisation. And as such, in contrast with other jurisdictions that pared down the strength of their formal employment laws, negative *functional* harmonisation is undoubtedly the most appropriate way of describing the UK's labour law reaction to the GFC crisis in any comparison with countries such as Spain, Portugal, Greece and Italy.

The GFC lasted from 2008 until 2013. During that period, it has been estimated that around 'more than one-third of OECD countries undertook some relaxation of the[ir employment protection] regulations'.[32] But, as well as economic and social consequences, its effects were also political. For example, it is no stretch of the imagination to claim that the decision of the British electorate to exit the European Union was partly a political response to the economic and social hardships wrought by the GFC. And as such, it is to Brexit that we now turn.

3.2 Brexit

One of the many claims advanced by the 'Leave' campaign during the EU membership referendum in the summer of 2016 was that Brexit would enable the UK to exercise sovereignty by pivoting its laws and policies away from those of the EU in order to compete and attract business. In terms of labour law and social protection—bearing in mind that there was a high level of harmonisation of employment laws across the EU and the UK prior to the UK's exit from the EU – Brexit clearly opened up the theoretical scope for labour laws in the EU and UK to formally and functionally diverge. This would involve both bottom-up and top-down divergence of employment rights at the level of market actors, organisations and the courts and the UK Government. However, as will become clear, as a result of the terms of article 387 of the EU-UK Trade and Co-operation Agreement ('EUUKCA'), there are limits.[33]

Taken at face value, formal divergence in employment laws would appear to be already happening. In 2019, the EU introduced the Transparent and Predictable Working Conditions Directive ('TPWCD').[34] The TPWCD is applicable to apprentices, trainees, short-term employees, intermittent workers and a whole cast of casual labourers, provided that they are working for a minimum period of three hours per

[32] Ibid.

[33] See OJ 2021 L 149/10.

[34] 2019/1152/EU (OJ 2019 L186/105).

week and twelve hours every four weeks on average.[35] Part of the apparatus of the TPWCD is to confer entitlements to enhanced information about the terms of their employment,[36] including a right to a predictable pattern of working and to transition to an alternative working pattern and a maximum six-month probationary period.[37] There is also an embargo on contractual terms which prevent parallel employment, i.e. the situation where an 'exclusivity clause' prohibits an employee from taking up employment with a second employer outside of his/her working hours.[38] Since the UK is under no obligation to transpose the terms of the TPWCD into domestic labour law, divergence is clearly possible here. But the most pressing question is whether that is actually occurring in practice.

This takes us towards consideration of the nature and depth of employment protection measures introduced by the UK Parliament prior to the implementation of the TPWCD as well as those currently in the pipeline. For only then can a meaningful comparative assessment be conducted. First, the UK recently legislated to enhance the quantity and quality of information given to all workers about their employment, as well as restrictions on what the employers of zero-hours contract workers can impose in their contracts.[39] For example, an 'exclusivity clause' is banned in the case of a zero-hours work contract.[40] Moreover, the Workers (Predictable Terms and Conditions) Bill is currently in the final stages of its consideration by the UK Parliament, in terms of which workers will have an entitlement to 'request' a contract with the undertaking after 12 months continuous employment.[41] Workers are also to be given a right to (i) switch to a contract that is more predictable and stable, reflective of their actual working hours, (ii) reasonable notice of their work schedule in advance and, (iii) compensation in respect of any of their shifts which are either cancelled or shortened by the employer without reasonable notice. Taken as a package, although perhaps not as deep and broad as the EU requirements, the domestic UK measures are broadly equivalent to the provisions of the TPWCD in terms of their protective effects. To that extent, although theoretically, there is the power for the UK and the EU to formally or functionally diverge in social policy terms, this example underscores how there has been an element of functional harmonisation in labour laws between the UK and EU. One can also speculate that some part of the motivation behind this phenomenon may be a desire on the part of

---

[35] Article 1(3). For a comprehensive account of the provisions of the TPWCD, see Bednarowicz (2019); Roisin (2021), pp. 158–159.

[36] Articles 4(2), 5 and 7 and Bednarowicz (2019), pp. 616–617.

[37] Articles 8, 10, 11 and 12 and Bednarowicz (2019), p. 619.

[38] Article 9 and Bednarowicz (2019), p. 619.

[39] See the Employment Rights (Miscellaneous Amendments) Regulations 2019/731, amending sections 1 to 7B of the Employment Rights Act 1996 ('ERA'), with effect from April 2020.

[40] Section 27A of the ERA, introduced by the Small Business, Enterprise and Employment Act 2015.

[41] See Good Work: One-Sided Flexibility (2019), https://assets.publishing.service.gov.uk/government/uploads/system/uploads/attachment_data/file/818674/Good_Work_Plan_one_sided_flexibility-consultation_.pdf.

the UK not to take any action that would detract from a level playing field in trade and investment.[42]

The EU's enactment of the Whistleblowing Directive ('WD')[43] in 2019 is another testbed for the thesis positing that the post-Brexit EU/UK relationship is one of potential functional or formal divergence of labour laws, but in reality, an extension of the position ex ante tending towards functional and/or formal harmonisation or convergence. On the face of matters, this piece of European legislation could be conceived of as the EU simply catching up with the UK, to the extent that the UK took legislative steps to protect whistleblowers in employment as long ago as 1998.[44] However, that would be too crude a conclusion. Instead, the devil is in the detail of the provisions of the WD and the PIDA. Although both share the same concern to improve the conditions for individual voluntary reporting of breaches of Labour Laws and their effective enforcement (including protection for whistleblowers from harassment, victimisation or retaliation), the question is how extensive the divergences are between the respective terms of the WD and the PIDA. Too many (in terms of depth and breadth of substance) and the thesis capitulates. Of course, this necessitates some forensic engagement with the provisions in the WD. For example, its protective scope—in terms of the kinds of working relationships covered—is much broader than that envisaged by the PIDA to the extent that it includes everyone in receipt of information in a work-related context.[45] This will cover friends and relatives to whom disclosure is made, as well as shareholders, company directors and the self-employed. This can be contrasted with the PIDA which applies to 'workers', which is arguably a much more restricted personal scope of application.[46] However, the domestic British regime is clearly more inclusive in terms of the subject-matter of what is deemed to constitute a relevant disclosure. Protection from harassment, victimisation and retaliation extends to any worker who divulges a breach of *any legal obligation, or criminal offence committed, by an employer that,* in the reasonable belief of the worker, would be in in the public interest to disclose.[47] However, the WD's terms are limited to *breaches (and potential breaches, very likely to occur) of EU law within specified fields and sectors only*, e.g. state aid law, competition law, financial services, environmental law, health and safety law, data protection law, amongst many others.[48] Moreover, there is an objective element to the assessment of what is, and is not, a qualifying

---

[42] See Article 387 of the EUUKCA. The EU has the power to take appropriate rebalancing measures if there is too much formal divergence in labour and social standards.

[43] 2019/1937/EU (OJ 2019 L305/17).

[44] The Public Interest Disclosure Act 1998 ('PIDA'), whose provisions amended the terms of the ERA.

[45] Article 4. See Abazi (2019), pp. 647–648; Gerdemann and Colneric (2021), pp. 199–200.

[46] See section 43K ERA.

[47] See section 43B(1) ERA.

[48] Articles 2 and 5(1) and (2). See Abazi (2019), pp. 646 and 648; Gerdemann and Colneric (2021), pp. 196–198.

disclosure, viz that an objective assessment would reveal that the whistleblower had reasonable grounds that the disclosure was both true when it was made, as well as one that fell within the scope of the WD.[49] As for the nature and scope of the reporting lines, the PIDA's terms are marginally more protective than those contained in the WD. The main ground for such a contention lies in the degree to which the WD's application is limited in the private sector,[50] which is not the case for the UK regime under the PIDA.[51] However, both are consistent in terms of the prescription that protection from retaliation, victimisation or harassment is only available where internal reporting channels are exhausted, whereupon disclosure to external organisations is permitted.[52] As for the protections in respect of employer victimisation, retaliation or harassment,[53] in UK law, the equivalents are more subtle. For example, any "dismissals" and/or 'detriments' (adverse action short of dismissal) taken by the employer against whistleblowing employees are treated as actionable in law.[54] As such, the relevant safeguards stipulated in the WD are similar, with no great deviation in the protective ambit here. In conclusion, taken in aggregate on a systematic basis and adopting a bird's eye perspective, although there is clearly some deviation, what passes for divergence is of such a limited nature that it would be uncharitable to claim that there is a lack of functional harmonisation as regards the relative whistleblowing regimes in the EU and the UK.

Additional evidence for convergence between European and British Labour Law is also provided by the EU's proposal for a Pay Transparency Directive ('PPTD').[55] The terms of the PPTD are concerned with the external reporting of discrepancies in pay between the sexes in the workplace. And they are broadly comparable with the reporting requirements imposed on British employers by the Equality Act 2010 (Gender Pay Gap Information) Regulations 2017.[56] For example, in the UK, private[57] and voluntary sector employers with 250 employees or more are bound to publish the difference between the average hourly rate of pay paid to male and female employees, the difference between the average bonus paid to male and female employees, the proportions of male and of female employees who receive

---

[49] See Recital 32 and Articles 5(2) and 6(1). See Abazi (2019), p. 648; Gerdemann and Colneric (2021), pp. 201–202.

[50] Both the WD and the PIDA apply to the public sector.

[51] The WD is restricted to private sector organisations employing 50 or more employees, with the exception of entities in the financial services industry: see recital (48) and article 8(3) WD. For discussion, see Gerdemann and Colneric (2021), p. 195; Abazi (2019), pp. 646; 650.

[52] See Articles 6(1)(b) and 7–13 of the WD and sections 43C to 43J of the ERA. For analysis, see Abazi (2019), pp. 649–653; Gerdemann and Colneric (2021), pp. 201–207.

[53] See Article 19 and Gerdemann and Colneric (2021), pp. 255–258; Abazi (2019), p. 648.

[54] See sections 47B and 103A of the ERA.

[55] See COM(2021) 93 final, https://eur-lex.europa.eu/legal-content/EN/TXT/PDF/?uri=CELEX:52021PC0093&from=EN. See also Common Position document, pdf (europa.eu).

[56] SI 2017/172.

[57] Public sector employers with 250 employees or more are covered by The Equality Act 2010 (Specific Duties and Public Authorities) Regulations 2017 (SI 2017/353).

bonuses, and the relative proportions of male and female employees in each quartile pay band of the workforce. These legislative provisions share many similarities with the PPTD, which also governs private and public sector employers with 250 employees or more. The information that must be reported is also extensive, covering many imaginable methodologies that can be employed towards calculating pay gaps between female and male workers.[58]

A recent domestic episode also lends further support to the functional harmonisation/convergence thesis. Buoyed by the formal Brexit date of 31st January 2020, the UK Government's Department of Business and Industrial Strategy announced in early January 2021 that there would be a review of UK Labour Laws. Owing to the fact that the relevant Government Minister Kwasi Kwarteng had penned a book in the early stages of his political career, lamenting the negative economic effects of labour standards,[59] speculation grew that the UK Government would use Brexit to pursue a deregulatory employment law reform agenda.[60] However, the UK Government abandoned its plan in late January 2021 after a backlash from trade unions, company bosses and the media. Hence, in the final analysis, there is little evidence so far of any divergence between the UK and EU, which is constrained by extraneous factors anyway, such as article 387 of the EUUKCA trade agreement. Exactly the same can be said in respect of the UK Government's proposed stripping away of large chunks of subordinate UK legislation derived from EU law in terms of the Retained EU Law (Revocation and Reform) Act 2023. Having originally included a number of employment laws constituting secondary legislation (that had EU law as their source) that were slated for repeal, the passage of the Bill through Parliament was fraught, with the end result that the Act's impact on employment legislation turned out to be negligible. However, rather than 'reform denied', this is more likely to be a case of 'reform delayed'. In other words, owing to the lifestyle squeeze on living costs imposed on the British public by the COVID-19 pandemic, it was felt that it was not an opportune time to set about stripping away employment rights: well, not yet anyway.

Having subjected the headline measures in the TPWCD, WD and PPTD to scrutiny relative to their domestic equivalents in UK Labour law, is there any compelling, clear-cut answer to the question that poses whether there has been

---

[58] See COM(2021) 93 final, Articles 3(1) and 8(1), https://eur-lex.europa.eu/legal-content/EN/TXT/PDF/?uri=CELEX:52021PC0093&from=EN.

[59] Kwarteng et al. (2012).

[60] In particular, the following employment rights found in the Working Time Regulations 1998 (SI 1998/1833) ('WTR') were slated for removal: (i) the 48-hour working week limit (see regulation 4(1) of the WTR and article 6(b) of Directive 2003/88/EC of the European Parliament and of the Council of 4 November 2003 concerning certain aspects of the organisation of working time O.J. L 299 ('WTD')); (ii) the inclusion of overtime pay when calculating paid holiday under regulations 13–16 of the WTR and article 7 of the WTD (see *East of England Ambulance Service NHS Trust v Flowers* [2019] IRLR 798, *Patterson v Castlereagh Borough Council* [2015] IRLR 721 and *Dudley Metropolitan Borough Council v Willetts* [2017] IRLR 870); (iii) the requirement for businesses to log employees' working hours (see *Federacion de Servicios de Comisiones Obreras v Deutsche Bank SAE* [2019] 3 CMLR 32).

divergence or harmonisation as a result of Brexit? What the analysis reveals is that the scope for negative formal or functional divergence has been exchanged for a complex amalgam of formal and functional harmonisation to date, depending on the particular employment laws under consideration. In this way, it is impossible at this stage to conclude that Brexit has opened up a chasm between the degree of social and labour protections in the UK and the EU. Instead, it would be premature to reach such a conclusion.

3.3 The COVID-19 Pandemic and the Response

The unprecedented crisis in commercial and labour markets caused by the health, medical and social crisis that was the COVID-19 pandemic and the associated government-mandated 'lockdowns' precipitated various policies and laws designed to protect the jobs of employees and workers. In European legal systems the regulatory responses were very similar in terms of the techniques that were prescribed. And that is despite the fact that they were each national in origin and the formal black-letter laws were very different. For example, countries in Europe introduced income support measures that benefitted their employees in order to ensure that businesses could retain their staff pending the conclusion of the crisis.[61] In the Continental European jurisdictions, many of the targeted worker income support schemes were broadly based on the German 'Kuzarbeit'. This entailed publicly financed temporary wage subsidies paid to qualifying employers for short-term work, i.e. where there were reductions in the working hours of their staff. The quid pro quo for these state payments was the introduction of legislation embargoing such qualifying employers from dismissing those workers for the duration of the scheme, e.g. in the case of Luxembourg, Spain, the Netherlands and Italy.

The approach described above can be contrasted with the British deployment of income support measures. This was referred to as the 'Coronavirus job retention scheme' (CJRS).[62] What set it apart from the European schemes was its failure to prescribe a prohibition on the dismissal of employees as a precondition for qualifying employers to access 'furlough' money from the UK Government.[63] The scheme envisaged that employers would continue to pay wages to their employees, but that qualifying employers under the CJRS would then be entitled to claim 80% of the value from the UK Government, subject to a maximum of £2500 per month per employee. Like the income support regimes operated in European countries, the

[61] See Mangan et al. (2020).

[62] See The Coronavirus Act 2020 Functions of Her Majesty's Revenue and Customs (Coronavirus Job Retention Scheme) Direction.

[63] Mangan et al. (2020), pp. 334–339.

purpose of the CJRS was to disincentivise employers from dismissing their staff during the lockdown period, so that they remained in employment and were ready to resume work once normal business resumed. At the inception of the scheme, the CJRS did not permit short-term working. As such, while employees would be kept on the payroll of employers who qualified under the CJRS, they were specifically instructed to stop all work.[64] However, that changed with effect from July 2020, when the British Government altered the terms of the CJRS to enable employers to bring back their furloughed employees on a part-time basis. Furlough was then paid at the rate of 80% of the salaries of those employees in respect of the hours they did not work.[65]

The policy consideration underpinning both the CJRS in the UK and the Kuzarbeit-related schemes in continental Europe was the same: that of sustaining the businesses of employers with as much of their existing workforce as possible, so that on the resumption of standard commercial activity, employees would still be on the payroll. As such, when probed against the backdrop of this policy objective, across jurisdictions, what we witnessed was variety in form, but consistency in function, i.e. positive functional harmonisation. This outcome—functional harmonisation—is consistent with that in play in the other crises reviewed by this chapter, i.e. in the context of the GFC and Brexit, albeit with differentiations in their effects on social protection. A pressing question is why these findings are so uniform, which is an issue to which we now turn in Sect. 4.

4 Analysis and Theorisation Surrounding Preceding Findings

The preceding discussion concerning the GFC, Brexit and the Covid Pandemic and their consequences for the relationship between the differing labour laws of European legal systems reveals that harmonisation or convergence—whether formal or functional—has been the principal, albeit not the most obvious, outcome. In brief, the findings were that the GFC gave rise to negative functional harmonisation, with a complex mixture of formal and functional convergence/harmonisation in the case of Brexit, and clear evidence of positive functional harmonisation in response to the Covid pandemic. And if these forms of convergence or harmonisation are endemic irrespective of the internal or external crises being studied, certain inferences may be drawn. First, the results reinforce a notion that there are particular forces that have a chilling effect on, or serve to prevent, the adoption of policy prescriptions that secure formal and functional divergence in labour laws. This suggests the existence of

[64] Paragraph 6.1(a) of the Coronavirus Act 2020 Functions of Her Majesty's Revenue and Customs (Coronavirus Job Retention Scheme) Direction directed that employees or limb (b) workers must 'cease all work in relation to their employment'.

[65] By October 2020, the 80% threshold had dropped to 60%.

various factors that militate against forms of protectionist labour policies and laws designed to protect 'inside' labour against 'outside' labour.[66] For example, one might conjecture that the recent incremental disempowerment of national-level interest groups such as trade unions has stunted their ability to promote positively formal or functional divergent labour law reforms.[67] And as such, that this has translated into the weakening of national pressures that seek to deviate from the comparative norm as a means of effecting localized responses.[68]

Building on this theme, the question that must be posed is what might explain this phenomenon? One suggestion is that organisations such as national legislatures, policy-makers and courts exhibit an implicit *tendency towards copying*, particularly where the relevant law has been successful and resulted in strong performance. In the field of sociology, the force of example has been cited as a cogent explanation for imitation, or 'mimetic processes' in the direction of isomorphism. Paul DiMaggio and Walter Powell have remarked that models 'may be diffused unintentionally, indirectly through employee transfer or turnover, or explicitly by organizations'.[69] And what drives this mimetic process is a quest for legitimacy on the part of an organisation. For example, in the case of corporate law, it has been claimed that the Anglo-American 'shareholder primacy' corporate governance framework was copied throughout the world in the post-Cold War period based on its perceived positive economic outcomes.[70] Likewise, the pervasiveness of imitation and isomorphism in labour law has already been noted in the context of formal systems for the resolution and adjudication of employment disputes.[71]

Another view propounds that in the teeth of crises, certain informal pressures coerce jurisdictions to take action deprioritising economically protectionist policies, and in the direction of maintaining the same or similar labour standards as other countries. For example, it has been remarked that globalisation has unleashed *competitive forces* that prioritise a 'level playing field' in labour regulatory standards.[72] A marked reluctance to move away from a level playing field for fear of an adverse retaliatory market response may exercise a grip on a jurisdiction's agenda for labour law. Likewise, commercial players in the market may intimate such a clear preference. As such, any claim that divergent labour laws is the natural state for jurisdictions lacks substance and is overstated.

Finally, different jurisdictions may be driven along the same (or a similar) path in labour law reform (as a response to various crises) by *the force of logic*. For instance,

---

[66] For the relationship between nationalism, protectionism and populism in the context of comparative labour law, see Campbell (2021).

[67] See Pontusson (2013), p. 800; Charlwood (2004); Blanchflower (2007); Raday (2002).

[68] For the traditional power of national trade unions in shaping labour laws and the relationship with corporate governance, see Gourevitch and Shin (2005); Pargendler (2021), p. 536.

[69] DiMaggio and Powell (1983), p. 150.

[70] See Hansmann and Kraakman (2001), p. 450; Rasheed and Yoshikawa (2012).

[71] See Corby and Latreille (2012).

[72] See DiMaggio and Powell (1983), p. 150; Hansmann and Kraakman (2001), p. 450.

the form and shape of the legal interventions in the area of employment law may be consistent across a number of countries for the reason that they have developed a *particular normative status or legitimacy.*[73] In this way, the perception arises that the model adopted is the correct reform agenda owing to its moral capacity to inspire widespread acceptance.

If we turn to consider which of the above processes can best describe the three crises of the GFC, Brexit and the COVID-19 pandemic, the latter can be presented as a particular illustration of the *normative* pressures variable. As discussed, the principal labour law response observed across many jurisdictions constituted the introduction of income support schemes. This phenomenon largely owed its existence to a lively sense that these schemes amounted to shared best practice on the part of policy makers and legislatures in differing countries. However, arguably, *normative force* was not the only factor in play in relation to the legal responses to COVID-19. *Memetic pressures* tending towards *imitation* also had a role in influencing the legislative scheme. Although, having said that, the forces of copying and imitation were arguably weaker in strength than the normative pressures in this instance, to the extent that there was evidence of some formal divergence in the legal schemes, albeit large elements of harmonisation in function, e.g. the deviations in the nature and content of the British and European income support schemes.

As for Brexit, there are considerable outside pressures inclining towards the maintenance of functional parity of labour standards (via harmonisation and/or convergence)—such as the desire for British businesses to remain *competitive* vis-a-vis the EU—and the UK being reluctant to impose further austerity on the general public immediately after the Covid experience. This is undergirded by the significant economic considerations presented by article 387 of the EUUKCA, whereby the EU retains the potential to take retaliatory measures against the UK where labour and other standards are pared down so materially that trade is distorted. Seen from this angle, the functional harmonisation/convergence of labour laws as a response to Brexit displays the purchase of the *competitive forces* variable.

Finally, turning to the GFC, there was a great deal of normative power in the view that the costs imposed by the crisis should be passed on to and absorbed by all in society, including workers and the public, rather than being borne solely by the banks who caused the problem in the first place. This was the austerity agenda in action, which in the area of labour law could be articulated and applied more overtly or covertly, as the case may be. One illustration of the latter is the UK employment law response whereby it was considered best practice to marginalise employment laws by making their enforcement more difficult. In this way, the actual and potential costs associated with employment rights would be reduced for employers, albeit in an indirect manner. This can be contrasted with the much blunter solution adopted by various jurisdictions in the EU, where the costs and risks of employment rights were

[73] DiMaggio and Powell (1983), pp. 152–154.

passed onto workers and demutualised away from employers (and banks) by simply removing or diluting certain employment law protections.[74]

A second insight from this work is how divergence in times of crises may be more difficult to achieve than might be initially supposed. One explanation is that democratic constraints may exert a hold on the capacity of differing jurisdictions to deviate in their labour laws. For example, to remain in power in a democracy, the ruling parties have a duty to 'sell' viable policy solutions to crises (as and when they arise) to their electorates. It may prove easier to do so, commanding greater popular acceptance (and enhanced political stability) in the eyes of the voting electorate if the applicable response is one which is copied from other neighbouring countries, i.e. assimilation of what is understood to be the most fitting way out of the crisis. This was particularly visible in the case of the COVID-19 pandemic, where a great deal of imitation of solutions was palpable.

5 Conclusion

How do labour laws in neighbouring jurisdictions evolve in reaction to major crises and are those various responses convergent in some formal or functional respects? This is the principal question to which this chapter has been devoted. Three recent prominent crises were taken as the lens through which this question would be considered, namely the GFC, Brexit and Covid. Somewhat surprisingly, in each of the three crises, what was particularly striking about the relationship between the legal developments in the countries under consideration was how formally or functionally convergent they were in practice, either through top-down harmonisation or bottom-up forms of convergence. In essence, in the case of the GFC, there was evidence of the negative functional harmonisation of labour laws, which could be contrasted with an amalgam of formal and functional convergence/harmonisation in the case of Brexit, followed by a consistent reaction of positive functional harmonisation in relation to the COVID-19 pandemic. As such, where crises strike, this chapter suggests that there are various factors at work in the case of labour law reforms that render it challenging for law-makers to respond in ways that are formally divergent to one's neighbours. To the extent that the discussion charts and classifies the comparative legal responses of jurisdictions in the field of labour law in crisis-related contexts, this chapter is undoubtedly novel and important in aiding understanding. Of course, an altogether different question is whether there might be any contrast between the findings of this chapter and the comparative legal responses in *non-crisis related* contexts, and if so, why. This chapter's parting shot is the suggestion that this is a task to which additional research ought to be dedicated.

[74] For a discussion of the 'demutualisation' strategy, see Countouris and Freedland (2013), pp. 7–9.

References

Abazi V (2019) The European Union whistleblowing directive: a "game changer" for whistleblowing protection? Ind Law J 49:640–656

Adams A, Prassl J (2017) Vexatious claims: challenging the case for employment tribunal fees. Mod Law Rev 80:412–442

Antokolskaia M (2006) Harmonisation of family law in Europe: a historical perspective. Intersentia, Antwerpen/Oxford

Avdagic S (2015) Does deregulation work? Reassessing the unemployment effects of employment protection. Br J Ind Relat 53:6–26

Barmes L (2016) Bullying and behavioural conflict at work. Oxford University Press, Oxford/UK

Barnard C, Deakin S (2002) "Negative" and "positive" harmonisation of labor law in the European Union. Colum J Eur Union Law 8:389–413

Bednarowicz B (2019) Delivering on the European pillar of social rights: the new directive on transparent and predictable working conditions in the European Union. Ind Law J 48:604–623

Blanchflower D (2007) International patterns of union membership. Br J Ind Relat 45:1–28

Blyth M (2013) Austerity. Oxford University Press, Oxford

Bradley S et al (2014) Employment protection, threat and incentive effects on worker absence. Br J Ind Relat 52:333–358

Busby N, McDermont M (2012) Workers, marginalised voices and the employment tribunal system: some preliminary findings. Ind Law J 41:166–183

Busby N, McDermont M (2020) Fighting with the wind: claimants' experiences and perceptions of the employment tribunal. Ind Law J 49:159–198

Campbell JL (2021) Nationalism, populism, and labour market reform today. Comp Labor Law Policy J 42:1–15

Charlwood A (2004) The new generation of trade union leaders and prospects for union revitalisation. Br J Ind Relat 42:379–397

Clarke T (2016) The continuing diversity of corporate governance: theories of convergence and variety. Ephemera 16:19–52

Corby S, Latreille PL (2012) Employment tribunals and the civil courts: isomorphism exemplified. Ind Law J 41:387–406

Countouris N, Freedland M (eds) (2013) Resocialising Europe in a time of crisis. Cambridge University Press, Cambridge

Davidov G (2021) Compliance with and enforcement of labour laws: an overview and some timely challenges. Soziales Recht 3:111–127

Davidov G, Eshet E (2022) Improving compliance with labor laws: the role of courts'. Comp Labor Law Policy J (forthcoming) 42

Deakin S et al (2014a) How do labour laws affect unemployment and the labour share of national income? The experience of six OECD countries, 1970–2010'. Int Labour Rev 153:1–27

Deakin S et al (2014b) Labour law and inclusive development: the economic effects of industrial relations laws in middle-income countries. In: Schmiegelow M, Schmiegelow H (eds) Institutional competition between common law and civil law. Springer-Verlag, pp 185–210

Department for Business, Energy & Industrial Strategy (2019) Good work: one-sided flexibility. https://assets.publishing.service.gov.uk/government/uploads/system/uploads/attachment_data/file/818674/Good_Work_Plan_one_sided_flexibility-consultation_.pdf

Dickens L (2012) Making employment rights effective-issues of enforcement and compliance. Hart, UK

DiMaggio PJ, Powell WW (1983) The iron cage revisited: institutional isomorphism and collective rationality in organizational fields. Am Sociol Rev 48:147–160

Edmans A et al (2014) Employee satisfaction, labor market flexibility, and stock returns around the world. European Corporate Governance Institute (ECGI)—Finance Working Paper Series No. 433/2014

Ewing K (1988) The death of labour law? Oxf J Leg Stud 8:293–300

Gerdemann S, Colneric N (2021) The EU whistleblower directive and its transposition: Part 1. Eur Labour Law J 12:193–210
Gilson RJ (2001) Globalizing corporate governance: convergence of form or function. Am J Comp Law 49:329–357
Gilson RJ (2004) Globalizing corporate governance: convergence of form or function. In: Gordon J, Roe M (eds) Convergence and persistence in corporate governance. Cambridge University Press, Cambridge, pp 128–158
Gordon JN (2018) Convergence and persistence in corporate law and governance. In: Gordon JN, Ringe W (eds) The Oxford handbook of corporate law and governance. Oxford University Press, Oxford/UK, pp 28–55
Gourevitch PA, Shin JJ (eds) (2005) Political power and corporate control – the new global politics of corporate governance. Princeton University Press, Princeton
Hansmann H, Kraakman R (2001) The end of history for corporate law'. Georgetown Law J 89: 439–468
Hepple B (2013) Back to the future: employment law under the coalition government. Ind Law J 42: 203–223
Hyde A (2011) The idea of the idea of labour law: a parable. In: Davidov G, Langille B (eds) The idea of labour law. Oxford University Press, Oxford, pp 88–98
Kwarteng K et al (2012) Britannia unchained: global lessons for growth and prosperity. Palgrave MacMillan, New York
La Porta R et al (2000) Investor protection and corporate governance. J Financ Econ 58:3–27
Lohse E (2011) The meaning of harmonisation in the context of European Union law – a process in need of definition. In: Andenas M, Andersen CB (eds) Theory and practice of harmonisation. Edward Elgar Publishing, UK, pp 282–313
Mangan D (2013) Employment tribunal reforms to boost the economy. Ind Law J 42:409–421
Mangan D et al (2020) An unprecedented social solidarity stress test. Eur Labour Law J 11:247–275
Marshall S (2014) Shifting responsibility: how the burden of the European financial crisis shifted away from the financial sector and onto labour. Comp Labor Law Policy J 35:449–478
Nelken D (2002) Legal transplants and beyond: of disciplines and metaphors. In: Harding A, Örücü E (eds) Comparative law in the 21st century. Kluwer Law International, Netherlands, pp 19–34
OECD (2013) Employment Outlook 2013, OECD Employment Outlook 2013 (oecd-ilibrary.org)
Pargendler M (2021) The grip of nationalism on corporate law. Indiana Law J 95:533–590
Pontusson J (2013) Unionization, inequality and redistribution. Br J Ind Relat 51:797–825
Raday F (2002) The decline of union power – structural inevitability or policy choice? In: Conaghen J et al (eds) Labour law in an era of globalization. Oxford University Press, Oxford, pp 353–378
Rasheed AA, Yoshikawa T (2012) The convergence of corporate governance: promise and prospects. In: Rasheed AA, Yoshikawa T (eds) The convergence of corporate governance. Palgrave MacMillan, Basingstoke/UK, pp 1–31
Renton D (2012) Struck out. Pluto Press
Roisin R (2021) Platform work and fixed-term employment regulation. Eur Labour Law J 12:156–176
Wilmot-Smith F (2019) Equal justice. Harvard University Press, London

David Cabrelli is a professor of employment law at the University of Edinburgh, Scotland, United Kingdom.

Consumer Law in Ghana

Nuhu Yidana and Lydia A. Nkansah

1 Introduction

The lack of adequate laws is a well-known driving force of law reform, especially when dealing with emerging social concerns. The gradual emergence of new societal developments often reflects existing functional deficiencies and flaws in legal provisions. Such diverse arrays of developments essentially leave the prevailing laws archaic, obsolete or outdated. Crises also trigger law reform initiatives; they constitute one of the catalysts for reforming the regulatory architecture, with a view to bringing the law up to speed with the crises-engendered challenges of society. Such a regulatory response is not only confined to the national level, but is also a common practice internationally, especially where such crises transcend national borders or are of a global dimension.[1] As one of the principal triggers of law reform, it is arguable that crises can shake the moral foundations of society's so-called time-tested complacent status quo and provide space for legal development in many jurisdictions, including Ghana. This rightly underscores the observation that the upshot of crises often reveals the inherent limitations of the existing regulatory

The authors are deeply grateful to the editors and reviewers for their well-thought-out comments and suggestions for improvement to earlier draft of this chapter. However, the authors remain responsible for errors and omissions found in the manuscript.

[1] Plotnic (2021); Cseres and Reyna (2021); Pagliari and Wilf (2021); Lane (2013); Krugman (2017).

N. Yidana (✉)
School of Law, SOAS University of London, London, UK
e-mail: ny4@soas.ac.uk

L. A. Nkansah
Faculty of Law, Kwame Nkrumah University of Science and Technology, Kumasi, Ghana

E. Ghio, R. Perlingeiro (eds.), *Are Legal Systems Converging or Diverging?*,
https://doi.org/10.1007/978-3-031-38180-5_7

frameworks and creates a window of opportunity for introducing and promoting new regulatory reforms.[2]

Crises-motivated reforms may lead to the convergence of national laws with regional or international protocols or measures of other jurisdictions. However, the reforms may also serve as a conduit for divergent regulatory action with a national focus. Although the forces of globalisation are increasingly driving legal systems toward convergence, country-specific optima impose inherent limits on convergence, leading to some degree of positive divergence.[3] Some scholars argue, however, that a purely national focus is untenable due to the exponential growth of cross-border trade.[4]

This chapter critically investigates the evolution of consumer law and policy in Ghana against the contextual backdrop of whether crises-connected law reforms converge with or diverge from international standards, protocols and initiatives of other jurisdictions with respect to identical crises. The analysis covers crises that have actively or passively shaped the framework of consumer law and policy evolution in Ghana in the last two decades.

It is trite that before Ghana's return to constitutional rule in 1993 (i.e. Ghana's Fourth Republic), the country's political history had been marked by a number of coup d'états.[5] However, since 1993 the story has been different. In the last twenty years, Ghana has had some true civilian governments where the two dominant political parties in the country, the New Patriotic Party (NPP) and the National Democratic Congress (NDC), between whom the constitutional power to rule has alternated, have been led by civilians. The first eight years of Ghana's return to constitutional political order (1993–2000) were controlled by a soldier-turned-civilian whose belief in the rule of law was generally perceived to be questionable. Therefore, it is reasonable to exclude this period of constitutional rule in trying to trace the evolution of consumer law and policy responses to crises in Ghana. Second, arguably, in the last twenty years, Ghana has been plagued by unpreceded forms of crises, ranging from economic and financial crises to energy crises. Consequently, it is contended that discussing these crises and the legal and policy responses to them has the potential to expand the frontiers of the existing literature on consumer law and policy. Third, the last twenty years constitute the first twenty years of the twenty-first century, a century characterised by astounding advances in technology, information explosion and heightened globalisation. Thus, crises and their concomitant consumer law and policy responses to them in the last twenty years satisfy the twin requirement of recency and relevancy of data in academic discourse.

This chapter focuses on consumer law and policy responses encompassing product safety regulation, financial services regulation, and issues regarding the COVID-19 pandemic. It discusses the various crises-oriented reforms that ensued

[2] Pagliari and Wilf (2021).

[3] Crettez et al. (2014).

[4] Menon (2013).

[5] Nkansah (2015).

in Ghana over the last two decades and the extent to which international, regional and sub-regional standards or protocols and initiatives of other jurisdictions have instrumentally shaped such reforms. Overall, the chapter demonstrates that crises motivated consumer law and policy responses in Ghana over the last two decades broadly converged with international, regional and sub-regional standards and initiatives of other jurisdictions as regards identical crises of a global character, except in the case of COVID-19 where there was some level of divergence between various jurisdictions. Consequently, this chapter argues that convergence is predicated on the existence of well-developed international standards and protocols that serve as guidelines, which did not exist in the heydays of the COVID-19 crisis, when national action was urgently needed. As such, each country was grappling to fashion-out measures to deal with the crisis head-on, bearing in mind the peculiar challenges the pandemic brought onto consumers in the domestic setting, leading to a divergence of approaches. It is, therefore, submitted that while the existence of international standards or initiatives elsewhere is a bedrock for possible convergence of national legal systems in dealing with crises of identical character, the non-availability of such international standards provides space for the divergence of measures bearing in mind the peculiar national circumstances of various countries dealing with similar crises.

The chapter is divided into six sections. Section two provides an overview of the architecture of consumer law and policy in Ghana and highlights the principal scope of the substantive analysis of this chapter. The third section considers product safety regulation taking into consideration the safety of communication equipment and public health products with a particular focus on tobacco regulation. The extent to which measures in these fields are consistent or otherwise with global guidelines or other jurisdictional initiatives is appraised. The fourth section considers the legislative and regulatory response to the recent financial crises that disturbed the country. An attempt is made in this section to evaluate the degree to which the legislative and regulatory responses converge with, or diverge from, other jurisdictions' initiatives or international standards or guidelines. The fifth section covers the legislative and regulatory responses to the constraints that are exerted on the rights of consumers in Ghana under the prevailing COVID-19 crisis. The sixth section provides a conclusion providing a summary of the argument in this chapter.

2 The Architecture of Consumer Law and Policy in Ghana

2.1 The Current Law on Consumer Protection

Ghana currently has no uniform consumer legislation that is tailored for the protection of the rights of consumers. Rather, there are several pieces of laws that cumulatively regulate the regime of consumer law in Ghana, encompassing both private and public law regulatory regimes.[6] The question as to what constitutes the private law aspect of consumer law in Ghana brings into sharp focus the general principles of the law of contract and the law of torts which are supplemented with statutes such as the Sale of Goods Act 1962, the Hire-purchase Decree 1974 and some provisions of the Electronic Transactions Act 2008.[7] The public law facet of consumer law embodies the exercise of regulatory oversight by various regulatory institutions targeted at the protection of the consuming public in Ghana.[8] The architecture of consumer law, therefore, represents the amalgamation of the diverse laws drawing from private and public law regimes.

While private law statutes relevant to consumer protection in Ghana have not yet witnessed reforms in response to crises in the past two decades, the public law dimension of consumer protection has greatly benefitted from some reforms inspired by crises over the last two decades. Therefore, the discussion in this chapter focuses primarily on some key reforms within the public law regime that contributed to shaping the contours of consumer law in Ghana. The recent COVID-19 pandemic also occasioned responses that touched upon consumer law and policy in Ghana, and this will not be excluded from the lens of the current appraisal.

2.2 *Policy on Consumer Protection in Ghana*

As noted earlier, there is no uniform consumer protection regime in Ghana. The prevailing laws for the protection of the rights of consumers are fragmented and contained in diverse pieces of law. These include both private law devices and public regulatory mechanisms. The scattered pieces of laws are generally inadequate, complex, and difficult to access. A concerted effort to resolve the inherent deficiencies of the regime led to the government's inclusion of 'consumer protection and fair trade' as one of the key policy instruments under the Ghana National Trade Policy since 2005. The principal focus of the government's policy instrument on consumer protection was to 'develop clear, transparent, comprehensive and consolidated consumer protection rules to facilitate the exercising of consumer rights', and also, 'establish mechanisms and instruments such as small claims courts to provide speedy remedies which are accessible to all consumers.'[9] This sought to give force to one of the central objects of Ghana's Trade Policy whose target is 'to ensure a consistent and stable policy environment within which the private sector and consumers can operate effectively and with certainty.'[10] The overall objective of the

[6] Yidana (2021).

[7] Yidana (2020).

[8] For details, see Yidana (2023).

[9] Ghana National Trade Policy, p. 31.

[10] Ghana National Trade Policy, p. 'v'.

policy instrument on consumer protection rests on the growing importance '[t]o ensure the well-being and rights of consumers'.[11]

This National Trade Policy instrument was further given a boost with the adoption of a Consumer Protection Policy in 2014.[12] It is important to note that the framework of Consumer Protection Policy 2014 is consistent with the United Nations (UN) Guideline on Consumer Protection.[13] The central target of the Policy is to achieve seven principal goals which broadly include the quest to:

> [e]stablish a fair, transparent and efficient marketplace in line with Ghana's Trade Policy; provide a consistent, predictable and effective framework that fosters consumer confidence and capacity, in particular among vulnerable consumers; provide access to redress for all sections of the consuming public; Empower Ghanaian consumers to assert their rights in the marketplace; promote customer responsiveness in both public and private sectors of the economy; harmonise and streamline the regulatory and institutional environment, and align and harmonise national consumer protection policy with international best practices.[14]

While the adoption of the Policy was celebrated as a welcomed development,[15] the Policy is yet to be fully implemented for consumers to reap the intended benefits. Nonetheless, the Drafting Department of the Ministry of Justice and Attorney has since been working on drafting a Consumer Protection Bill for both government and parliamentary consideration. However, the process has so far been very slow and in 2018, Dowuona-Hammond noted that the drafting process was still in its initial stages and that it would take a little while for the parliament to enact the law.[16] The situation has not changed much since 2018. With Accra, the national capital of Ghana, serving as the Secretariat of the African Continental Free Trade Area (ACFTA),[17] it is imperative for the government to speed up the enactment process to offer the needed protection to consumers in their transactional relationships in Ghana under the aegis of the ACFTA. This is highly critical as the ACFTA regime does not presently cover issues of consumer protection, including the ACFTA protocol on rules and procedures for the settlement of disputes.[18] This implies that

---

[11] Ghana National Trade Policy, p. 31.

[12] Ghana News Agency (12th March 2015) Cabinet Passes Law On Consumer Protection, https://m.peacefmonline.com/pages/local/news/201503/235191.php.

[13] UN Guideline on Consumer Protection 1985 and expanded in 1999 (as superseded by the UN Guidelines for Consumer Protection 2016).

[14] Government of Ghana (2014) Draft Consumer Protection Policy, http://www.cacghana.org/images/documents/consumer_protection_policy_central_hotel_may_9_atuahene_2.pdf.

[15] Ghana News Agency (12th March 2015) Cabinet Passes Law On Consumer Protection, https://m.peacefmonline.com/pages/local/news/201503/235191.php.

[16] Dowuona-Hammond (2018).

[17] Ighobor K (2020) AfCFTA Secretariat commissioned in Accra as free trade is set to begin in January 2021. African Renewal, https://www.un.org/africarenewal/magazine/august-2020/arz/afcfta-secretariat-commissioned-accra-free-trade-set-begin-january-2021.

[18] Article 1, Protocol on Rules and Procedures on the Settlement of Disputes; see also, Erasmus (2019), Dispute Settlement in the African Continental Free Trade Area, https://www.tralac.org/blog/article/14150-dispute-settlement-in-the-african-continental-free-trade-area.html#_ftn15.

consumers will have to resort to domestic law to defend their rights in transactions that occurred in Ghana under the current dispensation of the ACFTA. It is hoped that the enactment of consumer-tailored consolidated legislation will help address the myriad of deficiencies of the current regime on consumer protection in Ghana.

3 Product Safety Regulation

As noted above, product safety regulation is one of the key areas of consumer law that has profited from concerted regulatory reforms over the last two decades. Some of these reforms are rooted in the emergence of crises over the years.

It is first important to note that the various reforms on product safety regulation are sector-specific and are linked to the mandate of different sector regulatory establishments. Some of these regulatory institutions include the Ghana Standards Authority, the Food and Drugs Authority, the Energy Commission and the National Communications Authority. The discussion in this chapter is confined to product safety regulation under the aegis of the Food and Drugs Authority and the National Communications Authority where the reforms are attributable to specific crises.

3.1 Public Health Product Safety Reforms

Safety regulations of public health products are enshrined in the Public Health Act 2012 and the Standards Decree 1973. This chapter focuses on the former, which revised and consolidated 'the law relating to public health to prevent disease, promote, safeguard, maintain and protect the health of humans and animals and to provide for related matters' as provided under the preamble of the statute. In doing so, the Public Health Act repealed the Food and Drugs Act 1993, PNDL 305B[19] which hitherto created the Food and Drugs Authority (FDA) and brought the FDA under its ambit. The Public Health Act 2012 mandates the FDA 'to provide and enforce standards for the sale of food, herbal medicinal products, cosmetics, drugs, medical devices and household chemical substances.'[20] While this is a transposition of the predecessor Food and Drugs Act 1993 provision on the mandate of the FDA, the Public Health Act 2012 extends the scope of the mandate of the Food and Drugs Authority to cover the regulation of tobacco and tobacco products among others.

Part Six of the Act sets out the control devices for the regulation of tobacco and tobacco product usage in Ghana by the Food and Drugs Authority. The framework for the control of tobacco and tobacco products under the 2012 Act was arguably introduced as a response to the alarming global health impact of tobacco

[19] Section 175, Public Health Act 2012, Act 851.

[20] Section 81, the Public Health Act 2012, Act 851.

consumption and the usage of tobacco and tobacco products by the youth in Ghana.[21] During the twentieth century, over 100 million deaths were attributed to tobacco consumption. While these deaths were mostly recorded in developed countries, studies have revealed that the twenty-first century will see the death of a further one billion persons in low- and middle-income countries if current tobacco consumption patterns persist.[22] However, over 200 million of these estimated deaths could be avoided if the current tobacco consumption is reduced by a third by 2025 according to the World Health Assembly in its call to governments to take drastic actions through effective regulatory control.[23]

To effectively reduce the use of tobacco and tobacco products in the broader interest of the health and safety of consumers, Ghana introduced stringent measures into the Public Health Act 2012,[24] supplemented by the Tobacco Control Regulation 2016.[25] In October 2021, Ghana also acceded to the Protocol to Eliminate Illicit Trade in Tobacco Products and this came into force in January 2022.[26]

The 2012 Act prohibited all forms of tobacco promotion, sponsorship and advertising that promote tobacco products in a manner that is 'false, misleading or deceptive or likely to create an erroneous impression about its characteristics, health effects, hazards or emissions'.[27] While imposing on persons who manufacture, import or sell a tobacco product to ensure that the product packaging carries a health warning including a conspicuous display of the health warning at the point of sale as determined by the Food and Drugs Authority,[28] the statute further prohibited packaging, labelling or offering for sale a product that looks like or is likely to be identified or associated with tobacco or a tobacco product.[29] The Act equally outlawed the exposure of minors to tobacco or tobacco products including selling or offering for sale tobacco or tobacco product to a child or sending a child to buy or requesting a child to light tobacco or tobacco product.[30]

The above prescriptions of the Public Health Act 2012 and its subsidiary legislation regarding tobacco implemented the 2003 World Health Organisation (WHO) Framework Convention on Tobacco Control. It is instructive to note that the

---

[21] Owusu-Dabo et al. (2009); VALD (2012) Public Health Bill (Tobacco Control Measures) Passed by Parliament. Modern Ghana, https://www.modernghana.com/news/405747/public-health-bill-tobacco-control-measures-pass.html.

[22] Jha and Peto (2014); Peto and Lopez (2004); Jha (2009).

[23] World Health Organization (2013) Global action plan for the prevention and control of noncommunicable diseases 2013-2020. World Health Organization.

[24] Part Six of the Public Health Act 2012, Act 851.

[25] L. I. 2247.

[26] FDA, Ghana completes the ratification process for the illicit trade in tobacco products protocol, http://www.fdaghana.gov.gh/news-media.php?page=119.

[27] Section 62 (2), Public Health Act, 2012.

[28] Sections 63 (1) and 64, Public Health Act, 2012.

[29] Section 62 (1), Public Health Act, 2012; See also, Regulation 16, Tobacco Control Regulation 2016, L. I. 2247.

[30] Section 65, Public Health Act, 2012.

Convention on Tobacco Control is provided under the Public Health Act 2012 as the Third Schedule to the Act. Arguably, in considering the import of the provisions relating to tobacco control under the Public Health Act, the courts are likely to draw guidance not only from the Convention and its protocols but also from how other jurisdictions have implemented and construed the provisions of the Convention. The primary purpose of the Convention and its protocols is:

> to protect present and future generations from the devastating health, social, environmental and economic consequences of tobacco consumption and exposure to tobacco smoke by providing a framework for tobacco control measures to be implemented by the Parties at the national, regional and international levels in order to reduce continually and substantially the prevalence of tobacco use and exposure to tobacco smoke.[31]

The WHO Framework Convention on Tobacco Control, which Ghana implemented under the Public Health Act, became necessary upon the shared recognition that 'the spread of the tobacco epidemic is a global problem with serious consequences for public health that calls for the widest possible international cooperation and the participation of all countries in an effective, appropriate and comprehensive international response'.[32]

Aside from the convergence of the regulatory control of tobacco and tobacco products of the Public Health Act of Ghana with the WHO Framework Convention on Tobacco Control, the statutory measures regarding food and food supplements, drugs, herbal and homeopathic medicines, veterinary medicines, cosmetics, medical devices, domestic chemical substances equally have strong connections with other international devices. It is worth stressing that the regulatory oversight of the FDA over the latter class of products existed under the Food and Drugs Act as not earlier.

However, the novel part of the Public Health Act 2012 is the creation of the Technical Advisory Committee to operate under the FDA in the evaluation of 'the safety, efficacy, purity and quality' of drugs, herbal medicinal products, medical devices or cosmetics' and approval for a clinical trial, subject to the satisfaction that 'the drugs, products or devices are reasonably safe, efficacious and of acceptable quality'.[33] The Committee essentially 'serves as a forum/platform that provides requisite timely expert advice to the FDA on both current and emerging issues relating to a pre-market conformity assessment as well as post-market monitoring of diverse medical devices including in vitro diagnostics manufactured, imported, distributed, sold and/or used in Ghana.'[34]

The establishment of the Technical Advisory Committee which draws on the expertise of diverse health professionals makes it an important division within the

---

[31] Article 3, WHA 56.1 WHO Framework Convention on Tobacco Control 2003.

[32] See Paragraph 1 of the Preamble to the WHA 56.1 WHO Framework Convention on Tobacco Control 2003.

[33] Section 150, Public Health Act 2012.

[34] FDA, The Technical Advisory Committee on medical devices (TAC-MD), http://fdaghana.gov.gh/images/stories/pdfs/downloads/THE%20TECHNICAL%20ADVISORY%20COMMITTEE%20ON%20MEDICAL%20DEVICES.pdf.

Committee, capable of helping Ghana to deal with the menace of substandard products. Studies reveal that a substantial percentage of medical products on the Ghanaian market are of substandard quality, thus exposing consumers to health consequences.[35] The FDA's recent notice of a 'seizure of substandard and falsified drugs as well as body enhancement products' at the Madina market in Accra exemplified the menace of substandard medical products in the market in Ghana.[36] Sadly, the use of these poor-quality drugs is a recipe for disastrous consequences such as poor treatment, prolonged patient illness and a boost to drug resistance not excluding the waste of patient financial resources.[37] The WHO has also recorded that substandard and falsified antimalarial drugs alone account for an estimated 116,000 annual deaths in sub-Saharan Africa.[38] The work of the Committee is therefore critical to help control the widespread menace of substandard medical products in Ghana.

In the dispensation of the Technical Advisory Committee work, it is required to ensure that its investigations comply with 'Good Clinical Practice as recommended by the International Conference on Harmonization Guidelines and Helsinki Declaration'.[39] Additionally, Schedule Four to the Public Health Act requires that regard be had to publications of:

> (a) the British Pharmacopoeia; (b) the Extra Pharmacopoeia; (c) the United States Pharmacopoeia; (d) the International Pharmacopoeia; (e) the standards, codes of practice, guidelines and recommendations issued by the Codex Alimentarius Commission, and (f) any other work of reference adopted and approved by the Authority' in considering the standard of drugs.

In effect, the reading of the provisions regarding the determination of the safety, quality, purity and efficacy of drugs, medical devices, cosmetics, and herbal medicinal products under the Public Health Act is consistent with both international guidelines and other jurisdictional measures. Since 2014, the FDA is also the designated Regional Centre of Regulatory Excellence (RCORE) in Clinical Trials and Drug Registration by both the New Partnership for African Development and the African Regulatory Harmonisation. As such, the FDA 'seeks to build regulatory capacity in Africa to facilitate quality review of clinical trials and harmonise existing clinical trial processes in the sub-region in line with globally accepted standards.'[40]

---

[35] Bekoe et al. (2020) found that 66.38% of sampled antibiotics were of substandard quality.; Namboodiri et al. (2011); Forson et al. (2010); Donkor and Nartey (2008).

[36] FDA (2021) Seizure of unregistered medicinal products at the Madina market in Accra, http://www.fdaghana.gov.gh/press.php?page=40.

[37] Fadeyi et al. (2015).

[38] Vorrath and Voss (2019).

[39] Section 152 (e), Public Health Act 2012, Act 851.

[40] BERC Africa, RCORE – Training Experience. See https://berc-africa.wixsite.com/berc-africa/post/rcore-training-experience.

This ensures that not only Ghanaians 'have access to quality, safe and efficacious medication, medical devices and health products' but all African citizens.[41]

It is therefore clear that the measures under the Public Health Act promote the convergence of statutory regulation of public health product safety in Ghana with standard guidelines at both international and other jurisdictional levels.

3.2 Product Safety and Quality Regulation of Communication Equipment

One of the major reforms that occurred in the domain of product safety is the regulation of communication equipment. The regulation of the safety of communication equipment in Ghana is under the mandate of the National Communication Authority (NCA), established by the National Communications Authority Act 2008.[42] The role of the NCA is to regulate communications services in Ghana.[43] To achieve this objective, the NCA is empowered to certify and ensure the testing of communications equipment for compliance with (i) international standards; and (ii) environmental health and safety standards including electromagnetic radiation and emissions'[44] while having regard 'to the protection of the interests of consumers or users of communications networks or communications services and in particular to the interests of consumers' choice, quality of service and value for money.[45]

To bolster its regulatory oversight of ensuring the compliance of communications equipment to international health and safety standards for the protection of consumers, the NCA formulated the Type Approval Guidelines 2015 leveraging on its power to issue guidelines under the instruction of section 3 (r) of the statute.[46] The Type Approval Guidelines 2015 (TAG 2015) provide detailed rules that regulate the importation and sale of internationally acceptable, safe and quality standards of communication equipment. Clause 2 (2) of the TAG 2015 states that the Guidelines are set out 'to ensure that all Electronic Communication Equipment (ECE) that are used in Ghana comply with the applicable technical standards'.[47] The TAG 2015 specifically provide examples of telecommunications terminal equipment that are covered under the regime. These include, but are not limited to, 'ADSL modems,

[41] Ibid.

[42] (Act 769). The National Communications Authority Act, 2008, Act 769 repealed the National Communications Act, 1996, Act 524.

[43] Section 2, National Communications Authority Act, 2008, Act 769.

[44] Section 3 (n), National Communications Authority Act, 2008, Act 769.

[45] Section 5 (c), National Communications Authority Act, 2008, Act 769.

[46] The NCA is empowered under section 3 (r), The National Communications Authority Act 2008, Act 769 to 'issue guidelines and standards from time to time'.

[47] Clause 2.2, Type Approval Guidelines 2015.

PBX, phones connected to PSTN, Fax machines, answering machines, mobile handsets, set-top boxes, etc'.[48]

Under the TAG 2015, dealers and importers are prohibited from trading in non-Type Approved communication equipment in Ghana. The TAG 2015 are broadly meant to combat the wanton brisk trading in substandard and counterfeit communication equipment. The TAG 2015 explicitly stipulate that the regime is meant to ensure that '(a) no substandard ECE which can present health and safety hazards are operating in Ghana'.[49] It has aptly been observed that the 'Type Approval of equipment ensures that no sub-standard equipment which may present health and safety hazards to users and electronic communication infrastructure are allowed in Ghana.'[50] Therefore, the TAG 2015 bans both manufacturers and dealers or traders from bringing into the market communication equipment which is not compliant with the established Type Approval standards. The overriding goal is the protection of the interests of consumers.[51]

This commendable regulatory development became necessary on account of the growing prevalence of substandard and counterfeiting communication equipment on the Ghanaian market. For example, the Communications Minister recently observed that one of the most popular Information Communication Technology (ICT) products on the Ghanaian market are mobile phone communication equipment with over 34 million mobile device subscribers.[52] Over five million mobile phones are annually recorded to enter the Ghanaian market[53] and about 60% of these devices are either of substandard quality or counterfeit.[54] This situation poses hazardous health and safety risks to unsuspecting consumers in Ghana.[55] The enforcement of the TAG 2015 will therefore go a long way to safeguard and protect innocent consumers.

---

[48] For details, see, Definition of Terms under the term 'Telecommunications Terminal Equipment' as captured.

[49] Clause 2.3 (a), Type Approval Guidelines 2015.

[50] Ghana News Agency (26 May 2016) NCA to improve standardisation space in Ghana, https://newsghana.com.gh/nca-to-improve-standardisation-space-in-ghana/.

[51] Section 5, NCA 2008, Act 769.; See also, paragraph 2.3, Type Approval Guidelines 2015.

[52] GhanaWeb (2019) "Fake" phones to be banned in Ghana soon – Communications Minister, https://www.ghanaweb.com/GhanaHomePage/NewsArchive/Fake-phones-to-be-banned-in-Ghana-soon-Communications-Minister-788900.

[53] Graphic.com.gh (2019) Ghana to clamp down on fake/substandard mobile devices. BusinessGhana, http://www.businessghana.com/site/news/Business/187706/Ghana-to-clamp-down-on-fake-substandard-mobile-devices access on the 02/10/2021.

[54] Ngnenbe (2019) Communications Ministry to stop importation of fake phones in Ghana. Graphic Online, https://www.graphic.com.gh/news/general-news/ghana-news-communications-ministry-to-stop-importation-of-fake-phones-in-ghana.html; Boateng (2015) Counterfeit ICT Products and Certification Regime in Ghana. WSC Workshop on Conformance Assessment - Geneva, Switzerland.

[55] GhanaWeb (2019) "Fake" phones to be banned in Ghana soon – Communications Minister, https://www.ghanaweb.com/GhanaHomePage/NewsArchive/Fake-phones-to-be-banned-in-Ghana-soon-Communications-Minister-788900.

In order to give force to the TAG 2015, the NCA can conduct market surveillance which supplements its pre-market supervision of mobile phone communication equipment. The above enforcement measures will undoubtedly contribute to bringing appreciable control of the influx of substandard communication equipment into the market in Ghana.

The key question is to what extent do the TAG 2015 converge with, or diverge from, international or supranational and other jurisdictions' approaches to dealing with substandard or counterfeit communication equipment crises of similar proportions. The TAG 2015 approach to combating the rampant trading in substandard or counterfeit communication equipment is not an isolated measure in Ghana. The Guidelines are a prototype of the standards of the US Federal Communications Commission (FCC), the European Telecommunication Standards Institute (ETSI), Infocomm Development Authority of Singapore (IDA) and Industry Canada (IC). As such, communications equipment that is consistent with the standards of these bodies is also recognised as equipment complying with the TAG 2015 of Ghana.[56] The Type Approval Standards of the Nigeria Communications Commission, which are based on international standards such as the International Electrotechnical Commission (IEC) and its International Special Committee on Radio Interference (CISPR), including the European Committee for Electrotechnical Standardization (CENELEC) are equally consistent with the Type Approval Guidelines of the NCA in Ghana.[57] More importantly, other jurisdictions in Africa have mirrored the Ghanaian TAG 2015 in their jurisdictions.

It is therefore submitted that the TAG 2015 introduced in Ghana under the aegis of the NCA promotes the convergence of international, supranational and other jurisdictional approaches dealing with the problems of substandard and counterfeit communication equipment, for the broader benefit of consumers.

4 Regulatory Reforms in Response to Financial Crises

Crises impacting the Ghanaian financial industry have been unprecedented in the last few years. This has triggered both legislative and regulatory responses aimed at restoring viability in the system and protecting depositors or consumers of financial services. The finance catastrophe under review started with the Bank of Ghana's 2015 exposure of the regulatory breaches of the defunct DKM Financial Services, Care for Humanity International, and Little Drops Financial Services. These institutions lured large crowds of customers into depositing substantial sums of money

[56] See Appendix 5, Type Approval Guidelines 2015. Here, the appendix provide the various bodies as recognized bodies whose Type Approval standards are satisfactory to the NCA standards.

[57] Schedule 1, Part 'A', Type Approval Guidelines, Nigeria, https://www.ncc.gov.ng/docman-main/legal-regulatory/guidelines/67-guidelines-on-type-approval/file.

with their companies on the planes of unrealistic interest rate promises,[58] which the managers subsequently diverted into private channels against the dictates of regulatory stipulations.[59] This led to the institutions' inability to honour promised payments to their clients resulting in the central bank intervention and the eventual collapse of the institutions affecting a total of about 101,958 customers.[60] In response to this development, the parliament of Ghana conferred on the Bank of Ghana the power to supervise and regulate banks and specialised deposit-taking institutions. The Bank of Ghana has since been empowered to establish a Supervision Department and other similar structures necessary for the effective supervision of banks and specialised deposit-taking entities.[61] This welcomed development mended the legislative deficiencies that existed in the regulatory architecture of the Central Bank.

The regulatory and supervisory oversight of the Bank of Ghana was further emboldened by the Banks and Specialised Deposit-Taking Institutions Act 2016[62] highlighting the Central Bank's role over specialised deposit-taking entities, as regulated under section 3 of the statute. The 2016 Act stipulates that 'the Bank of Ghana shall have overall supervisory and regulatory authority in all matters relating to deposit-taking business', including promoting the safety and soundness of banks and specialised deposit-taking institutions.[63] This is a clear extension of the supervisory and regulatory function the Bank of Ghana has over matters relating to banking business under section 2 of the Banking Act 2004.[64] It is also worth noting that section 31 of the Non-Banking Financial Institutions Act 2008[65] equally entrusted the regulatory burden of the Non-Banking Financial Institutions to the Bank of Ghana and its appointed representatives. It is evident from the provisions of the statutes that the Bank of Ghana has vast regulatory and supervisory control over the activities of the various financial establishments—both banking, specialised deposit-taking entities, and non-banking financial institutions in Ghana. The enhanced regulatory and supervisory powers of the Bank of Ghana arguably positioned the Bank to swiftly take pragmatic administrative measures against statutory non-compliance financial institutions.

[58] DKM Financial Services offered 50% rates on deposits; Care for Humanity International was offering 70% on two months deposit to clients and Little Drops Financial Services promised customers who deposited GH¢450.00 for a period of five months, GH¢5000.00 in return.

[59] DKM Financial Services inappropriately invested about $29.7million and could not return customers' monies. For detail see, Oxford Business Group (2017) The Report: Ghana 2017, p. 46; see also, Amenu-Tekaa (2021).

[60] Ofori-Atta (2018) The budget statement and economic policy 2019 financial year of the government of Ghana, https://mofep.gov.gh/sites/default/files/budget-statements/2019-Budget-Statement-and-Economic-Policy_.pdf.

[61] Section 54, Bank of Ghana (Amendment) Act 2016 (Act 918).

[62] Act 930.

[63] Section 3.

[64] Act 673.

[65] Act 774.

At the time of the passage of both the Bank of Ghana (Amendment) Act 2016 (Act 918) and the Banks and Specialised Deposit-Taking Institutions Act 2016 (Act 930), an Asset Quality Review (AQR) of commercial banks which the Bank of Ghana conducted in 2015 and 2016 found several indigenous banks plagued with inadequate capital, high levels of non-performing loans, weak corporate governance practices and other signals of distress.[66] The compelling force of the poor financial state of most of the banking institutions and the broader ramifications to depositors, potential depositors, the general public and the growth and development of the financial industry resulted in the activation of the Bank of Ghana enforcement powers. Consequently, the licenses of seven banks were revoked on account of the crisis within the industry which the AQR discovered. The Bank of Ghana first closed UT Bank and Capital Bank down and approved the acquisition of some of their assets and liabilities by the Ghana Commercial Bank (GCB) under a Purchase and Assumption Agreement in August 2017.[67]

UniBank, Royal Bank, Beige Bank, Sovereign Bank, and Construction Bank were the next culprits that had their operating licences withdrawn by the Bank of Ghana. At the same time, a newly created Consolidated Ghana Bank Ltd with a universal banking licence took over some of the assets and liabilities of the expunged banks alongside an approval of a Purchase and Assumption Agreement between the Consolidated Bank and the receiver of the Banks.[68] The period also witnessed the merger of six other banks into three and the downgrading of one of the banks into a micro-finance institution. Arguably, the drastic measures that saw the downfall of the various banks were necessary to protect the deposits of customers of the banks in question. The Bank of Ghana unequivocally stated that its decisions were largely 'in the interest of promoting financial stability, protecting the interests of depositors and lenders, minimising the costs to the taxpayer, and restoring integrity in the financial sector'.[69] From this observation, it seems clear that aside from the object of sanitising the financial service sector for the building of a more confident and resilient economy, the Bank of Ghana's regulatory response overwhelmingly targeted the protection of financial consumers in Ghana.

It is worth noting that the crisis was not limited to the banking sector. The remit of the financial downturn equally led to the collapse of several deposit-taking non--banking financial institutions. As highlighted earlier, following the DKM Financial Service turbulence in 2015, the then Governor of the Bank of Ghana, appealed to

[66] Bank of Ghana (1st August 2018) Government establishes new indigenous Bank; Bank of Ghana revokes licences of five Banks and appoints receiver in respect of their Assets and Liabilities, https://www.bog.gov.gh/wp-content/uploads/2019/07/PRESS-RELEASE-Grand-Final-August-2018.pdf.

[67] Communications Department (2017) GCB Bank Ltd takes over UT Bank Ltd and Capital Bank Ltd, https://www.annualreportsghana.com/wp-content/uploads/2020/04/GCB-Bank-takes-over-UT-and-Capital-Bank.pdf.

[68] Bank of Ghana (2018) Government establishes new indigenous Bank; Bank of Ghana revokes licences of five Banks and appoints receiver in respect of their Assets and Liabilities.

[69] Ibid.

parliament to raise the level of protection for banks and microfinance depositors, especially in the Banks and Special Deposit-Taking Bill that was before parliament at the time.[70] Consequently, the Banks and Specialised Deposit-Taking Institutions Act 2016 enhanced the regulatory and supervisory powers of the Bank of Ghana as noted earlier. More importantly, section 123(1) of the Banks and Specialised Deposit-Taking Institutions Act 2016 (Act 930) equally conferred on the Bank of Ghana the authority to revoke the licence of a Bank or Specialised Deposit-Taking Institution where the Bank of Ghana determines that the institution is insolvent. In the Bank of Ghana's comprehensive assessment of the functional viability of the savings and loans and finance house sub-sectors of the economy spanning between 2018 and 2019, it emerged that some of the institutions were beset with 'severe undercapitalization, poor lending and risk management practices, and poor corporate governance practices among many other reasons.'[71] On account of this, the Bank of Ghana asserted its authority under section 123(1) of the Banks and Specialised Deposit-Taking Institutions Act 2016[72] to revoke the licences of 64 affected institutions.[73] For instance, 39 microcredit companies' licences were revoked in May 2019, 29 as a result of severe undercapitalization, poor lending and risk management practices, and poor corporate governance practices among many other reasons as noted earlier.[74]

The revocation of the licences of these microcredit companies was followed swiftly by the renunciation of the licences of 23 insolvent saving and loans companies and two non-banking financial companies in August 2019.[75] The Central Bank categorically stated that the revocation of the licences of the institutions was necessary as their continued existence posed risks not only to the financial system stability but also to the interest of depositors. As part of the regulatory response, the Bank of Ghana noted that with the commitment to safeguard and protect depositors' funds, the Government had made funds available to enable the Receiver to pay depositors after their claims are validated.[76] These measures by the Bank of Ghana

[70] The Economist (2016) Microfinance crisis highlights problems with regulation, http://country.eiu.com/article.aspx?articleid=704041454&Country=Ghana&topic=Economy&subtopic=Forecast&subsubtopic=Economic+growth&u=1&pid=1294014513&oid=1294014513&uid=1.

[71] Bank of Ghana (31 May 2019) Notice of revocation of licences of insolvent microcredit companies, https://www.bog.gov.gh/wp-content/uploads/2019/07/NOTICE-OF-REVOCATION-OF-LICENCES-OF-INSOLVENT-MICROCREDIT-COMPANIES.pdf.

[72] Act 930.

[73] Bank of Ghana (31 May 2019) Notice of revocation of licences of insolvent microcredit companies; Bank of Ghana (16 August 2019) Notice of revocation of licences of insolvent savings and loans companies and finance houses, and appointment of a receiver, https://www.bog.gov.gh/wp-content/uploads/2019/08/Revocation-of-Licenses-of-SDIs-16.8.19.pdf.

[74] Bank of Ghana (31 May 2019) Notice of revocation of licences of insolvent microcredit companies.

[75] Bank of Ghana (16 August 2019) Notice of revocation of licences of insolvent savings and loans companies and finance houses, and appointment of a receiver.

[76] Ibid.

are consistent with its clearly defined mandate under section 3 of the Banks and Specialised Deposit-Taking Institutions Act 2016 which dictates that the regulation and supervision of financial institutions should be targeted at ‘ensuring the soundness and stability of the financial system and the protection of depositors’. The provision goes on to stress that the Bank of Ghana’s responsibility includes ‘developing appropriate consumer protection measures to ensure that the interests of clients of the banks and the specialised deposit-taking institutions are adequately protected’.[77]

The key question is to what extent are the legislative and regulatory measures converged with, or diverged from, international or supranational or other jurisdictional institutions. This calls for the interrogation of the domestic reforms and their alignment or otherwise with international, supranational, and foreign jurisdictional initiatives. In the case of international or supranational guidelines, the responses appear to be consistent with the Basel III Framework which calls on member countries to make provisions for capital requirements above the minimum capital requirements to create buffers against unannounced shocks.[78] One of the measures which succeeded in addressing the poor financial state of the Ghanaian financial institutions was the increase of the minimum capital requirements from Gh¢170 million to Gh¢400 million in September 2017 by the Bank of Ghana as per its statutory mandate[79] in order to create buffers to mitigate crises. The institutions which had more than a year to demonstrate their solvency, failed, leading to the revocation of their licences after earlier bailouts could not salvage their financial situation. It is therefore submitted that the regulatory venture by the Bank of Ghana which gave force to the statutory provisions converges with the Basel III Framework of the BIS. The Bank of Ghana itself confirmed that its regulatory architecture is largely ‘consistent with the Basel Core Principles for Effective Banking Supervision.’[80]

It may be argued that the financial institutions could have been saved with the Bank of Ghana bailout instead of the outright revocation of their licences manifested through the over 200% newly adjusted minimum capital requirement. This argument seems consistent with the responses to banks that were near collapse in the United States (US), the United Kingdom (UK), and Brazil during the great economic and financial global crisis of the late 2000s. In the US, for example, the financial crisis ‘resulted in an unprecedented federal intervention to rescue banks and restore confidence to the finance sector.’[81] Similar measures were pursued in the UK

---

[77] Section 3, Banks and Specialised Deposit-Taking Institutions Act, 2016, Act 930.

[78] BIS (2010) Basel III: A global regulatory framework for more resilient banks and banking systems. Bank for International Settlements Communications, Switzerland.

[79] Section 28 (1) of the Banks and Specialised Deposit-Taking Institutions Act, 2016.

[80] Bank of Ghana, Regulatory Framework: Supervisory and regulatory authority. See: https://www.bog.gov.gh/supervision-regulation/regulatory-framework/.

[81] Davis (2021) U.S. Government Financial Bailouts’ Investopedia, https://www.investopedia.com/articles/economics/08/government-financial-bailout.asp.

where 'the government announced guarantee arrangements in respect of all existing retail savings in, and certain existing wholesale liabilities' as of September 2007 during the early period of the turbulence.[82] The spill over effects of the crisis also led Brazil to opt for capital injection into its National Development Bank to strengthen the bank lending capacity.

While admitting that a similar approach could have been adopted in saving the collapsed banks in Ghana, it remained that those banks were besieged with an unprecedented financial crisis, as noted earlier, in the Bank of Ghana's submission. Indeed, the government created the Ghana Amalgamated Trust (GAT) as a special-purpose vehicle to support banks deemed solvent yet struggling to meet the new capital requirement.[83] The banks that had their licences revoked fell below the solvency threshold to benefit from the GAT package. In effect, the GAT programme which supports the beneficiary banks converges with the bailout measures adopted by the US, the UK, and Brazil to salvage domestic banks hit by the global financial crisis.

5 The Advent of the COVID-19 Pandemic and Consumer Law in Ghana

The discussion on consumer law reforms triggered by crises would be incomplete without commenting on the COVID-19 pandemic which besieged most countries around the world and significantly impacted the terrain of consumer law worldwide, including Ghana. The COVID-19 virus emerged at the end of 2019 and quickly spread to most countries in the world. The first two positive cases in Ghana emerged in March 2020,[84] at a time the WHO declared COVID-19 to be a global pandemic.[85] The President of the Republic of Ghana quickly addressed the nation detailing measures targeted at the safety and protection of Ghanaians. Specifically, the President instructed the Attorney General to submit emergency legislation to parliament under Article 21(4)(c), (d) and (e) of the 1992 Constitution, as well as the Minister for Health to activate section 169 of the Public Health Act, 2012 (Act 851)

---

[82] House of Commons Treasury Committee (2009) Banking Crisis: dealing with the failure of the UK banks, https://publications.parliament.uk/pa/cm200809/cmselect/cmtreasy/416/416.pdf.

[83] Ministry of Finance (2019) Support for Solvent Indigenous Banks to meet new Minimum Capital Requirement, https://www.mofep.gov.gh/news-and-events/2018-01-05/support-for-solvent-indigenous-banks-to-meet-new-minimum-capital-requirement.

[84] Ministry of Health (2020) Ghana Covid-19 Emergency Preparedness and Response Project & Additional Financing Environmental And Social Management Framework, https://www.moh.gov.gh/wp-content/uploads/2016/02/FINAL-COVID-19-ESMF.pdf.

[85] World Health Organisation (2020) WHO Director-General's opening remarks at the media briefing on COVID-19 - 11 March 2020, https://www.who.int/director-general/speeches/detail/who-director-general-s-opening-remarks-at-the-media-briefing-on-covid-19%2D%2D-11-march-2020.

by declaring a public health emergence respectively to give force to the measures.[86] The instruction to the Attorney General eventually led to the Imposition of Restrictions Act 2020 (Act 1012) which was passed into law within 48 hours after the Bill was laid before Parliament under a certificate of urgency.[87] The Act legitimated the imposition of restrictions on persons with the object of ensuring 'public safety, public health, and protection' as stated under section 1.

While the constitutional legitimacy and the overall relevance of the Act have been questioned by commentators on account of existing laws providing similar powers through presidential proclamations,[88] this is not the focus of the current discourse. The primary basis of the present commentary rests on the extent to which the statute laid the foundation for measures that directly relate to consumer protection within the context of the COVID-19 crisis. In this regard, the statute vested in the President of the Republic of Ghana the powers to impose restrictions that are reasonably necessary to uphold public safety, public health, and protection and for the running of essential services. In exercising these powers, several Executive Instruments (EI) have since been published notably including the Imposition of Restrictions (Coronavirus Disease (Covid 19) Pandemic) Instrument, 2020 (E.I. 64), as well as E.I. 65 and E.I. 66 among others.[89]

Through these various EI, the government instituted measures within its Coronavirus Alleviation Programme (CAP) that greatly impacted consumer law and policy in Ghana.[90] One crucial policy response that directly resonates with the agenda of consumer protection rests with government free water and electricity subsidy for consumers during the zenith stages of the first wave of the COVID-19 pandemic in Ghana.[91] Where infection rates were high, the crux of national measures

[86] The Presidency Republic of Ghana, President Akufo-Addo Addresses Nation On Measures Taken By Gov't To Combat The Coronavirus Pandemic (2020), https://www.presidency.gov.gh/index.php/briefing-room/speeches/1535-president-akufo-addo-addresses-nation-on-measures-taken-by-gov-t-to-combat-the-coronavirus-pandemic.

[87] Parliament passes Imposition of Restrictions Bill (2020) MyJoyOnline, https://www.myjoyonline.com/parliament-passes-imposition-of-restrictions-bill/.

[88] Addadzi-Koom (2020), pp. 311–327; Kwasi Prempeh (2020) Executive Powers and Domestic Responses to the Coronavirus Pandemic: Is the Imposition of Restrictions Bill Necessary?, https://ghanalawhub.com/executive-powers-and-domestic-responses-to-the-coronavirus-pandemic-is-the-imposition-of-restrictions-bill-necessary/.

[89] Imposition of Restrictions (Coronavirus Disease (COVID-19) Pandemic) (No. 3) Instrument, 2020, Executive Instrument 66 of 2020; Imposition of Restrictions (Coronavirus Disease (COVID-19) Pandemic) (No. 4) Instrument, 2020, Executive Instrument 67 of 2020; Imposition of Restrictions (Coronavirus Disease (COVID-19) Pandemic) (No. 5) Instrument, 2020, Executive Instrument 68 of 2020; Imposition of Restrictions (Coronavirus Disease (COVID-19) Pandemic) (No. 3) Instrument, 2020, Executive Instrument 66 of 2020.

[90] Ministry of Finance, Ghana Covid-19 Alleviation And Revitalization Of Enterprises Support (Cares) Obaatanpa Programme, https://www.mofep.gov.gh/sites/default/files/news/care-program.pdf.

[91] CNBCAfrica (2020) Ghana lifts lockdown on key regions as COVID-19 cases reach 1042, https://www.cnbcafrica.com/2020/ghana-lifts-lockdown-on-key-regions-as-covid-19-cases-reach-1042/.

was social distancing, resulting in partial or national lockdowns in several countries. In the case of Ghana, a partial lockdown was imposed, covering mainly the Greater Accra Metropolitan Area and Kasoa and the Greater Kumasi Metropolitan Area and its contiguous districts.[92] Even where lockdowns were not imposed, social gatherings were banned across the country and various institutions like schools and universities were closed.

The lockdown, closure of institutions and bans on social gatherings meant that people were to stay at home for most of their daily affairs. Another important protocol that emerged since the inception of the crisis with the impetus of limiting the spread of the virus was heightened hygiene etiquette, including the regular washing of hands with soap under running water.

While the protocols such as lockdowns, social distancing, and closure of institutions during the early days of the first wave of the novel virus were crucial to nib in the bud the spread of the virus, staying at, and working from home increased pressure on utility expenses such as water and electricity. More importantly, persons whose work could not be carried out at home became financially distressed. While it may be argued that these experiences were not confined to Ghana, it is submitted that the level of (financial) distress was particularly high for workers within the informal sector[93] in Ghana in areas where there was complete lockdown.

In order to alleviate these financial burdens, the government froze water and electricity payments for lifeline consumers and covered 50% of consumers whose bills exceeded the lifeline threshold. Moreover, commercial users of electricity for business purposes had 50% of their bills covered by the government possibly to sustain the operation of such business entities.

Another significant intervention directed at alleviating the impact of COVID-19 on consumers was the provision of hot meals for the vulnerable segment of the society in Ghana during the lockdown period.[94] This was a particularly welcomed intervention for the vulnerable 'kayayei' population in the lockdown cities.[95] In

---

[92] MoH (2020) Address To The Nation By President Of The Republic, Nana Addo Dankwa Akufo-Addo, On Updates To Ghana's Enhanced Response To The Coronavirus Pandemic On Sunday, 5th April 2020, https://www.moh.gov.gh/address-to-the-nation-by-pres-akufo-addo/.

[93] Informal sector in Ghana is broadly construed to mean the unregulated sector of the economy where persons are mainly self-employed in small-scaled and micro-level economic activities such as petty traders, hairdressers, artisans, and wholesalers and retailers. For details, see, Ghana Statistical Service (2021) Ghana 2021 Population and Housing Census Publications, General Report Vol. 3E, Economy Activity, para. 3.9, https://statsghana.gov.gh/gssmain/fileUpload/pressrelease/2021%20PHC%20General%20Report%20Vol%203E_Economic%20Activity.pdf. See also, Osei-Boateng and Ampratwum (2011).

[94] Ministry of Finance (2020) Government Distributes Food Items to Needy Individuals and Households affected by Lockdown through Faith-Based Organisations, https://mofep.gov.gh/news-and-events/2020-04-07/government-distributes-food-items-to-needy-individuals-and-households-affected-by-lockdown-through-faith-based-organisations.

[95] CitiNews (2020) Gender Ministry, NADMO to offer further support to stranded Kayayei, https://citinewsroom.com/2020/04/gender-ministry-nadmo-to-offer-further-support-to-stranded-kayayei-ama/; See also, SEND West Africa (2020) COVID-19: AMA Provides Stranded Kayayei

Ghana, it is a common phenomenon for young girls from the rural communities to migrate to regional capitals to work as head porters, popularly known in the Ghanaian parlance as 'kayayei'. Most of these head porters often had no decent accommodation in the cities.[96] The COVID-19 alleviation programme saw that a hot meal was provided once daily to the head porters at the venues where some of them converged during the lockdown.

While the electricity subsidy and water reliefs were rolled out throughout the country until mid-2021, the hot meal provision to the vulnerable population was confined to Accra, Kumasi and Kasoa, where the EI imposed a total lockdown of those areas to prevent the spread of the virus. It is instructive to note that these reliefs were crucial to the agenda of consumer law and policy as many consumers of services such as electricity and water whose livelihoods were being curtailed on account of the lockdown struggled to meet their financial commitments with respect to those services.

Another policy intervention worth noting is the provision of stimulus facilities to businesses. While acknowledging the severe difficulties the COVID-19 restrictions caused many, the government argued that this underscored the introduction of the CAP with GH¢600 million being allocated to assist micro, small and medium-scale businesses.[97] While it may be argued that this intervention is not within the purview of consumer law and policy, it is submitted that the micro, small and medium-scale enterprises are the mainstay of the economy and the collapse of these businesses would be devastating to consumers. Moreover, the absence of such intervention could have had a rippling effect on consumers with respect to those businesses dealing with consumers afterwards. Thus, businesses experiencing difficulties may have negatively impacted consumers as regards the goods and services those businesses deliver or supply to consumers.

The key question is to what extent do the measures in Ghana converge with, or diverge from, measures of other jurisdictions during the heydays of the first wave of COVID-19? It is important to note that some of the measures adopted in Ghana to ease the burden of the broader effect of COVID-19 on the average consumer in Ghana were similarly introduced by most countries around the world.

In Benin, for instance, measures introduced to support vulnerable consumers included electricity and water bill subsidies and cash transfers to vulnerable households. Another comparable measure targeted at fostering micro, small and medium enterprises' access to finance reflected the government public guarantee plan and credit lines and refinancing plans of 1.0 per cent GDP and 0.7 per cent GDP

Temporary Shelter, Food, https://www.sendwestafrica.org/nu/blog/covid-19-ama-provides-stranded-kayayei-temporary-shelter-food/; see also, Mbamba et al. (2021), pp. 1–11.

[96] Ungruhe (2020); Kapere et al. (2021).

[97] MoH (2020) Address To The Nation By President Of The Republic, Nana Addo Dankwa Akufo-Addo, On Updates To Ghana's Enhanced Response To The Coronavirus Pandemic.

respectively.[98] Additionally, Togo adopted similar measures including water and electricity subsidies for social tariffs paying groups, and allocation of funds for the strengthening of fertilizer, seed and food stocks for the overall benefit of vulnerable consumers. The United Arab Emirates also provided water and electricity subsidies to consumers as well as credit guarantees and liquidity support to small- and medium-sized enterprises. Other countries with similar policy responses aiming at alleviating the severity of the pandemic included Armenia and Bahrain, among others.[99] In Armenia, the support of the policy came in a form of lump-sum transfers to vulnerable persons including the unemployed following the outbreak of the COVID-19, families with or expecting children, and the general population in need of help to pay bills, micro-business, and persons on temporary part-time employment. In the case of Bahrain, the policy for the mitigation of the impact of the COVID-19 crisis came in the form of electricity and water subsidies for individuals and companies, salaries for workers in the private sector financed by the Unemployment Fund, and support for adversely affected micro and small enterprises by Tamkeen, a government agency that finances SMEs among other measures.

While the policy measures in the reviewed jurisdictions similarly cover electricity, water, and stimulus packages to micro, small and medium enterprises as was the case in Ghana, there is a slight departure point. Thus, while in the case of Ghana, the government fully absorbed the electricity and water tariffs, the other jurisdictions mentioned above only provided subsidies to cover tariffs. Moreover, whereas Ghana provided a hot meal daily to the vulnerable segment of the society during the lockdown period, some of the reviewed jurisdictions transferred funds to support the vulnerable population. In effect, while there are areas of convergence in the policy measures in Ghana and the other jurisdictions, there are equally other policy measures that demonstrate a point of divergence in respect of the protection of consumers during the heydays of the first wave of the COVID-19.

A similar trend appears to dominate when we further consider introduced policy initiatives of other jurisdictions such as the UK. The UK government introduced several interventions to minimise the devastating effect of the pandemic. One of these measures was the Coronavirus Job Retention Scheme. The purpose of the intervention was ‘to provide grants to employers to ensure that they could retain and continue to pay staff, despite the effects of the COVID-19 pandemic’. The Job Retention Scheme started in March 2020 and came to an end in September 2021.[100] The UK intervention measures also covered the self-employed segment of the population under the Self-Employment Income Support Scheme (SEISS). The Scheme provided for the payment of 80% of the taxable monthly trading profits to eligible persons up to a maximum of £7500 in total. The SEISS scheme which

[98] IMF (2021) Policy Responses To COVID-19’, https://www.imf.org/en/Topics/imf-and-covid19/Policy-Responses-to-COVID-19.

[99] Ibid.

[100] Ferguson (2021) FAQs: Coronavirus Job Retention Scheme. House of Commons Library, Briefing Paper, https://researchbriefings.files.parliament.uk/documents/CBP-8880/CBP-8880.pdf.

started in March 2020, equally benefited from quarterly renewals with modifications until the end of September 2021.[101] The UK Coronavirus response measures appeared to have sustainable imprints by requiring that benefiting businesses limit any negative impact on consumers.

Looking at both the UK policy responses and the Ghanaian measures against the COVID-19 pandemic, while the UK did not adopt any measure vis-à-vis electricity or water, it seems that a point of convergence existed within the remit of the support granted to businesses. It is clear that the landscape of consumer protection during the COVID-19 crisis across jurisdictions witnessed both points of convergence and divergence in the instituted policy measures to contain the ramifications of the pandemic on consumers. This is an obvious departure from most situations of crises where the regulatory responses of different jurisdictions converged as exemplified earlier.

6 Conclusion

This chapter appraised the landscape of consumer law and policy evolution in Ghana in response to the emergence of crises over the last two decades and whether crises provoked reforms converged with, or diverged from, international, regional, sub-regional or initiatives of other jurisdictions. The discussion demonstrates that whereas crises have played a significant role in the reform of the law and policy on consumer protection in Ghana, the areas of reforms are inclined towards public regulatory dispensation of consumer law and policy.

Beyond this, the analysis has brought into sharp focus two competing findings that deserves highlighting. The first fundamental construct is that a crisis can act as a conduit for the uniform harmonisation of legal regimes across diverse jurisdictions. This is especially the case where the crisis imminently provides a platform for the development of international or supranational instruments, guidelines and protocols that national regimes conscientiously implement to deal with the crisis head-on. This is precisely the case regarding the tobacco regulation, the TAG 2015 and the financial service regulatory dispensations.

The second outstanding theoretical construct that emerges from the analysis rests with the contention that policy response to crises invites diverse approaches across jurisdictions subject to domestic circumstances. These varied approaches have a higher propensity of producing converging or diverging solutions across jurisdictions. This is typical of the policy responses of the various jurisdictions considered in the analysis regarding the COVID-19 pandemic. This contrasting theory equally underscores both the functional divergence and convergence of the policy responses

[101] Browning et al. (2022) Coronavirus: Support for businesses. House of Commons Library, Research Briefing Research Briefing, https://researchbriefings.files.parliament.uk/documents/CBP-8847/CBP-8847.pdf.

in reaction to the COVID-19 pandemic across various jurisdictions. The overall chapter argues that whereas consumer laws and policies in Ghana predominately converge with international -instruments and guidelines, there are instances where Ghana, as well as other jurisdictions, have diverged, especially regarding the policy responses to the COVID-19 pandemic.

In summary, this chapter demonstrates that Ghana's crisis-connected consumer law convergence with international standards and other initiatives is predicated on instances where well-established international standards and protocols as guidelines already exist. These standards did not exist during the heydays of the COVID-19 crisis. As such, each country was grappling to fashion-out measures to deal with the crisis head-on, bearing in mind the peculiar challenges the pandemic brought on consumers in the domestic setting, leading to the divergence of approaches. It is, therefore, submitted that while the existence of international standards or initiatives elsewhere is a bedrock for possible convergence of national legal systems in dealing with crises of identical character, the non-availability of such international standards provides space for the divergence of measures bearing in mind the peculiar national circumstances of various countries dealing with similar crises.

References

Addadzi-Koom M-E (2020) Quasi-state of emergency: assessing the constitutionality of Ghana's legislative response to Covid-19. Theory Pract Legis 8:311–327

Amenu-Tekaa K-S (2021) Financial regulation and the financial crisis in Ghana. Academia Letters 2

Bekoe S-O et al (2020) Exposure of consumers to substandard antibiotics from selected authorised and unauthorised medicine sales outlets in Ghana. Trop Med Int Health 25:962–975

BIS (2010) Basel III: a global regulatory framework for more resilient banks and banking systems. Bank for International Settlements Communications, Switzerland

Boateng I (2015) Counterfeit ICT products and certification regime in Ghana. WSC Workshop on Conformance Assessment, Geneva, Switzerland. http://de6xtht0gd5sw.cloudfront.net/wp-content/uploads/2015/11/2-WSCCAWorkshop-Isaac_Boateng-Counterfeit.pdf

Browning S et al (2022) Coronavirus: support for businesses. House of Commons Library. https://researchbriefings.files.parliament.uk/documents/CBP-8847/CBP-8847.pdf

Communications Department (2017) GCB Bank Ltd takes over UT Bank Ltd and Capital Bank Ltd. https://www.annualreportsghana.com/wp-content/uploads/2020/04/GCB-Bank-takes-over-UT-and-Capital-Bank.pdf

Crettez B, Deffains B, Musy O (2014) Legal convergence and endogenous preferences. Int Rev Law Econ 39:20–27

Cseres K-J, Reyna A (2021) EU State aid law and consumer protection: an unsettled relationship in times of crisis. J Eur Compet Law Pract 12:617–629

Donkor E-S, Nartey E (2008) Nasal colonisation of drug-resistant bacteria in Ghanaian children less than five years. Internet J Microbiol 5

Dowuona-Hammond C (2018) Consumer law and policy in Ghana. J Consum Policy 41:333–354

Fadeyi I, Lalani M, Mailk N, Van Wyk A, Kaur H (2015) Quality of the antibiotics—amoxicillin and co-trimoxazole from Ghana, Nigeria, and the United Kingdom. Am J Trop Med Hygiene 92:87–94

Ferguson D (2021) FAQs: coronavirus job retention scheme. House of Commons Library, Briefing Paper. https://researchbriefings.files.parliament.uk/documents/CBP-8880/CBP-8880.pdf

Forson A, Kudzawu S, Kwara A, Flanigan T (2010) High frequency of first-line anti-tuberculosis drug resistance among persons with chronic pulmonary tuberculosis at a teaching hospital chest clinic. Ghana Med J 44:42–46

Jha P (2009) Avoidable global cancer deaths and total deaths from smoking. Nat Rev Cancer 9:655–664

Jha P, Peto R (2014) Global effects of smoking, quitting, and of taxing tobacco. N Engl J Med 370: 60–68

Kapere F, Kyere K, Maphumulo M, Moussié R (2021) Women informal traders and child care during the COVID-19 Pandemic. WIEGO Resource Document No 20. WIEGO Limited, United Kingdom

Krugman P (2017) Crises: the price of globalisation? In: Gangopadhyay P, Chatterji M (eds) Economics of globalisation. Routledge, London, pp 31–50

Lane PR (2013) Financial globalisation and the crisis. Open Econ Rev 24:555–580

Mbamba C-R, Ndemole I-K, Hassan M-S, Gabuljah S-G, Okpattah D-S (2021) 'I don't think anyone thinks of us': experiences of teenage head porters amidst COVID-19 in Ghana. Vulnerable Child Youth Stud:1–11

Menon S (2013) Transnational commercial law: realities, challenges and a call for meaningful convergence. Sing J Leg Stud:231–252

Ministry of Health (2020) Ghana Covid-19 Emergency Preparedness and Response Project & Additional Financing Environmental And Social Management Framework (ESMF). https://www.moh.gov.gh/wp-content/uploads/2016/02/FINAL-COVID-19-ESMF.pdf

Mofep.gov.gh and MoF, GHANA COVID-19 Alleviation And Revitalization Of Enterprises Support (Cares) Obaatanpa Programme. https://www.mofep.gov.gh/sites/default/files/news/care-program.pdf

Namboodiri S-S, Opintan J-A, Lijek R-S, Newman M-J, Okeke I-N (2011) Quinolone resistance in Escherichia coli from Accra, Ghana. BMC Microbiol 11:1–9

Nkansah LA (2015) Transfer of power to a new administration in Ghana's democratic system: the way forward. In: Apt NA (ed) Positioning Ghana: challenges and innovations. IFRA-IBADAN, Institut Francais de Rechercheen Afrique, Nigeria, pp 35–57

Ofori-Atta K (2018) The budget statement and economic policy of the Government of Ghana for the 2019 financial year. http://ir.parliament.gh/bitstream/handle/123456789/1058/2019-Budget-Statement-and-Economic-Policy_.pdf?sequence=1&isAllowed=y

Osei-Boateng C, Ampratwum E (2011) The informal sector in Ghana. Friedrich-Ebert-Stiftung, Ghana Office, Accra

Owusu-Dabo E, Lewis S, McNeill A, Gilmore A, Britton J (2009) Smoking uptake and prevalence in Ghana. Tobacco Control 18:365–370

Oxford Business Group (2017) The Report: Ghana 2017

Pagliari S, Wilf M (2021) Regulatory novelty after financial crises: evidence from international banking and securities standards, 1975–2016. Regul Gov 15:933–951

Peto R, Lopez A-D (2004) The future worldwide health effects of current smoking patterns. In: Boyle P, Gray N, Henningfield J, Seffrin J, Zatonski W (eds) Tobacco and public health: science and policy, pp 281–286

Plotnic O (2021) Interaction between consumer law and competition law in pandemic times. ECLIC 5:387–400

Ungruhe C (2020) A lesson in composure: learning from migrants in times of Covid-19. UCL Medical Anthropology

Vorrath J, Voss M (2019) The hidden dangers of falsified and substandard medicines: developing countries are most affected by the illegal trade. SWP Comment 2019/C 25, 4

World Health Organization (2013) Global action plan for the prevention and control of noncommunicable diseases 2013-2020. World Health Organization

Yidana N (2020) Enacting a consumer protection law in Ghana: possible lessons from the UK Consumer Rights Act 2015. Law Res Rev Q 6:323–342

Yidana N (2021) Consumer protection in Ghana: oversight, enforcement and recommendations. Commercial Law Network of Nigeria – Interview Transcript. https://www.clrnn.net/2021/11/18/consumer-protection-in-ghana-oversight-enforcement-and-recommendations/

Yidana N (2023) Regulatory remedies in the enforcement of product quality and safety standards in Ghana: a case for reform from a comparative analysis. Bus Law Rev 44:2–11

Nuhu Yidana is a lecturer in law, School of Law, SOAS University of London, UK.

Lydia A. Nkansah is an associate professor of law and former dean of the Faculty of Law at the Kwame Nkrumah University of Science and Technology, Ghana.

Family and Child Law in Chile

Fabiola Lathrop Gómez

1 Introduction

Since the beginning of the 2000s, three crises have impacted and influenced Chilean family and child law: (i) the sit-ins during student protests in 2006; (ii) the social outburst in 2019 which sparked the current constitutional process to revise the Chilean constitution; and (iii) the COVID-19 pandemic which started in 2020.

This chapter discusses whether, in the context of these events, Chilean family and child law has converged or diverged with national rules, other legal systems and/or international standards. Were Chilean laws and courts able to adequately address the problems arising from these events? Were the conflicts that arose resolved through appropriate and flexible solutions? Did these solutions consider family relationships and the children's rights involved?

This chapter explains how the Chilean legal system ended up dealing with some of the legal and social issues that these three crises triggered. Indeed, this work describes how, in general, the country's political, legislative and judicial authorities considered constitutional norms and principles, as well as international standards, when resolving these issues.

Judicial decisions converged towards constitutional guarantees and principles of International Law in dealing with the crisis triggered by the student demonstrations in 2006 ('Penguin Revolution'), and the laws passed after this event converged in the same direction.

This work is part of the Fondecyt (Fondo Nacional de Desarrollo Cientifico y Tecnologico) Regular Project 1190580, entitled 'The right to family life for children deprived of parental care: towards strengthening alternative care arrangements', for which the author is the responsible researcher.

F. Lathrop Gómez (✉)
University of Chile, Santiago, RM, Chile
e-mail: flathrop@derecho.uchile.cl

E. Ghio, R. Perlingeiro (eds.), *Are Legal Systems Converging or Diverging?*,
https://doi.org/10.1007/978-3-031-38180-5_8

The current constitutional process seems to converge with principles of International Law and demands for greater participation of some vulnerable groups, such as women and children, that emerged with the social outburst of 2019.

Finally, during the COVID-19 pandemic, the justice system adopted administrative adjustments that made some legal rules and family court proceedings more flexible, although some judicial decisions diverged from some International Law principles when resolving conflicts of visitation regimes; while some family laws passed after the COVID-19 crisis, especially in child support matters, converged with these judicial practices and towards the civil society demands.

2 Crisis 1: Student Protests

In April 2006, the first large-scale protests in Chile after the reinstatement of democracy in 1990 came in the form of an unprecedented secondary student movement, also known as the 'Penguin Revolution'.[1] The movement created turmoil in Chile's educational system, and country generally, by mobilising thousands of secondary school students against the neoliberal education model. Students occupied schools, barricading the entrances with desks, while riots raged for over 10 h in Santiago. Over 300 people were arrested.

The mobilisations and sit-ins at schools were promoted, initially, by economic concerns, i.e. the demands for free use of public transport and lower fees for college entrance exams. However, after several weeks of protests, the unswerving commitment of the 'Penguins' forced a substantial discussion of the education system as a whole. At the root of the students' protests were the demand for a potent upgrade of the public school system, the questioning of State's subsidiary role in educational funding and generally, the perception that education had become a consumer commodity, regulated as a traditional supply and demand model.[2]

Sit-ins have, and remain, a staple tool in students' efforts to pressure school—and more broadly, the country—into accepting their demands. While the original protests, and later mobilisations, questioned the authority of school leadership and created considerable difficulties for the government at the time, they also brought the parents into the political line of fire.

The 2006 crisis involved the students' parents in one of two ways: parents of students expelled for taking part in the school sit-ins advocated for their children's reinstatement, while others urged authorities to dislodge the protesters so that their children could attend school. Legally, the issue was parental responsibility, while socially, the issue focused on how parents can support their children's development and autonomy. In dealing with these two issues, the court primarily invoked the

[1] The reference to penguins comes from the fact that Chilean students wear a uniform made of a jacket, jumper, and a tie, in shades of white and dark blue.

[2] See Aguilera (2017).

principles of constitutional guarantees, as well as the protection of a child's best interests, in which family and child law is rooted.[3]

2.1 Parents in Favour of Mobilisation

Of particular relevance is a 2009 ruling by the Supreme Court of Chile[4] on an appeal for protection filed by the mother of a 15-year-old student who had been expelled from school for calling meetings and engaging in outreach activities to protest the amendments to the General Education Act.[5] The school principal decided against renewing the student's enrolment at the establishment, arguing that the boy was not a good fit for the school because he was allegedly more interested in political activities than academics.

The Court of Appeal of Antofagasta had originally stated that 'there [was] no evidence of any arbitrary or illegal act or omission on the part of the principal [...] that violates any of the constitutional guarantees referred to.'[6] On 23 April 2009, the Supreme Court reversed the decision, holding that there was no evidence of the student's alleged disruptive behaviour. The Court took the view that the student's engagement in the protests was a manifestation of the freedom of expression guaranteed to all persons by the constitution and concluded that the school had infringed on that student's freedom of expression. The Supreme Court stated that 'there [was] no justification for the school's actions, as it is clear that they did not take into account the best interests of the child, in this case, the preservation and strengthening of his formative development, but only the negative appraisal of his opinions.'[7]

On 18 February 2011, the Court of Appeal of Temuco similarly found that:

> the best interests of the child entail, then, a limitation, an obligation, a mandate of an imperative nature for the authorities, that is, all such entities , authorities, public and private institutions, must consider the best interests of the child as a primary consideration in the exercise of their power, since, before any decisions are made about children, they are entitled to require [the individual decision-making authorities to adopt measures first to promote and protect their rights rather than measures that violate them.[8,9]

---

[3] The principle is recognised, for example, in Article 16 of Law 19.968 of 2004, creating the Family Courts.

[4] Rol 1.740.

[5] This law (20.370), published in 2009, provides for a new framework for the educational system; it repealed the Constitutional Organic Law of Education (18.962 of 1990) with regard to elementary and secondary general education, maintaining the regulations for higher education.

[6] 06/03/2009, Rol 36, Recitals 3, 4 and 5.

[7] Rol 1.740, Recitals 2, 3 and 4.

[8] Rol 59-2011, Recitals 4 to 6.

[9] Court of Appeal of Punta Arenas, Resolution 5189 of 1 October 2011, Recitals 5 and 8.

In a similar vein, Resolution 5189 of the Court of Appeal of Punta Arenas dated 1 October 2011, ruling on the disciplinary measures imposed, reads as follows:

> That the rights of children, precisely because they are vulnerable as persons who are in a developmental stage and do not enjoy full autonomy, must be effectively protected in a way that goes beyond a mere declaration of principles, in accordance with the Inter-American Convention on Human Rights [. . .] The protection of their rights has been raised to the level of a guarantee enshrined in the Convention on the Rights of the Child, Article 3 of which stipulates that the best interests of the child, which are a "primary consideration," in terms of the child's welfare and must be the central objective of any measure in respect of children. It is a consideration that is directly binding on judges in their decisions affecting children, and it is obviously necessary to determine the child's best interests for the sake of proper orientation [. . .]
>
> The current treatment of minors, typical of a democratic State under the rule of law, requires a new vision and approach as opposed to the traditional criteria that assume that children should be seen but not heard. It is understood that, according to both the international system of civil rights treaties and the Chilean Political Constitution, children and adolescents share rights with adults, but in case of children, such rights are reinforced by greater guarantees and protection to make them effective. By understanding them, we will be able to conduct ourselves in a way that decisively allows us to prevent regrettable facts or situations, such as those alleged by the appellants and which should not occur in the context of student mobilizations and demands that have recently been officially characterized as a noble movement before the General Assembly of the Organization of American States and certainly there is a recognition of the citizen rights of children since it is a well-known public fact that they have been invited to dialogue with the nation's highest educational authorities.

Later appellate rulings have also found in favour of protection from expulsion on grounds of, inter alia, the violation of property rights (enrolment) and the right to equal treatment before the law. Insofar as the latter is concerned, the courts have identified two primary sources of infringement: (i) discrimination, since only some of the students who participated in the demonstrations were punished; and (ii) violation of due process, since the procedures set forth in the schools' internal regulations were not followed in the cases considered (although they were adhered to in other cases of school misconduct).[10]

2.2 *Parents Against the Sit-Ins*

On the other hand, cases were also brought before the courts by parents opposed to the protests, on the grounds that the sit-ins had prevented their children from receiving adequate education. However, on 3 November 2011, the Court of Appeal of Arica found that the sit-ins did not interfere with the freedom of education or the right to choose an educational establishment, adding that:

---

[10]Matte (2012), pp. 371–372.

> obviously, the fact that classes are not being held at that school can be linked to its occupation by part of the student body of the same. However, according to our interpretation, in such a predicament, a party who has entrusted the education of their children to a private (non-governmental) entity and who feels that the educational project that was offered and accepted is not being provided, must turn to the supplier of said project and not replace it in an effort to secure the commodity offered, as apparently happened in the instant case.[11]

Ultimately, the Court of Appeal was arguing that sit-ins were allowed and that parents should be merely discussing their options with schools.

On 4 November 2014,[12] the Supreme Court overturned a judgment on appeal, noting that the claim could not succeed because the Court could not possibly adopt measures conducive of the restoration of the pre-infringement status. Parents requested the eviction of students from the school and that students be ordered not to incite sit-ins with a view to resuming academic activities within schools. It stated that 'notwithstanding the illegitimacy of a sit-in, the courts of justice cannot be compelled to order the students [. . .] to refrain from discussing nor holding sit-ins as [they would] any other form of suspension of academic activities.'[13] Nonetheless, the ruling upheld the appeal with regard to omissions by the school principal, stating that:

> insofar as the principal against whom the claim was filed has failed to explain or show willingness to consider any of the measures that the internal regulations empower him to take or those that experience suggests effective in cases of student conduct at odds with the law and internal regulations of schools – which measures range from negotiation to forcible eviction – and given the potential, real and current threat of compromising the appellants' fundamental rights, the claim filed against the principal [. . .] must be upheld.[14]

From the judgments discussed in this section, it is clear that the reasoning of the courts has been to allow sit-ins and disruption of academic activities, rather than siding with the discontent of parents and their request to resume academic activities.

2.3 *The Concept of Parental Responsibility*

A fundamental concept, linked to the changing nature of the family, is that of childhood. The notion that children and adolescents are social agents, holders of fundamental rights and able to shape their own circumstances influenced by institutions such as the family and school, has been gaining ground in Chile. Since the promulgation of the Convention on the Rights of the Child ('CRC'), ratified by Chile in August 1990, a series of legal, doctrinal, and jurisprudential decisions have

---

[11] Resolution 12008, Recital 8.

[12] Resolution 240813.

[13] Ibid, Recitals 4 and 7.

[14] Ibid, Recital 17.

consolidated the evolving concept of childhood. Children and adolescents are now deemed to be both right-holders and beneficiaries of comprehensive protection.

This dual position of minors creates tensions both within and beyond the family. Their rights are simultaneously protected through the concept of parental responsibility while guaranteed in their own right, through the freedom to exercise their right for autonomy. Therefore, understood as relational rights, children's rights are intwined with the lives and rights of adults, as is exemplified through the cases discussed in the previous sections.

On the one hand, parental responsibility dictated that parents fight against the disruption of their children's education, whether their children were themselves in favour of it or not. On the other hand, the cases also uncovered the emergence of the concept of freedom of expression and conscience, as elements of the formative process of children. For example, commentators have noted that the 2009 Court of Appeal of Antofagasta ruling cited both the special protection afforded to voicing political discontent and to the protection of children's autonomy.[15]

While other forms of freedom are also protected in the educational context, their protection, unlike the right of political freedom, is more demanding. Whenever restrictions are imposed in the name of protecting an adolescent's formative process, these are deemed unconstitutional. However, this is an inadequate way of understanding the concept of the best interests of the child.

On the other hand, other parents found the radicalisation of the demands by students, epitomised in the sit-ins, unacceptable and unjustified, even though their own children may have agreed with the coercive action agreed upon by a majority of students. For this group of parents, the teaching process should not be disrupted, nor interrupted, and school authorities should have taken all necessary measures to resume its normal operation.

The student protests and the legal cases which ensued reflect the challenges within family life of striking a balance between the rights and interests of all family members, including minors. In striking that balance, the Chilean legal system has ultimately engaged with some of the legal and social aspects that the crisis triggered by the student demonstrations brought to light. For example, on 15 March 2022, Law 21.430 on Guarantees and Comprehensive Protection of the Rights of Children and Adolescents was passed. The law establishes a guarantee and protection statute that makes possible the enjoyment and effective exercise of the rights of children and adolescents with emphasis on the human rights recognised by the constitution, the CRC and other international treaties ratified by Chile.

In particular, the law has introduced four provisions that reflect a change in the way the issues discussed in the previous sections are addressed. Article 10 states that parents have the right to educate, care for, protect and guide their children, while children and adolescents have the right to be cared for, protected, trained, educated and supported at all stages of their development, preferably by their parents or alternatively, by legal guardians or caregivers. They also have the right to be guided

[15] Lovera (2009), p. 223.

and counselled by them in the exercise of their rights, and for their best interests to be taken into account at all times.

Paragraph 3 of Article 11 stipulates that children and adolescents have the right to be active protagonists in their own lives. Therefore, they need to strike a balance between autonomy in the exercise of their rights and the need to receive protection. In this context, parents, legal guardians or caregivers must guide and direct them in the exercise of their rights.

The final paragraph of Article 28 states that schools, health centres, or any other institution that provides services for the protection or fulfilment of the rights of the child or adolescent must have the means to give a fair hearing to children and adolescents whose rights are at stake. When it is not possible to heed the views of the child or adolescent, the relevant authority must explain the reasons why in a comprehensible manner and provide a reasoned statement of grounds for the resulting decision.

Finally, Article 42, which refers to the right to education, is particularly important in the context of the student protests and sit-ins discussed above. Paragraph 8 provides that the pedagogical and disciplinary measures that may be adopted in accordance with existing laws and regulations with respect to children and adolescents in the context of their educational activities, must always follow a procedure that ensures full respect of their rights and be compatible with the purposes of education, and the dignity of the child.

In the numerous proceedings that have arisen as a result of the student demonstrations and sit-ins since 2006, rights such as equality and non-discrimination, due process, freedom of expression, freedom of education, the right to property, the right to choose a school have been invoked. In their analyses, most court rulings have interpreted these rights in the context of the CRC, in terms of prioritising the right of children and adolescents to participate in the proceedings in keeping with their level of development and best interests. As the Court of Appeal of Punta Arenas stated: 'the law provides us with sufficient elements to interpret the best interests of the young appellants, as well as the right and duty of parents and guardians, in terms of their right to education and the scope to be given to their well-being.' [16] The impact of this particular social crisis on family and child law may well be found in a broader understanding to the effect that political deliberation and critical demonstrations against a deeply segregated educational system are an exercise of the right to participation, recognised in the Chilean legislation through the right to be heard.[17] Moreover, any eventual clash between the child's interest in political participation and the parents' interest in their children receiving an education and demand that the State protect this educational process, can and should be resolved in the light of the CRC.

[16] Court of Appeal of Punta Arenas, Resolution 5189 of 1 October 2011, Recital 6.

[17] Article 242.2 of the Civil Code establishes since 1998 that 'In all cases, in making its decisions, the judge shall consider, as a primary consideration, the best interests of the child, and shall take due account of the child's views, in accordance with his or her age and maturity'.

The CRC is based on a democratic logic; it does not pit the rights of children against that of their parents. The Committee on the Rights of the Child has strongly emphasised that upholding children's rights within the family does not imply going against the rights of 'other persons', especially the rights of parents, but, on the contrary, reinforcing the rights of the whole family.[18] In this context:

> [. . .] it is important, in striving to implement the provisions of the Convention, to promote the real spirit of that legal instrument, which is not merely to empower the child but also to show that upholding the rights of the child reinforces the rights of the whole family, and that, as far as parents are concerned, the emphasis should not be on authority but on responsibility.[19]

Thus, it is possible to conclude that Chilean family and child law, after the crisis discussed above, has converged towards International Law that protects the rights of the child. Chile has applied article 19 of the American Convention on Human Rights (Rights of the Child), which establishes that every minor child has the right to the measures of protection required by his condition as a minor on the part of his family, society, and the state. Likewise, the aforementioned articles of Law 21.430 reflect the spirit and content of the CRC standards, such as article 5 (progressive autonomy), article 12 (participation), article 18.1 (primary parental responsibility), article 28 (education and guidance) and articles 40 and 37 letter d) (due process).

3 Crisis 2: A New Constitution

The new constitution is an opportunity for Chile to align its existing constitutional norms, especially in the area of family and child law, with other Latin American constitutions but also, with international human rights standards.

3.1 Social Upheaval and the New Constitution

In October 2019, Chile experienced one of the most important social upheavals since the return to democracy in the 1990s,[20] the 'estallido social'. A series of

[18]Discussing the interrelationship between the rights of children and their parents, Bainham wonders if there is anything left of 'parental rights.' In this regard, the author postulates that parents have interests parallel to those of their children; that these interests go hand in hand with the satisfaction of how they themselves understand that they must fulfil their parental responsibility; and finally, he points out that the interests of the child do not always prevail. Bainham (2009), pp. 23–42.

[19]UNICEF (2004), p. 104.

[20]See Morales (2020).

protests—originally led by teenagers[21]—and riots that started in the capital city of Santiago, and later spread throughout the country, were met with brutal police repression.[22]

While the original cause of this social crisis was the increase in the capital's public transportation fares, the protests were also a cry for more justice and more dignity for all people, as well as a denunciation of deep economic and social inequalities Millions of Chileans filled the country's streets and public squares to demand change.

One year after the protests, this crisis was channelled into building up the Chilean democracy when Chileans citizens voted overwhelmingly (78.27%) in favour of drafting a new constitution. The drafting process began on 25 October 2020 and was unprecedented for its participatory mechanisms, which allowed the involvement of minorities and communities historically discriminated against. These groups included women, children, and adolescents, as well as indigenous peoples and disabled persons. However, the draft constitutional text was rejected in a plebiscite on 4 September 2022. At the time of writing, meetings are taking place in parliament to decide on the mechanism through which a new constitutional proposal will be drafted.

3.2 *Family and Children in the New Constitution*

Following the restoration of democracy in several Latin American countries in the 1980s, a phenomenon of legal convergence occurred among these countries in the 1990s and early 2000s. Legal convergence took place through constitutional and legislative reforms and one of the main outcomes was the increased integration of human rights within family and child law. Several principles, rules, and obligations directly applicable to family life were included in South American constitutions, such as the 'integral protection of the family',[23] the 'special rights and duties of parents towards their children',[24] and the 'equality between children in, and out of, wedlock.'[25] Some constitutions also came to grant parents the 'preferential right and

---

[21] High school students jumped the turnstiles of the subway to express their general discontent with the rise in subway fares (despite being exempt from the fare increase).

[22] According to data reported by the Public Prosecutor's Office to the Childhood Ombudsman's Office, between 18 October 2019 and 31 March 2020, 8,510 cases of victims of institutional violence were admitted, 1,315 of which corresponded to children and adolescents: Office of the Ombudsman for Children (2020), p. 153.

[23] Federal Constitution of Argentina, Article 14 bis; Constitution of Colombia, Article 42.

[24] Federal Constitution of Brazil, Article 229; Constitution of Costa Rica, Article 53; Constitution of Paraguay, Article 53; Constitution of Colombia Article 42(4).

[25] Constitution of Peru, Article 6; Constitution of Uruguay, Article 42; Constitution of Costa Rica, Article 53; Constitution of Colombia, Article 42.

duty to educate their children,'[26] as well as the 'inviolability of the home' and the 'intimacy' of family life.[27] Others, finally, granted a broader right to children to 'be free from abuse and violence.'[28]

These constitutional reforms were complemented by a number of legal amendments in Latin America, designed to carry out changes in the structure, composition, and expectations of family members. These included reforms in rules governing divorce, the recognition of 'consensual unions' (or de facto couples), same-sex marriage, shared custody between divorced parents, restrictions on corporal punishment of children and the obligation to safeguard the child's best interests in judicial proceedings.

However, in the 1990s and 2000s, Chile remained largely absent from this phenomenon of legal convergence and specially, from the process of constitutionalisation of family relations.[29] Although the Chilean Civil Code of 1855 served as a source of inspiration for the Latin American codification process of the nineteenth century, the Code, as well as the Chilean constitution of 1980, remained firmly anchored in a matrimonial, heterosexual, and patriarchal vision of the family.

It is only now that the new constitution of Chile is being written against this phenomenon of legal convergence which has occurred since the 1990s across the South American continent, as well as against context of the social crisis of 2019, which exposed strong inequalities originating in a macroeconomic model for which equality was never an objective. Existing family and child laws were crafted with the upper-middle class family in mind and rooted in the assumption of a fair and impartial patriarch.

Against these backgrounds, Peña has proposed a set of principles that would accommodate the changing nature of family relationships and the transformative social context has been proposed, to enshrine fundamental rights within the next constitution. These principles include the right to privacy and family life, the right to form a family and to marry, and the right to be free from discrimination. Privacy is understood as a sphere of personal self-governance which allows for the normative acceptance of various forms of family life. The right to marry is advocated as encompassing a variety of personal partnerships which must be recognised by the State. Freedom from discrimination, finally, ensures that individuals from state mistreatment based on specific characteristics or decisions which shape their

[26] Constitution of Chile, Article 19 n° 10; Constitution of Peru, Article 13.

[27] Constitution of Chile, Article 19 n° 5; Constitution of Ecuador, Article23.8; Constitution of Colombia, Article 42.

[28] Federal Constitution of Brazil, Article 227; Constitution of Colombia, Article 44; Constitution of Uruguay, Article 41.

[29] In Chile, the constitutional norms relating to the family are: Article 1, paragraph 2: 'The family is the fundamental nucleus of society'; Article 1, final paragraph: 'It is the duty of the State [. . .] to protect the people and the family and to encourage its strengthening'; and, indirectly, the primary responsibility of parents towards their children (Article 19, paragraph 10: 'Parents have the preferential right and duty to educate their children.')

lifestyle. These principles reflect the evolution of contemporary societies wherein family ties are conceived as elective relationships.[30]

This phenomenon of convergence of social and legal norms is also supplemented by a phenomenon of constitutional convergence. The new constitution is considering recognising and protecting minors as right-holders, as per the CRC which it ratified over 30 years ago. This is somewhat logical since the constitution is the founding document legitimising the State and its institutions, through which the power, immunity, and authority of the People of Chile, including children, are recognised.[31]

While at the time of writing, it remains unclear whether Chile will adopt a new constitution down the line, this development is to be welcomed as historically, children have been excluded from social participation and denied the possibility of acting as right-holders in the matters that affect them most. This highlights the inequalities faced by children regarding their citizenship, social inclusion vis-à-vis adults, and their legal protection. If democracy, through the constitution, is to provide equal dignity, protection and justice for all, it is only natural that children should be perceived as relevant political actors within their communities. In this context, the opportunity to recognise and uphold the right of children in the constitution is unprecedented in Chilean history and would set a legal and ethical framework in line with international human rights standards.[32]

4 Crisis 3: The COVID-19 Pandemic

4.1 Government, Court Action, and the Law in Relation to Family and Child Law

On 18 March 2020, the state of emergency was declared in Chile because of the COVID-19 pandemic[33] and on 25 March 2020, a strict lockdown was instated in seven townships for seven days (renewable for seven more days). Relevant for the topic discussed in chapter is the statement made by the issuing authority: 'We seek to protect the lives of children and families. Therefore, in the best interests of the child, it has been decided that parental visitation will be suspended during these seven days. On that note, we call on parents to make up for the lost days once the lockdown is lifted.'[34]

---

[30] Peña (2020).

[31] Espejo (2017), pp. 11 and 13.

[32] Cortés and Morales (2021).

[33] Supreme Decree 104 of 18 March 2020 of the Ministry of the Interior and Public Security, which remained in place until 30 September 2021.

[34] The strict, rolling, stay-at-home orders evolved throughout 2020. Eventually, an online permit system was developed in which residents in 'Phase 1' (the strictest quarantine) were entitled to leave their homes only for two hours, twice a week, to purchase essentials. Exceptions were made for essential workers.

The government later issued 'lockdown instructions' that prohibited children from moving from one household to another. As time went by, new townships were added to the lockdown list. As of May 2020, 42 towns and cities were subject to isolation, i.e. 7,467,820 people (almost 40% of Chile's total population).

During that time, the Supreme Court did not suspend its proceedings and cases continued to be dealt with. To facilitate this, the High Court authorised remote working for staff and hearings by videoconference.[35] However, in practice, setting up the necessary systems within courts was challenging and family courts ended up suspending all scheduled hearings for two months, leaving only a few courtrooms open for urgent matters.[36]

Nevertheless, during the COVID-19 pandemic, Chilean family and childhood law demonstrated its capacity to adapt by adopting necessary changes, in line with national rules and international standards. On 8 April 2020, the Supreme Court issued Resolution 53-2020, which established a consolidated text on the operation of the judicial branch during the state of emergency. The text was rooted in the principles of the protection of life and public health, continuity of judicial services, the protection of the rights of vulnerable persons, due process, and the use of electronic means of communication.[37]

Echoing the flexibility adopted in other courts in terms of videoconferencing of hearings and the streamlining of non-complex cases, Law 21.394 was published on 30 November 2021 with a view to adjust the procedures in cases of 'constitutional exception' such as public disasters. Relevant to family and child law matters was the modifications made to Law 19.968 on family courts. First, regarding family proceedings, the Law allowed the courts to immediately grant joint petitions for divorce if the parties agreed to it. According to Article 64 bis, the petitioners had to submit the required documentation via the judiciary's e-portal, including two affidavits from witnesses attesting that the spouses had not resumed co-habitation. Second, Article 103 of the Law provided that mediation could be conducted remotely, by videoconference, if both parties agreed to it and if the mediator had the technological means to do so. Both parties could appear remotely, or one of them could appear remotely while the other was present at the mediator's office or at the Mediation Centre, if so agreed.

[35] Resolution 42-2020 and Agreed Order 41-2020 of 13 March 2020. On 22 April 2020, Law 21.226 ('Establishing a legal regime of exception for judicial processes in hearings and judicial proceedings regarding the deadlines and actions indicated as a result of COVID-19 in Chile') allowed the Supreme Court to order the suspension and rescheduling of oral proceedings in family courts, with the sole exception of those that required urgent intervention by the court and those that the courts order or the parties requested to be held remotely.

[36] The matters considered urgent were those related to the protection and precautionary measures for children's rights, immediate surrender of children, authorisation to leave the country, domestic violence, and temporary support (Resolution 42-2020).

[37] Articles. 1 to 6.16, paragraph 1, read as follows: 'The country's courts with jurisdiction in family matters must carry out an ex officio review of the interim protective measures that were issued in favour of persons in vulnerable situations, such as the measures ordered in favour of women, children or adolescents who are victims of violence and that are currently in force and pending expiration, so that the most expeditious possible means may be found to review and renew them.'

4.2 *Visitation*

4.2.1 Visitation Permits

At the onset of the pandemic, visitation rules were confusing. Different family courts took different approaches to sanctioning applications for the suspension of contact and allegations of non-compliance. Supreme Court Resolution 42-20 of 16 March 2020 did not include visitation among the category of 'urgent matters' and therefore, hearings to address visitation issues were eligible for postponement.

On 8 April 2020, the Supreme Court issued Resolution 53-20 which included, among urgent matters, '[t]hose hearings that relate to [. . .] routine contact with the non-custodial parent and provision support, according to the circumstances of the case.' However, the phrase 'according to the circumstances of the case' was ambiguous and caused further confusion among users of the judicial system.[38]

From 17 April to 15 May 2020, two different permits were made available electronically to parents in order for them to leave their home during the lockdown period with a view to permitting routine visitation. However, no instructions were provided as to the use of these permits by government officials who also proved quite erratic in managing these permits, granting and suspending them for no apparent reason.

The only clear indication of why these temporary permits were created was given by the Intersectoral Technical Committee on Mental Health and Psychosocial Support in Disaster Risk Management (*Consideraciones de Salud Mental y Apoyo Psicosocial durante COVID-19: Recomendaciones para la acción*),[39] according to which: 'In cases of epidemic/pandemics, people are often under stress and anxious. Some anticipated reactions include fear of being separated from loved ones and caregivers due to lockdowns or isolation.'

The permits read as follows:

> 13. Individual Temporary Permit - Transfer of children or adolescents between the homes of their parents or guardians. Temporary authorisation for the transfer of children or adolescents under 18 years of age between the homes of their parents or guardians pursuant to an existing agreement between the father, mother and/or caregiver, as appropriate, or in accordance with the regime of routine contact established in the resolution issued by the relevant competent court. Permit not valid if: (i) the father, mother or relative living on the premises displays symptoms; or (ii) the child or adolescent displays symptoms. Permit not valid during curfew hours.

Interestingly, the language used in these permits did not mirror the existing legal terminology in use in Chile. It spoke of 'homes' not 'dwellings' and used the term '*tutor*' instead of '*guardador*' for guardians.

---

[38] Muñoz (2021), p. 304.

[39] Intersectoral Technical Committee on Mental Health and Psychosocial Support in Disaster Risk Management. Ministry of Health and the National Emergency Office (2020).

Ministry of Health and the National Emergency Office.

> 14. Temporary Individual Permit – Authorises the minor's exercise of the right to maintain contact with his or her parent. Temporary authorisations to exercise the right of the child or adolescent under 18 years of age to maintain personal ties and contact with his or her parent or the person or persons responsible for his or her care when there is no previously established regime of routine contact. Permit not valid if: (i) the parent or relative living on the premises displays symptoms; or (ii) the child or adolescent displays symptoms. Permit not valid during curfew hours.

This type-14 permit did not mention transfers, which may be why the wording was broader than that of the type-13 permit. However, the description erroneously referred to the 'parent or person(s) responsible for [the] care' rather than specifying that contact is to be maintained with the non-custodial parent/guardian (who could be a grandparent for example).

4.2.2 The Impact of Lockdowns on Children and Adolescents: Reaction of Family Courts

The COVID-19 pandemic radically transformed children's lives. Schools and kindergartens were closed; difficulties arose concerning access to distance learning; children were prohibited from playing outside; family relationships were subject to stressful situations due to uncertainty around employment and the economy; relationships with non-custodial parents and other caregivers waved; and the process of reconnecting with parents or grandparents lapsed.

The initial response of governmental authorities was geared towards protecting the collective interest in preventing the spread of COVID-19, while sacrificing the interests of individuals whose contact was interrupted. This had a severe impact on the interests of children and adolescents, whose family ties were thwarted.

Several legal issues arose as a consequence of these decisions. First, while court rulings and agreements on routine visitation remained binding, changes to these rulings and agreements were not formulated in an equally legally binding way. Support for this position can be found in Article 229 of Chile's Civil Code, which states that visitation is a right and an obligation, with a view to ensure that the family bond between the non-custodial parent and the child is maintained through routine and periodic interaction. The article also requires that, when suspending or restricting this right, courts should provide clear grounds for doing so, including an explanation of how such visitation would be manifestly prejudicial to the child's welfare.[40] Another issue was flagged by the Chilean Bar Association in a statement dated 16 May 2020, which expressed the following warning against the withdrawal of permits which allowed parents to visit their children: 'this withdrawal fails to safeguard the best interests of the children or the will of the parents, whose rights pertaining to the care, education and guidance of their children should override the

[40] 'The exercise of this right shall be suspended or restricted when it is manifestly prejudicial to the welfare of the child, which shall be declared by a finding of fact by the court on the basis of a reasoned decision.'

decision of any governmental authority.'[41] Finally, as noted above, court decisions were not always consistent. For example, the decisions handed down in the Santiago Metropolitan Region between 18 March and 17 April 2020 were dissimilar, as will be explained below.[42]

Some courts did not resort to the prescribed substantive modifications to visitation orders and kept the face-to-face system in place, while others did substantively modify visitation procedures.[43] In a judgment dated 18 March 2020, the second family court of Santiago stated, in a case where the father had custody of the child:

> [b]earing in mind the above, notwithstanding and in light of the fact that routine visitation is a right of the child, and that the lockdown of the minor has not been decreed by the corresponding health authority, so that there is no legal reason for failure to comply with visitation system, so ordered: Comply with the established system of interaction, with both parents taking the corresponding precautions and following recommendations to protect the health of the child and both families.

In its judgment of 14 April 2020, the same court ruled as follows:

> considering that the sole circumstance of the health emergency does not justify by itself in an arbitrary and unilateral manner the provisional suspension of the system of contact, especially if the non-custodial parent provides all assurances in terms of adopting safety protocols for the children and thus avoiding contagion in such a way as to ensure safe on-site personal contact with both parents subject to taking a maximum number of precautions, there is no reason for the suspension of such visits. With regard to compensation for the loss of the days requested by the non-custodial parent, the parties are urged to reach an agreement for the benefit of the children, requiring the cooperation and collaboration of the adults involved and, without which, in the end, any system or procedure will be futile.

However, in a ruling dated 30 March 2020, the court said that:

> [h]aving reviewed the background information, the arguments put forward by the parties, the report by the Technical Committee and in light of present health emergency, so ordered: The request to modify the current provisional system of visitation is granted to allow for interaction between the father and the child by any electronic means including image, on a daily basis, the mother must facilitate conditions for such contact for a period of seven days as of Friday, March 27th which shall be automatically renewed should the complete lockdown be extended in the townships in which the parties live.

---

[41] See Consejo General del Colegio de Abogados de Chile A.G. (2020) Declaración Colegio de Abogados de Chile A.G., 16/05/2020 http://colegioabogados.cl/declaracion-colegio-de-abogados-de-chile-a-g-4/.

[42] Case information omitted to protect the privacy of the parties, especially of the children.

[43] In a ruling dated March 30, 2020, the court said: "Having reviewed the background information, the arguments put forward by the parties, the report by the Technical Committee and in light of present health emergency, so ordered: The request to modify the current provisional system of visitation is granted to allow for interaction between the father and the child by any electronic means including image, on a daily basis, the mother must facilitate conditions for such contact for a period of seven days as of Friday, March 27th which shall be automatically renewed should the complete lockdown be extended in the townships in which the parties live." This ruling clearly reflects the intent of the court to substantively modify the existing procedure for contact with the non-custodial parent.

Other courts simply encouraged parents to agree on a form of interaction that did not involve personal contact. In a judgement dated 7 April 2020, the second family court of Santiago stated that:

> [i]n response to the presentation of 24 March, made by the plaintiff: Bearing in mind that compliance with the regime could be detrimental to the health of the child or adolescent, in view of the recommendations of the health authority to remain at home, the parties are urged to allow and maintain expeditious channels of communication such as e-mail and telephone or similar, so as not to interrupt communications between the child or adolescent and his or her non-custodial parent. The parties are informed that the above decision is an exceptional measure, in view of the health alert, the state of emergency and total isolation, to ensure the continuity of judicial services in accordance with Resolutions s42-2020 and 21.226.

Over time, most decisions in this area of law adopted similar rules and principles of Chilean family and childhood law in trying to resolve these conflicts through conciliation.[44] Indeed, once the functioning of these courts during the pandemic was regulated by Resolution 53-2020 and Law 21.394, as mentioned above, family judges were actively participating in remote hearings, as used to happen before the health emergency, always with the support of their technical advisory council.

4.3 *Child Support*

The high rate of default of payment for child support is a core issue in family and child law in Chile. Despite the existence of legal mechanisms to ensure payment,[45] as of April 2019, these debts amounted to over USD 220 million, a situation which affected around 70,000 children and adolescents.[46] The COVID-19 crisis and the ensuing economic crisis exacerbated this issue. To alleviate the economic challenges on the general population, several measures were taken.

First, Chileans were authorised to withdraw up to 10% of the funds accumulated in individual retirement capitalisation accounts run by the Pension Fund Administrators (known as the AFPs) on three occasions.[47] Second, family courts were

---

[44] Muñoz (2021), pp. 318, 319. Article 9 of Law 19.968 of 2004, which creates the Family Courts, establishes that the procedure applied by the family courts will be oral, concentrated and informal, and that the principles of immediacy, ex officio action and the search for collaborative solutions between the parties shall prevail.

[45] Some of the enforcement mechanisms established in Law 14.908 on parental abandonment of the family and payment of support, include, inter alia, the suspension of the debtor's driver's license for up to 6 months; the withholding of income tax refund; night arrest for up to 15 days; full arrest for up to 15 days; arrest or prohibition to leave the country until payment of the amount owed.

[46] See https://www.elmostrador.cl/braga/2020/12/02/crisis-en-las-pensiones-de-alimentos-un-derecho-no-garantizado-para-ninas-ninos-y-madres/.

[47] Law 21.248, Constitutional reform that allows the exceptional withdrawal of accumulated individual capitalisation funds under the conditions indicated, of 30 July 2020; Law 21.295, establishing a one-time extraordinary withdrawal of pension funds under the conditions indicated, of 10 December 2020; and Law 21.330, modifying the Constitution so as to establish and provide

empowered to withdraw all, or part of, the amount of pending child support payments from the second or third withdrawals. The law also allowed the beneficiaries of pending support to file a petition in court for the withdrawal to be made on their behalf. In other words, at the request of the child support beneficiary, a court could order that the total amount of overdue support be withdrawn from the debtor's retirement savings, even if the pension account holder had not requested the withdrawal of pension funds.[48] The impact of these laws far exceeded expectations. As of September 2021, some 552,754 judgments ordering payment had been issued and USD 513,797,664 in pension funds had been withdrawn from debtors and transferred to support recipients.[49]

However, the avalanche of requests by child support beneficiaries created a significant and unforeseen burden on family courts, prompting the judiciary to adopt measures that proved effective, such as increasing the number of judges in these courts, turning to criminal judges for backup, creating a working group with different stakeholders, and setting up an online platform to process requests for pension fund withdrawal.[50]

As a result of the public outcry during the pandemic against support payment defaults, new legislation was enacted on 5 October 2021, which introduced two important measures. The first was the modification of Law 14.908 on parental abandonment of the family and default on child support payments. The modification established that the judgment setting or approving support should be expressed in monthly tax units, or UTM (Monthly Tax Unit, which automatically adjust with inflation)[51] and that the court, *sua sponte* or at the request of the plaintiff, may order public and private entities to provide background information with a view to determining the defendant's income and ability to provide child support.

The second and most important, was the new legislation which created a National Registry of Support Debtors, to be maintained by the Office of Vital Records. This Registry listed people who either (i) were required to pay child support—provisional or final—set or approved by a court; or (ii) owed, totally or partially, at least three consecutive monthly payments of provisional or final support, or a total of five monthly payments overall. The effects of this registration are varied. For example, a listed debtor cannot obtain a passport or driver's license unless he or she can prove to the court the need to obtain such documents. Similarly, if an individual requests a loan from a financial institution for more than USD 1,835, the service provider is

---

rules for an exceptional mechanism for the withdrawal of pension funds and advance of life annuities, under the conditions indicated, of 28 April 28.

[48] Section 3 and subsequent sections of the sole Article of Law 21.295; and section 3 et seq. of the Sole Article of Law 21.330.

[49] See https://www.pjud.cl/prensa-y-comunicaciones/noticias-del-poder-judicial/61471.

[50] See https://www.latercera.com/nacional/noticia/poder-judicial-recibio-mas-de-900-mil-solicitudes-de-retencion-de-fondos-de-afp-por-deudas-de-pensiones-de-alimentos-en-los-tres-procesos-y-facilito-el-pago-de-mas-de-417-mil-millones-de-pesos/TYDWXOS4GJAVFHGM25EUSR4KPA/.

[51] One UTM is equivalent to approximately USD 56.

required to query the Registry and, if the applicant is listed, to withhold the equivalent of 50% of the loan or enough to pay the support owed.[52] The system of automatic withholding, which started as an emergency measure during the COVID-19 pandemic, has since been made permanent.

4.4 International Standards

International human rights law is a source of family and child law in Chile and has become an essential element in the process of constitutionalisation.[53] The principles and rights recognised by the CRC and other universal and regional legal instruments, as well as the case law of the Inter-American Court of Human Rights, constitute mandatory standards in the national legal system. Ultimately, they have led to a phenomenon of legal convergence whereby Chile national rules have adapted to these international standards.

These standards were particularly important during the COVID-19 pandemic, especially in its early days, given the above-mentioned erratic actions by the government—and to a lesser extent, by the judiciary. International organisations issued statements that guided the Chilean administration, particularly government officials and the family courts, in the determination of measures restricting freedom of movement and the resolution of conflicts between individuals in matters such as routine contact and support payments.

In its statement of 8 April 2020,[54] the United Nations Committee on the Rights of the Child called on states to protect the rights of children and adolescents from the COVID-19 pandemic considering the physical, emotional, and psychological effects that prolonged confinement was having on them.

At the inter-American level, it should be noted that Article 27 of the American Convention on Human Rights, also known as the 1969 Pact of San José (an international human rights instrument adopted by several Western Hemisphere countries)[55] refers to the suspension of guarantees, stating that in time of war, public danger, or other emergency threatening the independence or security of a state party to the Convention, the state party may take measures derogating from its obligations under the Convention to such an extent and for such a period of time as is strictly required by the exigencies of the situation. The second paragraph adds that the preceding provision does not authorise the suspension of the rights set out in the articles listed therein, including Article 19 on the Rights of the Child.

---

[52] Barría (2021).

[53] Lathrop and Espejo (2019), pp. 128–157.

[54] See https://tbinternet.ohchr.org/Treaties/CRC/Shared%20Documents/1_Global/INT_CRC_STA_9095_E.pdf.

[55] Chile ratified the Convention in August 1990.

On 10 April 2020, the Inter-American Commission on Human Rights (one of the bodies responsible for overseeing compliance with the Convention) issued Resolution 1/2020 on the Pandemic and Human Rights in the Americas. It recommended that states

> [r]einforce protection for children and adolescents, most notably for those who are not cared for by their families and who are in care institutions, and prevent COVID19 contagion by implementing measures that take into account that they are still developing, and that look as broadly as possible to their best interests. Protection should, to the extent possible, ensure that family and community ties are maintained.

In a similar vein, Standard 16 of the 2019 Minimum Standards for the Protection of Children and Adolescents in Humanitarian Action states that '[f]amily and caregiving environments are strengthened to promote children's healthy development and to protect them from maltreatment and other negative effects of adversity.' Building on Standard 16, the Alliance for Child Protection in Humanitarian Action noted that it should '[e]ncourage and create safe opportunities to support routine contact between children and family members who are physically separated.'[56]

These guidelines call for the adoption of health measures applicable in family contexts, taking into consideration the unique aspects and socio-economic conditions of each family, LGTBIQ+ children and adolescents, those separated from their families, belonging to ethnic groups, or in situations of homelessness, migration, or requiring safe harbour.

4.5 Conclusion on the COVID-19 Crisis

It is clear that the COVID-19 crisis brought the law and Chile's institutions into the forefront of debate. There is no doubt that the country is experiencing extraordinarily difficult times due to the pandemic and that the consequences of this deadly disease will continue to be felt in family relationships for the foreseeable future. The crisis required states around the world to adopt measures to mitigate the damages caused, to prevent harm that occurred in the medium and long term, and to make administrative and legal adjustments as necessary and appropriate.

Unfortunately, in terms of the family relations of children and adolescents in contexts of separation from their parents, especially regarding the right to maintain routine visitation with their significant adult caregivers, the government of Chile failed to live up to its ethical and international duties during the pandemic. Authorities reacted belatedly and erratically, with poorly grounded decisions, an approach biased towards adults, and a disproportionately heavy hand. By limiting certain individual freedoms in an effort to protect the broader public interest, the government unreasonably curtailed the rights of children and adolescents. Living in

[56] In its technical note: Protecting children during the Coronavirus pandemic, Version 1, March 2019.

exceptional circumstances also requires exceptional solutions; ones that are tailored to the reality of members of society such as children and adolescents who have special needs.

The courts did somewhat better in isolated cases, although initially a number of rulings followed the government lead and sacrificed the right of the child to maintain direct contact with the non-custodial parent in accordance with an 'all or nothing' approach, that is, without evaluating whether the circumstances of a particular case merited continued direct, routine contact. In short, the best interests of the child, which should be a primary consideration in judicial decisions as per international standards, were not always duly weighed nor were the specifics of the case always taken into account. This demonstrated a case of legal divergence from international standards during the COVID-19 pandemic.

Fortunately, in the area of child support, urgent measures were adopted that proved to be effective, to the point of being subsequently recognised by law as a permanent mechanism for ensuring compliance. This success was particularly due to the timely reaction of the judiciary, who, working together with other authorities, instituted a system to allow funds to be withheld from pension fund withdrawals drawdowns.

However, one area in which action was sorely lacking in the context of the COVID-19 crisis was international collaboration in family and child law, especially in the context of child abduction. In Chile, international child abduction proceedings are uniquely expeditious: a single hearing is held within five days of filing the application. This expediency often prevents the party seeking the abducted child's return from travelling to participate in the hearing. One positive impact of the transition to online proceedings has been that such parties have been able to attend the hearing, engage in dialogue and reach an agreement.[57] In June and July 2020, the Colombian consulate arranged for humanitarian flights that allowed two girls who had been abducted in Chile to return to Colombia. In other cases, the Chilean central authority requested that provisional contact regimes be established until it was possible to comply with the order to return the children. [58] While this was a positive experience with Colombia in fighting against international child abduction, that example is unfortunately an outlier.

5 Conclusion

Despite the shortcomings, Chile's system of family and child Law has generally proven resilient during times of crisis and adapted to them. The underlying principles on which the system is based have allowed the courts to continue resolving conflicts involving family relationships and the rights of children and adolescents.

[57] Verdugo (2021), p. 92.

[58] Ibid, p. 93.

Furthermore, the guidance and application of international human rights standards has been decisive in Chile's ability to weather the storms of recent decades, thanks both to the incorporation of such regulations into domestic law and to their ability to allow creative solutions to be forged in cases of unprecedented emergency.

Today, Chile stands at a crossroads, faced with a unique, historic opportunity to enshrine protections for family relationships at the highest level of law, regardless of their origin and composition. Such protections at the constitutional level for children and adolescents would also necessarily lead to much needed changes at lower levels to rectify the dearth of comprehensive legal protections for the rights of children and adolescents.

Case Law

Court of Appeal of Punta Arenas, Resolution 5189 of 1 October 2011, Recital 6.
Court of Appeals of Antofagasta 06/03/2009, Rol 36
Resolution 12008, Recital 8.
Resolution 42-2020
Supreme Court 04/11/2014, Resolution 240813
Supreme Court 23/04/2009, Rol 1.740
Temuco Court of Appeals 02/18/2011, Rol 59-2011

References

Aguilera O (2017) The student movement in Chile, 2006-2014. An approach from culture and identities. Nueva Antropología 30:131–152

Bainham A (2009) Is anything now left of parental rights? In: Probert R et al (eds) Responsible parents and parental responsibility. Hart Publishing, Oxford, pp 23–42

Barría M (2021) The creation of the National Registry of Alimony Debtors. El Mercurio Legal, 19/10/2021

Cortés S, Morales C (2021) Outbreak over outbreak: children living the pandemic in the aftermath of Chile's social unrest. Children's Geographies, https://www.tandfonline.com/action/showCitFormats?doi=10.1080/14733285.2021.1900543

Espejo E (2017) El reconocimiento de la infancia y de los derechos de los derechos de los niños en la Constitución Política de la República. In: UNICEF Constitución e Infancia. UNICEF-Chile, pp 11–43

Intersectoral Technical Committee on Mental Health and Psychosocial Support in Disaster Risk Management. Ministry of Health and the National Emergency Office (2020) Consideraciones de Salud Mental y Apoyo Psicosocial durante COVID-19: Recomendaciones para la acción

Lathrop F, Espejo N (2019) Towards the constitutionalization of family law in Latin America. In: Choudhry S, Herring J (eds) The Cambridge companion to comparative family law. Cambridge University Press, Cambridge, pp 128–157

Lovera D (2009) Libertad de expresión e interés superior del niño, a propósito de la sentencia de la Corte de Apelaciones de Antofagasta de 6 de marzo de 2009 y Corte Suprema de 23 de abril de 2009. Revista Chilena de Derecho Privado 12:215–225

Matte A (2012) Recursos de protección y movilizaciones estudiantiles. Sentencias Destacadas 2012, Libertad y Desarrollo, https://lyd.org/sentencias-destacadas-back/, pp 371–372

Morales M (2020) Social outburst in Chile 2019: participation, representation, institutional trust and public scandals. Análisis político 98:3–25

Muñoz G (2021) Routine relationship in times of quarantine in Chile and comparative law. In: Ravetllat I et al (eds) Covid-19 y Derecho de Familia. Tirant lo Blanch, Valencia, pp 318 and 319

Office of the Ombudsman for Children (2020) Annual Report, www.defensorianinez.cl/informe-anual/

Peña C (2020) Family and constitution. Notes for debate. Seminar on Families and Children in the New Constitution, Department of Private Law, University of Chile Law School, 16/12/2020

UNICEF (2004) Implementation Handbook for the Convention on the Rights of the Child. UNICEF, New York

Verdugo J (2021) La sustracción internacional de niños, niñas y adolescentes y el Covid-19. In: Lathrop F et al. Challenges of Covid-19 for Family Law. Tirant lo Blanch Valencia, pp 87–96

Web

Consejo General del Colegio de Abogados de Chile A.G. (2020) Declaración Colegio de Abogados de Chile A.G., 16/05/2020, http://colegioabogados.cl/declaracion-colegio-de-abogados-de-chile-a-g-4/

https://www.latercera.com/nacional/noticia/poder-judicial-recibio-mas-de-900-mil-solicitudes-de-retencion-de-fondos-de-afp-pordeudas-de-pensiones-de-alimentos-en-los-tres-procesos-y-facilito-el-pago-de-mas-de-417-mil-millones-depesos/TYDWXOS4GJAVFHGM25EUSR4KPA/

https://www.pjud.cl/prensa-y-comunicaciones/noticias-del-poder-judicial/61471

Fabiola Lathrop Gómez is professor of civil law at the University of Chile, Chile.

Contract Law in Germany

Hannes Henke

1 Introduction

Contracts are the main instrument by which individuals shape law by which the parties regularly commit to a performance that can be legally enforced. The obligations to perform are thus at the heart of every contract. In Germany, § 241 (1) of the *Bürgerliches Gesetzbuch* (BGB), the German Civil Code, states that the obligee is entitled, by virtue of the obligation, to demand performance from the obligor. Unlike in common law,[1] for example, the obligee thus primarily has a contractual claim to performance in kind. Of course, contract law is not limited to specifying such contractual obligations and classifying them into special types of contracts. Rather, it is also and precisely the purpose of contract law to stipulate legal consequences in the event that the contractual relationship is disrupted, i.e. the performance is not (or cannot be) effected as promised. Depending on the type of contract and the impairment of the performance of an obligation, the termination of the contract, a claim for damages, or a reduction may be considered. Contract law is thus designed primarily with a view to regulating the non-performance of an obligation. The fact that the circumstances for an originally made commitment change should therefore, in principle, not challenge contract law to any particular extent. Rather, it is precisely the task of contract law to allocate the risks of fulfilment of the contract between the parties involved *ex ante* and to safeguard the promised performance. However, such a contractual risk allocation can become unstable if circumstances change systemically. Here, the question is quite justified as to how such a change will affect concluded contracts and contract law in general.

[1] See, for example, Tröger (2014), p. 57.

H. Henke (✉)
Martin-Luther-University Halle-Wittenberg, Halle (Saale), Germany
e-mail: hannes.henke@jura.uni-halle.de

E. Ghio, R. Perlingeiro (eds.), *Are Legal Systems Converging or Diverging?*,
https://doi.org/10.1007/978-3-031-38180-5_9

Systemic changes occur particularly in the form of crises, although this is not absolutely necessary. The digital revolution, for instance, can hardly be described as a crisis, even though the increasing digitalisation throws a completely new light on familiar questions of risk allocation and poses entirely new challenges for legal regulation. Digitalisation is unlikely to be classified as a crisis, because it is a long-term and, at least in principle, also a predictable development. Moreover, digitalisation is not generally seen as a negative development. Crises, in contrast, are characterised by adjustment processes as a result of disappointed expectations, whereby the disappointment follows the disruption of an entire system.[2] As is well known, there has been no shortage of such crises in recent years. The global financial crisis (2008/09), the refugee crisis (2015/16), the crisis of the European Union (EU) due to Brexit (2016–2020), the COVID-19 pandemic (2019–2023) and the Russia-Ukraine war (from 2022) can be mentioned here.

Chronologically, these crises have framed by two major reforms of German contract law. The starting point for the present study of the influence of crises on German contract law will therefore be the Act on the Modernisation of the Law of Obligations from 2001, discussed in Sect. 2. Subsequently, the financial crisis (Sect. 3), Brexit (Sect. 4) and the COVID-19 pandemic (Sect. 5) are provided as examples with a view to determining the influence that these events have had on the development of contract law in Germany. In each case, a distinction is made between the application of contract law, which already existed at that time, and the creation of new law by the legislator in response to the respective crises. Finally, Sect. 6 discusses the most recent reform of the law of obligations in 2022 and current legislative projects. Overall, it will be shown that large parts of German contract law are developed through European harmonisation. Beyond this process of institutionalised convergence, it will also be evident that German contract law converges in particular with that of the Member States of the EU, without EU law being imposed on them. However, crises are only of secondary importance in this process.

2 Reform of the Law of Obligations (2001)

The central codification of German private law in general, and contract law in particular, is based on the BGB, which came into force on 1 January 1900. In the following years, the BGB as a whole remained almost unamended, despite the advent of the First World War and the hyperinflation in 1923/24.[3] Even during the National Socialist era (1933–1945), while changes in regulatory interpretation occurred through the inclusion of racially motivated content,[4] there were few actual

[2] See Finke (2020), pp. 152 et seq.

[3] Dannemann and Schulze (2020), para. 22.

[4] Säcker (2021), para. 16.

legislative changes in contract law. Thus it can be seen that the BGB as a codification instrument, inclusive of contract law rules, already proved to be extremely resistant to crises. As a consequence of the Second World War and the resulting housing shortage, the tenancy law witnessed a reform,[5] which was intended to improve the protection of residential tenants. After the amendment of individual aspects of contract law by the Act on the Regulation of the Law of General Terms and Conditions of Business of 1976,[6] and the amendments to travel contract law of 1979,[7] the most extensive and important reform to the BGB came with the Act on the Modernisation of the Law of Obligations (*Gesetz zur Modernisierung des Schuldrechts*)[8] of 2001. This law fundamentally reformed German contract law, and the preparations for its implementation were correspondingly lengthy.

As early as 1984, the Federal Minister of Justice had convened a Commission to revise the Law of Obligations (*Schuldrechtskommission*). This had been prompted by the perception that the law of obligations was inadequate, particularly with regard to the legal consequences of non-performance of an obligation.[9] The Commission presented its final report in 1991 with a proposal for a new regulation, which was largely based on the model of the United Nations (UN) Convention on Contracts for the International Sale of Goods (CISG).[10] The reform project was put on hold yet resurrected in 1999 due to development in EU law. A total of three European directives had to be transposed into German law: the Consumer Sales Directive,[11] the Late Payments Directive,[12] and the E-Commerce Directive.[13] However, the modernisation of the law of obligations went beyond the mere transposition of these directives; rather, the reforms intended to standardise and simplify the legal consequences in general contract law. In addition, for the sake of legal certainty, previously practised judge-made law was to be codified. For this purpose, the legislator largely adopted the proposals made in the final report of the Commission of the Law of Obligations and thus, indirectly, to the CISG.[14]

---

[5] See, for example, the Act on Protection against Dismissal for Lease Agreements of Residential Spaces of 1971, BGBl. 1971 I, p. 1839, and the second Act on Protection against Dismissal for Lease Agreements of Residential Spaces of 1974, BGBl. 1974 I, p. 3603.

[6] BGBl. 1976 I, p. 3317.

[7] BGBl. 1979 I, p. 509.

[8] BGBl. 2001 I, p. 3137.

[9] Schuldrechtskommission (1992), pp. 16 et seq.

[10] Schuldrechtskommission (1992), p. 26.

[11] Directive 1999/44/EC of the European Parliament and of the Council of 25 May 1999 on certain aspects of the sale of consumer goods and associated guarantees.

[12] Directive 2000/35/EC of the European Parliament and of the Council of 29 June 2000 on combating late payment in commercial transactions.

[13] Directive 2000/31/EC of the European Parliament and of the Council of 8 June 2000 on certain legal aspects of information society services, in particular electronic commerce, in the Internal Market.

[14] See Bundestag document 14/6040, pp. 79; 86.

A point of focus was to regulate the legal consequences of frustration of contract (*Störung der Geschäftsgrundlage*). Until then, cases in which external circumstances which were decisive for the contract changed significantly were covered by case law through the objection of *clausula rebus sic stantibus*. Since 1922, despite dogmatic uncertainties,[15] case law had been based on the principle of good faith (§ 242 BGB), which also stipulated that the adjustment of a contract could be demanded if the basis of the transaction was disturbed.[16]

While the lack of corresponding provisions in the CISG prevented the German legislator to codify case law based on the Convention,[17] both the Commission of the Law of Obligations[18] and the German legislator itself[19] later expressly referred to the corresponding provisions in Italian law (Art. 1467 et seq. Codice Civile), Greek law (Art. 388 Civil Code), Dutch law (Book 6 Art. 258 of the Nieuw Burgerlijk Wetboek), as well as to the 'Principles for International Commercial Contracts' formulated by the 'International Institute for the Unification of Private Law' (UNIDROIT) (Art. 6.2.1, 6.2.2, 6.2.3 of the current version). Based on this, § 313 (1) BGB stipulates that the adaption of a contract can be demanded if the actual basis of the transaction has changed significantly since the contract was entered into, and if the parties would not have entered into the contract, or would have entered into it with different contents, had they foreseen this change. However, the prerequisite is that one of the parties cannot reasonably be expected to uphold the contract without alteration, taking into account all circumstances of the individual case, in particular the contractual or legal distribution of risks. Withdrawal or termination is only possible as *ultima ratio*. According to § 313 (3) BGB, this requires that the adjustment is either impossible or unreasonable for one party, for which strict requirements must be met.

The explanatory memorandum to the Act on the Modernisation of the Law of Obligations shows that the German legislator explicitly targeted 'social catastrophes such as war, currency collapse or environmental catastrophes', which were to be covered by the codified regulation.[20] This is the so-called 'large basis for the transaction' (*große Geschäftsgrundlage*), whereas other circumstances with limited effect are referred to as the 'small basis for the transaction' (*kleine Geschäftsgrundlage*).[21] However, the law itself does not differentiate between these two groups of cases. Rather, an assessment must always be made in each individual case, both on the part of the facts and on the part of the legal consequence.

[15] Finkenauer (2022), § 313 BGB para. 23 et seq.

[16] Reichsgericht, judgement of 3 February 1922, RGZ 103, p. 332; Federal Court of Justice, judgment of 14 July 1953, case V ZR 72/52; Federal Court of Justice, judgment of 25 September 1997, case II ZR 269/96.

[17] See Mankowski (2021), Art. 79 CISG para. 41.

[18] Schuldrechtskommission (1992), p. 149.

[19] Bundestag document 14/6040, p. 175.

[20] Ibid, p. 174.

[21] Ibid.

Overall, the 2001 reform thus created the central contract law provision for crisis management by way of international convergence—albeit absent the pressure of an actual crisis.

Another amendment made by the Act targeted the provision on the impossibility of performance according to § 275 BGB. According to this provision, the obligee can no longer demand performance in kind, if performance is impossible. Here, a distinction is made between the cases of objective and subjective impossibility (§ 275 (1) BGB), economic impossibility (§ 275 (2) BGB), and personal impossibility (§ 275 (3) BGB). What these cases have in common is that the obligee is only entitled to withdrawal from the contract, or—in the case of fault—a claim for damages. In the event of a crisis, these regulations will then also regularly be applied. Particularly problematic are those cases in which performance is only possible with grossly disproportionate effort (§ 275 (2) BGB). In contrast to Art. 7.2.2 lit. b of the UNIDROIT Principles for International Commercial Contracts, the obligee's interest in performance must also be taken into account. As a result, the interests involved must be weighed against each other. The distinction between frustration of contract (§ 313 BGB) and the right to refuse performance according to § 275 (2) BGB with their different legal consequences can be quite problematic in individual cases.[22] Nevertheless, crises prima facie create typical cases of application for both frustration of contract and the impossibility of performance. Both relevant provisions have remained unchanged since the 2001 reform.

3 Financial Crisis

3.1 Application of Existing Contract Law

The first time the reformed law of obligations, including the provisions of frustration of contract and impossibility, had to prove itself in a global crisis was in 2008. The financial crisis not only led to high unemployment and a loss of value, especially of real estate, but—due to the noticeable decline of the economy up to recession—ultimately called the entire economic growth model into question. It was particularly problematic that the financial crisis led to payment difficulties for both consumers and companies, so that monetary debts could no longer be adequately serviced. However, the adaption or termination of the contract in compliance with § 313 BGB due to payment difficulties was opposed to the dogma according to which the debtor of a monetary debt bears the risk of having sufficient financial means himself.[23]

[22] See, for example, Ernst (2022), para. 28 et seq.

[23] Finkenauer (2022), para. 209; Tröger (2014), p. 51 et seq.

Accordingly, German courts[24] have ruled that financing problems due to the financial crisis are the sole responsibility of the respective obligor.[25] It means there are only a few exceptional cases where there is room to adapt the contract due to financing difficulties.[26] This shows that the instrument of frustration of contract does not apply per se in the case of a crisis. Rather, the principle of *pacta sunt servanda* also applies in times of crisis.

In addition, according to § 275 BGB, mere financing difficulties due to unemployment or stagnating growth do not lead to a case of impossibility, as this is not applicable to monetary debts.[27] This illustrates a second principle of German contract law, which (despite its cynical tone) also claims validity even in times of crisis: 'Man has to have money'.[28] This alone expresses the fact that monetary debts are subject to unlimited asset liability, thus shifting the problem of lack of financing from contract law to enforcement and insolvency law.

3.2 Legislative Measures

Of course, it is incorrect to say that contract law did not react at all, or only defensively, to the financial crisis. However, considering the question of international convergence of responses, it should first be borne in mind that the financial crisis primarily affected an area that had already been shaped to a large extent by EU law. In particular, the 2004 Markets in Financial Instruments Directive (MiFID I)[29] and the 2007 Payment Services Directive[30] already applied. In addition, efforts to revise the Consumer Credit Directive from 1987[31] had already been underway since the 1990s.[32] The corresponding amendment (its first draft was from 2002) was

---

[24] However, German courts have not taken a special path with this. For comparable case law in Portugal, see Supreme Court of Justice Ruling of 23 January 2014, case 1117/10.9TVLSB.P1.S1 (reporting judge: Granja da Fonseca).

[25] Superior Court of Justice Berlin, judgement of 5 November 2012 - case 8 U 171/11; Regional Court Dortmund, judgment of 21 April 2010 - case 20 O 26/09; Regional Court Kaiserslautern, judgement of 13 January 2010 – case 4 O 260/09.

[26] See the comparable legal situation in France, Borghetti (2021), pp. 516–523.

[27] Schulze (2020), para. 10.

[28] See Ernst (2022), para. 13.

[29] Directive 2004/39/EC of the European Parliament and of the Council of 21 April 2004 on markets in financial instruments.

[30] Directive 2007/64/EC of the European Parliament and of the Council of 13 November 2007 on payment services in the internal market.

[31] Council Directive 87/102/EEC of 22 December 1986 for the approximation of the laws, regulations and administrative provisions of the Member States concerning consumer credit.

[32] See Green Book on Financial Services: Protecting Consumer Interests, COM (96) 209.

adopted in April 2008,[33] unaffected by the already ongoing crisis. Unlike general contract law, banking contract law—as well as consumer law—was thus already largely harmonised within the European Community without any specific reference to a crisis.[34] The directives mentioned were designed as full harmonisation measures,[35] so that the Member States could not deviate from the European requirements; they would only be free in the way they implemented them (Article 288 (3) Treaty on the Functioning of the EU (TFEU)). Hence, within the scope of application of the aforementioned directives, the German legislator could not have reacted on a purely national level.

Nevertheless, the financial crisis triggered a further push for international cooperation. After previous consultations between the finance ministers of the G7 countries, the heads of state and government, and the Member States of the Eurozone, the Financial Market Stabilisation Act was able to come into force in Germany in October 2008.[36] The intended goal was to ensure the solvency of financial institutions based in Germany and to avoid a general credit crunch. Subsequently, the regulatory framework for credit institutions and investment firms operating in the Union was also realigned at the European level, in particular through the Capital Requirements Regulation[37] and Capital Requirements Directives.[38] These measures were themselves based on the standards agreed upon by the Basel Committee on Banking Supervision in 2010 (the so-called Basel III).[39] However, direct measures at the level of contract law in response to the financial crisis cannot be identified here.

Under the impact of the financial crisis and the subsequent recommendation of the newly founded Financial Stability Board,[40] in 2014 the Mortgage Credit Directive[41] was adopted at European level.[42] Among other things, this directive amended the Consumer Credit Directive and had a direct influence on the corresponding contract law. In the same year, MiFID I was amended, which also took into account

[33] Directive 2008/48/EC of the European Parliament and of the Council of 23 April 2008 on credit agreements for consumers.

[34] Grundmann, Atamer (2011), pp. 12 et seq.

[35] See Cherednychenko (2011), pp. 221 et seq.

[36] Winterfeld and Rümker (2017), para. 9.

[37] Regulation (EU) No 575/2013 of the European Parliament and of the Council of 26 June 2013 on prudential requirements for credit institutions and investment firms.

[38] Directive 2013/36/EU of the European Parliament and of the Council of 26 June 2013 on access to the activity of credit institutions and the prudential supervision of credit institutions and investment firms.

[39] See Recital 1 Regulation (EU) No 575/2013 and Recital 79 Directive No 2013/36/EU.

[40] FSB, Consumer Finance Protection with particular focus on credit, 26 October 2011, https://www.fsb.org/wp-content/uploads/r_111026a.pdf.

[41] Directive 2014/17/EU of the European Parliament and of the Council of 4 February 2014 on credit agreements for consumers relating to residential immovable property.

[42] See Recital 3 Mortgage Credit Directive.

the results of the G20 meeting in Pittsburgh (2009).[43] Through the new MiFID II,[44] investor protection—which was already pursued through MiFID I—was further expanded.[45] The central means for this is the obligation to provide information to investors. An important instrument in this regard is the obligation to create transparency (see for example Article 25, 25 MiFID II). MiFID II thus follows a general line of the European legislator, as is evident in consumer protection: the position of the weaker contracting party is to be improved above all by means of information before the conclusion of the contract.[46] However, unlike consumer protection law, MiFID II itself does not provide for any civil law consequences for breaches of transparency obligations, but only for regulatory sanctions.[47] As a consequence, the German regulations in §§ 63 et seq. WpHG (*Wertpapierhandelsgesetz*, German Securities Trading Act), which serve to implement MiFID II,[48] are only of a public law nature—which means that breaches of information obligations have no direct impact on the contracts concluded.[49]

However, regulatory requirements can also have indirect consequences for contract law.[50] In particular, vague legal terms and general clauses serve as a gateway for such standards in contract law.[51] For example, according to German contract law, an obligor has a duty to perform according to the requirements of 'good faith, taking customary practice into consideration' (§ 242 BGB). There is also a duty to take into account the interests of the other party even before the conclusion of the contract (§ 311 (2) BGB), which may be relevant for the information obligations under MiFID II. § 347 (1) HGB (*Handelsgesetzbuch*, German Commercial Code), according to which a commission agent must carry out an assumed transaction with the 'diligence of a prudent businessman', also offers a link between contract law and regulatory law. In this respect, the European harmonisation of regulatory law has not specifically led to a convergence of contract law. However, the (European) regulatory law has had a spillover effect, influencing, at least indirectly, the (pre-)contractual relationship between investment firms and clients.[52]

All in all, it can therefore be stated that the financial crisis has not brought about a new harmonisation of banking contract law. Nevertheless, the crisis strengthened and selectively expanded it. However, the cornerstones of (German) contract law remained untouched by the financial crisis.

---

[43] Comana et al. (2019), p. 2.

[44] Directive 2014/65/EU of the European Parliament and of the Council of 15 May 2014 on markets in financial instruments.

[45] Comana et al. (2019), pp. 141 et seq.

[46] Ibid, p. 148.

[47] Piwowarski (2020), p. 147.

[48] Poelzig (2022), para. 3.

[49] Ibid, para. 224.

[50] Gressler (2016), pp. 122 et seq.; Köndgen (2011), pp. 38 et seq.

[51] On the problematic relationship see Haar (2011), pp. 273 et seq.

[52] Poelzig (2022), para. 226; Zahrte (2019), para. 109.

4 Brexit

4.1 Application of Existing Contract Law

Unlike the financial crisis, Brexit, i.e. the withdrawal of the United Kingdom (UK) from the EU on 1 February 2020, took place within a legally regulated process. Brexit, as a crisis (of the EU) affected Germany, in particular, with regard to contractual relations between German and British companies. This initially raised questions of conflict of laws. Until then, the law applicable to contracts in the UK, as in all EU Member States (except Denmark),[53] was determined according to the Rome I Regulation.[54] While the situation remained unchanged for contracts concluded before the end of the transitional period on 31 December 2020,[55] the discussion took place regarding contracts concluded as of 1 January 2021. The question arose whether the previously applicable legal situation under the Convention on the law applicable to contractual obligations from 1980 (Rome Convention) should be revived regarding the UK. Despite legal policy concerns, this position was supported by commentators.[56] In this respect, Brexit has caused a step backwards in the area of conflict of laws.

Similar to any crisis, Brexit unearthed the question of the effects of crises on existing contracts. The reintroduction of customs duties, the levying of taxes, and an uncertain shift in the exchange rate between the British Pound and the Euro once again raised the question of frustration of contract. However, an adoption or even termination of the contract based on this was predominantly rejected in German law.[57] It is true that the basis of the transaction, within the meaning of § 313 BGB, can also be interfered by changes in national and foreign law.[58] However, once the result of the referendum was announced in June 2016, Brexit was no longer unpredictable. Due to the possibility of the UK leaving the EU, which ultimately took place almost four years later, it was in the hands of the contracting parties to contractually provide for a corresponding distribution of risk. Therefore, a subsequent correction of the affected contracts was ruled out. Frustration of contract could, at most (exceptionally), have been relevant in the case of long-term contracts already concluded. However, mere cost increases are not sufficient here either. This

[53] See Articles 1 and 2 of the Protocol (No 22) of the Treaty on European Union and the Treaty on the Functioning of the European Union on the position of Denmark, OJ 2008 C 155, pp. 299 et seq.

[54] Regulation (EC) No 593/2008 of the European Parliament and of the Council of 17 June 2008 on the law applicable to contractual obligations.

[55] Article 66(a) of the Agreement on the withdrawal of the United Kingdom of Great Britain and Northern Ireland from the European Union and the European Atomic Energy Community (2019)/C 384/01.

[56] Dickinson (2016), p. 203; Ungerer (2019), p. 403; Lehmann and Zetzsche (2017), pp. 64 et seq.

[57] Rüscher (2018), p. 941; Grupp (2017), p. 2066; Paulus (2020), § 10 para. 36 et seq.

[58] Federal Court of Justice, judgement of 8 February1984 - case VIII ZR 254/8; Federal Court of Justice, judgement of 6 July 2000 – case I ZR 243/97; Finkenauer (2022), § 313 BGB para. 232.

confirms the finding from the financial crisis that not every serious change in external circumstances leads to an adoption of the contract, even if this is regarded as a crisis.

4.2 Legislative Measures

Brexit did not result in any special legislative measures in the field of contract law in Germany, nor the EU. In view of the restrictive application of § 313 BGB, there were some calls for the principle of contractual continuity to be enshrined in law.[59] However, the German legislator did not follow this suggestion and continued to leave the examination of the individual case to the courts. In addition, it was proposed that the influence of Brexit on existing contracts relating to activities requiring a license should be legally established.[60] This is likely to be relevant for UK-based contractors whose activities in Germany have now become illegal due to the lack of recognition of a UK license, which in turn could have a direct impact on the contracts concerned. However, a subsequent illegality does not affect the effectiveness of a contract that has already been concluded. Only in the case of continuing obligations, which lose their validity *ex nunc* due to the entry into force of a legal prohibition, is the situation different.[61] The German legislator did not take up a proposal for a legal regulation of these cases either, which—as far as can be seen—has also remained without consequences in judicial practice. In any case, the lack of (effective) permission could mean an obstacle to the execution of the contract, so that ultimately there was a case of impossibility according to § 275 BGB. Here, it was up to the British obligor to avoid liability for this impossibility by taking suitable precautions. However, this did not require new mechanisms in contract law. Rather, the existing instruments of general contract law were already sufficient.

This applies not only to the transition phase, but also to the post-Brexit period. On closer examination, this is hardly surprising. Despite the extraordinary procedure itself, from the perspective of (European) contract law, Brexit merely resulted in the UK becoming a third state—like many other states—which, in itself, is not legally unique. From the perspective of contract law, there was thus no need to provide for a completely new legal situation. Whereas it is true that Brexit, by its very nature, led to a divergence between the British and the other legal systems within the EU, this did not result in any significant consequences for contract law, particularly not in Germany. This may be different for the practice of contract drafting, which is not the subject here.[62]

---

[59] Hirte and Schmidt-Kessel (2020), para. 153 et seq.

[60] Ibid, para. 151 et seq.

[61] Armbrüster (2021), para. 30 et seq.

[62] See Grupp (2017), pp. 2065 et seq.

5 COVID-19 Pandemic

5.1 Application of Existing Contract Law

In contrast to the crises examined so far, the Federal Court of Justice (*Bundesgerichtshof*) ruled, with regard to the 'systemic crisis'[63] caused by the COVID-19 pandemic, that due to frustration of contract, an adaption of concluded contracts according to § 313 BGB was generally possible.[64] This became relevant in the specific case of a commercial lease contract for retail, which had to remain closed due to an official order for the purpose of reducing contact. The Federal Court of Justice stated that:

> Due to the numerous measures taken to combat the COVID-19 pandemic, such as store closures, contact and access restrictions and the associated massive impact on social and economic life in Germany during the first lockdown in spring 2020, the so-called large basis of transaction is affected in the present case.[65]

On closer examination, it was not the pandemic itself that was the cause of the frustration, but rather, the governmental measures to combat the pandemic. Precisely for this reason, the tenant in the specific case had a claim against his landlord for adaption of the lease agreement, in particular with regard to the rent, the amount of which, in turn, had to be determined according to the specific circumstances of the individual case (including any state subsidy). However, this did not interfere with the contractually agreed distribution of the risk for the use of the leased premises. Rather, the Federal Court of Justice assumed that the contracting parties did not foresee the possibility of a pandemic and the associated danger of a state-ordered store closure and therefore also did not include this in the contractual distribution of risk. It is clear that, from a dogmatic point of view, frustration of contract is ultimately a supplementary interpretation of the contract,[66] in which gaps in the contractual distribution of risk (in this case in relation to a pandemic) are closed.

The comparison of the financial crisis, Brexit, and the COVID-19 pandemic and their respective influence on existing contracts, shows the difficulty of making general statements about whether a social crisis will lead to frustration of contract. Instead, it remains the case that, in addition to the change in circumstances (real element), it must be examined in each individual case whether the contracting parties would not have concluded or would have concluded the contract (hypothetical element) and whether it is unreasonable to adhere to the contract without amendment (normative element).

---

[63] Federal Court of Justice, judgement of 12 January 2022 – case XII ZR 8/21, para. 55; see also Federal Court of Justice, judgement of 2 March 2022 – case XII ZR 36/21, para. 32.

[64] See Prütting (2020), pp. 47 et seq.

[65] Federal Court of Justice, judgement of 12 January 2022 – case XII ZR 8/21, para. 45, translation by the author; see also Federal Court of Justice, judgement of 2 March 2022 – case XII ZR 36/21, para. 30.

[66] Oehm (2020), para. 2; Finkenauer (2022), para. 41 et seq.

5.2 Legislative Measures

All in all, the mechanism of frustration of contract is thus sufficiently flexible to cover crisis-related disturbances in the individual case. However, this flexibility comes at a price, namely that of legal certainty. For this reason, the German legislator felt compelled to enact a special provision for the COVID-19 pandemic. Thus, in accordance with Article 240 § 7 EGBGB (*Einführungsgesetz zum Bürgerlichen Gesetzbuche*, Introductory Act to the German Civil Code), it is presumed, in the case of lease and usufructuary lease agreements concerning commercial premises, that the basis of the transaction within the meaning of § 313 BGB has changed significantly, if the premises could not be used or could only be used with considerable restrictions as a result of the government measures to combat the COVID-19 pandemic. However, this clarification only concerns the real element of § 313 BGB.[67] A case-by-case examination of the hypothetical and normative element is still pending, so that legal uncertainty persists. Nevertheless, the German legal situation remains in line with the European Law Institute (ELI) Principles for the COVID-19 crisis.[68] According to Art. 13 (2) of these principles, the states should, for example, provide for an obligation to renegotiate between the contracting parties in case performance becomes excessively difficult due to the COVID-19 crisis and the countermeasures. However, there are no concrete preconditions defined for this. As in German law, the ELI Principles do not propose any concrete legal consequences beyond the mere obligation to renegotiate.[69]

Beyond clarifying the real element of frustration of contract, the German legislator has taken further measures in contract law to mitigate the consequences of the COVID-19 pandemic.[70] This alone indicates that the German legislator did not consider the case-by-case adoption of the contract according to the principles of frustration of contract—which, as has been seen, does not apply in principle to mere financing difficulties—to be sufficiently effective. Instead, the German legislator passed the Act to Mitigate the Consequences of the COVID-19 Pandemic under Civil, Insolvency and Criminal Procedure Law. With regard to contract law, the core element of the legislation was the moratorium on claims against consumers and micro-enterprises (Art. 240 § 1 EGBGB). According to this, until June 2020, consumers had the right to refuse performance with regard to continuing obligations if performance would have resulted in a situation in which consumers would have jeopardised their reasonable livelihood or that of their dependents as a result of the COVID-19 pandemic. However, this right of refusal only existed with regard to those continuing obligations that were necessary for the supply of services of general interest. A similar regulation applied to micro-entrepreneurs and their continuing

[67] Federal Court of Justice, judgement of 12 January 2022 – case XII ZR 8/21, para. 48.

[68] Available at: https://www.europeanlawinstitute.eu/fileadmin/user_upload/p_eli/Publications/ELI_Principles_for_the_COVID-19_Crisis.pdf.

[69] Wagner (2020), pp. 536 et seq.

[70] Schmidt-Kessel and Möllnitz (2021), pp. 699–718.

obligations, which was necessary to provide them with benefits for the reasonable continuation of their business (Article 240 § 1 (2) EGBGB). However, in the interest of creditors, this does not apply if the exercise of the right to refuse performance is unreasonable for the creditor for his part because the non-performance would jeopardise the economic basis of his business or his decent livelihood or that of his or her dependants (Article 240 § 1 (3) EGBGB).

However, the moratorium does not apply to claims under labour law or to lease and usufructuary lease agreements and loan agreements (Article 240 § 1 (4) EGBGB). Since tenants and lessees of land or premises cannot refuse to fulfil their payment obligations, in the event of default in payment they would be exposed to the risk of extraordinary termination. To prevent this, further special provisions have been provided. For example, Article 240 § 2 EGBGB provided for an exclusion of termination insofar as it concerned non-payment from April 2020 to June 2020 and the non-performance was caused by the effects of the COVID-19 pandemic. However, the entitlement to payment itself remained unaffected by the provision.

In addition, the German legislator provided for a deferral of claims arising from consumer loans due in April, May, and June 2020 if the consumer had suffered a loss of income due to the extraordinary circumstances caused by the spread of the COVID-19 pandemic, that made it unreasonable for the consumer to make the contractually agreed payment (Article 240 § 3 EGBGB). Once again, an exception applied if the deferral was unreasonable for the lender (para. 6). This deferral was accompanied by the protection against termination (para. 3) and options for adjusting the contract (para. 2, 4).

Furthermore, a regulation was made for cancelled leisure events (e.g. concerts or sports competitions) and closed leisure facilities, according to which the organisers and operators did not have to reimburse the price of the tickets, but could offer the entitled person a voucher as a replacement (Article 240 § 4 EGBGB). The aim was to save the event organisers and operators from running out of liquidity and thus, from imminent insolvency. The same also applied to tour operators who also feared an outflow of liquidity threatening their existence due to cancelled package tours and the associated refunds to customers (§ 651h BGB). The fact that other EU Member States, including France, Italy, and Spain, introduced a voucher solution in travel law put the German legislature under political pressure.[71] However, the German legislator saw itself prevented from such a solution due to Union law requirements. Article 12 (4) of the Package Travel Directive[72] stipulates that in the event of cancellation, a tour operator must immediately reimburse all payments made by the traveller. This does not include the right to reimbursement in the form of a voucher. The German government has therefore called on the EU Commission to clarify the admissibility of a voucher solution under European travel law. The Commission then published a formal recommendation stating that vouchers may

---

[71] Tonner (2021), Art. 240 § 6 EGBGB para. 5.

[72] Directive (EU) 2015/2302 of the European Parliament and of the Council of 25 November 2015 on package travel and linked travel arrangements.

be offered to the traveller as an alternative to a repayment claim, but that the traveller must retain the right to repayment.[73] The recommendation also contains detailed rules on the specific design of the voucher, which the German legislature largely followed. According to Article 240 § 6 EGBGB, a tour operator could also offer the customer a voucher as a replacement for a cancelled trip. However, the customer then had the choice of accepting the voucher or demanding a refund. Other European Member States did not provide such a choice, which the EU Commission saw as a violation of the Package Travel Directive. Accordingly, the Commission initiated infringement proceedings against several states (such as France, Italy, Croatia and Portugal) and requested the states concerned to remedy the deficiencies identified. This shows that the requirements of EU law for harmonisation of the internal market remain fully valid, even in times of crisis.

With regard to the other measures mentioned in contract law, in the absence of relevant provisions of EU law, the German legislator was free in its design. Nevertheless, in certain areas, a *de facto* convergence can be identified. As such, the German regulation on deferment of consumer loans served as a model[74] for the corresponding Austrian regulation.[75] In addition, moratoria comparable to German law can also be found in other legal systems, such as Spanish,[76] Italian, and Portuguese law.[77] However, these laws differ in detail, in some cases fundamentally, so that convergence can only be seen in the choice of instruments, but not in their specific design. The reason for this may have been the need for a quick response to impending defaults and the associated chain reactions. This would probably have been difficult to achieve through a coordinated approach and the necessary decision-making process, for example between the European Member States. The fact that the German legislator saw reason to act with particular haste is demonstrated in the short duration of the legislative process. On the part of the German government, a formulation aid[78] was only published on 23 March 2020. Already on 27 March 2020, the Act to Mitigate the Consequences of the COVID-19 Pandemic in Civil, Insolvency and Criminal Procedure Law was passed. Both the exceptionally fast legislative process and the limitation of the various regulations show that the measures were rightly described as emergency legislation, which was ultimately intended to prevent long-term damage through a short-term response in the form of selective measures. However, this was not accompanied by a lasting change in German contract law.

[73] C(2020) 3125 final.

[74] See explicitly in the corresponding motion, No. 403/A XXVII. GP, p. 43.

[75] See § 2 of the Federal Law on Accompanying Measures to Covid-19 in the Judiciary, BGBl. I Nr. 24/2020.

[76] Luna and Salvador Coderch (2021), pp. 836 et seq.

[77] See Ganuza and Gómez Pomar (2021), pp. 577 et seq.

[78] Available at: https://www.bmjv.de/SharedDocs/Gesetzgebungsverfahren/Dokumente/Corona-Pandemie.pdf.

6 Reform of the Law of Obligations (2022) and Outlook

The most comprehensive reform of contract law since the 2001 Act on the Modernisation of the Law of Obligations came into force on 1 January 2022. §§ 327-327u BGB introduced a whole new title on 'contracts on digital products' into the BGB, which regulates the rights of consumers in contracts for the provision of digital content or digital services in detail. An example of this is the consumer's right to update the purchased digital product (§ 327f BGB). The Act on the Regulation of the Sale of Goods with Digital Elements and Other Aspects of the Sales Contract of the same date also fundamentally restructured the warranty for defects under sales law, especially in the sale of consumer goods (§§ 474 et seq. BGB).

As with the 2001 amendment, this reform was also triggered by European directives. On the one hand, the reform served to implement the Digital Content Directive;[79] on the other hand, the legislator hereby implemented the Sale of Goods Directive,[80] which in turn repealed the Consumer Sales Directive of 1999. With both directives, the European legislator reacted to the developments in the field of digitalisation. In this respect, the impulse of European convergence in contract law, similar to what occurred 20 years earlier, was not a crisis, but the (predictable) development in the EU's Digital Single Market. The aim of the European measures was to achieve the highest possible level of consumer protection while at the same time creating legal certainty for businesses, especially for their cross-border activities, which are particularly prevalent in the digital sector.[81]

These directives are, again, full harmonisation instruments, so that the Member States may not maintain or introduce divergent provisions in national law.[82] However, this requirement is limited to the respective scope of application of the directives. Hence, they do not lead to a complete harmonisation of contract law. Article 3 (6) of the Sale of Goods Directive explicitly states that:

> this Directive shall not affect the freedom of Member States to regulate aspects of general contract law, such as rules on the formation, validity, nullity or effects of contracts, including the consequences of the termination of a contract, in so far as they are not regulated in this Directive, or the right to damages.

An almost identical wording can be found in the Digital Content Directive (Article 3 (10)) and the Mortgage Credit Directive, adopted after the financial crisis (Recital 21). The European legislator thus continues to promote the harmonisation of European contract law, yet only selectively (above all in favour of consumer protection). Thus, the provisions of § 313 BGB (frustration of contract) and §

---

[79] Directive (EU) 2019/770 of the European Parliament and of the Council of 20 May 2019 on certain aspects concerning contracts for the supply of digital content and digital services.

[80] Directive (EU) 2019/771 of the European Parliament and of the Council of 20 May 2019 on certain aspects concerning contracts for the sale of goods.

[81] See, for example, Recital 3 of the Digital Content Directive and Article 3 of the Sale of Goods Directive.

[82] Article 4 of the Sale of Goods Directive and Art. 4 of the Digital Content Directive.

275 BGB (impossibility), which are particularly relevant in times of crisis, are not prescribed by European law. Rather, they are subject to the free design of the national legislator.

Even the most recent European directives in the area of contract law cannot hide the fact that a broad diversity within the systems of contract law of the Member States persists.[83] This remains unchanged despite the various efforts of the last 20 years. In 2003, for example, the EU Commission proposed an action plan entitled 'A more coherent European contract law',[84] which aimed, among other things, at the coherent structuring of existing and future rules in the area of European contract law. In 2007, a commissioned research group came up with the 'Draft Common Frame of Reference' (DCFR).[85] However, contrary to its stated aim, the Commission did not use this as preparation for the creation of a common contract law as an optional instrument alongside the legal systems of the Member States.[86] The efforts were limited in content to the law relating to sales, so that in 2011, the Commission published a draft of a directly applicable regulation on a Common European Sales Law (CESL), which was to take its place (again as an optional instrument) alongside the national sales laws.[87] However, due to the opposition of the Member States, this proposal was rejected as well. Instead, in December 2015, the proposals for the Digital Content Directive[88] and the proposal the Sales of Goods Directive[89] were announced, which ultimately led to the directives relevant to the German reform of the law of obligations.

This outline of the development from the ambitious (and at the same time vague) idea of codifying a common European contract law to merely fragmentary regulations that primarily focus on the Digital Single Market suggests that there will probably not be a uniform European contract law in the near future.[90] It can be observed that there is a lack of sufficient competence on the part of the EU,[91] as well as a lack of political will on part of the Member States.[92] The past crises have not changed this. Nonetheless, as in the past, the EU will continue to strive for a successive adaptation of national contract law regulations through the selective harmonisation of the internal market. This view is based on the consideration that the existing diversity of national contract law regulations poses a challenge to cross-border trade and thus impairs a central objective of the EU, the establishment of an

[83] Kötz (2017), p. 1; Weatherill (2016), p. 3.
[84] COM(2003) 68 final.
[85] Schulze and Zoll (2021), Chap. 1 para. 50.
[86] Ibid, Chap. 1 para. 52.
[87] COM(2011) 635 final.
[88] COM(2015) 634 final.
[89] COM(2015) 635 final.
[90] Kötz (2017), p. 11.
[91] Weatherill (2016), p. 54.
[92] Kötz (2017), p. 11.

internal market (Article 3(3) Treaty on the EU (TEU)).[93] This is because transnational contracts always entail additional transaction costs on the part of the contracting parties due to different regulatory systems and the associated uncertainty. Of course, it cannot be ruled out that future crises will bring such uncertainties to the fore. However, the need for European convergence exists simply because of increasing economic interdependence, which is—also in view of the recent reform of German contract law—additionally driven by digitalisation.

This is also shown by the proposal for the Data Act, which the EU Commission published on 23 February 2022 as part of the European data strategy.[94] This affects contract design in particular, insofar as it significantly restricts the freedom of the parties to draft contracts concerning the access to and use of data by prohibiting certain contractual terms.[95] At the same time, the proposal for the Data Act provides for provisions to reduce contractual obstacles that make it difficult for customers to change data processing services (e.g. long notice periods).[96] However, the proposal again only provides selective provisions for contracts on data use and data access, so that the proposal remains true to the line of only fragmentary regulation of certain areas of contract law. However, with regard to the other measures to harmonise European contract law, it is noticeable that the European legislator wants to resort to a regulation which—unlike directives—claims direct applicability in the Member States (Article 288 (2) TFEU). In this respect, an even higher degree of convergence of contract law within the EU can be expected, at least in qualitative terms.

7 Conclusion

The divergent application of the principles of frustration of contract has shown, by way of example, that every crisis has its own peculiarities. Therefore, it is not possible to make general statements about the treatment of crises in German contract law. What the crises considered here have in common is that they did not give rise to fundamental reforms of German contract law. The existing provisions of the BGB thus once again prove to be resistant to crises. To the extent that there have been significant changes in German contract law in the past 20 years, these have tended to be triggered by European harmonisation. However, Union law is limited to only fragmentary regulation, so that national legislators can still shape contract law largely autonomously. Nevertheless, even in these areas which are left to the Member States, in isolated cases, a phenomenon of convergence of the national legal systems can be seen, as the example of the regulation of frustration of contract showed. The same can also be seen with regard to the legislative measures in the

[93] Weatherill (2016), p. 4.

[94] COM(2022) 68 final.

[95] Article 13 of the draft Data Act.

[96] Article 23 of the draft Data Act.

course of the COVID-19 pandemic. Admittedly, these were short-termed and time-limited reactions undertaken solely by national legislators. Nevertheless, comparable regulations were also found in other European Member States, at least to some extent, so that despite the lack of normative coordination, one can at least speak of *de facto* convergence.

However, with regard to the question of convergence of national regulations in contract law, it remains the case that the harmonisation of the internal market under Union law is of far greater importance. Interestingly, crises only have a minor impact on this development overall. On the one hand, the crises selected here have not inhibited the process of European harmonisation of contract law. On the contrary, the financial crisis has led to readjustments in European contract law while the European Commission is also urging for compliance with European law in the case of the COVID-19 pandemic with regard to the voucher infrastructure in travel law. Harmonisation should thus prevail even in the event of a crisis. On the other hand, it is not apparent that crises would significantly accelerate or expand European harmonisation in the area of contract law. Since contracts breathe life into the abstract goal of a European Single Market, efforts to harmonise Member State regulations on contract law will continue in the future, in small steps - even independently of crises.

References

Armbrüster C (2021) § 134 BGB. In: Säcker F, Rixecker R, Oetker H, Limperg B (eds) Münchener Kommentar zum Bürgerlichen Gesetzbuch, 9th edn. C.H. Beck, München

Borghetti J-S (2021) Non-performance and the change of circumstances under French law. In: Hondius E, Santos Silva M, Nicolussi A, Salvador Coderch P, Wendehorst C, Zoll F (eds) Coronavirus and the law in Europe. Intersentia, Cambridge, pp 509–526. https://doi.org/10.1017/9781839701801

Cherednychenko O (2011) Full harmonization of retail financial services contract law in Europe: a success or a failure. In: Grundmann S, Atamer Y (eds) Financial services, financial crisis and general European contract law. Wolters Kluwer Law International, Alphen aan den Rijn, pp 221–258

Comana M, Previtali D, Bellardini L (2019) The MiFID II Framework. Springer, Cham, https://doi.org/10.1007/978-3-030-12504-2

Dannemann G, Schulze R (2020) Introduction. In: Dannemann G, Schulze R (eds) German civil code, vol I. C.H. Beck, München

Dickinson A (2016) Back to the future: the UK's EU exit and the conflict of laws. J Priv Int Law 12: 2, https://doi.org/10.1080/17441048.2016.1209847, pp 195–210

Ernst W (2022) § 275 BGB. In: Säcker F, Rixecker R, Oetker H, Limperg B (eds) Münchener Kommentar zum Bürgerlichen Gesetzbuch, 9th edn. C.H. Beck, München

Finke J (2020) Krisen. Ein Erklärungsversuch dynamischer Rechtsentwicklungen in Krisenzeiten. Mohr Siebeck, Tübingen

Finkenauer T (2022) § 313 BGB. In: Säcker F, Rixecker R, Oetker H, Limperg B (eds) Münchener Kommentar zum Bürgerlichen Gesetzbuch, 9th edn. C.H. Beck, München

Ganuza JJ, Gómez Pomar F (2021) Government emergency intervention in private contracts in times of COVID-19. In: Hondius E, Santos Silva M, Nicolussi A, Salvador Coderch P,

Wendehorst C, Zoll F (eds) Coronavirus and the law in Europe. Intersentia, Cambridge, pp 567–602, https://doi.org/10.1017/9781839701801
Gressler (2016) Financial crisis and general contract law. In: Schmidt J, Esplugues Mota C, Arenas Garcia R (eds) EU law after the financial crisis. Intersentia, Cambridge, pp 117–132, https://doi.org/10.1017/9781780685205.010
Grundmann S, Atamer Y (2011) European contract law and banking contracts after the financial crisis: challenges for contracting and market transactions. In: Grundmann S, Atamer Y (eds) Financial services, financial crisis and general European contract law. Wolters Kluwer Law International, Alphen aan den Rijn, pp 3–31
Grupp TM (2017) Vertragsgestaltung in Zeiten von Brexit, Neue Juristische Wochenschrift (NJW), pp 2065–2070
Haar B (2011) From public law to private law: market supervision and contract law standards. In: Grundmann S, Atamer Y (eds) Financial services, financial crisis and general European contract law. Wolters Kluwer Law International, Alphen aan den Rijn, pp 259–277
Hirte H, Schmidt-Kessel M (2020) § 28 Legislative Vorsorge für den Brexit: Deutsche Begleitgesetzgebung zum Bexit und ungeregelte Felder. In: Kramme M, Baldus C, Schmidt-Kessel M (eds) Brexit, 2nd edn. Nomos, Baden-Baden, pp 709–777
Köndgen J (2011) Policy responses to credit crisis: does the law of contract provide an answer? In: Grundmann S, Atamer Y (eds) Financial services, financial crisis and general European contract law. Wolters Kluwer Law International, Alphen aan den Rijn, pp 35–59
Kötz H (2017) European contract law, 2nd edn. Oxford University Press
Lehmann M, Zetzsche DA (2017) Die Auswirkungen des Brexit auf das Zivil- und Wirtschaftsrecht, Juristen Zeitung (JZ), pp 62–71
Luna Á, Salvador Coderch P (2021) Spanish consumer law in the COVID-19 emergency. In: Hondius E, Santos Silva M, Nicolussi A, Salvador Coderch P, Wendehorst C, Zoll F (eds) Coronavirus and the law in Europe. Intersentia, Cambridge, pp 833–848, https://doi.org/10.1017/9781839701801
Mankowski P (2021) Art. 79 CISG. In: Drescher I, Fleischer H, Schmidt K (eds) Münchener Kommentar zum Handelsgesetzbuch, 5th edn. C.H. Beck, München
Oehm M (2020) § 313 BGB. In: Dannemann G, Schulze R (eds) German Civil Code, vol I. C.H. Beck, München
Paulus D (2020) § 10 Der Brexit als Störung der "politischen" Geschäftsgrundlage. In: Kramme M, Baldus C, Schmidt-Kessel M (eds) Brexit, 2nd edn. Nomos, Baden-Baden, pp 234–258
Piwowarski R (2020) Anlegerleitbilder und Anlegerschutz der MiFID II. Nomos, Baden-Baden
Poelzig D (2022) § 63 WpHG. In: Seibt CH, Buck-Heeb P, Harnos R (eds) Beckscher Online-Kommentar Wertpapierhandelsrecht, 6th edn. C.H. Beck, München
Prütting J (2020) Wegfall der Geschäftsgrundlage als Antwort des Zivilrechts auf Vertragsstörungen? In: Effer-Uhe D, Mohnert A (eds) Vertragsrecht in der Coronakrise. Nomos, Baden-Baden, pp 47–72, https://doi.org/10.5771/9783748909279-47
Rüscher D (2018) Vertragsanpassungen als Reaktion auf den Brexit nach deutschem, englischem, französischem, italienischem und spanischem Recht sowie nach UN-Kaufrecht, Europäische Zeitschrift für Wirtschaftsrecht (EuZW), pp 937–943
Säcker F (2021) Introduction. In: Säcker F, Rixecker R, Oetker H, Limperg B (eds) Münchener Kommentar zum Bürgerlichen Gesetzbuch, 9th edn. C.H. Beck, München
Schmidt-Kessel M, Möllnitz C (2021) Particular corona contract law in Germany. In: Hondius E, Santos Silva M, Nicolussi A, Salvador Coderch P, Wendehorst C, Zoll F (eds) Coronavirus and the law in Europe. Intersentia Cambridge, pp 699–718, https://doi.org/10.1017/9781839701801
Schuldrechtskommission (1992) Abschlußbericht der Kommission zur Überarbeitung des Schuldrechts. German Federal Gazette, Köln
Schulze R (2020) § 275 BGB. In: Dannemann G, Schulze R (eds) German Civil Code, vol I. C.H. Beck, München
Schulze R, Zoll F (2021) European contract law, 3rd edn. C.H. Beck, München

Tonner (2021) Art. 240 § 6 EGBGB. In: Säcker F, Rixecker R, Oetker H, Limperg B (eds) Münchener Kommentar zum Bürgerlichen Gesetzbuch, 8th edn. C.H. Beck, München
Tröger T (2014) Das Vertragsrecht der Krise: Vertragstheorie und -dogmatik im Lichte der Finanzkrise. In: Tobias T, Antonios K (eds) Gestaltung und Anpassung von Verträgen in Krisenzeiten. Mohr Siebeck, Tübingen, pp 49–74
Ungerer J (2019) Consequences of Brexit for European private international law, European Papers, 4(1), European Forum, Insight of 27 February 2019, pp 395–407, https://doi.org/10.15166/2499-8249/281
Wagner G (2020) Corona Law, Zeitschrift für Europäisches Privatrecht (ZEuP), pp 531–542
Weatherill S (2016) Contract law of the internal market. Intersentia, Cambridge, https://doi.org/10.1017/9781780687506
Winterfeld J, Rümker D (2017) § 124a Finanzmarktstabilisierungsgesetze. In: Schimansky H, Bunte H-J, Lwowski H-J (eds) Bankrechts-Handbuch, 5th edn. C.H. Beck, München
Zahrte K (2019) M. Anlageberatung. In: Drescher I, Fleischer H, Schmidt K (eds) Münchener Kommentar zum Handelsgesetzbuch, 4th edn. C.H. Beck, München

Hannes Henke is a postdoctoral researcher at Martin-Luther-University Halle-Wittenberg.

Part III
Thematic and Jurisdictional Case Studies 2: Public Law

Environmental Law in China

Wang Xi and Luo Wenjun

1 Introduction

In modern Chinese, 'convergence' is defined as 'things coming together and having similar characteristics.'[1] The Longman Dictionary of Contemporary Advanced English defines the verb 'to converge' as 'to come from different direction and meet at the same point to become one thing'; 'to focus, gather, assemble (if groups of people convergence in a particular place, they come there from many different places and meet together to form a large crowd)'.[2] Based on this understanding, the concept of convergence of environmental law in this chapter refers to the phenomenon whereby Chinese environmental law aligns with, to a certain extent, mainstream international environmental law. Here the phrase 'mainstream international environmental law' refers to the commonalities of the environmental laws of most industrialised countries, as well as international environmental law.

The development of China's environmental law over the past 40 years shows that it is not only a process of self-exploration to cope with environmental crises, but also

The authors would like to thank Zhang Haoyu for her great efforts in translating this article into English.

[1]Modern Chinese Dictionary (7th Edition). The Commercial Press: Beijing (2016), p. 1078.

[2]Longman Dictionary of Contemporary Advanced English (6th Edition). Foreign Language Teaching and Research Press, Pearson Education Limited, UK (2019), p. 551.

W. Xi (✉)
School of Law, Kunming University of Science and Technology, Platform for Promoting Research on Ecological Civilization and Environmental Rule of Law, Kunming, China

School of Law, Shanghai Jiao Tong University, Shanghai, China
e-mail: wangxi@sjtu.edu.cn

L. Wenjun
School of Law, Hubei University of Economics, Hubei, China

E. Ghio, R. Perlingeiro (eds.), *Are Legal Systems Converging or Diverging?*,
https://doi.org/10.1007/978-3-031-38180-5_10

a process of learning from mainstream global environmental laws. In this process, Chinese environmental law has converged with mainstream global environmental laws.

2 China's Environmental Crisis and Related Legislative Responses

Generally speaking, China experiences two types of interrelated environmental problems: pollution and ecological deterioration. These problems stem, notably, from China's rapid economic development in recent decades and they have been acknowledged as being the main issues hindering China's further development.[3] In 2008, then-President Hu Jintao declared that 'our economic growth is realized at an excessively high cost of resources and the environment.'[4] Although the situation has somewhat improved over the last decade, environmental deterioration remains a major issue in China. Mr Xi Jinping, the current President of the People's Republic of China and Chairman of the Chinese Communist Party, has emphasised that 'with the Chinese economy transitioning from high-speed growth to high-quality development, the building of ecological civilisation has entered a critical period. The country will fight a good battle against pollution and take its ecological civilization to a new level.'[5]

In the last four decades, China has attempted to respond to environmental issues by promulgating several laws dealing with the environment. In 1979, China enacted the Environmental Protection Law of the People's Republic of China, which allows the state to protect the environment and natural resources, while preventing and controlling pollution. In 1989, China enacted the Environmental Protection Law, which regulates environmental governance. This law was amended in 2014, strengthening the government's regulatory responsibility and polluters' liabilities. The amendment introduced the concept of environmental public interest litigation.[6] In 2018, an amendment introduced the concept of 'ecological civilisation' in the Constitution's Preamble and Article 89, which states that the State Council is responsible for the construction of this ecological civilisation. By 2019, China had 37 environmental laws in force, over 60 environmental administrative regulations of the State Council, and over 1000 departmental environmental rules.[7]

The COVID-19 outbreak has since brought other environmental issues to the fore, such as the protection of wildlife and biosecurity. China's response has been swift: in October 2020, the Biosafety Law was adopted with a view to protecting

[3] Li'an (2007), p. 37.

[4] Jintao (2008).

[5] Jinping (2018).

[6] Guangtao (2014).

[7] Youhai (2019), p. 7.

biological resources and ecological environment, preventing and responding to biosafety risks, safeguarding people's lives and health, and realising the harmonious coexistence between man and nature. In December 2020, China adopted the 11th Amendment to the Criminal Law of the People's Republic of China, in line with the enactment of the Biosafety Law.[8] At the time of writing, to tackle the global climate change crisis, China is drafting a Law on Climate Change.

In short, China's environmental law has made great progress in dealing with increasingly complex environmental crises. The development of China's environmental law has dealt with both domestic and international problems. In this process, Chinese environmental law has converged with mainstream international environmental law.

3 The Convergence of Chinese Environmental Law with Foreign Environmental Laws

A review of China's environmental legislation reveals that it is relatively similar to that of other countries, at least in its purpose, the type of legal instruments adopted, and China's overarching political and legal environmental governance.

3.1 The Convergence of Legislative Purposes

The purpose of a country's environmental law reflects the choices of values made by their legislature in the face of environmental challenges. In the words of Alexandre Kiss, a leading French environmental law scholar, 'the purpose of environmental laws is a reflection of the values of the legislators.'[9]

Comparing China's legislative purposes in environmental law with that of other countries (see Table 1) reveals that they are typically similar. Most environmental laws aim to prevent and control pollution and ecological deterioration, protect public health and welfare, and establish a national system of environmental regulation.[10]

---

[8] Ning (2020).

[9] Kiss and Shelton (1994), p. 30.

[10] Jianming et al. (2004), pp. 50–51.

Table 1 The convergence of legal purposes between Chinese environmental laws and foreign environmental laws

Country	Year	Legislation	Legislative purpose
China	1989	Environmental Protection Law	Article 1 states that the Law was formulated to protect and improve people's environment and the ecological environment generally, while preventing and controlling pollution and other public hazards, safeguarding human health and promoting the socialist development of the country.
Germany	1993	Environmental Code	Article 1 states that the aim is to preserve the environment with a view to protecting the viability and effectiveness of the biosphere and the availability of natural resources. Environmental protection measures aim to protect the health and safety of human beings.
Japan	1993	Environmental Law	Article 1 states that the purpose of this law is to impose a responsibility on the state, local public entities, and enterprises to protect the environment and promote future national health, life, and human welfare. It establishes the concept of national responsibility towards environmental protection.
United States	1969	National Environmental Policy Act	The purposes of this law are the promotion of the construction of a pleasant and harmonious relation between humans and the environment, the prevention and elimination of damages to the environment and biosphere, the improvement of human health and welfare, the deepening of national vital ecosystems, and the establishment of a national council regulating the quality of the environment.

3.2 *The Convergence of Legal Instruments Dealing with Environmental Protection*

3.2.1 Changes in Private Law as a Response to Environmental Challenges

Since the 1960s, in order to tackle growing environmental challenges, the private laws of many countries have undergone important changes. These changes have been particularly acute in the area of tort law. In the United States (US), for example, several environmental-related issues, such as nuisance, negligence, trespass and strict liability have led to new legislative developments.[11] In Japan, the rules on causal relation have changed. In many environmental tort cases, the burden of proof for causality has been shifted onto the defendants. If the defendant cannot disprove the existence of causality, they cannot be exempted from tort liability.[12] Similarly, in the face of growing environmental challenges, China's private law underwent

[11] Xi (1992), p. 123.

[12] Nohiko (1999), p. 27.

significant changes. In 2009, China promulgated the Tort Liability Law, which contained new provisions relating to environmental infringement, proof of causality, and inversion of the burden of proof. These provisions have since been incorporated into the Civil Code of the People's Republic of China, promulgated in May 2020. Therefore, since the 1960s, the changes in China's private law relating to environmental issues has mostly converged with that of other countries.

3.2.2 Changes in Public Law as a Response to the Needs for Environmental Regulation

Since the 1960s, environmental regulation has also become an elemental public law framework dealing with environmental protection in many countries in the world.[13] For example, the US has established a broad federal environmental framework through legislation on air, water, solid wastes, toxic substances, etc.[14] Countries in Europe and Japan have followed suit.[15] Similarly, since the promulgation of the Environmental Protection Law (Trial) in 1979, China has established a large legal system of environmental regulation. This system of public law consists of the Environmental Protection Law, which is based on the cause of environmental protection, and three types of laws concerning pollution prevention and control, nature protection and special matters. As a latecomer system of environmental regulation law, China is similar to other countries in terms of types and forms, as well as substantive regulatory measures.

3.3 *Convergence in the Political Relations in Environmental Governance*

In political sciences, the term 'governance' refers to the 'public management activity and public management process, including the necessary public authority,

[13] Mingyuan (2001), p. 73.

[14] Xi (1992), pp. 173–179; 213–435.

[15] For example, after the 1970s, Japan developed from a passive police administration that prevented and controlled public hazards and settled individual disputes to a comprehensive administration with positive contents such as preserving the environment itself in a good condition for future generations to inherit, manage and adjust the use of the environment. A large number of public law environmental regulations were passed. Another example is that after the 1970s, when Germany was transforming from an industrialised country to an ecological one, the central goal of most political decisions was to protect the environment. Environmental protection has become an important responsibility of state organs. The state enacted strict environmental public law to prohibit damage to the environment, to design permits for dangerous equipment (products, activities) and to regulate environmental taxation and public funds.

management rules, management mechanisms and methods.'[16] Against this understanding of the concept of governance, environmental governance can be defined as 'a political and legal process of implementing laws and policies by all parties involved in the cause of environmental protection in order to achieve the environmental protection goals set by the State.'[17] The major actors involved in environmental governance include governments as regulators, enterprises and other potential polluters as regulatees, and third-party actors as supervisors. Under environmental laws and policies, these actors interact with, and influence, each other for the exploitation and protection of the environment and natural resources.[18]

An examination of these political relations in environmental governance shows that environmental governance in China, the US, Japan and other countries exhibit three main similar political interactions, namely (i) a regulatory relation; (ii) a supervisory relation between the supervisors and regulators; and (iii) a supervisory relation between the supervisors and regulatees.[19] These political relations reveal that convergence has occurred within environmental governance across many countries in the world.

3.3.1 Regulatory Relation

The government is the initiator within regulatory relations. The government enjoys the power to adopt and enforce coercive measures as authorised by the law. Companies and other polluters are the regulated parties who, on the one hand, have the obligation to accept the government's regulation and, on the other hand, enjoy the right to lawful production and operation and the right to oppose improper governmental intervention in their activities. The purpose of environmental regulation is to address market failures and to reduce the negative environmental externality of a firm's production to a level permitted by statutory standards. Governments use statutory environmental standards, taxes, and any other regulatory instruments to push companies and other polluters to operate in compliance with the law and regulations and to internalise the costs of negative externalities associated with their operations and production.

Therefore, as a whole, environmental regulation is a fundamental public instrument for countries in order to eliminate market failures.[20] For example, in the US, this regulatory function manifests through the interaction between the government and parties such as companies as set out in federal statutes such as the Clean Air Act (1970), and the Toxic Substances Control Act (1976). In Japan, this regulatory function is governed by, inter alia, the Air Pollution Control Act (1968), the Water

---

[16] Keping (2015), p. 23.

[17] Xi (2012), p. 6.

[18] Ibid.

[19] Xi (2020), pp. 13–15.

[20] Xi (2020), p. 14.

Pollution Control Law (1970), and the Basic Environment Law (1993). In China, the laws regulating this area include the Environmental Protection Law (for Trial Implementation) (1979,), [21]the Water Pollution Prevention and Control Law (1984),[22] and the Atmospheric Pollution Prevention and Control Law (1987),[23] to name only a few.

3.3.2 Supervisory Relation (Supervisors-Regulators)

The purpose of governmental supervision in relation to environmental performance is to prevent and overcome governmental failures in environmental regulation. Governments juggle several responsibilities including promoting the economic development of their country, as well as social management and environmental protection. In the absence of incentives towards increased environmental protection, governments tend to focus more on economic development rather than environmental protection, which can lead to governmental failures in the area of environmental protection.

This problem was quite acute in China in the 1990s and 2000s, when many local governmental entities focused predominantly on GDP growth and disregarded the need to protect local ecological environments and resources. This led to these local entities being seen as 'environmental problem makers',[24] similar to companies. At the time, market failures and negative environmental externalities, characterised by increased pollution and ecological damage, were not only left unchecked but were also amplified and exacerbated by poor decision-making and regulatory failures on the part of these local governmental entities.[25]

Environmental protection supervision has developed as a means to overcome these governmental failures. Within these supervisory relations, the third-party supervisors are generally the legislature and the courts; supervised parties are the administrative authorities responsible for environmental regulation. These supervisory relations occur through various legal institutional measures. For example, the US enacted the National Environmental Policy Act in 1969. In addition to declaring environmental protection a federal policy of the US, the Act provides for an environmental impact assessment procedure (EIA). This EIA procedure consists of a supervisory mechanism which requires federal agencies to consider and accommodate environmental values in their decisions.[26] Other examples of this supervisory relation can be found in other statutes such as the Clean Air Act (42 U.S.C.A. 7410(a)(2)(A)-(K)) which requires a state to submit its plans for implementing the

[21] It was revised into the Environmental Protection Law in 1989 and revised in 2014.

[22] It was subsequently revised in 1996, 2008 and 2017.

[23] It was subsequently revised in 1995, 2000 and 2015.

[24] Xi (2020), p. 13.

[25] Ibid, pp. 14–15.

[26] Xi (1992), p. 221.

Act to the Environmental Protection Agency (EPA) for review and approval. The EPA has the power to oversee state enforcement and to withdraw a state's authority to carry out the implementation of the Act if the EPA is of the view that the state is violating federal environmental statutes. Additionally, citizens are authorised to bring civil lawsuits in their own names against the EPA or other administrative agencies.[27] In Japan, the Basic Law on the Environment sets out the responsibilities of local governmental entities in relation to environmental protection, as well as the mechanisms for environmental protection investigation and deliberation by these local governmental entities.[28] These entities, as well as the Minister of Environment, have a duty to disclose specific information related to environmental protection, as set out by the Air Pollution Control Law.[29] In China, typical provisions dealing with the supervisory relations include the environmental protection target responsibility system, and the system for assessment and evaluation of environmental performance of local governmental entities.[30] A mechanism of supervision over local environmental regulators by the local peoples' congresses is in place at local levels. [31] It is worth mentioning that since 2016, China has designed a system of central inspection regarding the ecological and environmental protection work carried out by local governmental entities. The Central Committee of the Communist Party of China (CPC) is responsible for organising a centralised, full-time inspectorate to inspect the performance of ecological and environmental protection by the Party committees and governments of provinces, autonomous regions, and municipalities, as well as the relevant departments of the State Council and selected companies which operate under the leadership of the Central Government.

3.3.3 Supervisory Relation (Supervisors-Regulatees)

This is a political relation between third-party actors, including the general public, environmental organisations, the media and the courts, and the regulatees, such as companies and other polluters. Third-party actors monitor whether companies and other polluters comply with their legal obligations to protect the environment. However, this supervisory relation is different from the previous two because the general public, environmental organisations, the media, the courts and other social forces participate in environmental governance through different channels provided by the law, such as reporting, complaint mechanisms, press coverage and environmental public interest litigation. The citizen suits provisions in several environmental statutes including the US Clean Air Act (Article 304) and the Clean Water Act

[27] Xi (1992), p. 296.

[28] Basic Law on the Environment, Articles 43(1) and 44. See also Xuhui and Yunxiao (2020), pp. 15–16.

[29] Xuhui and Yunxiao (2020), p. 235.

[30] Environmental Protection Law, Article 26.

[31] Environmental Protection Law, Article 27.

(Article 505) are examples of the provisions on the environmental public interest litigation. Citizens act as a watchdog for the government and corporations. In Japan, the Basic Environment Law (Article 24) establishes environmental information disclosure requirements whereby the state must provide necessary information related to environmental protection. This information is useful for environmental organisations that can monitor the environmental performance of corporations and other polluters. In China, the Environmental Protection Law contains a provision on environmental public interest litigation, which authorises non-governmental organisations to file environmental public interest litigation in courts.[32]

In 2013, a research group composed of Chinese and American scholars applied an equilateral triangle Model of Interaction of Parties in the Process of Environmental Protection (IPPEP Model)[33] to several major environmental law cases, from the 1970s onwards, relating to the Hudson River Basin in New York. They found that the three political relations discussed above, i.e. (i) regulatory relations; (ii) supervisory relations between the supervisors and regulators; and (iii) supervisor relations between the supervisors and regulatees, were fundamental to environmental governance in the US.

4 The Convergence of Chinese Environmental Law with International Environmental Law

Chinese environmental law has traditionally converged with international environmental law. The convergence has occurred through two processes: direct convergence and indirect convergence. Direct convergence has occurred through the conclusion of, and participation in, international treaties, which provide a direct source of international law for China. This process has resulted in legal harmonisation between the contracting parties. Indirect convergence occured through the incorporation of international principles into domestic law.

4.1 Direct Convergence

Since the 1970s, the world has witnessed an increase in transnational environmental problems such as global warming, ozone layer destruction, marine pollution, cross-border movement of hazardous wastes, acid rain, reduction in biodiversity, to name just a few. To tackle these challenges, the global community has developed a large body of international environmental law, which includes, inter alia, the Declaration

[32] Environmental Protection Law, Article 58.

[33] This model was first published by Wang Xi in 2012: Xi (2012), pp. 5–22. See also Xi (2020), pp. 12–18.

on the Human Environment (Stockholm Declaration, 1972), the World Charter for Nature (1982), the Rio Declaration on Environment and Development (1992), the Convention on Biological Diversity (1992), the United Nations Framework Convention on Climate Change (1992), the Kyoto Protocol (1997), the Paris Agreement (2016), and a series of other international environmental legal instruments. Several international environmental principles have been established, including the principle of sustainable development, the principle of common but differentiated responsibilities, the principle of precaution, the polluter pays principle and the principle of international cooperation on environmental matters. These international agreements and principle provide an important legal basis for all countries working on solving environmental problems, as well as a strong basis for the convergence of laws across countries.

China has always attached great importance to participating in the international community's effort to solve human environmental problems. Therefore, it has concluded, participated in, and ratified, almost all major international environmental conventions and other international environmental legal instruments such as the Amendment to Article 21 of the Convention on International Trade in Endangered Species of Wild Fauna and Flora signed by China in 1988, the Basel Convention on the Control of Transboundary Movements of Hazardous Wastes and their Disposal (signed by China in 1990) and its amendments (ratified by China in 2001), the Montreal Protocol on Substances that Deplete the Ozone Layer (signed by China in 1991) and the Kigali Amendment (accepted by China in 2021), the Convention on the Conservation and Management of High Seas Fishery Resources in the South Pacific Ocean (signed by China in 2010), the Convention on the Conservation and Management of High Seas Fishery Resources in the North Pacific Ocean (signed by China in 2012), the Stockholm Convention on Persistent Organic Pollutants Amendment to list nine new POPs (ratified by China in 2013), the Doha Amendment to the Kyoto Protocol (signed by China in 2014), the Minamata Convention on Mercury (ratified by China in 2016), the Nagoya Protocol on Access to Genetic Resources and the Fair and Equitable Sharing of Benefits Arising from their Utilization to the Convention on Biological Diversity (signed by China in 2016).

As Professor Veerle Heyvaert, Harold Samuel Chair in Law and Environmental Policy at the University of Cambridge said, '[t]he adoption of internationally recognized uniform standards or mutually recognized agreements, whereby different countries essentially recognize each other's legal provisions as having the same effect, can achieve approximation between laws.'[34] In accordance with the international principle of *pacta sunt servanda*, parties that have concluded and ratified international environmental conventions are bound to comply with the conventions' provisions and fulfil their corresponding legal obligations. As a result, through contracting and implementing international environmental conventions, China has witnessed a phenomenon of direct legal convergence with international law rules and principles.

---

[34] Heyvaert (2019), p. 772.

4.2 *Indirect Convergence*

In addition to direct convergence, much of the international community's efforts in environmental protection has had a significant impact on China's domestic environmental legislation, thereby promoting indirect legal convergence.

For example, in June 1972, a Chinese delegation attended the United Nations Conference on the Human Environment held in Stockholm. The conference served as an impetus for China to modernise and amend its environmental protection as it was realised that similar environmental problems existed across the country. This led to the convening of China's first National Conference on Environmental Protection in 1973 and the adoption of China's first programmatic document on environmental protection, namely the Draft Regulations on the Protection and Improvement of the Environment (for trial implementation). This document set out China's guidelines, principles, systems and basic measures to prevent and control pollution. It became the prototype for China's first environmental 'basic law', the Environmental Protection Law (for trial implementation) in 1979.[35]

Another example is the adoption of Agenda 21 at the United Nations Conference on Environment and Development in Rio de Janeiro (Brazil) in 1992. Agenda 21 is a broad action plan which can be adopted by governments, international organisations and non-governmental organisations in any country, with a view to promoting sustainable development. At the conference, then-Premier Li Peng committed, on behalf of the Chinese Government, to fulfil Agenda 21 and other legal documents adopted at the conference. Subsequently, China's Agenda 21 was formulated as an overall strategy to promote China's sustainable development. It serves as a guiding document for the Chinese Government in formulating its medium- and long-term plans for national economic and social development.

Finally, the development of international climate change law has served as an important driver for the development of climate change policies and laws in China. In September 2020, Xi Jinping, President of the People's Republic of China, delivered an important speech at the 75th General Debate of the United Nations General Assembly, indicating that China would increase its autonomous national contribution, adopt stronger policies and measures, strive to cap CO2 emissions by 2030, and work towards achieving carbon neutrality by 2060.

Additionally, the values developed by the international community and embedded in international environmental law have influenced China's domestic environmental landscape. Since the 1970s, several new concepts or principles have emerged on the international scene, including the concept of sustainable development, the protection of the intrinsic value of nature, the protection of the 'common heritage' of mankind and the balancing of the interests of current and future generations. These new concepts reflect a growing awareness of environmental issues and challenges and a change in human values. Therefore, they provide an ideological basis which

[35] Youhai (2019), p. 6.

serves for the convergence of environmental legislation around the world.[36] In particular, the concept of sustainable development has had a far-reaching impact over the years. From the 1990s onwards, the idea of sustainable development was slowly adopted by most countries around the world as a national strategy underpinning their social and economic development. Several jurisdictions around the world have now embedded the concept of sustainable development into their domestic laws.[37] Therefore, guided by the idea of sustainable development and the protection of the interests of mankind and the earth's ecosystems, environmental law has found itself at the heart of a phenomenon of legal convergence, which has intensified over the last few decades.

China has embedded the concept of sustainable development in its Environmental Protection Law as well as other domestic environmental laws. Article 1 of the Environmental Protection Law states that: 'this law is developed for the purposes of protecting and improving environment, preventing and controlling pollution and other public nuisances, safeguarding public health, promoting ecological civilization, and enhancing sustainable economic and social development.' Article 1 of the Atmospheric Pollution Prevention and Control Law provides that: 'this law is developed for the purpose of protecting and improving the environment, preventing and controlling atmospheric pollution, safeguarding the health of the general public, enhancing ecological civilization, and promoting the sustainable development of economy and society.'

Overall, several environmental protection laws in China have been heavily influenced by international rules, standards, and concepts. These influences have resulted in indirect legal convergence between international environmental law and that of China.

5 Reasons Behind Legal Convergence

Law is a complex social phenomenon and its development is influenced and constrained by a variety of factors. The convergence of Chinese environmental law with that of other countries and with international law can be explained by the following reasons.

5.1 Environmental Issues Are Caused by Similar Problems

When one looks at current environmental problems which have arisen over the years in China and other countries or regions in the world, one can easily see that most of

[36] Jin (1998), p. 34.
[37] Cai (1999), p. 15.

these issues have the same causes, notably neglecting the environment in the process of rapid industrialisation and the long-term, one-sided focus on economic development which has resulted in serious environmental pollution and ecological damage.

For example, in the 1950s and the 1960s, the US had to dealt with serious environmental problems which stemmed from the rapid economic development after the Second World War. At the time, the US saw a dramatic expansion of its industry, agriculture and cities, which resulted in the discharge of important amounts of untreated pollutants, including organic, inorganic, and radioactive chemicals into rivers, lakes and other bodies of water. Air and soil pollution issues arose as well.[38]

In a similar vein, after the Second World War, the focus of Japan was predominantly on reviving its industry through rapid economic growth. While it was a success, the adverse effects of these economic developments led to serious environmental degradation. Acute public health issues occurred in industrial zones across the country, with the general public experiencing bone pain, Minamata disease, and asthma.[39]

Environmental issues in China were caused by similar factors. While China has been hailed for the growth of its GDP over the last 40 years, the rapid industrialisation of the country and economic growth had generated serious problems of environmental pollution and ecological deterioration.[40]

The fact that countries in the world experience similar environmental problems, which are caused by similar factors, explains why national environmental laws around the world have mirrored each other, leading to a phenomenon of legal convergence.

5.2 China's Active and Constant Interests in Studying Mainstream International Environmental Laws of the World

The active study of mainstream international environmental laws by the Chinese legislature, as well as academics, has not only played an important role in the development of China's domestic environmental laws, but also promoted the convergence of environmental law in China with the environmental laws of other countries and international environmental law.

[38] Xi (1992), pp. 25–29.

[39] Nohiko (1999), p. 2.

[40] Li'an (2007), pp. 36–50.

5.2.1 The Role of the Chinese Legislature

The Chinese legislature has long played an active role in studying, comparing and learning about the legislative experiences of other countries against the domestic background of China's development. In fact, comparative jurisprudence has become an essential component of Chinese legislation.[41] In 2008, the Information Office of the State Council issued a *White Paper on China's Rule of Law Construction*, which stated that:

> China insists on carrying out the practice of the rule of law in light of its national conditions, while also paying attention to drawing on, and absorbing, the positive experiences of foreign rule of law constructions and the achievements of the rule of law civilization jointly created by mankind, so as to enrich and improve the socialist rule of law civilization with Chinese characteristics.[42]

The White Paper stressed that 'China has paid attention to, and drawn on, foreign legislative experiences, and has absorbed a lot of foreign legislative experiences in the areas of civil and commercial law, administrative law, criminal law, intellectual property protection and environmental protection.'[43] China's accession to the World Trade Organization in 2001 has further strengthened its ties and cooperation with other countries in the field of environmental protection, providing favourable conditions for China to learn from other countries in the area of environmental protection.

The environmental impact assessment system is a typical example of how China's national legislature and relevant administrative authorities have studied, and learned from, environmental laws of other countries. The system was first mandated by the US National Environmental Policy Act (1969), which required US federal agencies to conduct environmental impact assessments as part of their decision-making process. The law changed a long-standing approach to decision-making by federal agencies that did not consider environmental values much. China introduced a similar system in its Environmental Protection Law (for Trial Implementation), promulgated in 1979. Article 6 of the Law stipulates that environmental impact assessments should be conducted for construction projects.[44]

Additionally, in the 1990s, a number of countries developed an interest in Strategic Environmental Assessments, i.e. systematic processes for evaluating the environmental implications of a proposed policy, plan, or programme. China's legislature and relevant administrative organs released that the scope of the EIA in China should be expanded to cover governmental decision-making and that a special law on environmental impact assessment should be enacted. The National's People's Congress sent a delegation to the US and Mexico to study their respective legislation

---

[41] Mi (2018), p. 318.

[42] Information Office of the State Council of the People's Republic of China: China's rule of law (2008), http://www.gov.cn/zhengce/2008-02/28/content_2615764.htm.

[43] Ibid.

[44] Tao (2008).

on EIAs and their implementation. In 2002, China adopted its Environmental Impact Assessment Law, which includes procedures for assessing environmental impacts of construction projects (Sect. 3) and governmental planning (Sect. 2).[45] As Professor Sun Youhai puts it, China's ability to learn 'from successful legislative experience of other countries has led to a world-renowned achievement in environmental protection law in the new era.'[46] This active studying and learning by Chinese authorities has contributed to the convergence of domestic environmental law with the environmental laws of other countries.

5.2.2 The Role of Academia

Academic contributions have played an important role in the legal convergence experienced by China in environmental law. As early as 1981, Professor Jin Ruilin from Beijing University, wrote an article promoting the study of the environmental legal systems of other countries. He pointed out that 'the laws of each country differ from one another according to political, economic and social circumstances. However, in the field of environmental law, the existence of certain common issues reflecting the laws of nature and economy has led to a number of countries having broadly similar legal norms and the gradual development of certain common legal systems. China is a late starter in environmental protection law, and a comparative study of the basic institutions dealing with the environmental laws of other countries would be useful.'[47] Professor Ma Xiangcong of the Chinese Academy of Social Science believes that:

> the reason why China's environmental rule of law, environmental law and environmental jurisprudence have developed relatively quickly is not only because we base our legislation on the needs of China and start from Chinese reality, but also because we look at the world and learn from international advanced experience with an open mind [. . .] We, Chinese, are very good at learning from the advanced experience of human beings, so when developing environmental protection laws and conducting environmental jurisprudence research, we studied foreign environmental laws and international environmental law, and translated and published relevant materials. At the same time, we sent people abroad to study and invited foreign experts to come to China for lectures and exchanges, so we have made important achievements and these have played a good role in promoting the development of environmental jurisprudence in our country. We now have many scholars who are very accomplished and successful in the study of foreign environmental laws and international environmental law.[48]

In 1994, Professor Wang Xi, then at Wuhan University, devoted a discussion to the basic principles of comparative environmental jurisprudence, including concepts and methods. He pointed out that:

---

[45] Tao (2008).

[46] Youhai (2007), p. 22.

[47] Ruilin (1981), p. 51.

[48] Xiancong (2021), p. 134.

> comparative environmental jurisprudence can compare the environmental protection legal methods and legislative techniques of various countries, thus promoting the progress of our environmental protection legal methods and legislative techniques. Comparative environmental jurisprudence can enrich our legal thinking on environmental protection by comparing the legal ideas of various countries on environmental protection and it can compare the legislative effects of various countries in the market economy, so as for China to learn from them. Comparative environmental jurisprudence can even recommend those environmental laws or some of their provisions to our legislature for transplantation into our country on the basis of comparison and verification.[49]

In the last 40 years, research on comparative environmental jurisprudence in China has yielded fruitful results. These results have contributed to the legislature's and academic community's understanding of the environmental laws of other countries. The list of publication given in Table 2 reflects the major achievements of Chinese academia in comparative environmental law research in the last four decades.

6 Conclusions

This chapter has examined the convergence of Chinese environmental law with mainstream international environmental law from the perspective of legislative purposes, legal instruments, and the political relations present in environmental governance. In terms of legislative purposes, just as in any other country, the substance of Chinese environmental laws is primarily focused on establishing environmental regulation and providing legal remedies, in order to maintain social justice. In terms of legal instruments, China, similarly to other countries, has experienced visible changes in both its public and private law spheres with a view to addressing environmental challenges. In the public law sphere, in particular, a new system of environmental regulation has emerged, providing a sufficient legal basis for governmental intervention in the field of environmental protection in case of market failures. In terms of the political-legal relations in the process of environmental governance, Chinese environmental law exhibits a similar pattern to other countries; three basic political relations exist. Therefore, Chinese environmental law has directly and indirectly converged with mainstream international environmental laws.

Two main reasons explain this convergence. The first is that environmental problems typically have the same causes. Similar problems lead to similar legal reactions. The second is the active and constant study and learning of mainstream international environmental law by China.

Several concluding points can be drawn from the discussion in this chapter.

First, the political system of a country is neither the cause nor the decisive factor in solving domestic environmental problems. Although China and other countries exhibit remarkable differences in their political systems, their environmental laws

[49] Xi (1994), p. 54.

Table 2 Selected Chinese books on comparative environmental law, written or translated by Chinese scholars between 1988 and 2022

	Book	Author or translator	Publisher and date
1	Environmental Law in Western Countries	Wen Boping	Law Press of China, 1988
2	Environmental Law in the Soviet Union and Eastern European Countries	Ma Xiangcong	China Environmental Science Press, 1990
3	Hard to Escape the Ghost City – The Tragedy of Chemical Pollution that Shocked the World (Original Title: Love Canal: My Story)	Written by Lois Gibbs, translated by Wang Xi	China University of Geosciences Press, 1991
4	Introduction to Environmental Law in the United States	Wang Xi	Wuhan University Press, 1992
5	Environmental Law in Japan	Wang Jin	Wuhan University Press, 1994
6	Principles of Environmental Law Enforcement	EPA (US), translated by Wang Xi et al.	Democracy and Construction Press, 1999
7	Ecological Law in Russia	Wang Shuyi	Wuhan University Press, 2011
8	Comparative Environmental Law	Xiao Jianming	China Procuratorial Press, 2001
9	Legal Studies on Environmental Policy in the European Union	Cai Shouqiu	Wuhan University Press, 2002
10	Weaving the Web of Environmental Law: Contributions of the IUCN Environmental Law Program (2012)	Written by Barbara J. Lausche, translated by Wang Xi et al.	Law Press of China, 2012
11	Dictionary of Environmental and Climate Change Law	Edited by Wang Xi and Nicholas Robinson	Edward Elgar Publishing, 2013
12	Environmental Law Stories	Written by Richard J Lazarus, Oliver A Houck, translated by Cao Minde et al.	Press of Renmin University of China, 2013
13	A Comparative Study of Environmental Legal Systems	Peng Feng	Law Press of China, 2013
14	A guide for U.S. NPDES Permit System	EPA (US), translated by Ye Weili et al.	China Environmental Press, 2014
15	US Environmental Law: Training Manual for Judges	Written by Robert Percival, translated by Zhao Huiyu	Law Press of China, 2014
16	Study of U.S. Superfund Law	Jia Feng et al.	China Environmental Press, 2015
17	IUCN Guide to Protected areas Legislation	Written by Barbara J. Lausche, translated by Wang Xi et al.	Law Press of China, 2016

(continued)

Table 2 (continued)

	Book	Author or translator	Publisher and date
18	Reform of U.S. Environmental Law – Regulatory Efficiency and Effective Enforcement	Written by Edward Stewart, translated by Wang Hui	Law Press of China, 2016
19	200 Questions on the U.S. Emission Permit System	Dai Weiping et al.	China Environmental Press, 2016
20	Environmental Encyclopedia of China: Environmental Jurisprudence	Edited by Wang Xi et al.	China Environmental Press, 2017
21	200 Questions on Enforcement of US Environmental Law	Environmental Supervision Bureau of the Ministry of Environment Protection and the Centre of Environmental Engineering Assessment of the Ministry of Environmental Protection	China Environmental Press, 2018
22	Oxford Handbook of Comparative Environmental Law	Edited by Emma Lees and Jorge E. Vinuales, translated by Wang Xi et al.	Oxford University Press (forthcoming, 2023)

tend to be relatively similar. Faced with similar environmental challenges, countries with different political systems will nonetheless apply similar legal tools to address these common challenges.

Second, because political systems are not a decisive factor in environmental protection, it is possible for countries to cooperate legally to ensure environmental protection.

Third, the convergence of laws across the world on the matter of environmental protection provides a strong basis for the development of 'a community with a shared future for mankind', as proposed and promoted by China in recent years.

Although each country has its own unique legal, political, and cultural traditions, the Earth is the common home of mankind. China, as well as other countries in the world, should strive to find a mutually acceptable combination of environmental protection rules and standards and integrate each other's law and policy on environmental protection. They should, jointly, develop adequate standards of environmental protection in order to protect the common home of mankind.

References

Cai S (1999) Globalization and convergence of contemporary environmental law. World Environment, Cambridge

Guangtao W (2014) Regarding Amendments to the Environmental Protection Law of the People's Republic of China (draft), http://www.npc.gov.cn/wxzl/gongbao/2014-06/23/content_1879667.htm
Heyvaert V (2019) Chapter 34 transnational networks. In: Lees E, Vinualies JE (eds) The Oxford handbook of comparative environmental law. Oxford University Press, pp 769–789
Jianming X, Guangming O et al (2004) Comparative environmental law monographs. China Environmental Science Press, Beijing
Jin W (1998) On the convergence of global environmental legislation. Chinese Foreign Law 2:32–42
Jinping X (2018) Speech at the National Conference on Ecological and Environmental Protection, 18 May 2018 (in Chinese), http://www.qstheory.cn/dukan/qs/2019-01/31/c_1124054331.htm
Jintao H (2008) Speech at the Conference for Celebrating the 30 Years Anniversary of the Third Plenary Meeting of the Eleventh Central Committee of the Chinese Communist Party of China, Part I The work of the past five years, 18 Dec. 2008, http://news.xinhuanet.com/english/2007-10/24/content_6938749.htm
Keping Y (2015) On modernising state governance, revised edn. Social Science Literature Press, Princeton
Kiss A, Shelton D (1994) Manual of European environmental law. Cambridge University of Press, Cambridge
Li'an Z (2007) A study on the promotion tournament model of local officials in China. Econ Res J 7:36–50
Mi J (2018) Introduction to comparative jurisprudence. Commercial Press, Beijing
Mingyuan W (2001) The legal system on environmental tort relief. China Legal Publishing House, Beijing
Ning L (2020) Notes on the Amendment to the Criminal Law of the People's Republic of China (11) (draft), http://www.npc.gov.cn/npc/c30834/202012/f16fedb673644b35936580d25287a564.shtml
Nohiko H (1999) Environmental law (trans: Yu Min). Law Press, Beijing
Ruilin J (1981) Several basic institutions on foreign environmental law. Foreign Jurisprud 6:51–58
Tao W (2008) Notes on the (Draft) Law of the People's Republic of China on Environmental Impact Assessment, http://www.npc.gov.cn/zgrdw/npc/zfjc/hpjc/2008-08/12/content_1442080.htm
Xi W (1992) Introduction to American environmental law. Wuhan University Press, Wuhan
Xi W (1994) A preliminary exploration of comparative environmental law in China. Law Rev 4:53–55
Xi W (2012) The theory of the interaction of environmental protection subjects in the rule of law. J Shanghai Jiaotong Univ (Philosophy and Social Sciences Edition) 1:5–22
Xi W (2020) A conceptual model of environmental governance in China: a new paradigm tool. Environ Prot 48:12–18
Xiancong M (2021) Forty years of reform and opening up: a review and prospect of environmental law - speech at the 2019 Zhongda environmental law forum. In: Xi W (ed) Forty years of reform and opening up: a review and prospect of environmental law. Shanghai Sanlian Bookstore, Shanghai, p 134
Xuhui D, Yunxiao Z (eds) (2020) Compilation of Japanese environmental laws and regulations. China Environment Publishing Group, China
Youhai S (2007) A review of China's environmental protection laws and basic experiences in the new era. China's Environ Rule Law 1:19–26
Youhai S (2019) 70 years of environmental protection laws in China: review, reflection and prospects. China Environ Manage 6:5–10

Wang Xi is a professor of law and the director of the Platform for Research on Ecological Civilization and Environmental Rule of Law (PRECERL) at the Kunming University of Science and Technology, China.

Luo Wenjun is an associate professor in the School of Law at Hubei University of Economics, China as well as the vice director of the Hubei Research Centre for Water Law and Policy.

Healthcare Law in Denmark

Katharina Ó Cathaoir

1 Introduction

This chapter explores the theme of the book through examining whether two crises have led to the convergence or divergence of Danish law with international human rights law, in particular, the extent to which the State has respected its obligations to uphold the right to health. The Danish parliament has been careful to comply with its obligations under the European Convention on Human Rights. Yet, overall, one can observe that domestic migration law has moved towards a minimalist view of the State's international obligations. This can still be viewed in terms of convergence, in that the State continues to approximate its laws to international norms. It can furthermore be observed that while Denmark initially diverged from neighbouring countries when adopting strict immigration rules, Sweden and Norway are increasingly inspired by the Danish approach, leading to growing convergence. Beyond this finding, the chapter submits that changes in access to interpretation have resulted in divergence from the right to health as guaranteed by the International Covenant on Economic, Social and Cultural Rights.

The chapter focuses on the COVID-19 pandemic (2020–2023) and the European migration/refugee crisis (2015–2019) as these have coincided with amendments to the Health Act that, it is submitted, go against the Act's ethos. It first explores how entitlements to healthcare under the Act have developed, in particular in light of these crises. While amendments to the Communicable Diseases Act 2020–2021 were a direct response to the pressure facing the healthcare system due to the COVID-19 pandemic, it is less clear whether changes adopted in 2018 targeting non-nationals can be directly attributed to the 2015 migration crisis.

K. Ó Cathaoir (✉)
Faculty of Law, University of Copenhagen, Copenhagen, Denmark
e-mail: Katharina.o.cathaoir@jur.ku.dk

E. Ghio, R. Perlingeiro (eds.), *Are Legal Systems Converging or Diverging?*,
https://doi.org/10.1007/978-3-031-38180-5_11

The COVID-19 pandemic and the 2015–2019 migration crisis are two of the most significant crises that European states have faced this century. Both events have been highly mediatised and politicised but have had very different impacts on Danish healthcare. The unprecedented numbers of Syrians (and other nationalities) travelling to Europe to seek asylum predominantly in 2015 has not had a seismic impact on the healthcare system. In contrast, the COVID-19 pandemic transformed society's daily life and interactions, including, but not limited to, access to healthcare. Interestingly, both crises have coincided with changes to legal entitlements to healthcare under the Danish Health Act (*Sundhedsloven*).

In Denmark, healthcare is tax financed and typically free at the point of purchase. However, since 2018, patients who have been resident in Denmark for over three years must pay for interpretation in healthcare, if necessary. This provision has been criticised by doctors and human rights organisations for undermining safe access to healthcare. Separately, in response to COVID-19, new possibilities to limit patients' rights have been introduced. Under the Health Act, patients normally have rights to timely treatment such as the right to a diagnosis within 30 days. However, due to the pressure on the healthcare system caused by COVID-19, the Minister for Health was empowered to suspend certain entitlements when the health care system is under pressure.

As discussed below, despite the influence of international human rights and patients' rights on Danish law in the 1980s and 1990s, successive Danish governments have approached human rights with a view to fulfilling minimum international obligations, not their full realisation. Yet, the pandemic has driven home the interconnectedness of public health and how, by excluding some groups of people, the majority can be impacted. It remains to be seen whether the pandemic will be a catalyst for greater solidarity or heighten the fear of 'foreign' pathogens.

2 International Patients' Rights and Human Rights

All patients hold a catalogue of rights by virtue of their status as patients and, separately, as human beings. Since the 1970s, patients' rights have been recognised and strengthened under international and national law. The traditional ethos of 'doctor knows best' has been replaced by an emphasis on patients' rights to determine what happens to their bodies.[1] Similarly, although some form of human rights have existed for centuries, since World War II, inalienable rights have been legally codified through successive human rights treaties.

The Declaration on Patients' Rights of the World Health Organization's Regional Office for Europe[2] recognises rights to: (i) information; (ii) consent; (iii)

[1] Sinding Aasen and Hartlev (2022), pp. 53–87.

[2] WHO (Europe), 'A declaration on the promotion of patients' rights in Europe,' Copenhagen, World Health Organization Office for Europe, 1994.

confidentiality and privacy; (iv) care and treatment; and (v) justice and compensation.[3] While the declaration is non-binding, informed consent and the right to information are protected by Article 5 of the binding Biomedicine Convention, which Denmark has ratified.[4] Patients' rights span rights to become a patient, receive treatment and rights after treatment.[5] Meanwhile, many patients' rights are also simultaneously human rights. For example, informed consent is protected by the International Covenant on Civil and Political Rights ('ICCPR'),[6] European Convention on Human Rights ('ECHR')[7] and the EU Charter on Fundamental Rights.[8] Individuals also hold rights to privacy and data protection under European Union (EU) and international law.[9]

The right to health, stemming from the International Covenant on Economic, Social and Cultural Rights (ICESCR),[10] as well as the Convention on the Rights of the Child (CRC),[11] the Convention on the Elimination of Racial Discrimination (CERD)[12] and the Convention on Elimination of Discrimination against women (CEDAW),[13] protects the right to informed consent. Furthermore, the right to health goes beyond negative obligations to non-interference and places positive obligations on the state. This, according to the Committee on Economic, Social and Cultural Rights (CESCR), includes the 'AAAQ principles': availability of health services, accessibility of healthcare, including non-discrimination, physical and economic accessibility, information accessibility; cultural and ethical acceptability, and quality.[14] While this expert Committee's interpretation is non-binding, as it is tasked with supervising the Covenant, its analyses of states' obligations should be taken

[3] Sinding Aasen and Hartlev (2022), pp. 53–87.

[4] Council of Europe, Convention for the Protection of Human Rights and Dignity of the Human Being with regard to the Application of Biology and Medicine: Convention on Human Rights and Biomedicine, Oviedo, 4.IV.1997, ETS no. 164.

[5] Sinding Aasen and Hartlev (2022), pp. 53–87.

[6] Article 7, UN General Assembly, International Covenant on Civil and Political Rights, 16 December 1966.

[7] Article 8, Council of Europe, European Convention for the Protection of Human Rights and Fundamental Freedoms, as amended by Protocols Nos. 11 and 14, 4 November 1950.

[8] Article 3.2(a), European Union: Council of the European Union, Charter of Fundamental Rights of the European Union.

[9] Charter of Fundamental Rights of the European Union, articles 7 and 8; ECHR, article 8; ICCPR, Article 17.

[10] UN General Assembly, International Covenant on Economic, Social and Cultural Rights, 16 December 1966.

[11] UN General Assembly, Convention on the Rights of the Child, 20 November 1989.

[12] UN General Assembly, International Convention on the Elimination of All Forms of Racial Discrimination.

[13] UN General Assembly, Convention on the Elimination of All Forms of Discrimination Against Women, 18 December 1979.

[14] Toebes and Ó Cathaoir (2022), p. 34.

seriously.[15] Meanwhile the right to healthcare is also protected by the European Social Charter.[16]

While international human rights and patients' rights set out fundamental principles and entitlements, as they are phrased broadly, it is largely for the individual state to interpret and apply these in law. Healthcare at European and international level varies among member states, spanning public, private and mixed systems. Furthermore, the rights introduced above are not absolute. Following ICESCR, the right to health can be limited by law and only 'so far as this may be compatible with the nature of these rights and solely for the purpose of the general welfare in a democratic society'.[17] The Committee on Economic, Social and Cultural Rights further states that such restrictions must be strictly necessary.[18] Restrictions should not affect the 'core' of the right.[19] Despite the promise of universality of rights, as Lougarre points out, there is 'ambiguous protection of non-nationals' [. . .] rights' [to health].[20] Still, states' obligations to avoid adopting deliberately retrogressive measures,[21] i.e. backtracking on the protections provided, apply to all people under the state's jurisdiction.

3 Introduction to Denmark as a Welfare State

Denmark is a Northern European state with a population of 5.8 million.[22] In 2021, slightly under 11% of the population were non-citizens.[23] As a welfare state based on a universalist model, social services provided by the state are funded through taxation. This includes most health services, such as access to general practitioners as well as in-patient and outpatient care, which are run by the five regions of Denmark. The regions' obligations are set out in the Danish Health Act and include the obligation to provide free treatment through general practitioners,[24] free advice

[15] Ó Cathaoir (2022).

[16] Articles 11, 13, Council of Europe, European Social Charter of 1961.

[17] Article 4, ICESCR.

[18] Committee on Economic, Social and Cultural Rights (ICESCR Committee), General Comment No. 14: The Right to the Highest Attainable Standard of Health (Art. 12), E/C.12/2000/4, 2000, para. 28.

[19] Toebes and Ó Cathaoir (2022), p. 369.

[20] Lougarre (2020), pp. 252–290.

[21] CESCR General Comment No. 3: The Nature of States Parties' Obligations (Art. 2, Para. 1, of the Covenant), adopted at the Fifth Session of the Committee on Economic, Social and Cultural Rights, on 14 December 1990.

[22] www.dst.dk/en/Statistik/emner/borgere/befolkning/befolkningstal.

[23] Ibid.

[24] § 60, Sundhedsloven, consolidated act of 903 of 26.08.2019.

on contraception,[25] free check-ups for children[26] and hospital treatment.[27] Other healthcare services, like dental care and physiotherapy, are subject to co-pay for most adults.

Following this model, the central criterion for determining access to healthcare is residency, not citizenship.[28] So long as an individual is registered as living in Denmark, they can access treatment, which is not contingent on paying taxes or contributing to a health insurance fund. In contrast, non-residents are only entitled to acute or emergency treatment,[29] and fees can be levied.[30] There are some exceptions for European Union citizens, who may be able to access treatment without payment or receive reimbursement following EU social security and free movement law.[31] Asylum seekers are not considered residents and are therefore only entitled to 'necessary treatment', which is paid for by the Danish immigration office.[32]

As detailed further below, these variations in entitlements within the Danish welfare state have been framed as a shift from 'universalism' to 'welfare chauvinism',[33] whereby ethnic Danes are perceived as entitled to benefit from the welfare state, whereas outsiders, particularly third country nationals, are viewed as 'undeserving' of the state's benefits. Notably, the migration crisis and COVID-19 have both been framed as threats to the welfare state, although this narrative has also been challenged.[34] By securitising these two tragedies, far-reaching restrictions on rights and entitlements can be justified.[35] Another perspective is that, far from unexpected crises, the migration crisis and COVID-19 were foreseeable events spurred by political and human actions, i.e. the EU's failure to create a sustainable legal framework in the field of asylum, and in relation to COVID-19, failure to adequately prepare and react to a long warned pandemic.[36] Scipioni has held that the refugee crisis can be attributed to 'weak monitoring, lack of policy harmonization, low solidarity, and absence of central institutions'.[37] The same factors have likely contributed to the rapid spread of COVID-19.

The right to health is not constitutionally enshrined in Denmark and parliament can thereby alter health entitlements by a parliamentary majority. While this allows for flexibility in the face of a healthcare crisis like COVID-19, it also allows politics

[25] § 62(1) Sundhedsloven.

[26] § 63(1) Sundhedsloven.

[27] § 81(1) Sundhedsloven.

[28] § 7(1) Sundhedsloven.

[29] § 80(1) Sundhedsloven.

[30] § 81(2) Sundhedsloven.

[31] § 7(3) Sundhedsloven.

[32] § 42 a, Udlændingeloven, consolidated act no. 1910 of 26.09.2021.

[33] Vitus and Jarlby (2021).

[34] Bak Jørgensen (2020), p. 72.

[35] Ibid, p. 73.

[36] Singh et al. (2021).

[37] Scipioni (2018).

to filter into healthcare entitlements. Thus, in the case of non-citizens who lack political power, it can mean that permanent reductions in entitlements are adopted, contrary to the interests of public health and against the advice of human rights bodies.

3.1 The Danish Health Act

The aims of the Health Act are listed in section 2 of the Act and include the objectives 'to ensure respect for the individual, their integrity and self-determination' and, inter alia, treatment of high quality, easy access to information, choice and short wait times for treatment.[38] The Health Act entered into force in 2007, replacing and consolidating several laws that had previously regulated access to healthcare and patients' rights.

The preparatory works of the 2007 Health Act and the repealed Patient Rights Act (which entered into force 1998) draw upon Denmark's international obligations under the UN Covenant on Civil and Political Rights, the UN Convention on Children's Rights, and the Council of Europe Biomedicine Convention.[39] While Denmark has ratified these conventions, as well as the ICESCR, only the ECHR has been incorporated into domestic law. As the Danish legal system is a dualist model, the state is bound by the treaties it has ratified, but a Danish court will not strike down a law solely based on non-compliance with international treaties. As courts will usually not intervene in such cases, this means that Danish compliance with treaty obligations is largely dealt with as a political question.

Alongside the Health Act, the Communicable Disease Act (*Epidemiloven*) provides for the measures that can be adopted to fight communicable diseases. At the start of the pandemic, the Communicable Disease Act of 1979 was in force. It quickly became clear that the Act did not contain the legal bases to allow the government to adopt far-reaching restrictions and therefore, it was amended twice during 2020, before being repealed and replaced with a new 2021 Communicable Diseases Act. The speed with which the amendments have been adopted has been criticised as being, inter alia, contrary to the principles of foreseeability and transparency.[40]

In terms of convergence, while Denmark's international obligations did not provide a basis for the 2021 Act as was the case with the 1998 Patients' Rights Act, such considerations were also not completely absent from the parliamentary discussions. For instance, when presenting the 2021 Bill, the Ministry of Health referred several times to the World Health Organization (WHO) to support the case

---

[38] § 2 Sundhedsloven.

[39] See, 1997–1998, 2. samling - L 15, Forslag til lov om patienters retsstilling; L 74, Forslag til Sundhedsloven. See further, Mourby et al. (2021).

[40] Ó Cathaoir et al. (2021), pp. 417–444.

for adopting the proposed measures. For example, it noted that WHO (as well as the national health authority, *Sundhedsstyrelsen*), supported use of facemasks.[41] The International Health Regulations (the WHO's treaty on the spread of infectious diseases) is also briefly mentioned.[42] Furthermore, the government provided an assessment of the bill's compliance with the ECHR. Regrettably, again in contrast to the Health Act, other international conventions to which Denmark is a party are not included in this assessment. Only the bill's compliance with the following rights was evaluated: Article 11 (freedom of assembly), Article 5 (liberty), Article 8 (private life), Article 9 (religion), Article 2 of the Fourth Additional Protocol to the ECHR (freedom of movement) and Article 1 of the First Additional Protocol (property).[43] It is noted that several safeguards are included in the legislation to pursue compliance with these obligations, such as, that restrictions on liberty must be tried before a court, that restrictions must suitable, necessary and in place for as short as possible. However, important questions, like risk of discrimination or differential impact on certain groups are not analysed. In summary, human rights, such as the right to health, are not viewed as a basis for adopting restrictions but instead civil and political rights are identified as obstacles to adopting restrictions with which the legislature must comply. There is thereby an attempt to converge with ECHR rights, though international rights are neglected.

3.2 *Rights Under the Health Act*

While the Health Act is not explicitly a patients' rights act, it does enshrine certain rights and entitlements for patients. As noted above, these can be amended by the parliament, as the right to health is not constitutionally protected. With the exception of abortion and sterilisation,[44] patient entitlements are generally framed as obligations on the regions or on healthcare professionals. Furthermore, patients do not have an absolute right to treatment, as this is primarily a medical determination.[45] Unlike Norway,[46] for example, patients in Denmark do not have a right to a second opinion if a doctor determines that they are ineligible for/do not need treatment.

Patients aged over 15 years must give informed consent before treatment can be commenced, although there are exceptions, such as emergencies, or where a patient lacks capacity because of age or disability.[47] Patients also have rights to information about their health, as well as the proposed treatment, including expected benefits and

[41] Para 2.4.10.2.

[42] Lovforslag nr. L 134 Folketinget 2020-21, section 2.5.1.

[43] Ibid, section 7.2.

[44] See chapter VII and VIII, Sundhedsloven.

[45] See Hartlev et al. (2022), Chapter 12.

[46] Lov om pasient- og brukerrettigheter, LOV-1999-07-02-63, § 2-3.

[47] § 15 – 20, Sundhedsloven.

side effects. The right to confidentiality means that patients must normally also give consent to information regarding their health or other confidential matters being shared, though as with informed consent, there are exceptions.[48] As seen above, these rights and obligations converge with those found in international human rights and biomedicine law.

Patients also have more specific entitlements under the Health Act. This includes, inter alia, access to help from a midwife if homebirth is chosen[49] and the right to certain cancer screenings.[50] Furthermore, a patient referred to a hospital can choose by which hospital they wish to be seen,[51] subject to exceptions like limited capacity.[52] A patient can also choose to be diagnosed or treated in a private hospital if the regional council, due to capacity issues, cannot diagnose or treat the patient within 1 month of referral.[53] Furthermore, for patients suffering from a life threatening illness, such as cancer, the Health Authority can set maximum waiting times for treatment. If the region cannot offer timely treatment, the patient must be offered treatment at a different region, private hospital or abroad.[54] Finally, the region is required to inform the patient, inter alia, of when treatment will take place and of the above rights if relevant, at the latest 8 days after referral.[55] Furthermore, patients can, subject to certain conditions, claim compensation through a no fault system if they are injured during treatment.[56] This includes injury due to delay in treatment.[57] Normally delays in treatment due to resource shortages cannot be compensated,[58] though the legislature recently amended the law on compensation to allow for compensation of injuries caused by delayed cancer screenings.[59]

3.3 Limitations on Patients' Rights Under the Communicable Diseases Act

The 1979 Act allowed for patients' physical integrity and confidentiality to be limited in certain circumstances. These powers were expanded in response to the

---

[48] § 40-48, Sundhedsloven.

[49] § 83, Sundhedsloven.

[50] § 85, § 85a, § 85b, Sundhedsloven.

[51] § 86, Sundhedsloven.

[52] § 86(2),(3), Sundhedsloven.

[53] § 87, Sundhedsloven.

[54] § 88, Sundhedsloven.

[55] § 90, Sundhedsloven.

[56] Lov om klage- og erstatningsadgang inden for sundhedsvæsenet (KEL), no. 995 of 14.06.2018.

[57] Patienterstatning, complaint no. 195074, 08-10-2019, https://pebl.dk/da/afgoerelser/afgjorte-behandlingsskader/195074.

[58] U 2018.3572 H.

[59] § 20(2), KEL.

COVID-19 crisis through 2020 revisions of the Communicable Diseases Act and the adoption of the current 2021 Act, which introduces further possibilities to limit certain patient rights if required due to the spread of a communicable disease.

Following the 1979 Act, the Communicable Diseases Commission could order that an individual infected, or presumed to be infected, with a generally dangerous disease be examined by a doctor, admitted to hospital, enter isolation or, if isolation proved insufficient, be treated without consent.[60] If the individual refused to comply with the relevant order, the police could assist through use of force. It was also possible for the Minister of the Interior, upon recommendation from the Health Authority, to order forced vaccination within a specific area or group of people to prevent the spread of a generally dangerous disease.[61]

The 2021 Act altered the manner in which such powers can be applied. While the Communicable Disease Commission is retained, it is now an advisory body instead of a decision maker.[62] The 2021 Act gives the Patient Safety Authority the power to order a person to be examined by a healthcare professional,[63] to be admitted to hospital,[64] to be placed in isolation at home or in a suitable facility[65] or to be treated by a healthcare professional.[66] If an individual does not comply with these orders the police shall, using the necessary force, provide assistance.[67] Prior to such a decision being adopted, the person must be encouraged to voluntarily comply with the order.[68] The person must be suffering from or suspected to suffer from a generally dangerous or societally critical disease. Bødker Madsen has criticised the latter formulation as providing an insufficiently clear legal basis given that 'presumed' infected is not defined.[69]

The law stipulates that any measure must be necessary, in place as short as possible and proportionate to the aim. The least restrictive measure must be applied if sufficient to achieve the purpose. Measures must be suspended if no longer necessary.[70] The Patient Safety Authority must review such measures on day 3, 10, 20 and 30 to ensure the conditions are still met.[71] Furthermore, new to the act is an extended protection of the right to liberty in case of deprivation of liberty, which requires the Patient Safety Authority to bring the decision before a court

[60] § 5-7, Epidemiloven no. 114 of 21.03.1979.
[61] § 9, Epidemiloven 1979.
[62] § 7-8, § 10, Epidemiloven no. 285 of 27.02.2021.
[63] § 13, Epidemiloven 2021.
[64] § 14, Epidemiloven 2021.
[65] § 15-17, Epidemiloven 2021.
[66] § 18, Epidemiloven 2021.
[67] § 22(1), Epidemiloven 2021.
[68] § 12(2), Epidemiloven 2021.
[69] Bødker Madsen (2021), p. 207.
[70] § 12(3), Epidemiloven 2021.
[71] § 12(4), Epidemiloven 2021.

within 5 days.[72] These sections converge with international standards regarding protection from, inter alia, deprivation of liberty and the principle of proportionality.

Furthermore, the 2021 Act allows the Minister for Health to adopt secondary legislation allowing for deviation from health entitlements if necessary due to a 'societally critical disease' for ensuring capacity to treat and care for persons with acute or critical treatment needs, provided the obligations and entitlements can be seen as of minor importance in relation to the need to create capacity.[73] As a starting point, the rules can only last for four weeks but they may be extended in exceptional situations.[74] The Minister has used this power several times since the beginning of the pandemic. Already from 18 March 2020, the regional council could prioritise capacity to treat acute patients or patients with a life-threatening illness, as well as, to prioritise tasks directly connected therewith, such as logistical and hygiene measures. It was possible to postpone a range of rights and obligations, such as children's entitlement to preventative health examinations and the right to midwife help during home birth.[75] Originally, it was not possible to appeal such decisions, [76] although this restriction was removed on 5 April 2020.[77]

The secondary legislation in place in January 2022 allowed a Regional Council to prioritise capacity for, inter alia, diagnosing and treating patients with acute and life-threatening illnesses, including patients with COVID-19 who need hospital treatment, including intensive care.[78] Following this power, the regional council could postpose planned or future examinations, treatments or appointments. This includes the time limits and obligations set under the Health Act, such as the right to freely choose a hospital, the right to a timely diagnosis and the right to extended hospital choice.[79] The regional council may also deviate from its information obligations under the Health Act, i.e. regarding date and time of treatment.[80] Certain safeguards are provided, including that the regional council must continuously evaluate the necessity of the suspension of the guarantees and whether the requirements for doing so continue to be present. The restrictions must be repealed as soon as the criteria are no longer present.[81] The health authority guidelines on postponing treatment stipulate that patients with illnesses that are not acute or life threatening, or where delayed

---

[72] § 65(1), Epidemiloven 2021.

[73] §55(1), (2) Epidemiloven 2021.

[74] §54, Epidemiloven 2021.

[75] § 2(2), Bekendtgørelse om begrænsning af rettigheder på sundheds- og ældreområdet i forbindelse med håndtering af Coronavirussygdom 2019 (COVID-19) no. 219 of 17.03.2020.

[76] § 13, no. 219 of 17.03.2020.

[77] Bekendtgørelse om begrænsning af rettigheder på sundheds- og ældreområdet i forbindelse med håndtering af Coronavirussygdom 2019 (COVID-19) no. 364 of 04.04.2020.

[78] § 2(1),(1), Begrænsning af rettigheder på sundhedsområdet i forbindelse med håndtering af covid-19, no. 2574 of 12.22.2021.

[79] § 2(2), no. 2574 of 12.22.2021.

[80] § 2(3), no. 2574 of 12.22.2021.

[81] § 2(6) no. 2574 of 12.22.2021.

treatment will not result in a risk of loss of functionality and where it is professionally responsible to delay treatment, may have their treatment delayed.[82] A concrete clinical assessment must always be carried out as to whether the examination or treatment can be postponed, taking into account the seriousness and severity of the illness, as well as the risk of increased medicine use and the risk of the condition becoming chronic, as well as the extent to which quality of life and functionality will be affected.[83]

It is expected that such regulations have resulted in delays in patients receiving necessary treatment in 2020 and 2021. For example, one complaint to the Authority for Patient Complaints (a body that can criticise a hospital or clinic but does not provide compensation), describes how a 21-year-old patient presented at an accident and emergency department. She had pains in her stomach, breasts and body, as well as diarrhoea and vomiting. The physicians determined that she probably had a cold and she was told to isolate and contact her general practitioner or an out of hours doctor if she deteriorated. In its decision, the Authority noted that the treatment took place during the pandemic where the healthcare system was under great pressure and that this should be taken into account in its decision. The Authority noted that at this point of the pandemic, patients who were not acutely or life threateningly ill should be sent home. Based on this, the Authority declined to criticise the department for its failure to diagnose that the patient was actually suffering from an ectopic pregnancy.[84] While such a decision may have been understandable at the start of the pandemic, when there was greater panic and pressure, it seems that this should have been emphasised in the decision, given that such oversights seem less defensible the longer the pandemic continues.

Beyond hospital treatment, during the pandemic, the Danish Health Authority (*Sundhedsstyrelsen*) issued guidelines regarding COVID-19. It recommended that patients with respiratory symptoms, such as coughing and fever, be treated over the telephone or through video consultation as far as possible. In one instance, a patient made a complaint to the Authority for Patient Complaints as he had not received a physical consultation. The Authority found that as the patient's symptoms (a long-lasting cough) were mild, the clinic had not acted contrary to the normally recognised standard of treatment.[85]

In summary, due to the COVID-19 pandemic, the power to limit patients' rights to access healthcare has been expanded. As under the 1979 Act, patients' rights to informed consent and bodily integrity can be limited if a patient refuses to be tested or isolate and this intervention is deemed necessary. Furthermore, patients' access to

---

[82] Sundhedsstyrelsen (2021) Rammer for udskydelse af sygehusaktivitet grundet COVID-19, 12.01.2021, p. 2.

[83] Ibid.

[84] Styrelsen for Patientklager, case no. 21SFP60, 19 April 2021, https://stpk.dk/afgorelser-og-domme/afgorelser-fra-styrelsen-for-patientklager/21sfp60/.

[85] Styrelsen for Patientklager, case no. 21SFP73, 21 May 2021, https://stpk.dk/afgorelser-og-domme/afgorelser-fra-styrelsen-for-patientklager/21sfp73/.

treatment can be limited based on medical need. The law does not permit discriminatory determinations, based on age, race or ethnicity. That is not to say however, that the law has not resulted in harm to patients' health, as operations and examinations have been cancelled or postponed. Overall, it does not seem that the parliament has tried to diverge from international rules. In Sect. 5, an assessment will be made as to whether the limitations identified in this chapter are compatible with the right to health.

4 The Migration Crisis (2015–2019)

4.1 The Rights of Migrants and Asylum Seekers in Denmark

Asylum and immigration law is one of the most politically charged areas of Danish law.[86] While in the 1980s, Danish immigration and asylum law was liberal despite an 'asylum crisis', Danish politicians now compete to promote a hard line. Denmark has thus been described as 'Hungary light'[87] and earned the title of the Hungary of Northern Europe.[88] The main piece of legislation, the Aliens Act, is frequently amended, skyrocketing to 40 times between 2016 and 2018.[89] Thus, as with COVID-19 legislation, the pace at which legislation in this area is amended and updated threatens the principles of legal foreseeability and rule of law.

Once a liberal frontrunner,[90] Danish politicians now express a desire to 'approximate Danish [migration] legislation with a minimum interpretation of international law'.[91] The same approach could be seen in relation to the Communicable Diseases Act, where, as noted above, political focus appears to be on avoiding conflict with the ECHR, not fulfilling the state's obligations under human rights treaties. As with the Health Act, references to UN and European rights law are found in the preparatory works to the original 1983 Aliens Act.[92] Yet in recent years, human rights are viewed as barriers to political aims, not obligations to ensure evolving protections over time. Gammeltoft-Hansen and Scott Ford furthermore note that Denmark has been subject to 89 immigration-related complaints sent to UN human rights treaty bodies; In 42 of which, a committee found a violation.[93] The majority of these cases are from 2015 to 2018.

[86] Gammeltoft-Hansen and Scott Ford (2022).
[87] Bak Jørgensen (2020), p. 71.
[88] Kjærum (2018). Hungary has a reputation for a hard line against immigrants.
[89] Gammeltoft-Hansen and Scott Ford (2022).
[90] Ibid.
[91] Ibid.
[92] Ibid.
[93] Ibid.

Gammeltoft-Hansen and Madsen posit that the tide in Danish asylum and immigration law turned in 2001 when a new right wing government took power supported by the nationalist and anti-immigration Danish People's Party.[94] While the hardest-line Scandinavian country, Denmark, has since inspired its neighbours, Sweden and Norway, to pursue deterrence policies in migration.[95] Gammeltoft-Hansen concludes that such policies have at least been partially successful, leading to a fall in asylum claims.[96] In 2015, the number of asylum applications peaked in Denmark, when over 21,000 applied. In 2020, only 1515 people applied, likely due to COVID-19 border restrictions.[97]

Although Denmark was relatively isolated from the 2015 migration crisis, its location between Sweden and Germany (two of the EU countries that accepted the most asylum seekers) left it vulnerable to secondary migration.[98] Denmark, like other states, introduced temporary border controls under the Schengen Agreement in 2016 in response to the increase in migration. Similarly, one of Denmark's first responses to the COVID-19 pandemic was to unilaterally reintroduce border controls and drastically curtail entry. Although Danish citizens and residents were not subject to these provisions, until June 2020, their families and loved ones were not able to enter the country.[99]

As noted above, Denmark has long pursued 'welfare dualism,' whereby welfare entitlements are adjusted based on years of residence.[100] Hagelund details how Denmark reduced social benefits available to refugees in 2015, although many of the changes preceded the crisis, as Denmark already took a hard line on immigration.[101] Crucially, social welfare for immigrants was cut by up to 50% with the intention to target asylum seekers and refugees.[102] In political documents, the necessity of keeping refugee numbers low is tied to the prospects of successful integration[103]—suggesting that the more diversity, the less successful amalgamation will be. This frames refugees and other outsiders as threats to the welfare state, and therefore benefits to them must be limited to ensure the state's survival and its ability to provide for its 'own' people.[104] Policies thereby focus on preservation of the Danish collective, not international solidarity.[105] Danish measures in response to the migration crisis can be seen to converge with the minimum requirements of human

[94] Ibid.

[95] Gammeltoft-Hansen (2017).

[96] Ibid.

[97] Available at: www.dst.dk/da/Statistik/nyheder-analyser-publ/nyt/NytHtml?cid=32660.

[98] Gammeltoft-Hansen (2017).

[99] Hagelund (2020).

[100] Ibid.

[101] Ibid.

[102] Hernes (2018).

[103] Hagelund (2020).

[104] Abdelhady et al. (2020), p. 89.

[105] Hagelund (2020).

rights law. While they once diverged from neighbouring countries, they now serve as inspiration to these states.

4.2 The Entitlement to Interpretation in Healthcare

In 2018, the Danish government introduced an amendment to the Health Act to allow for the levying of fees for interpretation in healthcare in hospitals and private practice. The fees apply to those who have resided in Denmark for over three years. The basis for introducing this requirement was the claim that foreigners should have the necessary language abilities after three years and that it is unreasonable to require the state to pay if they do not.[106] The government highlighted that the amendment did not remove the right to interpretation but instead the service is no longer free, subject to exceptions.[107] It was claimed that the cost of interpretation in the healthcare sector was 170 million Danish crowns in 2017 (approximately € 22 million), which was determined to be unreasonably high.[108] According to the government, the basis for introducing the rule is to encourage foreigners to learn Danish, which will improve their integration, thereby benefitting the individual and society.[109] The government declined to provide evidence for this claim.[110]

Although the 2018 amendment came during the refugee/migration crisis, the crisis is not mentioned in the preparatory works to the bill. Notably, in 2011, a government led by a centre-right party had introduced a requirement to pay for interpretation,[111] only for the law to be repealed months later when a Social Democrat government came to power.[112] When introducing the bill to repeal payment for interpretation in December 2011, the government stated that while foreigners should still be given incentives to learn Danish, interpretation in healthcare should not be the driving force.[113] The Regions opposed the 2018 amendment, as the previous requirement to pay for interpretation had been administratively costly and created inequality.[114]

[106] Sundheds- og Ældreudvalget 2017-18 L 213 endeligt svar på spørgsmål 10, 9 May 2018, https://www.ft.dk/samling/20171/lovforslag/l213/spm/10/svar/1487528/1891700.pdf.

[107] Sundheds- og Ældreudvalget 2018-19, SUU Alm.del - endeligt svar på spørgsmål 127, https://www.ft.dk/samling/20181/almdel/suu/spm/127/svar/1538739/1984091.pdf.

[108] Ibid.

[109] Ibid.

[110] Sundheds- og Ældreudvalget 2017-18 L 213 endeligt svar på spørgsmål 11.

[111] Bekendtgørelse om tolkebistand efter sundhedsloven no. 446 of 12.05.2011.

[112] Bekendtgørelse om tolkebistand efter sundhedsloven no. 1413 of 28.12.2011.

[113] LFB 2011-12-13 nr 37 Ændring af sundhedsloven (Ophævelse af regler om egenbetaling for behandling med kunstig befrugtning, refertilisation og sterilisation i det offentlige sundhedsvæsen og tolkebistand m.v.).

[114] Sundheds- og Ældreudvalget 2017-18 L 213 endeligt svar på spørgsmål 37.

The Social Democrats regained control of the Danish Parliament in 2019 but have allowed the measure to remain. Reasons given for the Social Democrats' changed stance towards immigrants include a desire to win back voters from the far-right Danish People's Party, a return to the Party's pre-1980s restrictive attitude to immigration and a desire to protect the welfare state.[115] The 2015 crisis is also frequently referred to in the Social Democrats' 2018 immigration policy. For example, referring to the 2018 asylum system, the plan declares 'we are failing our own unique model of society if Denmark does not regain control'.[116] It furthermore notes that as of 2018, never have so many people been in flight and that 85 % of such people come from developing countries.[117] This is an example of reframing international crises as a domestic threat, given that only 2600 people applied for asylum in Denmark in 2018.[118] The perceived crisis appears to have influenced the party's approach to immigration, integration and as a corollary interpretation in healthcare.

Secondary legislation establishes that patients have a right to interpretation when a doctor determines that an interpreter is necessary for the treatment.[119] The patient will be charged for this service where they have been resident in Denmark for more than three years, subject to exceptions.[120] The charges that can be levelled are: outpatient video/online interpretation: 191 DKK (approximately €25), in person, 334 DKK (approximately €45); inpatient interpretation video/telephone or in person 957 DKK (approximately €130) and 1675 DKK (approximately €225), respectively.[121] Due to lobbying by non-governmental organisations ('NGOs'), fees are not charged for patients who due to physical or mental capacity have permanently or temporarily lost the ability to acquire or use acquired Danish skills. This can include refugees suffering from post-traumatic stress disorder ('PTSD').[122] Furthermore, fees are not charged for children or parents in connection with their children's health. No charges are levied on the German-speaking minority in Denmark,[123] as well as in relation to Faroese and Greenlandic languages.[124] In the preparatory works to the bill, the Ministry indicates that these exceptions mean that the amendment complies with the Convention on the Rights of the Child and the Convention on the Rights of Persons with Disabilities, thus evidencing an attempt to approximate with international standards.[125]

---

115 Nedergaard (2018).

116 Socialdemokratiet (2018), p. 7.

117 Socialdemokratiet (2018), p. 10.

118 www.dst.dk/en/Statistik/emner/borgere/befolkning/indvandrere-og-efterkommere.

119 § 1, Bekendtgørelse om tolkebistand efter sundhedsloven, no. 855 of 23.06.2018.

120 §2(1) no. 855 of 23.06.2018.

121 § 2(2) no. 855 of 23.06.2018.

122 Oasis (2019).

123 § 2(3(4) no. 855 of 23.06.2018.

124 § 2(4) no. 855 of 23.06.2018.

125 Section 3, LFF 2018-03-23 no. 213 Ændring af sundhedsloven.

Furthermore, children under 18 may only be used as interpreters in acute and life threatening cases, while children aged 15 or over may act as interpreters in easy and unproblematic cases.[126] In a complaint to the Authority for Patient Complaints, a clinic was criticised for prohibiting patients from bringing their own interpreter.[127] In another instance, an interpreter was automatically ordered for a patient referred for the first time to a hospital and this was found to be contrary to the Health Act, as a doctor had not assessed the need for an interpreter.[128] These cases thereby demonstrate that the rules are being incorrectly applied, at least in some cases. There may also been underreporting, as it is difficult for people who do not understand Danish to lodge a complaint.

The provision continues to be criticised. In 2019, the Danish Institute for Human Rights and the Danish Doctor's Association released a report on the impact of the law. It is based on a survey of 623 doctors who have contact with a patient at least once a week who requires the use of an interpreter. The majority of respondents claimed that the co-pay negatively affected the quality of the appointment with the patient due to lack of or poor interpretation. This affected the quality of the treatment, led to increased risk of mistakes and risk of incorrect or mistake-laden diagnoses or treatment.[129] The majority of doctors (53%) had experienced that patients, due to the co-pay, did not attend a consultation or treatment.[130] Doctors furthermore felt pressured to accept family members as interpreters where a patient lacked the resources to pay for a professional interpreter.[131] As a result, relatives were used more frequently than when interpretation was paid for by the Regions. There are risks associated with use of family members as interpreters, such as that the relative will miscommunicate or communicate in a manner that that suits their interests or wishes, e.g. between couples in cases of pregnancy or contraception.[132] It may thereby undermine patient rights, like confidentiality and informed consent. Furthermore, doctors report that the new charges increase administrative burdens, the rules are difficult to work with and the consultation takes longer.[133] Another report claimed that administration of the rules had already after six months cost a region 1.4 million DKK.[134]

When questioned before a parliamentary hearing, the Minister for Health argued, in response to the report, that it was not up to the patient to decide whether they could

[126] § 4(2) no. 855 of 23.06.2018.

[127] Styrelsen for Patientklager (2019) Reglerne Om Gebyr For Tolkebistand Har Ikke Ændret På Muligheden For At Medbringe Egen Tolk, 20 October 2019.

[128] Styrelsen for Patientklager (2019) Det er en betingelse for opkrævning af gebyr for tolkebistand, at tolken er rekvireret efter et lægeligt skøn, case no. 19SFP10, 10 September 2019.

[129] Institut for Menneskerettigheder (2019), p. 10.

[130] Ibid, p. 15.

[131] Ibid, p. 17.

[132] Ibid, p. 21.

[133] Ibid, p. 25.

[134] Oasis (2019).

afford an interpreter, but instead, up to the doctor. Previously, when asked about responsibility regarding mistakes where a patient rejects interpretation as they cannot afford it, the Minister for Health claimed that the patient would not be able to refuse interpretation based on economic considerations.[135] Although it is the responsibility of the doctor to determine whether interpretation is needed,[136] following the principle of informed consent (see Sect. 2), a patient may refuse treatment for any reason, including if they do not have finances to pay for an interpreter, provided they have capacity. The fact that a patient is sent a bill for the interpretation after treatment does not resolve this concern. Fundamentally, the doctor must balance their obligations to provide medical assistance[137] with the obligation to ensure that a valid consent has been given, i.e. that the patient understands to what they were consenting, as well as the benefits and risks of the treatment. Furthermore, if a doctor insists on the use of an interpreter for which the patient must pay, this can affect the patient-doctor relationship.[138]

In terms of the convergence/divergence dichotomy, the obligation to pay for interpretation varies in the EU.[139] The government referenced Germany and the Netherlands in support of their proposal, where interpretation is only free for a limited period.[140] Yet, this selection of comparators is not robust, given that the German and Dutch healthcare systems are insurance based and vastly different to the Danish system. The government did not note that Denmark's neighbours, Sweden, Norway and Finland, do not require payment to access an interpreter in healthcare. In contrast to Denmark, Swedish patients can be considered to have a right to an interpreter.[141] The rules thereby diverge from comparable countries.

Furthermore, the government's justification of the measure by reference to integration seems at odds with the government's approach that integration should be abandoned and that refugees can be sent home at any point.[142] This paradigm shift, it has been argued, has been justified with reference to the refugee crisis, although one can question whether the latter truly ever has been a crisis in Denmark.[143] As claimed, 'temporariness is the central concern in the policy framework' and integration is 'basically not possible'.[144] While integration is difficult for refugees, the requirement is consistent with other immigration laws that do place, among other things, a strong emphasis on the requirement to learn the Danish

[135] Sundheds- og Ældreudvalget 2017-18 SUU Alm.del endeligt svar på spørgsmål 463.
[136] § 4 no. 855 of 23.06.2018.
[137] § 17, Autorisationsloven, no. 731 of 8.07.2019.
[138] Institut for Menneskerettigheder (2019), p. 29.
[139] Sundheds- og Ældreudvalget 2017-18 SUU Alm.del endeligt svar på spørgsmål 463.
[140] Sundheds- og Ældreudvalget 2019-20 SUU Alm.del - endeligt svar på spørgsmål 1275.
[141] Skåne (2019).
[142] Bak Jørgensen (2020), p. 68.
[143] Ibid.
[144] Ibid, p. 75.

language, which is necessary to gain permanent residence[145] and family reunification,[146] and of benefit when applying for resettlement as a refugee.[147] However, it can be asked whether it is appropriate to frame healthcare in terms of integration, as although a person may communicate well in a foreign language, in high stress situations, like illness, communicating in one's mother tongue may be more appropriate.[148] It should be noted that interpretation in relation to other public services remains free.

Finally, the issue of language and, in tandem ethnicity, played a part in the realisation of the right to health during the COVID-19 pandemic. From March 2020, the government held regular press conferences in Danish, with sign language interpretation only. Important recommendations and changes to the law were communicated during such briefings. The Danish Institute for Human Rights therefore called on the government to translate the briefings into different languages.[149] Information from the health authorities was also initially only available in Danish.[150] In response, civil society and multilingual Danes filled the gap in some instances.[151] However, as the crisis deepened, it became obvious that excluding minority groups is not in the interests of the collective society. More efforts were made to make information available in multiple languages based on public health considerations.[152] Still, the increased focus on minorities also came in the form of harassment, threats and blame for the virus.[153]

5 Do the Changes to the Health Act Comply with the Right to Health?

Denmark has ratified the ICESCR, as well as the CEDAW, CERD and CRC, and thereby is bound to respect, protect, and fulfil, inter alia, the right to health. Denmark has not ratified the Convention on the Protection of the Rights of All Migrant Workers and Members of their Families, which also recognises a right to medical care. This section argues that the introduction of charges for interpretation is a violation of the State's obligations under the right to health, while the limitations

[145] § 11(3)(7), Udlændingelov.

[146] Bekendtgørelse om danskprøve på A1-niveau og danskprøve på A2-niveau for familiesammenførte udlændinge, no 902 of 06.06.2020.

[147] § 8(4) Udlændingeloven.

[148] Patientsikkerhed (2019).

[149] Vikkelsø Slot and Krusaa (2020).

[150] Brønholt et al. (2021).

[151] Karrebæk and Sørensen (2020).

[152] Available at: https://ec.europa.eu/migrant-integration/news/denmark-covid-19-information-increasingly-accessible-minority-groups-and-non-danish-speakers_en.

[153] Steffensen and Sinja Laursen (2020).

on treatment guarantees appear to comply with state duties. Therefore, there is both convergence and divergence with international rules.

Turning firstly to the issue of interpretation in healthcare, the international and European human rights treaties negotiated in the latter half of the twentieth century were not negotiated with the purpose of endowing migrants with a wide class of human rights. Likewise, the right to health under European law originally allowed states to restrict access to healthcare benefits to non-nationals. Yet, it is increasingly clear that states hold obligations for the health of non-nationals on their territory. Since the 1980s, the European Court of Human Rights has dealt with an increasing body of migration cases.[154] Similarly, the European Social Committee has held that all individuals have a right to healthcare regardless of nationality.[155] International human rights bodies have also analysed non-nationals' rights to access to healthcare in a growing body of cases.[156]

Furthermore, as outlined above, General Comment No. 14 calls on states to make healthcare available, accessible, adequate and of good quality. While healthcare should be economically accessible, this does not mean free in all cases. Furthermore, healthcare should be timely, but the Committee has not prescribed in detail time limits and entitlements. This would be unwise given that conditions vary among states and that states have varied resources. Furthermore, the state can limit the right to health if necessary, such as, in a time of crisis like COVID-19.

Two questions arise in the literature on access to interpretation in healthcare, firstly, whether there is a right to interpretation and secondly, whether it must be provided free of charge. The right to medical interpretation is not formally guaranteed under the right to health for all persons.[157] However, persons with disabilities should be provided with interpreters following the Convention on the Rights of Persons with Disabilities. Phelan also notes that the WHO patients' rights declaration and the Council of Europe Health Committee of the Committee of Ministers urge that medical interpreters should be made available, although neither recommendation is binding.[158] Therefore, the fact that Denmark recognises a right to interpretation, even though this requires payment for some non-Danish speakers, goes beyond the basic requirements of international human rights law. The law also allows for exceptions for those who cannot speak Danish due to disability or age.

---

[154] Gammeltoft-Hansen and Rask Madsen (2021).

[155] Defence for Children International (DCI) v. Belgium, Complaint No. 69/2011, decision on the merits of 23 October 2012, para. 101–102; International Federation of Human Rights Leagues (FIDH) v. France, Complaint No.14/2003, 8 December 2004, para 31.

[156] For example, Committee on the Rights of the Child, Views adopted by the Committee under the Optional Protocol to the Convention on the Rights of the Child on a communications procedure concerning communication No. 56/2018, CRC/C/85/D/56/2018 30 October 2020; Committee on the Rights of the Child, Views adopted by the Committee under article 10 of the Optional Protocol, concerning communication No. 22/2017, CRC/C/81/D/22/2017, 9 July 2019.

[157] Dalton-Oates (2017), pp. 228–238.

[158] Phelan (2012), pp. 333–353.

However, the exceptions are limited. It is not possible to dispense of payment due to, for example, inability to pay due to poverty or frequent doctors' visits due to a chronic illness, which may undermine the right to health generally and the rights of persons with disabilities. For example, a person's disability may not prevent them from learning Danish but may cause frequent visits to the healthcare system, which are not exempted from payment for interpretation. Another situation that was brought up in the parliamentary debates but that has not been addressed, is the position of an individual who is or has been abused by their partner/a family member.[159] The victim could be put at risk if they attend a doctor and thereafter a bill for interpretation is sent to a shared address. Thus, the exceptions should be expanded to include intimate care, like anti-natal care, guidance on contraception and abortion, as well as instances where violence is suspected, to ensure that women are not disproportionately affected and to fully comply with international law.

In 2019, the Committee on Economic, Social and Cultural Rights noted with concern that Denmark had eroded refugees' rights, including the right to interpretation. It recommended that the state reinstate this entitlement.[160] The use of the word erode suggests that the Committee considers the amendment to run contrary to the obligation to not adopt deliberately retrogressive measures. According to the Committee, there is a 'strong presumption' against such measures and the state must prove that they were adopted after 'careful consideration of all alternatives' and justified.[161] Deliberately retrogressive measures in relation to core obligations are a violation of the right to health.[162] Core obligations include the right to access healthcare services, especially for vulnerable groups.[163]

The restriction of free medical interpretation is deliberately regressive,[164] given that experts warned that the bill would have retrogressive effects and that the previous act had not been economically justifiable. This was borne out in practice by evidence presented by the Danish Institute for Human Rights and Doctors' Association that the removal of the right to free interpretation has affected individuals' access to healthcare. Despite this evidence and widespread criticism of the measure, the government has refused to amend the rules. Furthermore, it should be seen in the context that, already in 2013, the Committee had noted with concern that refugees, asylum seekers and undocumented migrants encountered difficulties in accessing healthcare.[165] The Committee on the Elimination of Racial Discrimination

[159] Sundheds-og-Ældreministeriet, Høringsnotat – forslag til lov om ændring af sundhedsloven (Egenbetaling for tolkebistand), 23-03-2018, p. 7.

[160] Committee on Economic, Social and Cultural Rights Concluding observations on sixth periodic report of Denmark, E/C.12/DNK/CO/6, 12 November 2019, paras 25–26.

[161] General Comment No. 14, para 32.

[162] Ibid, para 48.

[163] Ibid, para 43(a).

[164] Warwick (2019), pp. 467–490.

[165] Concluding observations on the fifth periodic report of Denmark, adopted by the Committee at its fiftieth session (29 April-17 May 2013), E/C.12/DNK/CO/5, 6 June 2013, para 18.

has noted with concern that third country nationals face structural discrimination in accessing healthcare in Denmark,[166] while the Committee on the Elimination of Discrimination against Women has expressed concern that migrant women face multiple discriminations.[167]

Furthermore, while the law applies to all persons resident in Denmark for more than three years, it may have disproportionate impacts on some groups. The then Minister for Health pointed out that if the doctor speaks another language beyond Danish, the person can avoid paying for an interpreter.[168] This means that those who speak, in particular English (often immigrants from wealthy countries), are better placed than those who speak a minority language and thereby will be disproportionately affected despite the law seemingly being based on objective grounds. This could in turn increase ethnic inequality among non-fluent Danish/English speakers from countries where English is not widely spoken.[169] Furthermore, if a non-national cannot pay the fees due to poverty, they may end up owing money to the state. This can have knock-on effects for foreigners, as they cannot be granted permanent residency or citizenship if they have a debt to the state.[170]

In conclusion, it is submitted that the state is in violation of the right to health as the measure can be surmised as deliberately retrogressive. The state must prove that the measures adopted are not retrogressive, which to date it has not done. The arguments that the measure makes available resources and encourages integration, as noted, are not backed up by evidence. The government furthermore did not try to justify the limitation with reference to the refugee crisis, instead suggesting that there is an integration crisis, which the healthcare system, it is submitted, is ill suited to address. Furthermore, the measure should be seen in light of the fact that Denmark has been criticised repeatedly by the UN Human Rights Committee for its neglect of non-nationals' right to health. Therefore, the rules mark a divergence from international standards.

Turning to the amendments on access to treatment in response to COVID-19, these seem to be first and foremost limitations on the right to health which must thereby respect Article 4 ICESCR. At a general level, the state has sought to ensure that such limitations are not discriminatory and prioritise based on medical need. It has sought to avoid overburdening the health system and health workers by allowing for delays of some procedures and services. Still, individual cases could arise where the effects have been discriminatory or disproportionate or the rules have been

[166]Committee on the Elimination of Racial Discrimination Concluding observations on the combined twentieth and twenty-first periodic reports of Denmark, CERD/C/DNK/CO/20-21 12 June 2015, paras 20-21.

[167]Concluding observations on the eighth periodic report of Denmark, Adopted by the Committee at its sixtieth session (16 February-6 March 2015), para 33–34.

[168]LFF 2018-03-23 no. 213 Ændring af sundhedsloven; Sundheds-og-Ældreministeriet, Høringsnotat – forslag til lov om ændring af sundhedsloven (Egenbetaling for tolkebistand), 23-03-2018, p. 3.

[169]Hempler et al. (2020), p. 13.

[170]§ 9(15)(3); §11(3)(4), Udlændingelov.

applied in a manner that violated the individual's rights. There is an inherent arbitrariness and uncertainty in determining prioritisation among health conditions. It can tentatively be concluded that these rules thereby converge with international rules.

Besides being a limitation on the right to health, the measures are also potentially retrogressive. The decision does not however appear to be *deliberately* regressive but instead an attempt to find a proportionate response to the pressures on the healthcare system. There is a need to establish the extent to which the pandemic has resulted in violations of the right to health due to cancelled or postponed operations. To date anecdotal evidence suggests that cancelled operations have had serious impacts.[171] Fewer patients have furthermore been diagnosed with cancer, suggesting that mortality will increase in the coming years.[172]

6 Conclusion

When rights are subject to the whims of politicians, entitlements can be changed by political majority. As the right to health is not constitutionally enshrined in Denmark, parliament can alter health entitlements by a parliamentary majority. While this allows for flexibility in the face of a healthcare crisis like COVID-19, it also allows politics to filter into healthcare entitlements. In times of crisis, this can allow for suspending entitlements for the good of the collective without delay. Yet, challenges can also be capitalised upon to justify changes to meet political goals to the detriment of other rights and interests. In the case of non-citizens who lack political power, it can mean that permanent reductions in entitlements are adopted, contrary to the interests of public health and against the advice of human rights bodies.

In the case of the right to interpretation, the refugee/migration crisis is not mentioned in the preparatory works, instead, the purpose is claimed to be integration of foreigners and saving of resources. This aim can be questioned, given that overall, in particular in relation to refugees, Danish governments have decidedly moved away from integration and instead favour refugee status as a state of temporality. It seems that the 2015-2019 crisis has had an indirect impact on the decision to limit access to interpretation in healthcare. In contrast, entitlements to treatment that have been suspended at various times during the pandemic, have the express purpose of preserving the healthcare system due to the pressure caused by the pandemic. The two examples differ as the limitations related to the pandemic are of short-term character and based on a state of emergency. Of course, it can be questioned whether postponing treatment has at all times been justified or necessary. In the case of the right to interpretation, this retrogressive measure has not been justified as a state of

[171] Mathiassen (2021).

[172] Vestergaard (2021).

emergency and is a permanent change seen as necessary to preserve the welfare state. It thereby diverges from the standards guaranteed by the right to health.

The chapter concluded that the changes to the right to interpretation are deliberately retrogressive as the government was forewarned of the risks, which have come to pass and been ignored. Therefore, the state is found to be in violation of the right to health. Meanwhile, it is more difficult to assess whether the restrictions on access to treatment due to COVID-19 are proportionate limitations on the right to health, given that the effects are still understudied. While the legislation seeks to find a proportionate balance, in individual cases, the right to health may have been violated. It is therefore necessary for Denmark to take its right to health obligations seriously and thoroughly investigate the impacts of the pandemic on access to healthcare.

Despite the conclusion that Denmark is in violation of the ICESCR, there are limited means of holding the state accountable. Although the Committee on Economic, Social and Cultural Rights has repeatedly criticised Denmark for its treatment of refugees and non-nationals, it does not seem to have taken this criticism seriously. As Denmark has not ratified the Optional Protocol to the International Covenant on Economic, Social and Cultural Rights, individuals cannot complain directly to the Committee that their rights have been violated. Furthermore, as noted above, Danish courts are generally unwilling to examine questions related to the right to health, instead deferring to the legislature on what are deemed political questions. This thereby undermines the protection given to the right to health in Denmark.

References

Abdelhady D, Gren N, Joormann M (2020) Minimum rights policies targeting people seeking protection in Denmark and Sweden. In: Lindberg A (ed) Refugees and the violence of welfare bureaucracies in Northern Europe. Manchester University Press, Manchester, pp 85–102

Bak Jørgensen M (2020) Representations of the refugee crisis in Denmark: Deterrence policies and refugee strategies. Manchester University Press, Manchester

Bødker Madsen H (2021) Tvang som led i undersøgelse og behandling efter epidemiloven. Ugeskrift for Retsvæsen. U.2021B.205:205–212

Brønholt RLL, Langer Primdahl N, Jensen A, Verelst A, Derluyn I, Skovdal M (2021) I just want some clear answers: challenges and tactics adopted by migrants in Denmark when accessing health risk information about COVID-19. Int J Environ Res Public Health 18(17):8932

Dalton-Oates B (2017) Medical translation: the neglected human right. Int J Human Rights Healthc 10:228–238

Gammeltoft-Hansen T (2017) Refugee policy as 'Negative Nation Branding': the case of Denmark and the Nordics. Danish Foreign Policy Yearbook, pp 99–125

Gammeltoft-Hansen T, Rask Madsen M (2021) Regime Entanglement in the Emergence of Interstitial Legal Fields: Denmark and the Uneasy Marriage of Human Rights and Migration Law. iCourts Working Paper Series, 239

Gammeltoft-Hansen T, Scott Ford S (2022) An Introduction to Danish Immigration Law', In: Nielsen PA, Olsen J (eds) Danish Administrative and Constitutional Law, Hans Reitzel

Hagelund A (2020) After the refugee crisis: public discourse and policy change in Denmark, Norway and Sweden. Comp Migr Stud 8:13
Hartlev M, Jakobsen P, Ó Cathaoir K (2022) Sundhed og Jura, 3rd ed. Djøf, Copenhagen
Hempler NF, Jervelund SS, Ryom K, Villadsen SF (2020) Veje til etnisk lighed i sundhed. Dansk Selskab for Folkesundhed, Copenhagen
Hernes V (2018) Cross-country convergence in times of crisis? Integration policies before, during and after the refugee crisis. West Eur Polit 41(6):1305–1329
Karrebæk MS, Sørensen SH (2020) Covid-19 exposes language and migration tensions in Denmark. Language on the move. www.languageonthemove.com/covid-19-exposes-language-and-migration-tensions-in-denmark/
Kjærum M (2018) Er retsstaten Danmark ved at blive Nordens Ungarn?. Berlingske
Lougarre C (2020) The protection of non-nationals' economic, social and cultural rights in UN human rights treaties. Int Human Rights Law Rev 9(2):252–290
Mathiassen R (2021) Presset OUH udskyder kræftoperationer: - Patienterne kan dø i ventetiden. TV2 FYN, www.tv2fyn.dk/fyn/presset-ouh-udskyder-kraeftoperationer-patienterne-kan-doe-i-ventetiden
Menneskerettigheder LO (2019) Egenbetaling for Tolkebistand: Lægers Erfaringer med Ordningen. Institut for Menneskerettigheder, Copenhagen
Mourby M, Ó Cathaoir K, Collin CB (2021) Transparency of machine-learning in healthcare: the GDPR & European health law. Comput Law Secur Rev 43:105611
Nedergaard P (2018) Back to its roots: why do the Danish Social Democrats want a more restrictive immigration policy? Friedrich Ebert Stiftung, Budapest
Ó Cathaoir K (2022) UN institutions and health and human rights. In: Toebes B, Hartlev M, Hendriks A, Ó Cathaoir K, Herrmann J R, Aasen HS (eds) Health and human rights: global and European perspectives. Intersentia, Cambridge, pp 91–118
Ó Cathaoir K, Aasen HS, Gunnarsdóttir HD, Kimmel K, Lohiniva-Kerkelä M, Rognlien IG, Westerhäll LV (2021) Older persons and the right to health in the Nordics during COVID-19. Eur J Health Law 28(5):417–444
Oasis (2019, September) Tolkegebyret truer patientsikkerheden, forlænger forløb og koster i administration. Årsrapport 2017–18, pp 17–19
Patientsikkerhed DS (2019) Fredericksberg: Dansk Selskab for Patientsikkerhed
Phelan M (2012) Medical interpreting and the law in the European Union. Eur J Health Law 19(4): 333–353
Scipioni M (2018) Failing forward in EU migration policy? EU integration after the 2015 asylum and migration crisis. J Eur Public Policy 25(9):1357–1375
Sinding Aasen H, Hartlev M (2022) Human rights principles and patient rights. In: Toebes B, Hartlev M, Hendriks A, Ó Cathaoir K, Herrmann J R, Aasen HS (eds) Health and human rights: global and European perspectives. Intersentia, Cambridge, pp 53–87
Singh S, McNab C, Olson RM, Bristol N, Nolan C, Bergstrøm E, Bartos MM-Q (2021) How an outbreak became a pandemic: a chronological analysis of crucial junctures and international obligations in the early months of the COVID-19 pandemic. Lancet Health Policy 398:2109–2124
Skåne R (2019) Språktolkning inom hälso-och sjukvård – en fråga om mänskliga rättigheter. Region Skåne, Malmö
Socialdemokratiet (2018) Retfærdig og Realistisk: Helhedsplan for Dansk Udlændingepolitik. Socialdemokratiet, Copenhagen
Steffensen T, Sinja Laursen S (2020) Had i det offentlige rum under covid-19-epidemien – en analyse af minoriteters oplevelser. Institut for Menneskerettigheder, Copenhagen
Toebes B, Ó Cathaoir K (2022) Public Health and Human Rights. In: Toebes B, Hartlev M, Hendriks A, Ó Cathaoir K, Herrmann JR, Aasen HS (eds) Health and human rights: global and European perspectives. Intersentia, Cambridge, pp 359–389
Vestergaard C (2021) COVID-19 vil få store konsekvenser for kræftområdet, Patientsikkerhed. https://patientsikkerhed.dk/covid-19-faa-store-konsekvenser-kraeftomraadet/

Vikkelsø Slot L, Krusaa NM (2020). Pressemøder om corona bør oversættes til udvalgte fremmedsprog. Altinget, 14 December 2020.
Vitus K, Jarlby F (2021) Between integration and repatriation – frontline experiences of how conflicting immigrant integration policies hamper the integration of young refugees in Denmark. J Ethnic Migr Stud:1–19
Warwick BTC (2019) Unwinding retrogression: examining the practice of the committee on economic, social and cultural rights? Human Rights Law Rev 19(3):467–490

Katharina Ó Cathaoir is an associate professor of health law in the Faculty of Law at the University of Copenhagen, Denmark.

Immigration Law in Russia

Natalia A. Voronina

1 Introduction

Despite the rapid development of migration laws in Russia in recent years, especially in the field of external labour migration, migration legislation has not yet emerged as an independent branch of law[1] and rather, it has been described as an 'integrated legal institute'.[2] Migration relations are regulated by a combination of constitutional, administrative, labour, financial, civil, criminal, social and other branches of the Russian legal system. At present the prevailing view amongst Russian lawyers is that migration should be classified under administrative law (as a sub-branch of administrative legislation).

This chapter addresses the process of regulatory development in migration law in Russia in recent decades and the social and legal responsibility by the state towards migrants. An analysis of the main stages of development of the Russian immigration legislation is given and peculiarities of the legal regulation of migration relations in the Russian Federation are studied. Borrowings and implementation into national legislation of foreign legal norms, institutions and principles are discussed, uncovering a phenomenon of legal convergence in the area of migration law.

The chapter shows that crises, including the Russian immigration crisis and the COVID-19 pandemic, have uncovered problems in the migration sphere. This

The author has limited the scientific study period to the years 1991–2021. Latest developments are thus not considered.

[1] Хабриева (2008).

[2] Ibid.

N. A. Voronina (✉)
Institute of Migration and Inter-Ethnic Relations (Институт миграции и межнациональных отношений), An Autonomous Non-Commercial Organisation, Moscow, Russia
e-mail: igpran@igpran.ru

E. Ghio, R. Perlingeiro (eds.), *Are Legal Systems Converging or Diverging?*,
https://doi.org/10.1007/978-3-031-38180-5_12

chapter also reveals certain shortcomings of the current Russian migration normative acts, especially contradictions between laws, duplication of norms, gaps and collisions. It is argued that the main drawback is the fragmentation of elements in the system of migration laws: existing migration norms are not clear enough and insufficiently unified. Issues concerning further development of interstate (transnational) integration processes and the exit of constitutionalism beyond the framework of national states are considered, with a view to determining whether further convergence could assist in optimising Russian immigration law.

2 The Initial Development of Russian Immigration Law (1990s–2000s): Regulating the Exodus Crisis

In the early 1990s, the Russian Federation dramatically changed its former Soviet legal system. The new socio-economic conditions required new approaches, concepts, and principles of law and at the time, Russia borrowed significantly from the Romano Germanic legal system. Today, modern Russian law still bears the stamp of foreign experience, although the influence of such experience should not be overestimated. As Rene David and Camille Jauffret-Spinosi wrote, '[o]n the one hand, the reception of the Romano Germanic models was incomplete and not defining. But on the other, national legal culture was not always ready to integrate innovative laws.'[3]

After the dissolution of the Soviet Union, immigration law did not develop systematically and thoughtfully. Rather, it developed spontaneously, as a response to emerging external challenges and crises. The changes were exacerbated by an unprecedented crisis which occurred in the first half of the 1990s, when an important forced exodus of Russians from the former Soviet republics took place. Because of the nature of the borders and the lack of border control,[4] a high level of refugees from Afghanistan, as well as Asian and African countries, arrived. This crisis required regulation of migration, in turn requiring the creation and adoption of completely new laws and normative acts, previously unfamiliar to the Soviet legal system.

At first, the focus was placed on finding solutions regarding returning Russian expatriates from the former Soviet republics.[5] It then turned to the problems of thousands of refugees and asylum seekers from all over the world.[6] Indeed, according to official data, more than 5 million immigrants, of which 3.3 million ethnic Russians, arrived in Russia in the 1900s. The state supported these forced

[3] Давид and Жоффре-Спинози (2021), p. 183.

[4] Due to the dissolution of the Union of Soviet Socialist Republics (USSR) and the emergence of new independent states, administrative borders turned into state borders.

[5] In the early 1990s, about 25 million ethnic Russians found themselves living in other CIS countries and in the three Baltic Republics.

[6] Воронина (2010), pp. 8–132.

migrants in finding accommodation, arranging their settlements, and creating jobs. For example, a network of centers and locations for temporary accommodation of refugees and forced resettlers was created.

As a response to this emerging crisis, the state bodies responsible for migration management had to adopt measures on the settlement of forced migrants and refugees. However, at the time, there was no Concept of the state migration policy (a comprehensive document defining the goals, directions, and mechanisms for implementing migration policies in Russia), which impeded law-making efforts and practical work in this area. Interestingly, when drafting laws in this area, a new legal category of migrants, 'forced resettlers' (also referred to as 'forced migrants'), was introduced into Russian law.[7] This concept was, at the time, unknown to Western immigrations laws and norms, as well as to the international community.

Over the first half of the 1990s, various components of migration legislation were created. As a result, a fairly extensive and ramified legal framework regulating migration processes, mostly regulating forced migration, was created. In May 1992, the first National Long-Term Migration Programme was approved, followed by the creation of the Federal Migration Service in June 1992. In subsequent years, the institutional affiliation of the migration sphere has been repeatedly changed.[8] Over the following years, several laws were passed in this area, including rules on entering the country and travelling abroad, citizenship, refugee status, as well as rules regulating the status of forced migrants, their rights, and obligations. For example, Law N. 524-1 'On the Right of Citizens of the Russian Federation to freedom of movement, choice of place of stay and residence within the Russian Federation' was passed in 2003 to ensure the freedom of movement of Russians.

At this stage, Russia had shifted from a closed state into an active participant in the regulation of international migration processes. The Russian Federation had assumed obligations under numerous international and interstate legal treaties in the field of migration. Russia had joined the intergovernmental agreements on regulation of resettlement processes and protection of migrants' rights within the framework of the Commonwealth of Independent States (CIS) countries. For

---

[7]The Federal law of the Russian Federation 'On Forced Migrants' of 1993 (as amended) contains the definition of a refugee. The Law provides that anyone, regardless of citizenship, who had been forced to leave their place of residence on the grounds of race, citizenship, confession, language, social affiliation, political convictions, etc. could acquire the status of forced migrant.

[8]In 1992, the Federal Migration Service (FMS) was established as a state institution in the field of migration with territorial services. In May 2000, the FMS was dismantled, and its functions transferred to the newly created Ministry of Federation, National and Migration issues. In October 2001, the Ministry was abolished and its functions in the field of migration passed to the Ministry of Interior. From 2004 until 2012, the FMS was under the Ministry of Interior but by a President's decree of 2012, the FMS was then removed from Ministry of Interior and its functions expanded. By the same decree, a number of its functions were given to the Ministry of Labour and social protection and to the Ministry of Health. In April 2016, the FMS was abolished, and its functions were transferred back to the Ministry of Interior. At present, the Ministry of Internal Affairs of the Russian Federation is responsible for the direct regulation of migration processes.

example, Russia had concluded agreements on visa-free travel with several CIS countries and in 2001, the Concept of Demographic Development of the Russian Federation was adopted. This instrument called for the creation of effective mechanisms to replace the population decline through migration and build tolerance for migrants. However, several issues remained, which Russia tackled in a trial-and-error manner over the following years.

3 Further Developments in Immigration Legislation (2000s–2010s): Regulating the Rise in Illegal Immigration

From the early 2000s onwards, the nature of immigration flows towards Russia changed significantly. Forced migrants were replaced by economically motivated, temporary, labour immigrants from the CIS countries such as Ukraine, Moldova, Azerbaijan, Tajikistan, Uzbekistan and Kirgizia, as well as from Turkey, China, and Vietnam. For the most part, immigrants were young people from rural areas, unskilled or poorly qualified, and not fluent in the Russian language. They were employed in jobs with low wages and unfavourable working conditions. The attractiveness of Russia lied in its more favourable economic development compared to most CIS countries. As a result, the country saw a sharp increase in the number of illegal immigrants, which led to an immigration crisis. Consequently, new and more effective methods and legal acts were sought to regulate external labour migration and combat illegal migration. Because illegal immigration intensified, cooperation between states was required to tackle this crisis (joint working groups/commissions, data base exchange, etc.).

Therefore, several federal laws were introduced,[9] chief among which was Federal Law N. 115-FL of 25 July 2002 'On foreign citizens regulated the procedure for the stay and employment of foreign citizens on the territory of Russia', which introduced a system of job quotas. A Russian citizen could benefit from a preferential right to employment compared to a non-citizen with equal professional training and qualifications. The law also set up the share of foreign workers employed in various sectors of the economy by economic entities (e.g. trade, pharmaceuticals). Law N. 62-FL abolished the simplified procedure for obtaining Russian citizenship, and negatively affected those expatriates who had returned to Russia but did not upgrade their legal status. In 2007, Law N. 109-FL simplified the procedure for registering and attracting labour migrants from countries with visa-free entry, which stimulated the growth of labour migration from the CIS countries. Finally, Law N. 86-FL 'On

[9]Law N. 115-FL 'On the Legal Status of Foreign Citizens' (as amended). See also, inter alia, Law N. 114-FL 'On the Procedure for Leaving the Russian Federation and Entering the Russian Federation' (1996), Law N. 62-FL 'On Citizenship of the Russian Federation' (2002, as amended in 2020), Law N. 109-FL 'On Migration Registration of Foreign Citizens and Stateless Persons in the Russian Federation (2006).

Amendments to the Federal Law On the Legal Status of Foreign Citizens in the Russian Federation and Certain Legislative Acts of the Russian Federation' entered into force in July 2010. It created two categories of migrant workers: (i) those employed by individuals; and (ii) highly qualified specialists.

From the early 2000s onward, Russia has been prolific in upgrading its immigration legislation. Russia also launched numerous policy initiatives aimed at increasing the recruitment of foreign highly skilled professionals, as well as at encouraging Russian expatriates to return to Russia. In doing so, immigration procedures were made simpler, and stricter sanctions were imposed on employers hiring undocumented labour migrants.

Similar to the constitutional traditions and principles of Romano-Germanic law (with its broad scope and provision of fundamental rights and freedoms), the Constitution of the Russian Federation proclaims that the Russian Federation is a social state, whose policy is aimed at creating conditions that ensure a decent life and free human development (Chapter 12). The idea of a social state is the responsibility of the state to ensure a decent standard of living for *everyone*. In accordance with Article 2 of the Constitution of the Russian Federation, immigrants exercise their constitutional rights and freedoms as equal members of society. To ensure that these provisions are implemented adequately, the state has created special bodies for the protection of their rights, which include, courts, especially the Constitutional Court of the Russian Federation, law enforcement agencies, the prosecutor's office and the Institute of the Commissioner for Human Rights.

4 Recent Developments: Further Crises and Legal Shortcomings

4.1 The Force Migration Crisis: Internally Displaced, Asylum Seekers and Refugees

The economic crisis that started in 2008 and continued in 2014 with economic sanctions by the EU and the US, made life more difficult for migrants. A double depreciation of the rouble against major world currencies led to a reduction in the number of migrants being received and a reduction in the demand for labour generally. The number of migrant workers decreased by at least a third for countries of origin such as Ukraine, Azerbaijan, Moldova, which saw a decrease of more than 50% in the number of their citizens moving to Russia. New regulations introduced in 2015 made it more difficult and expensive for migrants to access the labour market in Russia. All potential workers are now required to pass a Russian language and history test, undergo a medical examination and purchase health insurance.

Additionally, since the beginning of 2010, the nature of the migration fluxes towards Russia has changed dramatically. First, the ageing population in the Russian Federation has led to the need to replace the declining able-bodied population of the

Russian Federation with external labour migrants. This has resulted in a sharp rise in foreign labour force entering Russia. Over the last two decades, migrant workers have become an indispensable component of Russian city life. Most of the migrants from Central Asia work in the construction sector, while others are employed in commercial enterprises, service companies and agriculture.

However, these labour immigrants are mostly unqualified and have poor knowledge of the Russian language. The majority of migrant workers in Russia are irregular migrants who are particularly vulnerable to modern slavery. The collapse of the Soviet Union has led many people from the Central Asian Republics to move to Russia in search of opportunities and employment. Every year, about 10–12 million workers enter Russia. The geographical position of the Russian Federation, between the EU and some countries with a high rate of migration, as well as visa-free entry into most countries in the CIS and the existence of some 'permeable' parts of the Russian border, facilitate a high rate of irregular migration within the CIS. According to the OECD, Russia has the highest number of illegal migrants, representing almost 7% of the country's population.[10]

While these problems need to be regulated, the legislation in the field of labour migration is flawed in this regard. Considering the Russian legal system as a whole, 'there is a redundancy of legal regulation [. . .] In order for the law to cope with its social task, it is necessary to reinforce its norms with other regulators: traditions, customs, legal ideology, moral and moral norms, etc. [. . .] An excessive number of laws does not compensate for the absence or shortcomings of other regulators.'[11] This leads to several issues.

First, Russian migration legislation is quite complicated. It is often necessary for foreign workers and their employers to have recourse to qualified specialists in order to understand their rights and obligations. These specialists include executive authorities, lawyers, and non-governmental organisations (NGO) activists. However, some issues remain neglected.

Second, the current quota system (introduced by Federal Law N. 115-FL) does not meet the needs of the Russian economy for foreign labour. Procedures for obtaining temporary residence permits and residency status are complex, and the legislation does not support the recruitment of foreign workers on a long-term basis. Overall, with the exception of the 'State Program to Assist the Voluntary Resettlement of Compatriots Living Abroad to the Russian Federation', there are no legal mechanisms to ensure permanent immigration.

This is problematic as one of the most urgent problems facing the world community today is the problem of refugees. In 1993, the Russian Federation was the first of the post-Soviet countries to ratify the 1951 UN Convention Relating the Status of Refugees and the 1967 Protocol on the Status of Refugees. Compliance

---

[10] See Migrants Refugees, Country Profiles: Russia, https://migrants-refugees.va/country-profile/russia/#:~:text=Russia%20adheres%20to%20the%201951,extended%20from%20year%20to%20year.

[11] Сошникова (2015), p. 80.

with these international legal standards for the protection of refugees required incorporation of these norms into national legislation, or the creation of a procedure for granting refugee status, in order to protect the rights and freedoms of refugees.[12] This was done through Federal Law N. 4528-1 'On Refugees' of 19 February 1993. This law recognised the grounds and procedures for the recognition of refugee status on the territory of the Russian Federation, established economic, social and legal guarantees for the protection of the rights and legitimate interests of the refugees in accordance with the Constitution of the Russian Federation, the generally recognised principles and norms of international law and the international treaties to which Russia is a party.

The Law, in its Article 1, defines a refugee as:

> a person who is not a citizen of the Russian Federation and owing to well-founded fear of being persecuted for reasons of race, religion, nationality, ethnicity, membership of a particular social group or political opinion, is outside the country of his nationality and is unable or, owing to such fear, is unwilling to avail himself of the protection of that country; or who, not having a nationality and being outside the country of his former habitual residence as a result of such events, is unable or, owing to such fear, is unwilling to return to it.

Temporary asylum is defined as 'an opportunity for a foreign citizen or stateless person to stay temporarily in the territory of the Russian Federation [. . .].' Article 12 of the Federal Law on Refugees states that temporary asylum permits foreign nationals to reside temporarily in the territory of the Russian Federation. It is granted by the Ministry of the Interior if there are no requirements for refugee status but there are sufficient humanitarian reasons to guarantee the right of residence.

While Russia has aligned its migration standards to international practices, i.e. just as for Western countries, a refugee is someone who has a well-founded fear or persecution, not only for political but also racial, religious, ethnic and other reasons, refugee status remains difficult to obtain in Russia and temporary asylum status is not easily granted. For example, according to statistics from the Ministry of the Interior, in 2018, two Syrian refugees were granted asylum in Russia, and the number of those with temporary asylum status decreased from 1128 in January 2018 to 826 one year later, a drop of almost 30%. However, according to the Ministry of Interior, 9100 Syrian citizens were estimated to reside in the Russian Federation by the end of October 2018. Additionally, although every year, around 2,000 temporary asylum applications are received, only a few beneficiaries are granted each year. The presence of intermediate procedures (stages), such as preliminary consideration of the application, the decision to issue a certificate of consideration of the application on the merits or refusal to consider the application on the merits, creates delays and demonstrates the imperfection of the Law on Refugees from the point of view of law enforcement practice.[13]

---

[12] Зинченко (2016), p. 13.

[13] Цинделиани (2018), p. 184.

An analysis of judicial practice on appealing refusals to grant refugee status reveals a number of shortcomings with the process. First, the process of considering such cases can take several months. Second, the procedure is not easy to access for asylum seekers. Finally, recourse to a lawyer or interpreter has been refused in some cases. Additionally, the principle of non-refoulement has been violated as asylum seekers have been detained and deported while applying for asylum. Therefore, commentators have argued that the problems of ensuring and protecting the rights of foreign citizens in the Russian Federation lie not so much in legislation as in law enforcement practice.[14] In this regard, a draft of a new law ‘On asylum’ is currently being prepared, in which many shortcomings should be eliminated.

4.2 The COVID-19 Pandemic

Another crisis which has had an impact on labour immigrants and asylum seekers is the COVID-19 pandemic. The epidemiological crisis—the emergence of a new threat to the life and health of the world’s population—which was recognised by the World Health Organization (WHO) as a pandemic, has affected all spheres of economic, political, and social life of society. Businesses across the world went insolvent and closed due to COVID-19, resulting in job losses. States took restrictive measures aimed at preventing the further spread of the infection, as well as to develop socio-economic programs to support businesses and provide medical and social assistance to the population of their countries. States were faced with the complex task of performing their usual functions, while solving a whole range of new and complex issues to counter the new COVID-19 pandemic, in order to protect the lives and health of their population as well as national economies. In these circumstances and under the imposed restrictions on movement, closure of state borders and transport links between states, migrants often found themselves in a very vulnerable situation.

In Europe, EU Member States were the first hit by COVID-19. The states quickly reacted by introducing different legal regimes (state of emergency, high alert, state of readiness, etc.), by closing national borders, limiting international transport and suspending immigration services and offices. At the same time many countries made exceptions for certain categories of migrants in key economic sectors and adopted temporary measures for those who could not leave the country in which they worked. For example, exceptions to the prohibition of movement were made for medics and transport workers. The EU also allowed for the free movement of seasonal and cross-border agricultural workers.

In Russia, the President of the Federation signed Decree N. 274 ‘On temporary measures to regulate the legal situation of foreign citizens who find themselves in a difficult life situation’ on 18 April 2020, with a view to solving the problems of

[14] Булатов and Андрейцо (2016), p. 21.

migrants with an unsettled legal status (the so-called 'COVID migration amnesty'). The Decree applied to foreigners in Russia and it stated that no decisions would be made against foreigners and stateless persons regarding the undesirability of their stay (i.e. residence) in, or administrative expulsion from, the Russian Federation, or their deportation or transfer to another state under an international repatriation agreement, until 15 June 2020. Migrant workers whose stay was lawful as of 15 March 2020 were permitted to remain in the Russian Federation and to continue engaging in the activities associated with their employment up to 15 June 2020. The term of visas held by foreigners was extended until 15 June 2020 and no residence permits held by foreigners, or residence entitlements held by stateless persons, would be cancelled or withdrawn if the person concerned had to stay abroad for longer than six months. Until 15 June 2020, no foreigner would see their refugee status or temporary asylum withdrawn.

5 Convergence Through Interstate and Comparative Migration Law

Comparative law provides an opportunity to get to know one's national law better and improve it. The analysis of the development of the Romano-Germanic and Anglo-Saxon legal systems shows that while their political systems continue to exhibit significant differences, a certain level of legal convergence has nonetheless occurred.[15] This has led authors to talk about a kind of unified ('Western') legal family that includes all private legal systems and families. In their opinion, this legal family is based primarily on a common 'Western European culture', which is manifested both in various legal and 'common liberal-democratic political values, and in existing legal norms, legal institutions, branches of law, in law-making, law enforcement and law enforcement activities.'[16] Commentators such as Marco Cappelletti, for example, speak of the merging of the Romano-Germanic and Anglo-Saxon legal systems into one legal family and of 'new prospects for the development of common law in Europe', within the framework of existing Romano-Germanic law.[17]

The legal regulation of migration processes is most effective when internal lawmaking is combined with the active use of international standards and contractual interstate interaction. This is due to the fact that interstate integration is increasingly developing today; international organisations are flourishing at regional, interregional, and global levels. Accordingly, legal rules supporting (transnational) integration are also developing, going beyond the framework of traditional

[15] Марченко (2001), p. 265.

[16] Bell (1995), pp. 63–64.

[17] Cappelletti (1978).

international law. Constitutional law acquires new properties, the internationalisation of which leads to forming up of a new supranational dimension.[18]

First, the Russian Federation has long been actively involved in the development of the legal framework for regulating migration relations. Since the establishment of the CIS, Russia has concluded a large number of bilateral and multilateral agreements in the field of migration with other CIS countries. The migration legislation of the CIS countries is rooted in international and European sources of law. Model laws adopted by the Interparliamentary Assembly (IPA) of the CIS states, including on labour migration, also play an important role. As a result, legal convergence has occurred and all CIS countries now possess laws on the status of foreigners, on the procedure for entering and leaving the country, and on the regulation of migration service authorities. The other CIS states largely follow the Russian model of the development of migration legislation (with countries' peculiarities) in terms of principles, categories of persons of migration legal relations, their status, etc.[19] Second, Russia also actively cooperates with different international organisations such as the United Nations High Commissioner on Refugees (UNHCR), the International Organization on Migration (IOM), the International Labour Organization (ILO) and the Organization for Security and Cooperation in Europe (OSCE) on a wide range of migration issues including migration and development, integration of migrants, smuggling of and trafficking in persons, irregular migration and so on. In addition to cooperating within the framework of international organisations, the Russian Federation has initiated international initiatives that do not impose international legal obligations on states (in the form of binding norms) but serve the promotion of ideas and practical interaction. Currently, interstate integration entities are developing, such as the Eurasian Economic Union (EAEU) and the Union State of Russia-Belarus. These entities also deal with immigration matters. For example, the EAEU Treaty states that foreign workers in the territory of the member states are guaranteed great preferences in the field of labour, pension, and social issues. While the Romano-Germanic legal tradition has evolved into the law of the European Union (EU) in recent decades,[20] EAEU law is still in its infancy. Therefore, EAEU law looks to both EU law and Western countries' legal systems with a view to borrowing legal solutions and concepts. However, this is not an easy task as 'modern state studies face the need to rethink both the role of the state as a social phenomenon and the processes of interstate interaction, which have clearly outgrown both the bilateral relations of sovereign states and the format of the activities of international associations.'[21]

In the specific context of migration, which is a social relationship caused by economic, political, social, demographic and other reasons, regulated by the norms

[18] Варламовой and Васильевой (2017).

[19] Воронина (2015), pp. 96–242.

[20] Lafitsky (2021), p. 190.

[21] Бабурин (2021), p. 5.

of law related to the movement (resettlement) of individuals, several conclusions can be made when comparing the legislation of the Russian Federation with Western countries and when determining whether legal convergence has occurred.

Generally, immigrations laws also tend to exhibit similarities in the aspects of immigration that they regulate, such as the presence of foreigners on their territory and the grounds for entry and stay of foreigners. They usually regulate elements such as the provision of visas, passports, and residence permits. These similarities can be explained by different elements.

First, Migration law is a relatively young branch of law, compared to other fields such as civil, criminal, and family law. Migration legislation in Western countries developed following different patterns and velocity, notably as a response to mass immigration in the mid–twentieth century. In France, for example, no immigration policy in the true sense of the word existed until 1945 and only individual, ad hoc measures were taken. In Italy, migration policy and legislation began to emerge in the late 1970s and 1980s, when Italy became an attractive immigration destination. In comparison, immigration laws in the Russian Federation developed much later. It is therefore argued that Russian migration legislation took into account the experience of legal regulation of migration relations in Western countries and is rooted in norms already in place in these countries. This process of legal emulation supported by the fact that at the beginning of the 1990s, a large number of legal consultants from Western countries worked within Russian institutions, including the Federal Migration Service of Russia. Consequently, norms and mechanisms introduced into the Russian legal system, notably relating to the protection of human rights within the context of migration law, had to dovetail with established and traditional rules and principles in place in Russia and its legal institutions.

Therefore, the world community has accumulated extensive experience in legal regulation of migration, protection of the rights and legitimate interests of refugees, forced migrants and persons engaged in professional activities outside its borders. As a result, the activities of states in the field of migration related to the development of goals and objectives of migration policy, functions and methods of their implementation, exhibit certain similarities. Countries generally identify similar priorities of migration policy, such as promoting economic and demographic growth, social and cultural development, fulfilling international obligations regarding refugees, internally displaced persons, asylum, non-discrimination, integration of migrants into society, attracting qualified specialists and investors into the country's economy, promoting family reunification, international cooperation on countering illegal immigration.

At EU level, the Schengen Agreement introduced uniform unified entry documents for most Member States, as well as a system of measures for effective border control and selective restriction of immigration', called 'controlled immigration policy. In general, the immigration policy of EU countries, despite some differences and national peculiarities, is characterised by a desire to develop uniform rules for regulating migration flows, the migration crisis that emerged in Europe in 2014-2015 contributed to a further revision of the regulation of asylum and reception of immigrants within the EU. European law includes not only the legal norms created as a result of the formation of the EU, but also the legal provisions, principles and norms of the European system of human rights protection, guaranteed by the European Convention for the Protection of Human Rights and Fundamental Freedoms (1950).[22] As a result, EU Member States are required to recognise migrants' rights, including migrant workers' rights, in their national systems. However, immigration policies across the EU are largely based on control and the provision of restrictive measures (restriction of entry into the country of low-skilled labour; countering illegal migration). National migration laws set out the different types of immigration, i.e. labour (socio-economic), humanitarian (refugees and asylum seekers) and family reunification, but countries also encourage the immigration of highly-skilled and qualified workers.

Another reason why national laws on asylum and refugee status are rather similar is because of the 1951 UN Convention on the Status of Refugees and its Protocol of 1967, the Dublin Convention on the Right of Asylum and Treatment of Refugees of 1990, as well as other international acts which are at the heart of the regulation of refugee status. In this case, legal convergence has occurred through the national alignment of laws with international rules and standards. By fixing certain progressive principles, norms, and provisions, international law has set a kind of example and encouraged states to adopt and implement them in practice. In other cases, international law indirectly assesses the positive and negative challenges of modern migration through the different structure of its norms, resorting to disposition when it comes to regular and controlled movements, and uses prohibitions in relation to illegal movements of people.[23] At the same time, some asylum issues remain regulated at the national level. For example, the granting of refugee status is decided by each country individually.

Rules relating to labour immigration also tend to exhibit common features. In Sweden, for example, labour immigration is allowed only if there are no specialists with the required qualifications on the domestic labour market. In a similar way, in order to obtain an entry visa into the US, it is necessary to have a 'labour certificate'—an official confirmation from the firm (company) of consent to provide a workplace. The certificate serves as evidence that American workers who have sufficient qualifications to perform the work provided to the foreigner are not currently applying for the same job. Similar norms exist in the Russian migration legislation. Additionally, States often implement various systems of selection of immigrants necessary, first of all, for the development of the economy, using different systems, such as quota systems or point selection. In labour importing countries, the regulation of the number of incoming migrants is carried out with the help of an immigration quota calculated annually. When calculating it, the economic needs of the country or its region, the demographic situation, and the political conjuncture are taken into account. A similar quota system exists in Russia. Western

[22] In this chapter, European law is understood not only as norms created at the EU level, but also those norms of national law that ensure the application of legal norms developed at the EU level.

[23] Ястребова (2014), p. 24.

labour importing countries also use the principle of selectivity and the provision of benefits/preferences of certain categories of migrants in their migration policy. In most Western countries, the entry of investors who invest certain funds in the country's economy is encouraged. This priority right of entry is also enjoyed by ‘business immigrants’ who create enterprises in the country with the provision of work to local citizens. In Russia, a similar principle of selectivity and the system of preferences have been introduced into migration legislation for highly qualified specialists and skilled workers.

At the same time, convergence has not resulted in the complete uniformity of legal norms and institutions. One might speak about unification, carried out not at the level of clear norms, but at the level of general principles or standards. For example, there is no legally accepted definition of the concepts of ‘migrant’, ‘alien’, and ‘foreigners’ at international level and definitions vary from state to state. The term ‘migrant’ is used mostly in areas such as economic and political sciences, as well as demography studies and sociology, rather than law. In the US, Sweden, and Germany, a ‘migrant’ is a person belonging to the citizenship of another state, or a stateless person. In Canada, on the other hand, it is a person who does not have Canadian citizenship and is not a permanent resident in the country. While in Germany and Sweden, the main concept is ‘foreigner’ (confirming the orientation of the migration policy of these countries on the temporary stay of these persons in their territories (on the basis of a visa or residence permit)), in the US and Canada, the main concept is ‘immigrant’, i.e. a foreigner entering the country to acquire permanent residence with a subsequent change of citizenship. In US law, the term ‘immigrant’ is used in relation to every foreigner (with the exception of diplomats; officials; persons permanently residing in another state and visiting the US temporarily for various purposes). In Russia, the main concept is ‘foreign citizen’. The CIS Agreement of April 1994 ‘On cooperation in the field of labour migration and social protection of migrant workers’ associates the concept with the term ‘migrant worker (or employee)’.

In addition, national differences exist when classifying ‘migrants’, ‘immigrants’, and ‘foreigners’. While in France, several dozen categories of migrants exist,[24] grouped within five main types (economic, family, students, humanitarian, others), the IOM sets out seven categories: (i) labour migrants; (ii) foreign students; (iii) refugees; (iv) irregular migrants; (v) migrant women; (vi) migrant children; (vii) environmental migrants Graff (2019). National laws have also created additional, ad hoc categories of migrants. For example, in Russia, ‘compatriots living abroad’ are considered to be migrants. In accordance with the ‘State Program of Support for the Resettlement in the Russian Federation of Compatriots Residing Abroad’, that recently became of unlimited duration,[25] these persons are those who have returned to their homeland. They benefit from a preferential status which translates into

[24] See Thibaut Fleury Graff. Les categories de migrants: refugies, etudiants, sans papiers... https://www.vie-publique/fr/parole-dexpert/271045.

[25] Adopted by President’s Decree of 22 June 22 2006, N 637.

simpler citizenship and residence permit procedures. The 1994 German Law on the Reception of Immigrants has created the status of 'late immigrants' for persons who received a long-term residence permit in Germany but had the status of foreigners regulated by the norms of the law on foreigners. These immigrants automatically receive German citizenship if they can demonstrate work experience and have gone through a German language course.

6 Conclusion

International migration is closely intertwined with globalisation and is one of the defining issues of this century. Migration increasingly entails economic, social, legal, cultural, demographic, security effects on both sending and receiving societies and because of the general internationalisation of economic, political and cultural ties, as well as the interaction of the legal systems of various states, close interpenetration is observed between the legal systems of states united in unions, communities, as well as participation in the activities of international organisations to achieve joint goals, including in the field of migration.

While Russia has adopted existing national and international standards and rules in the field of migration over the years, thereby contributing to a phenomenon of legal convergence in this area, the current migration legislation in Russia does not fully meet the socio-economic and demographic requirements of the Russian state. Accordingly, it is necessary to optimise migration legislation. This process is already underway. The current focus is on the introduction of rules governing the foreign labour force spontaneously arriving in Russia through a legally regulated channel and ensure that the professional and qualification requirements of foreign workers meet the needs of the Russian labour market. The Ministry of Internal Affairs of the Russian Federation (MVD of Russia) has prepared a consolidated draft federal law 'On the conditions of entry (exit) and stay (residence) in the Russian Federation of foreign citizens and stateless persons',[26] which would replace a number of federal laws on migration.

In this context, the study of the conceptual foundations of European law and its legal institutions can serve as one of the means of enriching the national legal systems of non-EU states. The positive experience of Western European integration can be used for, and adapted to, the processes of integrational development of the states of the former Soviet Union, in particular, the CIS countries, the EAEU and other integration associations emerging in the post-Soviet space, especially in the area of migration law.

[26]Federal Portal of draft regulatory legal Acts: 02/04/03-21/00113698, https://regulation.gov.ru/projects/List/AdvancedSearch#departments=7.

References

Bell J (1995) English Law and French Law – not so different? Curr Leg Probl 48:63–64. Part 2

Cappelletti M (1978) New perspectives for a common law of Europe. Publications of the European University Institute, London

Graff TF (2019) Les categories de migrants: refugies, etudiants, sans papiers... https://www.vie-publique/fr/parole-dexpert/271045

Lafitsky VL (2021) The worlds of law in the theory and practice of comparative law (in Russian): монография: в 2 т. – Москва: Проспект. I:191

Бабурин СН (2021) Интеграционный конституционализм: монография / С.Н. Бабурин. – Москва : Норма: ИНФРА-М. С. 5. [*Baburin S.N.* Integrational constitutionalizm]

Булатов РБ, Андрейцо СЮ (2016) Проблемы обеспечения и защиты прав иностранных граждан в России // Миграционное право. № 4. С. 21. [*Bulatov R.B, Andreitso S.Y.* Problems of ensuring and protection of foreign citizens' rights in Russia]

Воронина НА (2010) Миграционное законодательство России: состояние, проблемы, перспективы: Монография. – М.: Издательство «Спутник». С. 8-132. [*Voronina N.A.* Migration legislation in Russia: state, problems and prospects]

Воронина НА (2015) Международное право и миграционное законодательство стран СНГ. Монография / Институт государства и права РАН. – М.: Издательский дом ГУУ. С. 96-242. [*Voronina N.A.* International law and migration legislation of the CIS countries]/

Давид Р, Жоффре-Спинози К (2021) Основные правовые системы современности / пер. с фр. В.А. Туманов. – М.; Международные отношения. С. 183. [*Rene David, Camille Jauffret-Spinosi.*Les grands systemes de droit contemporains]

Зинченко НН (2016) Временная защита как рациональное и гуманное решение проблемы лиц, ищущих убежище // Миграционное право. № 1. С. 13.[*Zintchenko N.N.* Temporary protection as a rational and humane problem solving of asylum seekers]

Интернационализация конституционного права: современные тенденции / под ред. Н.В. Варламовой и Т.А. Васильевой. М., 2017. [Internatiolization of constitutional law. Ed. *Varlamova N.V., Vassilieva N.F.]*

Марченко МН (2001) Сравнительное правоведение. Общая часть. Учебник для юридических вузов. – М.: Издательство «Зерцало». С. 265. [Martchenko M.N. Comparative Law]

Пряхина ТМ (2015) Обращения граждан в Конституционный Суд РФ – индикатор состояния правовой системы России // Права человека – индикатор современного развития России / отв. ред. Т.А. Сошникова: материалы международной научн-о-практической конференции. – М.: Изд-во Моск. гуманит. ун-та. С. 80. [*Priakhina T.M.* Citizens' appeals to the Constitutional court]

Реализация миграционной политики уполномоченными органами в сфере миграции в ряде зарубежных стран. Под общ. Ред. А.С. Прудникова. Учебное пособие. Москва, 2019. С. 20. [Implementation of Migration Policy by the authorized bodies in the field of migration in foreign countries. Under the general editorship of A.S Prudnikov]

Хабриева ТЯ (2008) Миграционное право России: теория и практика. – М.: Юридическая фирма «Контракт». С. 2-5. [T.*Y. Khabrieva.* Migration Law of the Russian Federation: Theory and Practice. pp. 2–5]

Цинделиани ИА (2018) Миграционное право России \ под ред.. М.,. С. 184. [Migration Law of Russia. Ed. *Tsyndeliany I.A.]*

Ястребова АЮ (2014) Международно-правовые механизмы регулирования миграции: доктринальные подходы и опыт Российской Федерации. Монография. – М.: ВАКО, С.24. [Yastrebova A.Y. International Legal Mechenisms of Migration Regulation: Doctrinal Approaches and Experience of Russian Federation]

Natalia A. Voronina is a senior researcher in the Human Rights Department of the Institute of State and Law, in the Russian Academy of Sciences, Russia.

Social Rights in Australia

Beth Gaze

1 Introduction

Social rights in Australia are not systematically protected. Australia has no specific constitutional protection for human or individual rights,[1] nor has it adopted comprehensive domestic legislation to protect human rights, except for some privacy and non-discrimination rights.[2] As a result, it has no systemic and coherent protection for social rights. Instead, some rights are granted protection through legislative schemes, such as anti-discrimination laws or social security laws, or provision for disability services. This makes it different and divergent from almost every other Western democracy in the absence of a binding legal basis to ground social rights.

This chapter introduces the social and legal understandings of social rights in Australia and considers the extent of legal protection (or its absence) for some selected examples, as well as the factors that have influenced this situation. Because social rights demand resources, they are vulnerable to penny-pinching by governments. The absence of legal protection further leaves social rights vulnerable to incursions as a result of crises such as the COVID-19 pandemic or financial

[1] The Commonwealth of Australia Constitution contains a few specific rights, such as a right to trial by jury for an indictable offence (s. 80), and a prohibition on any state discriminating against residents of another state (s. 117). Section 116 protects the secular state by prohibiting the establishment of any religion, the use of a religious test for any public office, or the free exercise of religion, but does not go so far as to create an individual right to freedom of religion.

[2] Some limited protection against denial of rights by the commonwealth government or in territories is provided by the Australian Human Rights Commission Act 1986 (Cth) s. 3(1) definition of 'human rights,' 11(f) and 20. But this protection is not legally enforceable and can only result in conciliation and a report to the responsible Minister.

B. Gaze (✉)
University of Melbourne Law School, Carlton, VIC, Australia
e-mail: egaze@unimelb.edu.au

E. Ghio, R. Perlingeiro (eds.), *Are Legal Systems Converging or Diverging?*,
https://doi.org/10.1007/978-3-031-38180-5_13

stringency after budget crises like the global financial crisis of 2008. Because of the lack of legal grounding, political influences have taken on greater importance. The most important influences on the current state of social rights in Australia have been, at the political level, the pervasive influence of neoliberalism on both of Australia's major political parties,[3] and in the legal sphere, the long-standing Australian reluctance about rights.[4]

The chapter begins by examining the understanding of social rights in Australia and the legal context in which Australia engages with them. Australia engages with the international human rights system but is not subject to any binding obligations to protect social rights either through constitutional requirements or through a regional human rights organisation. In terms of law reform or policy, it does not directly engage with countries in its region (apart from New Zealand) due to their very different legal systems and social approaches. Australia still looks to the United Kingdom ('UK'), United States ('US') and Canada as the primary sources of ideas for law reform, but even this convergence has reduced over time as those jurisdictions have adjusted their policies and laws under the influence of binding rights obligations, whether in their constitutions or in binding conventions.[5] As a result, Australia's systems of legal protection for social rights, where they exist, tend to diverge from common insurance-based models found in these jurisdictions and the European Union.[6] Similarity is present only in very broad terms, for example in the development of the post war welfare state as a basis for unemployment benefits. But even here there is fundamental divergence—because social welfare benefits in Australia are not insurance based, they are not understood as rights-based or individual entitlements. Avoiding contributory schemes was intended to ensure universal coverage, but over time has led to them operating as contingent entitlements subject to an administrative process, with no enforceable rights. Further, Australia's federal structure (discussed below) creates complexity and brings it closer to models such as the US and Canada, diverging from approaches possible in unitary jurisdictions like the UK, New Zealand and the European Union ('EU'). The political and financial tensions between governments at two levels provide a further complication in protecting social rights.

The chapter moves on to examine how social rights are protected in Australia in the absence of adherence to an overriding conceptual or legal framework. The examples of disability discrimination and services, and social security rights will be used to illustrate the nature of protection available and its limitations. Their importance and the existence of legislative protection allows for evaluation of the legal approach and comparison with approaches in other countries.

---

[3] Solomon (2021), pp. 14–16.

[4] See Charlesworth (1993) and Otto (2001).

[5] Canada: Charter of Human Rights and Responsibilities, 1982, UK: Human Rights Act 1998, New Zealand: Bill of Rights Act 1990.

[6] See eg Maccabiani (2018), King (2012), Boyle (2020).

Finally, the social and political context for social rights is considered, as a major factor determining the treatment of social rights in Australia. All areas of social rights that rely on positive resources or actions by government have been adversely affected by the pervading neo-liberal and small government ideology of the Australian political system, which has been the dominant strand underpinning political action since the early 1980s.[7] It has influenced both conservative and progressive governments towards privatisation and outsourcing of services, accompanied by attempts to limit public expenditure on the vulnerable in the name of austerity and a balanced (national) budget, while at the same time providing tax reductions, mainly to higher income earners. The 'taken for granted' assumption that the expenditures of the state must be limited to allow taxes to be reduced has influenced the policies of both major political parties and remains a constant influence on policy, legislation, and protection for social rights. The dependence of social rights on implementation by the public sector makes it difficult to progress protection for rights in the face of this ideology. This dominant neoliberal orientation has made it difficult for claims for social rights and progressive policies to break through. Government responses to the impact of the COVID-19 pandemic on the unemployed and people with disability based on neoliberal approaches are in many ways similar to approaches in the US and UK but diverge in detail due to the different legal and political context in Australia.[8]

2 What Are Social Rights?

The clearest lists of social rights are those found in the various international and regional human rights conventions. These include the International Covenant on Economic Social and Cultural Rights ('ICESCR') and the European Social Charter. The main areas of rights listed in the IESCR are the rights to:

i. work under 'just and favourable conditions', including the right to form and join trade unions;[9]
ii. social security, including social insurance;[10]
iii. family life, including paid parental leave and the protection of children;[11]
iv. an adequate standard of living, including adequate food, clothing and housing, and the 'continuous improvement of living conditions';[12]

---

[7] Solomon (2021), pp. 11–17; Maccabiani (2018).

[8] See generally Wilson (2020).

[9] ICESCR (Articles 6, 7, and 8).

[10] Ibid. A 9.

[11] Ibid A 10.

[12] Ibid A 11.

v. health, expressed as "the highest attainable standard of physical and mental health;"[13]
vi. education, directed to 'the full development of the human personality and the sense of its dignity', to enable everyone to participate effectively in society; this includes free universal primary education, generally available secondary education and equally accessible higher education;[14]
vii. participation in cultural life.[15]

In contrast, the European Social Charter (1981, revised in 1996)[16] contains a more detailed list of rights that reflects the developing European community, including housing, health, education, labour rights, including full employment, reduction of working hours, equal pay for equal work, and parental leave, social security, social and legal protection from poverty and social exclusion, movement of persons, and non-discrimination, as well as rights for specific vulnerable groups such as migrant workers and people with disability. In other countries such as South Africa and Canada, the Constitution itself provides for protection of rights and for their enforcement, including some economic and social rights.[17] There is a vast difference between these approaches with enforceable legal rights and Australia's policies, which draw much more on developments in the UK and USA.

In Australia, there is no equivalent list of social rights because the Constitution has no systematic constitutional protection for individual human rights, unlike every other western liberal democracy. The Australian government has ratified all the United Nations ('UN') Human Rights Conventions including the International Covenant on Civil and Political Rights ('ICCPR') and the ICESCR, but these do not have any domestic legal effect until implemented, generally by legislation.[18] The UN documents generally oblige governments to create legally enforceable rights, but these international obligations are not enforceable. The Asia-Pacific is the only major region without a binding regional human rights agreement, unlike Europe, the Americas, and Africa, where a regional human rights convention creates enforceable obligations on governments to protect individual rights. Since Australia has no enforceable requirements to provide protection of human rights, such protection is entirely a matter of policy choice for the government. Governments' reluctance to act

[13] Ibid A 12.

[14] Ibid A 13 and 14.

[15] Ibid A 15.

[16] Council of Europe, European Social Charter, 18 October 1961, ETS 35.

[17] Constitution of South Africa ss. 26-29; The Canadian Charter does not expressly refer to social and economic rights, although the wording of some of its guarantees could be interpreted to include them and has sometimes been interpreted this way: Jackman and Porter (2017).

[18] Some rights can be implemented solely by executive action, but this is not sufficient where legal enforceability is needed. For example, the scheme for implementing the International Labour Organisation (ILO) Convention 111 on Discrimination in Employment and Occupation was non-legislative until it was incorporated in the Australian Human Rights Commission Act 1986 (Cth), where it has legislative support but is still not legally enforceable.

limits the space for ideas and discourse on social rights in Australian politics and law.

That is not to say that social rights have no protection in Australia. However, they are not protected legally as social rights or human rights. Instead, they are protected pragmatically as chosen by governments, in areas such as anti-discrimination legislation at state and federal levels, social security provision for unemployment, disability and child benefits, and work laws that may or may not address human rights.[19] Many of these laws are highly politicised in a partisan context. There are two major political parties in Australia. The conservative Liberal Party which governed from 2013–2022 was in coalition with the National Party, which represents the sectional interests of country voters, and has moved over time from representing farmers to large corporations engaged in mining. The second major party is the Australian Labor Party (ALP), which has been responsible for almost all of the anti-discrimination and human rights laws that do exist.[20] These parties could in the past be seen to represent the interests of capital and labour, but in recent years both have become adherents of neoliberal ideas of small government, outsourcing, and privatisation.

The two major parties look in different directions for ideas for policies and ideology. The conservative Liberal-National Party coalition government looked towards other states with conservative, neo-liberal governments, in particular the US and the UK. Progressive governments may look more broadly for ideas but are nevertheless committed to the precepts of neoliberalism and market fundamentalism, policies that undermine the role of the public sector which is an essential foundation for giving effect to economic social and cultural rights. These ideas suggest that government's role should be confined to providing policy guidance, and that the work of providing public services should generally be contracted out to private sector organisations. This shrinkage of the role of the public sector is currently the most distinctive feature of the protection of social rights in Australia, and given the dependence of social rights on implementation by the public sector, it does not bode well for the comprehensiveness or sufficiency of social rights protection in Australia.

While the ALP is generally more sympathetic to human rights, it has not been prepared to adopt systematic enforceable legislative protection for social rights. When last in government at Commonwealth level, it conducted a National Consultation on Human Rights which recommended adoption of a legislative bill of rights,[21] but the government did not act on that recommendation. Instead, it adopted a mechanism for parliamentary scrutiny of all legislation to identify potential

[19] Australia's national work law, the Fair Work Act 2009 (Cth), which is beyond the scope of this chapter, in fact fails to respect many human rights and ILO Convention rights: see e.g. Solomon (2021), Chapter 4.

[20] Only the Age Discrimination Act 2004 (Cth) was adopted by a conservative Liberal National Party coalition government. All other anti-discrimination and human rights laws in Australia have been introduced by ALP governments.

[21] National Human Rights Consultation Committee, Report (2009).

infringements of human rights,[22] based presumably on the assumption that if a risk to human rights is identified, governments will be more reluctant to proceed. In practice, although this process draws some attention to potential infringements of rights, it has not prevented politically expedient legislation from proceeding even if it is incompatible with human rights.[23]

In summary, Australia has no legal basis in the Constitution or in a binding external convention for requiring governments to comply with human rights or to provide positive protection for rights. It has ratified all the UN human rights conventions, and in particular the ICCPR and ICESCR, which impose obligations to provide legal protection for rights. However, the major influences on Australia's protections for social rights have been political. Policy ideas from the UK and US, as well as the country's general approaches, illustrate convergence with these jurisdictions, subject to the limitations of the legal context. However, specific approaches in Australia diverge from models in most other jurisdictions because of the absence of binding legal obligations to protect social rights and the absence of a contributory basis for benefits or services, which impedes understanding them as individual rights. The next section introduces the ways in which social rights are given some protection in Australian law, and considers the extent to which there is protection, and what factors have influenced this.

3 Protection for Social Rights in the Australian Legal Context

Australia's legal context is complicated by federalism. Because legislative protection is the only avenue available, protection for rights depends on the commitment of the party in government, and even when rights are protected, they can be repealed, reduced, or overridden by later laws, or their value allowed to reduce through lack of indexation or failure to adequately fund services. The political and social environment is not well educated on rights and their operation because the absence of

[22]Human Rights (Parliamentary Scrutiny) Act 2011 (Cth) (HRPSA) requires that every bill introduced into the parliament must be accompanied by a statement by its proponent of its compatibility with human rights and be assessed by the Parliamentary Joint Committee on Human Rights for compliance with human rights. The Committee reports back to the houses of parliament. The process includes the rights in all the UN human rights conventions: the ICCPR, ICESCR, the Conventions on the Elimination of All Forms of Racial Discrimination and All Forms of Discrimination Against Women, the Convention on the Rights of Persons with Disabilities, the Convention Against Torture and Convention on the Rights of the Child: HRPSA s. 3(1), definition of 'human rights.'

[23]There are many examples of legislation enacted despite reports from the Joint Committee on Human Rights identifying incompatibilities with human rights. Recent examples include laws authorising offshore detention of asylum seekers and expanding intelligence powers.

constitutional requirements means this is not part of education about the system of government.

The federal division of powers is not a bright line. The states, which pre-existed the Commonwealth as colonies, retain power to legislate in all areas. Under the Commonwealth Constitution, the Commonwealth (Australian) government, can legislate only in specific areas listed in ss 51 and 52 of the Constitution. Many responsibilities to provide basic services such as health and education remain with the states, while social security and the public health system of access to non-hospital medical care, which developed during the twentieth century are seen as Commonwealth responsibilities. Although both levels of government have taxing powers, over time the Commonwealth has come to exclusively control the most lucrative taxes, and its financial dominance has led to 'vertical fiscal imbalance.' The Commonwealth has greater financial resources but fewer obligations to provide services, while the states and territories retain responsibility for providing services such as health and education but have limited taxing and fundraising powers.

Despite its limited legislative powers, the Commonwealth has ample powers to legislate to give effect to the ICESCR if it chose to, but it has not protected human rights as such apart from its four anti-discrimination laws and a Privacy Act. The Australian Human Rights Commission Act 1986 (Cth) (AHRCA) contains limited and unenforceable protection for human rights, primarily those listed in the ICCPR.[24]

The main areas in which enforceable legislative protection for human rights has been adopted are anti-discrimination laws and some areas of privacy law. States and territories retain full power to legislate on any topic, and all have adopted anti-discrimination and privacy laws, and in several jurisdictions, legislative human rights charters.[25] Convergence is illustrated by the fact that these are based on the dialogue model of the UK Human Rights Act 1988 and the Canadian Charter, though divergence in detail emerges in the absence of any binding obligation to protect, leading to a weaker form of protection than the UK or Canadian models.

The earliest of these human rights charters covered only civil and political rights,[26] although recent tentative moves have been made to expand them to include some social rights. The Australian Capital Territory Human Rights Act 2004 (HRA ACT) has been amended to include the right to education and some work-related rights,[27] and the Queensland Human Rights Act 2019 (HRAQ) includes the rights to

[24] AHRC Act, s. 3(1) definition of 'human rights,' 11(f) and 20. See n 2 above. The limited scope to complain of a breach of the rights in the ICCPR is largely ineffective because it can only be conciliated, not taken to court. Other anti-discrimination acts are listed in n 37 below.

[25] Human Rights Act 2004 (ACT), Charter of Human Rights and Responsibilities Act 2006 (Vic), Human Rights Act 2019 (Qld).

[26] Human Rights Act 2004 (ACT) as passed in 2004, Charter of Human Rights and Responsibilities Act 2006 (Vic), ss. 8-27.

[27] HRA ACT, Part 3A Economic, social and cultural rights, s. 27A Right to education, s. 27B Right to work and other work-related rights.

education and health services.[28] All three laws also include some basic protection for rights applicable to work contexts, such as the right to protection against discrimination, freedom of association, and freedom from forced labour. Enforcement of these laws is constrained, due to the caution of the legislatures adopting them, so in fact these rights are better protected under anti-discrimination laws and the Commonwealth Fair Work Act 2009, which is the national labour regulation statute. As they are only legislative, they cannot limit the government's ability to pass other legislation that infringes on rights. Among their most important effects is the imposition of obligations on the judicial and executive branches to respect rights: the Acts make it unlawful for the executive to act incompatibly with human rights.[29] This has been a big step forward, and the laws have been used, for example, to declare it unlawful to move minors in youth detention into an adult prison after a riot at the youth justice centre.[30] Legislation is to be interpreted as far as possible compatibly with human rights, though it must be given effect even if it is incompatible with rights.[31] However, the High Court has treated this interpretive obligation as requiring no more than the common law principle of legality, in setting up a presumption that legislation does not intend to override rights that can be overridden by legislative intention implied from the wording of the law.[32]

In summary, the protection given by the few state and territory human rights acts is in its infancy and can be defeated by a parliament willing to override the rights protected. Australia 'has enacted laws and made policies in particular areas of [economic and social rights] often at odds with its international obligations.'[33] Such laws often receive little pushback because political discourse in Australia does not have an established space for human rights, especially economic, social, or cultural rights.

More important than any limits on legal powers to legislate for human rights is the political dynamic. Conservative governments have been reluctant to expand the government's responsibilities to protect further human rights or to provide support in terms of services or payments, even though power exists. As a result, legal protection for social rights remains piecemeal and patchwork, to be found in a wide range of laws, and often expressed without reference to human rights, as a privilege or benefit,[34] rather than an entitlement. Therefore, laws affecting social rights in Australia are quite diverse and can include social security laws, tenancy law, and public housing provision, the public health system, access and resources for

---

[28] HRAQ, Part 3 Division 3 Economic, social and cultural rights ss. 36 and 37.

[29] E.g. Charter (Vic), s. 38.

[30] *Certain Children v Minister for Families and Children (No 2)*[2017] VSC 251, upholding the decision in *Certain Children by their Litigation Guardian Sister Marie Brigid Arthur v Minister for Families and Children* [2016] VSC 796.

[31] E.g. Charter (Vic), s. 32.

[32] *Momcilovic v The Queen* (2011) 245 CLR 1; [2011] HCA 34.

[33] Solomon (2021), p. 1.

[34] Reich (1964).

education, especially for marginalised groups such as indigenous people and people with disability, laws against discrimination, and immigration law as it affects asylum seekers and temporary visa holders.[35]

Among the many disadvantages of this approach is that the absence of a focused list of rights makes education around human and social rights difficult and prevents the development of a culture of rights. In the next section the examples of disability discrimination laws, provision of disability services, and social security unemployment benefits are reviewed to trace modes of legal protection, the influences on them and how they have operated in response to crisis.

4 Examples: Convergence, Divergence and Crisis Response

The examples of social rights considered here illustrate differences in how social rights are protected and expressed by law. Some are dealt with explicitly as rights, such as the Disability Discrimination Act 1992 (Cth) (DDA). Others, such as social security unemployment benefits are not explicitly dealt with as rights but as privileges. In between lies the recent initiative of the National Disability Insurance Scheme (NDIS), which seeks to provide disability services on a nationally consistent basis. The key differences are whether or not the legislation explicitly identifies social or human rights and, if so, whether rights are framed as positive or negative rights, and what role if any is played by the idea of insurance. All these initiatives have been affected by responses to crisis, especially the COVID-19 pandemic, particularly through cost-cutting as the conservative government sought to cut expenditure in areas it saw as 'non-essential' in response to the budget demands of public health during the pandemic.

Both disability discrimination laws and the NDIS explicitly refer to rights, but neither the NDIS nor unemployment benefits laws confer a specific legal right to the benefit, merely a right to have proper process followed when an application for a benefit is made. Although the NDIS identifies itself as an 'insurance' scheme, it does not involve any contributory element. Similarly, and diverging from all Organisation for Economic Co-operation and Development ('OECD') countries (except New Zealand), Australia's social security system does not involve any contributory component.[36] Users and individuals do not pay into the scheme as insurance against unemployment or disability, and benefits are funded directly from government consolidated revenue. While this is desirable in universalising rights, it dilutes the idea that these schemes provide an entitlement that is 'bought' through individual contributions, undermining support for an individual rights claim.

[35] Solomon (2021) undertakes an extended consideration of social rights in Australia.

[36] See OECD, Social security contributions Total, % of GDP, 2000 – 2020, https://data.oecd.org/tax/social-security-contributions.htm.

However, the most recent of these schemes, the NDIS, explicitly relies on a human rights goal in the statutory purposes clause, and in particular, a claim to be giving effect to the social rights in the CRPD. This suggests that legal innovations in Australia are now more likely to move towards human rights thinking than in the past. Overall, however, policies are driven by local analysis and innovation albeit informed by choices made in other countries. Laws are most likely to be driven by local conditions and politics, and to diverge from the international consensus embodied in the UN conventions and OECD practices.

4.1 Disability Discrimination

The Disability Discrimination Act 1992 (Cth) ('DDA') is one of a series of anti-discrimination laws that, with privacy laws and the state Human Rights Acts and Charter are the main vehicles for specific protection of human rights. The DDA, like other Australian anti-discrimination laws, is modelled on the UK anti-discrimination laws which in turn were based on codifying US interpretations of the Civil Rights Act 1964.[37] The objects of the DDA are clearly within the realm of human rights. They are to 'eliminate, as far as possible, discrimination against persons on the ground of disability' in the major areas of activity, to 'ensure, as far as practicable, that persons with disabilities have the same rights to equality before the law as the rest of the community; and 'to promote recognition and acceptance within the community of the principle that persons with disabilities have the same fundamental rights as the rest of the community.'[38] Again, one can see convergence with UK and US approaches in the general policy of legislating against disability discrimination, but divergence in the details of the implementation of that policy. The DDA makes direct or indirect discrimination based on disability unlawful. Unlike comparable laws in the UK or US, the DDA has a broad definition of 'disability'[39] so establishing disability is not set up as a hurdle and access to the law is not narrowly restricted. Prohibition of disability discrimination operates as a negative right, but the DDA (and other Australian anti-discrimination laws) goes beyond that to create positive rights through at least two mechanisms. First, it requires duty holders to make reasonable adjustments for a person with disability unless it would impose 'unjustifiable hardship' on a respondent.[40] Second, it permits positive action

---

[37] Gaze and Smith (2017), pp. 33–34. The earliest federal anti-discrimination law, the Racial Discrimination Act 1975 (Cth) relied directly on the International Convention for the Elimination of all Forms of Racial Discrimination (ICERD). The next law, the Sex Discrimination Act 1984 (Cth) (SDA), was influenced by the then UK laws, the Sex Discrimination Act 1975 and the Race Relations Act 1976. The DDA was adopted in 1992 following the structure of the SDA, and in view of the Americans with Disabilities Act 1990, followed by the Age Discrimination Act 2004.

[38] DDA, s. 3.

[39] DDA, s. 4(1), definition of 'disability.'

[40] DDA, ss. 5(2) and 6(2), 11, 21B.

schemes for the purposes of achieving substantive equality for people with disability.[41] Such 'special measures' schemes are explicit recognition that equal treatment or formal equality is not a sufficient goal and that seeking substantive equality for people with disability is not discrimination.[42] The UK legislation of the time on which these laws were based did not allow for positive action, and these provisions were adapted from the US and Canadian approaches. The smorgasbord approach of Australian policy is illustrated by the way that different elements are chosen from the models usually considered.

In contrast with disability discrimination laws in comparable countries, none of the Australian anti-discrimination laws has a shifting onus of proof of the reason for a decision or action, leaving proof of direct discrimination difficult in the absence of direct evidence. All comparable jurisdictions have some mechanism to assist with proof, but Australian governments have resisted adopting such a provision so far, another divergence indicating the limits of influence of comparable jurisdictions.[43]

The pandemic revealed the impotence of the anti-discrimination laws against systematic failure to consider disabled people's interests. When vaccines against COVID-19 became available during 2021, the Commonwealth claimed to prioritise the elderly and people with disability as well as essential workers (e.g. in health care and food supply) for the first vaccinations, on the advice of its public health authorities. In practice, people with disability were not prioritised, and the DDA and similar state and territory laws did not assist in getting attention to their needs. Enforcement is too slow and too difficult to help in a crisis. The laws were insufficient to protect against a lack of respect for their health rights by government. Pro-active public policy to protect the health of people with disability is an essential element of their social rights, but in this case, it was overlooked by the government. There has subsequently been no change to this law or adoption of laws that would ensure prioritisation of these rights, despite claims to be doing so. The dangers of failing to protect social rights by law are evident. In contrast, where social rights are explicit in law, there is a better chance of ensuring attention is paid to such rights, for example through a mechanism such as the public sector equality duty in the UK.[44]

4.2 National Disability Insurance Scheme (NDIS): An Explicit Social Rights Objective

The NDIS is an initiative developed by the last ALP government and legislated in 2013 with the aim of providing support to people with disability to live to their

---

41 DDA, s. 45.

42 Fredman (2011), Degener (2016a, b).

43 See Allen (2009), p. 579.

44 Equality Act 2010 (UK) s 149.

potential. It is an original initiative[45] whose primary objective is to give effect to Australia's obligations under the CRPD as well as obligations undertaken under the other major human rights conventions.[46] Among its specific objectives are to:

(c) support the independence and social and economic participation of people with disability; and
(d) provide reasonable and necessary supports, including early intervention supports, for participants in the National Disability Insurance Scheme; and
(e) enable people with disability to exercise choice and control in the pursuit of their goals and the planning and delivery of their supports; and
(f) facilitate the development of a nationally consistent approach to the access to, and the planning and funding of, supports for people with disability . . .;[47]

The scheme is clearly based within the human rights field. The 'insurance' element seeks to 'give [. . .] all Australians peace of mind if they, their child or loved one is born with or acquires a permanent and significant disability, they will get the support they need.'[48] The scheme was developed after an 18 month inquiry into 'Disability Care and Support' by the Commonwealth Productivity Commission published in 2011.[49] It envisaged replacing the disparate and unequal state and territory disability services structures with a single scheme to provide consistent levels of services to people above a certain threshold of disability, on the basis of regular assessments of their needs. It provides funding to be spent on services, which are not provided by a public sector workforce but by an outsourced and privatised workforce engaged either directly (where the person with disability could or had support to do this) or by corporate providers who would take a management fee. Implementing the scheme has been a major undertaking, with many challenges and delays in getting assessments and plans, in seeking reviews of assessments and plans, and in access to services.[50] Outsourcing of the care workforce (which is female dominated) has led to minimum wage casual employment, with difficulty recruiting staff, and complaints about high management fees soaking up the funding for services, and the exploitation of the scheme by for-profit providers.[51] The NDIS replaced state and territory

[45] Ramcharan (2016), OECD 'Sickness and disability' at https://www.oecd.org/employment/sickness-and-disability.htm.

[46] National Disability Insurance Scheme Act 2013 (Cth) s 3(1)(i). The other conventions referred to are the ICCPR, IESCR, CROC, CEDAW and CERD.

[47] NDIS Act, s. 3(1)(c)-(f).

[48] NDIS: What Does it mean? https://www.ndis.gov.au/understanding/what-ndis.

[49] Productivity Commission (2011). The Productivity Commission is a national authority established to conduct research and provide advice to the government about 'matters relating to industry, industry development and productivity' as referred by the Minister, and on its own initiative: Productivity Commission Act 1998 (Cth), s. 6. On the NDIS see https://everyaustraliancounts.com.au/research-reports/where-did-the-ndis-come-from/#:~:text=The%20NDIS%20model%20was%20devised,countries%20that%20were%20working%20well.

[50] Lee (2017).

[51] Henriques-Gomes (2021a).

disability services provision (which often used public sector workers) with a single scheme that was intended to be better funded, consistent across the country, and provide a higher level of capacity for people with disability to live a full life.

When the scheme was designed, funding and numbers of administrative employees were projected by the Productivity Commission at a level appropriate to administer the scheme. However, the succeeding conservative government held employment in the National Disability Insurance Agency to around half of the planned level of employment, and this has slowed and impeded implementation of the scheme. The scheme is funded from consolidated revenue, and as a single program that involves very substantial expenditure, it is an easy target for governments seeking to reduce funding to the sector. This has been exacerbated as government sought to restrain expenditure because of the COVID-19 pandemic. Because services are contracted out, the government sees only the cost of the scheme. As a result, even though expenditure is either within or close to the cost projected in designing the scheme, the government has begun to seek to constrain expenditure of the scheme by making it more difficult to qualify and reducing expenditure per person. [52] Although the provision of services is structured as a market, information provision is not sufficient to allow the purchasers of services to choose services according to assessed quality as well as price. Employing their own service providers is a time-consuming activity which is really only realistic for those with extensive supports or who are particularly competent. For people with intellectual disability or mental illness, navigating the system is difficult.

A further consequence of contracting the service out is that accountability for the operation of the scheme and the quality of services provided is not governed by public law accountability requirements or administrative law but can only be based on contract. While there are mechanisms for review of decisions, these avenues are currently so overburdened that the slow responses are not adequate for people whose ability to operate in the community depends on the services they can access.

The human rights basis of the NDIS in seeking to protect the social rights of people with disability is expressed in its objectives, but not in its substantive provisions, which do not refer to rights to services, but only rights to apply for support and a process to seek review of decisions made by administrators.[53] This format, which also applies to social security rights, positions the schemes as providing privileges rather than rights. While the Act appears to echo the ICESCR obligation of progressive realisation of rights,[54] the language used avoids the issue by referring to 'progressive implementation' of the scheme, not of individual rights under the ICESCR or the CRPD.

---

[52] In mid-2021, a new mechanism was proposed for 'independent assessment' of plans and reductions of the amounts awarded to clients for their support services. See Henriques-Gomes (2021b).

[53] NDIS Act, Chapter 3 – Participants and their plans, e.g. ss. 18P, 20.

[54] See NDIS Act, s. 3(3)(a) 'progressive implementation' of the scheme.

This scheme is a clear example of local innovation being undermined by the political context of ideas adopted from elsewhere, in particular the ideologies of neo-liberalism, small government, privatisation and outsourcing followed in the UK, US and many OECD countries since the 1980s. It is not easy to track convergence and divergence in this context, because despite the scheme's originality and social rights orientation, these underlying ideas have dominated its operation. The absence of any legal basis for a claim to social rights perhaps makes this derogation easier to achieve in Australia than in countries where legal rights exist

4.3 Social Security Unemployment Payment: A Privilege Not a Right

As noted above, Australian social security laws diverge from the pattern in many countries, in not requiring any element of individual contribution. There is no contributory or social insurance element, as they are solely funded from general government revenue. Most benefits are available to everyone with the qualifying characteristics like unemployment or sole parenthood. Benefits such as unemployment benefit and the age pension are not linked to previous workforce participation. However, only some benefits are indexed to increases in the cost of living, so the age pension increases regularly, but the unemployment payment (Job Seeker) increases much less, and its payments are below the poverty line. Social security expenditure is a very large budget item, and under neoliberal influence it has been seen as an area for cost reductions, rather than an important area of human rights support. Over the past few decades eligibility for benefits has been constricted with the introduction of more onerous conditions to qualify for benefits (such as activity tests) and increasingly stringent targeting through various methods of income and assets testing. The real value of benefits not indexed to rises in the cost of living has fallen. Arguably the fact these benefits are not 'bought' by beneficiaries makes them more vulnerable to undermining by government. The absence of a sense of individual entitlements weakens the ability to oppose cost cutting, and provides another point of divergence in Australia's social security payment scheme from other OECD countries.[55]

The Commonwealth's power to provide welfare benefits was added in 1946 by constitutional amendment,[56] reflecting the rise of the welfare state after World War II, as well as the vertical fiscal imbalance that had been accelerated during that war, with the result that the states and territories no longer had the resources to provide such benefits. Australia thereafter adopted a range of benefits, including

[55] See OECD, note 36 above.

[56] Constitution s. 51(xxiiiA) gives the Commonwealth power to legislate for 'the provision of maternity allowances, widows' pensions, child endowment, unemployment, pharmaceutical, sickness and hospital benefits, medical and dental services (but not to authorise any form of civil conscription), benefits to students and family allowances.'

unemployment benefits, sole parent payments, parenting allowances, childcare subsidies, youth and student allowances, carer payments and various family benefits.[57]

Despite the absence of a contributory basis, convergence is present in underlying ideas adapted from overseas, with the development of the welfare state in the UK following the Beveridge Report the most obvious influence, while some ideas have been developed in Australia, like the National Disability Insurance Scheme. An example of such domestic policy innovation is the Higher Education Contribution Scheme ('HECS'),[58] whereby students do not pay fees at the time of tertiary study but incur a debt to the Commonwealth (which funds the tertiary education sector) for their fees which has to be repaid through the tax system only when their salary exceeds a certain level. However, like the NDIS, once a centralised scheme like HECS exists, it can become an easy target for an austerity-minded government to reduce funding by changing the parameters of the scheme. The fees charged to tertiary students through the HECS have increased substantially since it was introduced in 1989 and now create quite substantial student debts. This model has been followed, with variations, in other jurisdictions including the UK.

Like the NDIS, the laws relevant to social security benefits, the Social Security Act 1991 (Cth) and the Social Security (Administration) Act 1999 (Cth) do not create legal rights to benefits but set up a system that defines entitlements and provides a structured system for determining eligibility and appealing against adverse decisions. Decisions can be challenged though the Australian administrative law system, which has a distinctive system of no-cost merits review tribunals with powers to re-make decisions, including a new decision on the facts as well as the law, based on new evidence.[59] This creates strong protection for social security entitlements, but falls short of a legal right. The legislation has become more and more detailed over the years, and now leaves very little discretion to the departmental officer deciding on eligibility. The qualifications to receive payments have become stricter, and failure to maintain the value of benefits, especially unemployment benefits, leaves many recipients living below the poverty line.[60]

As the system has become increasingly targeted based on stringent means testing, it has moved away from a universal scheme (whereby child endowment, for example, was payable in respect of all children) towards a 'safety net' designed to provide minimal support to those most in need.[61] Narrowing eligibility for benefits can undermine community support as they come to be seen as a minority entitlement paid for by others. For unemployment payments, activity requirements have been introduced, like a need to apply for a minimum number of jobs each week, and compliance is supervised by outsourced job network providers, who can 'breach' a

[57] See Services Australia (2021).

[58] Higher Education Funding Act 1988 (Cth).

[59] This distinctive system was partly followed when the UK adopted its integrated two-tier tribunal system.

[60] Australian Council of Social Service (2021).

[61] Solomon (2021), p. 236.

recipient for non-compliance, with the possible consequences of suspension or cancellation of payments.[62]

Two examples demonstrate the impact of government policies in the context of crisis: the 'Robodebt' story shows government's determination to rein in expenditure, even in ways that are not lawful, while the COVID supplement demonstrates that the government could go a long way to eliminating poverty, but has chosen not to. 'Robodebt' as it is called, involved a program to claw back 'overpayments' from people who had received social security payments in previous years. Benefits like unemployment payments are paid fortnightly, with the amount adjusted based on the claimant's reported income for that fortnight. Beneficiaries are required to advise the relevant agency of their income every fortnight, and their payment is adjusted on this basis. People who have some casual or part time work can find this difficult if their shifts vary from week to week so that income can be difficult to predict. If income has to be predicted and later turns out to be inaccurate, or if inaccurate details of income are given, then any amount overpaid becomes a debt due to the Commonwealth and must be repaid.

The Commonwealth has always had a program that checked back over income details and matched them with Taxation Office income records to see whether an overpayment had occurred. In 2016, it decided to computerise this process, by taking reported annual income and averaging it over 26 fortnights. It calculated a benefit entitlement on that basis, and then issued a debt notice for any difference if more had been paid. Previously such discrepancies had been checked by staff with employers to ensure there was a genuine concern about overpayment. The 2016 programme omitted this and sent computer-generated letters to many people for alleged debts many years old, requiring them to prove that they had not incurred an overpayment. As it turned out, this process was not a lawful exercise of power; this method of calculation was not in accordance with the legislative requirements. The government had advice to that effect very early, but it persisted with the approach nevertheless.[63] Being presented with large debts and asked to disprove them caused many benefit recipients extreme stress and anxiety, and after it was declared unlawful by the Federal Court, the Commonwealth had to repay AUD720 million of wrongly collected debts.[64]

Robodebt involved an extreme level of government disregard for the health and rights of social welfare beneficiaries. It could be perceived to be a consequence of Australia's divergent failure to recognise the full range of human rights, both civil

---

[62] McKeever and Walsh (2020).

[63] Whiteford (2020), Solomon (2021), p. 248. The Senate Standing Committee on Community Affairs has been conducted an inquiry into Centrelink's Compliance Program, which reported in 2022 since June 2019. The reporting date has been postponed on several occasions and its currently May 2022: https://www.aph.gov.au/Parliamentary_Business/Committees/Senate/Community_Affairs/Centrelinkcompliance. Subsequently a Royal Commission into it was conducted in 2023 which reported adversely on the scheme and the role of the public service and ministers in devising and continuing it: Royal Commission into Robodebt, Report (July 2023).

[64] Henriques-Gomes (2021c).

and political and economic, social and cultural. If rights were better protected by law and generally better understood, such disregard would be more difficult. Although the scheme was declared unlawful and the government had to repay the overpayments it had collected, there has been no reform through greater recognition of rights. In contrast, a similar overreach in the Netherlands led to the resignation of the Prime Minister and cabinet, an indication of a different political context, and that legal rights may make a difference in the political and public perception of such actions.[65]

Finally, two further examples demonstrate the adoption of ideas from overseas (UK and US) with the support of Australian civil society, but where divergent details of implementation undermined the justice and respect for social rights of the program. During the COVID-19 lockdowns in 2020-2021 there was concern that people in essential but insecure casual and low paid work, such as food production and distribution and health care, might not isolate as required if they were symptomatic or after taking a covid test, for fear of losing their income or their job. Failure to isolate could result in much greater circulation of the virus with severe consequences for the health system and more deaths. The Commonwealth responded in two ways. Following the UK, and at the urging of the Australian Council of Trade Unions, the Job Keeper scheme paid money to employer organisations to retain their workers on their payroll even during furlough periods in order to keep their jobs on foot. Employers were eligible if they predicted a fall in revenue of 30% or more as a result of the lockdowns. Unlike the UK or New Zealand, which adopted similar programs, the scheme did not require employers to repay funds where the predicted downturn in revenue did not eventuate, and no public information was provided about how much funding had been paid to the entities that claimed. As a result, the government paid billions of dollars to companies that instead had increased turnover and profits. Despite some public pressure, the government has resisted requiring any return of funds, or even publishing the amounts of funds paid and the organisations that they were paid to.[66] In the second response, a COVID Supplement was added in 2020 to social security benefits such as Job Seeker (the unemployment payment) to ensure that self-employed and insecure workers who might lose income because their normal supplementary work was not possible during lockdown could continue to afford their normal expenses such as rent and food. The extra payment of AUD550 fortnightly for full time workers had the effect of greatly reducing child poverty in Australia, a major step forward in protecting social rights for the most vulnerable in society.[67] However the scheme was terminated in March 2021 with unemployment benefits returning to their pre-covid low amounts, even though further lockdowns occurred throughout 2021 with similar concerns about isolating and income. The contrast with the government's refusal to require companies that did not need Job Keeper funding to return it could not be clearer. It evidences a

---

[65] Corder (2021).

[66] Wright (2021).

[67] Bessell (2021).

government that could substantially reduce poverty in Australia, but chose not to, driven by its neoliberal preferences. Any divergence from actions elsewhere is the result of the varying political orientations of the elected governments in different jurisdictions. At the national elections in 2022, that government was replaced by an ALP government.

The neoliberal orientation that has shaped the social welfare system since the early 1980s under both parties, but especially since 2013, has been arguably more important than legal influences from other jurisdictions. Human rights imperatives have a reduced role in government policy making in Australia, partly because of their absence from the constitution and the consequent lack of broad understanding of human rights in the general community but also because of the lack of legal rights and the influence of political ideologies. These examples also illustrate the government's perception of human rights. The goal of the right to social security in the IESCR is prevention of poverty: '[s]ocial security is, at its core, a political issue about redistribution and as such is central to understanding the role of economic and social rights (ESR) in addressing social and economic concerns of people generally and, in particular, the most vulnerable.'[68] However, in practical terms in Australia, it has become about reducing public expenditures on individuals in need, while treating corporations generously at taxpayer expense.[69]

5 Conclusion: Convergence and Divergence in the Protection of Social Rights in Australia

The influences on these three examples are various. The DDA and the general objectives of the NDIS are based on UN Human Rights Conventions and follow UK and US developments, while the origins of the social security system lie in the development of the welfare state after the second world war. The original influences on Australia's social security regime were from the UK and US, but the Australian regime has never followed jurisdictions that rely on a contributory social insurance model. Even where the word 'insurance' is used to describe a scheme in Australia such as the National Disability Insurance Scheme, this is not to describe any individual contributions to the scheme, but only the protection it gives to individuals against the potentially enormous costs for any person of dealing with disability. The non-contributory approach, despite its potential benefit of universalism, risks such payments being seen as government beneficence rather than an individual right, and may be more readily subject to government control and restriction than a contributory scheme where the individual has 'bought' their entitlement.

Although the UN conventions are vitally important in developing and defining social rights, without a binding obligation to give effect to them it is difficult to

[68] Solomon (2021), p. 225.

[69] Arup (2022).

ensure adequate protection. This absence is the fundamental and most important divergence in Australia's legal environment from virtually every other developed country and OECD member state when considering social rights. The Australian approach has been shaped by the absence of familiarity with human rights claims in general political debate, resulting from the absence of such rights from our constitution and the relatively weak and patchy legislative protection for human rights beyond non-discrimination. This leaves Australia a divergent outlier in giving effect to human rights and social rights. This review illustrates the eclectic nature of influences in a field as wide as social rights, and the way in which governments choose approaches that are suited in their view to local social and economic conditions. This can lead to convergence at the level of general policies but substantial divergence in detail.

References

Allen D (2009) Reducing the Burden of proving discrimination in Australia. Sydney Law Rev 31: 579

Arup C (2022) Liberty or protection? Making law for employment and social security. Griffith Law Rev 31:361

Australian Council of Social Service (2021) Comparison of poverty lines with pension and Newstart (now JobSeeker) payments for singles and couples without children (in $2017-18 per annum)

Bessell S (2021) Australia was a model for protecting people from COVID-19 — and then we dumped half a million people back into poverty. The Conversation 12 August 2021

Boyle K (2020) Economic and social rights law: incorporation, justiciability and principles of adjudication. Routledge

Charlesworth H (1993) The Australian reluctance about rights. Osgoode Hall Law J 31:195–232

Corder M (2021) 'The buck stops here': Dutch PM, cabinet resign over welfare debt scandal'. The Age, 16 Jan 2021 https://www.theage.com.au/world/europe/the-buck-stops-here-dutch-pm-cabinet-resign-over-welfare-debt-scandal-20210116-p56ula.html

Degener T (2016a) Ch 3: A human rights model of disability. In: Blanck P, Flynn E (eds) Routledge handbook of disability law and human rights, Routledge, pp 31–50

Degener T (2016b) Disability in a human rights context. Laws 5:35

Fredman S (2011) Ch 1: Equality: concepts and controversies. In: Fredman S (ed) Discrimination law, 2nd edn. Clarendon Press, Oxford, pp 1–37

Henriques-Gomes L (2021a) Disability sector celebrates after Coalition forced to scrap NDIS independent assessments. The Guardian (Australia) 9 July 2021

Henriques-Gomes L (2021b) NDIS overhaul: a solution to a $60bn cost blowout or an attack on the scheme's soul? The Guardian (Australia) 9 July 2021

Henriques-Gomes L (2021c) Robodebt: court approves $1.8bn settlement for victims of government's 'shameful' failure. The Guardian (Australia) 11 June 2021

Jackman M, Porter B (2017) Social and economic rights. In: Oliver P, Macklem P, Des Rosiers, N (eds.) The Oxford handbook of the Canadian constitution (New York, Oxford University Press, 2017), pp 843-866.

King J (2012) Judging social rights. Cambridge University Press

Lee M (2017) The art of dependency: the NDIS promised choice and control. The Monthly, August 2017

Maccabiani N (2018) The effectiveness of social rights in the EU: social inclusion and European governance, a constitutional and methodological perspective. FrancoAngeli s.r.l, Milan

McKeever G, Walsh T (2020) The moral hazard of conditionality: restoring the integrity of social security law. Aust J Soc Issues 55:73

National Human Rights Consultation Committee (2009) National Human Rights Consultation Report

Otto D (2001) From 'reluctance' to 'exceptionalism': the Australian approach to domestic implementation of human rights. Alternat Law J 26:219–222

Productivity Commission (2011) Inquiry report - Disability Care and Support

Ramcharan P (2016) Understanding the NDIS: a history of disability welfare from 'deserving poor' to consumers in control. The Conversation 6 July 2016

Reich C (1964) The new property. Yale Law J 73:733–787

Services Australia (2021) A guide to Australian Government payments (20 September 2021 to 31 December 2021)

Solomon R (2021) Australia's engagement with economic and social rights: a case of institutional avoidance. Palgrave Macmillan, pp 14–16

Whiteford P (2020) Robodebt was a fiasco with a cost we have yet to fully appreciate. The Conversation 16 November 2020

Wilson S (2020) Rising pressures, new scaffolding, uncertain futures: Australia's social policy response to the COVID-19 pandemic. J Aust Polit Econ 85:183–192

Wright S (2021) Australians want JobKeeper overpayments given back to taxpayers. Sydney Morning Herald 28 August 2021

Beth Gaze is a Professor in the Law School at the University of Melbourne, Australia.

Part IV
Convergence and Divergence in Context

Harmonisation and European Integration in Times of Crisis

Emilie Ghio

1 Introduction

Globalisation generally, and European integration, more specifically, have led to calls for the minimisation of legal diversity which can result in transaction costs and the lack of level-playing field for cross-border actors. One of the prevailing methods to achieve such level-playing field is legal harmonisation.[1]

In the European Union (EU) in particular, harmonisation serves as a key tool for the integration of the internal market. The rationale behind such approach is that the EU would be more appealing to external economic actors and investors if they only had to tackle one regime, instead of twenty-eight (one supranational and twenty-seven national) different ones. Disparities between national legal systems are seen as obstacles to the proper functioning of the internal market because they produce competitive advantages for some actors with cross-border activities and deter foreign investment. It is thus not surprising that the harmonisation of several fields of law has been at the top of the European institutions since the creation of the EU.

However, legal harmonisation is not without its challenges. Although on the one hand, integrationists argue that European integration has achieved seminar milestones since the inception of the EU—Europe has enjoyed the longest period of peace in its history; the European Union is one of the world's most prosperous marketplaces; one of the largest trading entities; and an important source and recipient of foreign direct investment – Eurosceptics have claimed, on the other hand, that European integration has weakened national sovereignties, resulted in a

[1]The word 'harmonisation' in this chapter is understood as a top-down method of legal approximation.

E. Ghio (✉)
University of Edinburgh, Edinburgh, UK
e-mail: Emilie.ghio@ed.ac.uk

E. Ghio, R. Perlingeiro (eds.), *Are Legal Systems Converging or Diverging?*,
https://doi.org/10.1007/978-3-031-38180-5_14

lack of accountability and transparency on behalf of the European institutions, and that it operates from a circle of out-of-touch technocratic elites.

These challenges have been exacerbated by the multi-faceted crisis which has been hitting the EU for the last decade or so. European integration seems to have lost some of its shine and the EU is experiencing some 'integrational panic'.[2] The current across-the-board crisis has contributed to a politicisation of European integration and an increasing Eurosceptic mobilisation across borders. Because the Union's legitimacy is contested, Member States are reluctant to embrace further integration, including by means of harmonisation, accused of being the product of private legislators, heavily influenced by lobbying groups seeking to promote their own economic interests and working in an environment of scant accountability. It is therefore not surprising that in times of crises, Member States tend to fall back on state-centric solutions, rather than pursuing common, coordinated policies to tackle these crises.

The chapter proceeds as follows. Section 2 reviews the main challenges facing legal harmonisation. Section 3 analyses the current polycrisis in which the EU finds itself, notably by comparing the Eurozone and Schengen crises. The question at hand is not so much whether the EU is in a crisis but rather, whether crises are consistently bad for European integration and legal harmonisation?

2 Harmonisation in Crisis[3]

Harmonisation is about benefits, practicality, and utility.[4] In an ideal world, in the words of Platsas, 'the legal harmonisation thesis [would be] a thesis which gives recognition to the nation-state but [would] equally posit[s] that national considerations subside when wider legal considerations proceed beyond the local, the domestic and the national.'[5] Therefore, '[h]armonization is a delightful notion. How could one possibly be so unsophisticated as to oppose it?'[6] And yet, harmonisation is increasingly branded as a threat to national sovereignty, the enemy of national legal culture, and as an inefficient course of action for markets and the economy.

[2] Davis Cross and Ma (2015), p. 1056.

[3] Parts of this section have been explored in Ghio (2022).

[4] For an in-depth exploration of the benefits of legal harmonisation, see for example McCormack (2011), Chapter 2; La Porta et al. (2008).

[5] Platsas (2017), p. 2.

[6] Weatherill (2004), p. 633.

2.1 National Sovereignty and Loss of National Autonomy

Harmonisation is increasingly rejected for a number of reasons, including its conflict with national sovereignty and autonomy. Sovereignty and self-determination are closely related to the notion of law-making, which traditionally promotes a local process rather than the sourcing of legal rules from abroad. Hence, legal harmonisation can undermine national sovereignty and the concept of law-making.

'Sovereignty' comes from the Latin word *supremitas* and is commonly defined as 'absolute power'.[7] The sixteenth century French philosopher Bodin defined 'sovereignty' as a 'supreme principle of citizens and subjects, unbound by the law [. . .] a perpetual, humanly unlimited, and unconditional right to make, interpret and execute law.'[8] For him, legal sovereignty is the formal expression of a sovereignty that is inherent in the nature of a human association and is determined by its ends. On the other hand, British philosopher Hobbes, associated the concept with the role of the nation-state. In Hobbes' theory, the people should elect a government that will have supreme authority over the government.[9] Over time, popular sovereignty gradually aligned state jurisdictions with nations as personifications of the populi.[10] Thus, the original definition of sovereignty focused on nation-states' ability to craft domestic laws, but the concept has evolved to include a strong political component. The term 'sovereignty', today, generally refers to notions of legitimacy, power and authority, usually associated with a particular geographical area.[11] Sovereignty is defined as the ability of a state to control its own destiny, achieve its aims, and further its interests independently.[12]

This traditional view of law-making has been altered by globalisation. Globalisation has led to an increase in interconnected activities and increased interdependence and linkages between States. With a rise in cross-border activities came a need for cross-border rules. Globalization has driven harmonisation of law across borders, but tensions have also grown as a result. On the one hand, to satisfy popular consent and accountability, self-determination requires the lowest possible level of law. Conversely, there is a growing need for harmonised laws that facilitate

[7]For example, the American Heritage Dictionary (2021) defines sovereignty as 'supremacy of authority', 'complete independence and self-government' or 'a territory existing as an independent state.'

[8]Sabine (1961), pp. 405–407.

[9]Hobbes (1651).

[10]Hooghe and Marks (2008), pp. 22–23.

[11]One of the most comprehensive definitions of sovereignty, which combines international and national aspects can be found in the Academic American Encyclopaedia, volume 18 (Grolier, Inc., 1989), p. 113: 'a sovereign state is independent and free from all external control; enjoys full legal equality with other states; and has the power to enter into agreements with other nations, to exchange ambassadors, and to decide on war and peace. . . Although a sovereign state theoretically enjoys absolute freedom, its freedom is, in fact, often abridged by the need to coexist with other countries, as well as by treaties, international laws, and the strength of its military power.'

[12]Richardson (2000), p. 323.

economic exchanges by reducing transaction costs and increasing legal predictability. 'Globalization represents the reality that we live in at a time when the walls of sovereignty are no protection against the movement of capital, labor, information and ideas.'[13] In the EU, comprised of 27 Member States with varying levels of economic development, social priorities, and legal cultures, harmonisation is bound to challenge deep-rooted cultural differences and legal codes based on different principles, as countries are unwilling to allow laws made outside their national parliaments encroach on their national sovereignty.

The issue with harmonisation, therefore, is that the notion itself clashes with this prevailing idea of law-making as closely tied to a state's sovereignty and self-determination. Laws are produced locally, rather than sourced from a foreign supply. Harmonisation intrudes into the sovereignty of states and national legislatures and suppresses national differences for the sake of uniformity and to leave no opportunity for national autonomy and divergence.[14] This leads to discontent with harmonisation measures, perceived as necessary and useful only from the EU's perspective. Commentators have argued that '[m]any directives are only a harmonization success story from the perspective of Brussels: from the perspective of national legal systems, they lead to new fault lines.'[15]

As pointed out by McCormack, '[i]f harmonisation is merely intended to mean the identification of common approaches among existing national laws then this encroaches only minimally on States.'[16] However, 'a more proactive pose actively striving for the reform of [. . .] law [. . .] may involve [. . .] the rejection of existing law and the creation of new law [and] can represent a fairly sharp form of intrusion into the sovereignty of States and national legislatures.'[17] Globalisation, Europeanisation and the harmonisation measures that result from these processes, can 'stir up old nationalisms, exacerbate cultural conflict, and encourage post-modern scepticism about the universality of values and ideas.'[18]

The Brexit narrative is the perfect example. The Leave campaign in the UK used the 'Take Back Control' slogan repeatedly and relentlessly over several years. While this slogan was alluring, it masked an inaccurate description of decision-making in the EU. Evidently, in political campaigns, what matters is not what is accurate, but what works. The concept of a defenceless British Parliament stripped of its powers by the European Union became a pervasive topic during the run up to the referendum. Many denounced the loss of sovereignty brought about by European integration. Lord Denning even went as far as to compare EU laws to an incoming tide turning into a tidal wave:

---

[13] Higgins (1999), p. 82.

[14] See Legrand (2002, 2003a).

[15] Von Bar (2002), p. 385.

[16] McCormack (2021), p. 31.

[17] Ibid.

[18] Twinning (2000), p. 65.

> Our sovereignty has been taken away by the European Court of Justice [...] Our courts must no longer enforce our national laws. They must enforce Community law [...] No longer is European law an incoming tide flowing up the estuaries of England. It is now like a tidal wave bringing down our sea walls and flowing inland over our fields and houses – to the dismay of all.[19]

Comparing the Trade and Cooperation Agreement (TCA), Boris Johnson stated in December 2020 that '[t]he treaty banished the old concepts of uniformity and harmonisation, in favour of the right to make our own regulatory choices and deal with the consequences.'[20]

2.2 *Legal Cultures and Path-Dependence*

As legal systems become more globalised, another salient problem is bridging the gap between diverging national legal cultures. Law-making has historically been a function of the national legislature (and courts). Laws are usually made for relatively homogeneous societies with a common language and culture. As a result, law schools' curricula, popular culture, and domestic legislatures and government bodies all reflect distinctive national legal cultures.

Friedman describes legal culture as the 'ideas, attitudes, values, and opinions about law held by people in a society.'[21] These concepts are interrelated and arguably circular. Identity derives from the shared culture within the nation-state while 'nationhood, especially as conceived by the nationalists of early-nineteenth-century Europe, was explicitly cultural.'[22] This interdependence has been highlighted in different political, socio-economic and cultural contexts.[23] In the legal context, Montesquieu understood law as the product of the spirit of the people, cultural and political environment:

> should be so closely tailored to the people for whom they are made, that it could be pure chance if the laws of one nation could meet the needs of another [...] They should be relative to the geography of the country; to its climate [...] to the quality of the land, its situation, and its extent; to the form of life of the people [...]; they should be relative to the degree of liberty that the constitution can tolerate; to the religion of the inhabitants, to their inclinations, wealth, number, commerce, customs, manners.[24]

---

[19] Lord Denning (1990), p. 48.

[20] Johnson (2020).

[21] Friedman (1989), p. 1579.

[22] Herzfeld (2005), p. 75.

[23] Dedek (2011).

[24] Montesquieu (1949).

Savigny highlighted the significance of the *Volksgeist* (the spirit of the people).[25] Characteristics identifiable as common within the nation-state were invoked as dimensions of national (legal) culture.

These traditional views have evolved as a result of globalisation and European integration. This is quite logical: '[i]f the law is to retain its role of regulating society (be it no longer a national, but a global one), we have to find new ways of making law and enforcing this law.'[26] The increased rejection of harmonisation in the EU is due to the fact that laws are embedded within a specific domestic culture, related to the history and evolution of a state.[27] Kahn-Freund argued that 'we cannot take for granted that rules or institutions are transplantable. The criteria answering the question whether or how far they are, have changed since Montesquieu's day, but any attempt to use a pattern of law outside the environment of its origin continues to entail the risk of rejection.'[28]

Associated to legal culture is the concept of path dependence, which means that a decision is shaped by the historical path leading to it, implying that 'what happened at an earlier point in time will affect the possible outcomes of a sequence of events occurring at a later point in time.'[29] The economic literature[30] suggests that path dependence can be understood not just in terms of the interplay between economic forces, but also in terms of the way in which present decisions are shaped by the decisions and structures inherited from the past. Those past decisions and structures provide a context for understanding and evaluating current economic behaviour. It is assumed that what happens next is determined by what was chosen and decided in the past.

As a result, this reinforces the notion that legal rules exist within legal systems and are interconnected with rules, concepts, institutions, and practices within those systems. Wendell Holmes argued that 'if we want to know why a rule of law has taken its particular shape, and more or less if we want to know why it exists at all, we go for tradition'[31] while Richard Posner postulated that law 'venerates tradition, precedent, [. . .] custom, ancient practices, ancient texts, archaic terminology [. . .] and interpretation conceived of as a method of recovering history. It is suspicious of [. . .] discontinuities.'[32]

This is why La Porta and his colleagues claim that legal change is slow and is typically consistent with the original legal tradition:

> The central point is that the reason for persistence [of legal approaches] is that the beliefs and ideologies become incorporated in legal rules, institutions, and education and, as such, are

---

[25] von Savigny (2013).

[26] Smits (2007), p. 1181.

[27] Weatherill (2004).

[28] Kahn-Freund (1974), p. 27.

[29] Sewell Jr. (1996), pp. 262–263.

[30] Liebowitz and Margolis (1995).

[31] Collins (2010), p. 147.

[32] Posner (2000), p. 573.

> transmitted from one generation to the next. It is this incorporation of beliefs and ideologies into the legal and political infrastructure that enables legal origins to have such persistent consequences for rules, regulations, and economic outcomes.[33]

According to nationalist arguments, legal harmonisation undermines national culture and national identity and opposes the path-dependent nature of law. Hence, harmonisation, or so-called legal transplants, has become a well-known topic of debate. While Kahn-Freund argued that legal transplants are possible yet 'the use [of the comparative method] requires a knowledge not only of the foreign law, but also of its social, and above all its political, context,'[34] Legrand claims that law being 'outgrowth of local society [. . .] embedded holistically in local culture [. . .] mak [es] reception and assimilation of foreign ideas problematic.'[35] He argues that '[c] omparison must not have a unifying, but multiplying effect [. . .] It must avoid complicity in the disregard for different ways of doing things and the ensuring exclusion of alterity.'[36] In his view, harmonisation does not work. Legal rules cannot be transposed from one legal system to another and therefore, legal systems will never converge.[37] Similarly, Teubner rejects the idea that foreign transplants are easily absorbed by the host system. Basing his argument on sociological research, he sees transplants, and thus harmonisation, as a 'fundamental irritation which triggers a whole series of new and unexpected events, [which irritates] law's "binding arrangement" [and which] unleashes an evolutionary dynamic in which the external rule's meaning will be reconstructed and the internal context will undergo fundamental change.'[38]

More recently and in the context of the EU, Weatherhill wrote that European harmonisation is:

> driven by the perception that legal culture, represented in part by the shape of private law, has undergone a long-term, frequently unplanned evolution in the Member States, reflecting a range of influences. To confine such richness within the straightjacket of harmonization is to rob Europe of its past [. . .] More broadly still [. . .] this dissenting vein is nurtured by the profound belief that Europe is strengthened by its diversity.[39]

While path-dependence and the concept of legal culture are long-established debates, yet arguments are not entirely satisfactory, providing a rather static view of the legal system as something which is immutable. However, national identity is malleable, able to change as a result of regional and global factors.[40] As explained by Halpern and Johnson, '[r]elying on identity as a ground to resist harmonisation is simply a method of creating a "them" and an "us" [whereas] harmonisation is about

[33] La Porta et al. (2008), p. 308.

[34] Kahn-Freund (1974), p. 27.

[35] Legrand (2003b), p. 248.

[36] Ibid, p. 299.

[37] Legrand (1996).

[38] Teubner (1998), p. 12.

[39] Weatherill (2004), p. 647.

[40] Contrast with Sefton-Green (2012), p. 268.

everyone involved being an "us" and there being no "them" at all.'[41] They point out that in this context, nationalism is a belief that one's own national legal system is the best and superior to the others and that 'outside influence will taint that perfection.'[42] Chesterton also claims that '[t]radition [...] is the democracy of the dead. [It] means giving votes to the most obscure of all classes, our ancestors.'[43] Resisting harmonisation on the ground of protection of national legal rules for reasons of pure conservatism is, therefore, objectionable.

> Tradition, as an independent construct should not be an argument against *beneficial* change; just as change and departure from tradition should not be undertaken solely in the interests of a search for modernity. Societies do not live in the past and neither do lawyers [...] Law is always about evolution and change. Tradition [should not] dominate[] the law, but simply guide[] it to ensure the persistence of the good [...] Harmonisation is simply a way of fashioning a new axe made of iron rather than bronze.[44]

2.3 *Regulatory Competition*

Finally, opposition to harmonisation frequently rests on the premise that while legal diversity fosters rivalry among national legal systems, harmonisation eliminates these opportunities for competition. The process by which regulators work to create a more hospitable regulatory climate in order to enhance the competitiveness of domestic industries and draw in foreign business activity is known as regulatory competition. Competition between national legislatures takes place in the legal sphere to entice legal consumers (whether individuals or businesses) to operate on their territory. In order for regulatory *competition* to occur, customers must engage in regulatory *arbitrage*: that is, they select the law that governs their activities in a way that will minimise their costs of operation. If such arbitrage occurs, for regulatory competition to follow, individual jurisdictions must have something to offer to consumers; that is, generally, an attractive legal regime. If both conditions are met, jurisdictions will seek to enact laws encouraging customers to use their regulations, as opposed to those in other jurisdictions.

The theory of regulatory competition can be traced back to Tiebout's work on the economics of government, in which he made the case for a decentralised system of government in which local governments competed with one another to entice people and businesses by offering various benefits, including taxes.[45]

41 Halpern and Johnson (2014), p. 18.

42 Ibid.

43 Chesterston (2007), p. 39.

44 Halpern and Johnson (2014), pp. 18–19.

45 Tiebout (1956).

Since, the concept of regulatory competition has been predominantly discussed from a corporate law perspective,[46] usually relying on the United States (US) federal paradigm.[47] Claimed benefits of regulatory competition are: (i) the promotion of diversity and the following experimentation in the search for efficient laws; (ii) the increase of the flow of information on common issues, based on national practices; (iii) a better match between the preferences of local populations and corporations and the content of the legal rules and policies.[48] Van den Bergh explains that '[t]he advantages of competition between legal rules must not be underestimated: if rules differ, more preferences can be satisfied and learning processes remain possible.' [49] In addition, allowing individual Member States to experiment rather than searching for legal similarity across the EU means that several experiments can proceed at the same time and while not all these experiments will lead to efficient outcomes, the costs of unsuccessful attempts will be reduced if they are confined to a single country.[50]

Regulatory competition is frequently mentioned in discussions about whether or not harmonisation is desirable. Authors who support legal diversity over centralist legal systems almost always cite the benefits of regulatory and jurisdictional competition. In general, competition is only possible when top-down harmonisation has not resulted in the creation of a single legal system that is applied to all countries concerned. In this context, harmonisation is seen as a straitjacket stifling legal reform and the improvement of substantive law.

It is clear that the 'seductive appeal of harmonisation is today tarnished [and its] role is increasingly contested.'[51] However, this should not come as a surprise seeing as the EU itself has been confronted to some integrational panic in the last decade or so,[52] which has unfolded in a rather dramatic way for the EU, its market, and citizens.

3 The European Union in Crisis

3.1 The EU Polycrisis

While the rhetoric of crisis is not new for the EU, an entity predicted to be 'built through crises',[53] it also seems like the EU has never *not* been in a state of crisis—the

[46] Deakin (2000); Enriques and Gelter (2006); Armour (2005).

[47] Romano (1993); Romano (1998); Bebchuk (1992).

[48] Deakin (1999).

[49] Van den Bergh (2002), p. 267.

[50] Stephan (1999), p. 793.

[51] Weatherill (2004), p. 31.

[52] Davis Cross and Ma (2015), p. 1056.

[53] Monnet (1978), p. 417.

Luxembourg crisis in the 1960s; the Euro-sclerosis in the 1970s and early 1980s; the geopolitical crisis of the late 1980s; the global economic and financial crisis of the late 2000s; the Schengen crisis of the mid-2010s; and more recently, the COVID-19 pandemic which hit the world with full force in 2020.

It is against the backdrop of these regular challenges that the successes of European integration seem all the more extraordinary. Therefore, while history indicates that worries about the breakup of Europe are possibly even exaggerated. However, as the saying goes, "the best predictor of future behaviour (or performance) is past behaviour (or performance)", the threat of collapse can only be truly disregarded if the present polycrisis is similar to earlier crises. While some aspects of the present crisis are similar to earlier ones, others are new.

The first different trait is the multidimensional character of the crisis, which leads us to call it a 'polycrisis'. The current crisis started in 2009 with the Eurozone crisis, which reached tipping points in 2010, 2012, and 2015. While the tides were ebbing, the Ukrainian crisis broke out and escalated in 2013 and 2015 as Russia invaded Crimea, challenging the EU to find a response, which resulted in the 'Minsk Accords' in 2015. That year saw a large and sudden increase of people fleeing war and conflict zones in the Middle East and reaching Europe. The refugee crisis led to very different responses from the EU Member States. Many of them resorted to unilateral measures to control or stop the influx of refugees, putting a stop to the Schengen agreement of borderless travel in the 26-country area. Simultaneously, in May 2015, the British Conservative Party won an outright majority in the Parliament, and then-Prime Minister Cameron pledged to hold a referendum on the UK's membership to the EU. This set the path for the Brexit vote and EU disintegration crisis. At the time of writing, the EU is grappling with the effects of the COVID-19 pandemic which started in 2020, as well as the effects of the Russia-Ukraine conflict which peaked in February 2022 when Russia launched a full-scale invasion of Ukraine. Thus, although the EU has always been juggling a multiplicity of issues which generate conflicts with varying degrees of intensity, at no other time since its inception has the EU been confronted by as many simultaneous crises as it has since 2009.

Additionally, the longevity of the present polycrisis sets it apart from the majority of earlier crises. While it can be challenging to determine with absolute certainty when a crisis starts and ends, there is substantial evidence that the current crisis began in October 2009, making it the longest crisis in European history to date. The European Monetary System Crisis of 1992–1993 and the Empty Chair Crisis of 1965–1966 were both brief in contrast. The same could be said for the British budget crisis in the 1970s and the failed Constitutional Treaty problem in the 2000s. This crisis' length suggests that it is also the most difficult to resolve, presenting a greater risk of collapse than earlier crises.

The third aspect which differentiates the current crisis from past ones is the unprecedented mass politicisation of the events.[54] In the past, only the European

[54] Hooghe and Marks (2008); Parsons and Matthijs (2015), pp. 211; 223-224; 226.

Defence Community crisis of the 1950s involved a somewhat similar mobilisation of the mass public, yet mostly in France.[55] Until the 1990s, EU crises were exclusively managed within the political elites of Brussels and the Member States. Although domestic political incentives and constraints may have shaped the political classes' behaviours, mass participation of the public in these crises was minimal. The political party system in most Member States was dominated by Europhile movements and 'anti-EU' sentiments were relatively limited. This situation changed with the adoption of the Maastricht Treaty. Politicians started to resort to popular referenda more frequently than in the past to legitimise the transfer of decision-making powers in areas of national sovereignty, such as the currency. These fostered a mass politicisation of European integration. Since the outbreak of the Eurozone crisis in 2009, this mass politicisation has manifested in additional ways, thereby aggravating the current polycrisis. First, there has been an increase in the number of 'anti-EU' parties in several Member States, causing the mediation between Member States increasingly challenging. Second, demonstrations and protests against the EU have become more common, especially in southern European states as a response to the EU's imposition of economic austerity measures.

Finally, the costs of inaction are another aspect of the current crisis that was absent from earlier ones.[56] For instance, the crisis surrounding the dissolution of the European Defense Community was resolved by permitting West Germany to rearm within NATO. In some respects, it facilitated closer European integration in less sensitive areas even though it prevented the development of a European force. Similar to this, the EU would have continued to function based on the current treaties if the Constitutional Treaty had not led to the adoption of the Lisbon Treaty in 2009. The actual threat of European disintegration was rarely present.[57] In the words of Webber, the current polycrisis is different, 'perhaps even very different: it is unique and unprecedented in its gravity because it exhibits a combination of four traits of which no more than half characterised any of the earlier crises of European integration.'[58]

It should therefore come as no surprise that public opinion questions about the future of the EU, its institutions as well as its policies and integration tools, including harmonisation, continue to incite contentious discussions and draw sharp dividing lines in both the Member States and Brussels. In the words of former German President Steinmeier, 'I have come to learn that my belief, a belief shared by many of my generation, that the path of European integration was irreversible, was a fallacy. No, Europe's future is not set in stone.'[59] As summarised by Cotta and Isernia, a vicious circle has developed in the EU:

---

[55] Webber (2019), p. 11.

[56] Parsons and Matthijs (2015), pp. 211; 223–224.

[57] Webber (2019), p. 12.

[58] Ibid, p. 13.

[59] Steinmeier (2017).

> lasting negative effects of the crises → more national and centrifugal mobilization for the defence of national interests endangered by the crises → greater difficulty in achieving European decisions→ further loss of confidence in European solutions and greater readiness to explore national solutions → more European conflict.[60]

Therefore, successive crises are an integral part of the integration dynamic.[61] The question is not so much whether the EU is in a crisis but rather, whether crises are consistently bad for European integration and legal harmonisation?

3.2 Comparing the Eurozone Crisis and the Schengen Crisis

In some ways, the Eurozone crisis which started in 2009 and the refugee crisis, i.e. the Schengen crisis, which started in 2015, are similar: they were caused by exogenous shocks (the US subprime mortgage crisis and the armed conflicts and political repression in the Middle East) which exposed deficiencies in European integration, led to the domestic politicisation of the events, and produced important intergovernmental conflicts about how to share the burden of the crises.[62]

First, the European Monetary Union (EMU) resulted from an intergovernmental compromise about limited macroeconomic integration. It was designed to liberalise capital markets in the EU and to delegate monetary policy to an independent central bank with a primary mandate to ensure price stability. However, the regime lacked mechanisms for the rescue or resolution of systematically important banks and for the orderly dealing of insolvent Member States. Intergovernmental and supranational bailout and deficit financing were prohibited under EMU rules. When the financial crisis hit Europe, a dynamic sovereign-bank nexus developed. As governments bailed out domestic banks, sovereign credit risk increased, which made banks invested in sovereign bonds more vulnerable and contributed to higher interest rates for governments. In the absence of adequate policy instruments, there was a high risk that deficit countries would default and abandon the Euro. Similarly, when a high flux of refugees reached Europe, the Schengen regime was not adequately prepared to deal with the situation. While the Schengen agreements abolished internal border controls and established a common external border, the policing of external borders and the handling of asylum requests remained under the authority of the Member States. The differences in the asylum procedures and granting of refugee status encouraged 'asylum shopping' and secondary movement of refugees. The Schengen regime did not have a system of burden-sharing among Member States or supranational organisation which could have supported the countries most hit by the influx of refugees, i.e. Mediterranean Member States.

---

[60] Cotta and Isernia (2021), p. 12.

[61] Schmitter (1970).

[62] For an in-depth exploration of the two crises, see Schimmelfennig (2018).

Second, both crises were highly politicised. This is due to several factors, the first being that monetary and fiscal policies, as well as immigration and border control are areas of 'core state powers',[63] which are usually highly politicised. Additionally, both crises were politically salient across the EU. At their height, they topped the political agenda of the EU and its Member States as the economy and unemployment were the most important issues for the European citizenry during the Eurozone crisis while immigration moved to the top of the list in the autumn of 2015.[64] Finally, political contestation and outcry against the EU was high during both crises. According to Eurobarometer polls, public opinion (the trust, in and the image of, the EU) plunged toward historic lows at the height of the Eurozone crisis and, after a brief recovery in 2014 and early 2015, again during the peak of the Schengen crisis in the second half of 2015.[65] Therefore, during the Eurozone crisis, Eurosceptic parties benefited from their opposition to bailouts in the north and to austerity measures in the south. They also effectively mobilised against immigration (and Islam) during the Schengen crisis.

Notwithstanding these similarities, the outcomes of both crises have been remarkably different. The Eurozone crisis resulted in a major leap in integration, whereas the Schengen crisis did not.

3.2.1 The Eurozone Crisis: Deepened Integration

The measures adopted during and after the Eurozone crisis have deepened fiscal and financial integration among the Member States while preserving monetary integration. Importantly, no Member State left the European Union, even though this possibility was quite acute at the height of the crisis.

The no-bailout policy was replaced by institutions and procedures which provide deficit countries without enough public credit to keep them afloat. The European Financial Stability Facility (EFSF) was created in 2010, following an ad hoc emergency credit to Greece. The EFSF has provided financial assistance to Ireland, Portugal, and Greece through the issuance of EFSF bonds and other debt instruments on capital markets. The EFSF was superseded in 2012 by the European Stability Mechanism (ESM), a financial organisation assisting Eurozone countries to avoid and overcome financial crises and to maintain long-term financial stability. While the ESM is formally an intergovernmental institution, it has reinforced the financial commitment of the Eurozone countries.

Additionally, a number of legislative actions, notably the 'Six-Pack' and the 'Two-Pack' legislation were introduced. The Regulations and Directive which form the 'Six-Pack' were introduced in 2011 with the ambition of reducing macroeconomic imbalances and ensuring the viability of national finances through either

[63] Genschel and Jachtenfuchs (2014).

[64] Debomy (2015), pp. 42–43.

[65] Ibid. pp. 15–16.

preventive or corrective actions. The Regulations of the 'Two-Pack' were introduced in 2013 and were based on, while also enhancing, the 'Six-Pack' reforms by improving budgetary coordination through the introduction of a common budgetary timeline and common budgetary rules for Member States and a system of enhanced surveillance for those Member States experiencing serious difficulties with financial stability, receiving financial assistance, or emerging from adjustment programmes. The Treaty on Stability, Coordination and Governance in the EMU (Fiscal Compact) was signed in 2012 to reinforce the budget discipline of euro area governments following the Eurozone crisis.

Finally, the need for a banking union emerged from the financial crisis and subsequent sovereign debt crisis. It became clear that, especially in a monetary union such as the euro area, problems caused by close links between public sector finances and the banking sector can easily spill over national borders and cause financial distress in other countries. The banking union has two pillars, the Single Supervisory Mechanism (SSM) and the Single Resolution Mechanism (SRM). The SSM assigns supervision of systematically significant banks to a new supranational authority at the ECB while the SRM applies to the resolution of failing banks supervised by the European Central Bank and can draw on a Single Resolution Fund, which is being built up by the European banking sector over a period of 8 years (2016–2023).

In conclusion, the Eurozone was maintained and even consolidated through a major leap in European integration. Through the ESM and ECB programmes, the Member States responded to the crisis by introducing previously unexplored collective financial liabilities, reducing state autonomy in budgetary policy and centralising financial market regulation and supervision.

3.2.2 The Schengen Crisis: No Substantial Deepening

Similar to the Eurozone crisis, a number of institutional and policy reform proposals were sparked by the inadequacies of the EU's border and asylum policies. However, unlike the initiatives taken after the financial crisis, decisions taken following the Schengen crisis have neither consolidated nor deepened the regime.

First, several Schengen countries, including Austria, Denmark, France, Norway and Sweden, started implementing controls at some of their internal Schengen borders in September 2015, beginning with Germany. These measures were allowed under the Schengen Borders Code and authorised by the EU, yet they were extended several times—arguably without a threat to public order or security—and therefore amounted to an important and protracted restriction of the earlier state of European integration.

Second, the EU failed to replace, consolidate, or complement the Dublin rules (i.e. the system setting out which Member State is responsible for looking at an individual's asylum application) with a system of shared responsibility or reallocation. Member States merely agreed to a one-time reallocation of up to 160,000 refugees in May and September 2015 and even this ad-hoc measure was challenged by several Member States, including the Czech Republic, Hungary, Romania and Slovakia. Once the plan was launched, it was then poorly implemented. Only one-eighth of the expected relocations had taken place by summer 2017, a few months before the agree-upon relocation period was to end. A proposal by the Commission for a permanent quota system for allocating asylum seekers was rejected not only by Eastern Member States but also by France and Spain.[66]

While the European Asylum Support Office (EASO) and Frontex, the two EU agencies active in the EU's border and asylum regime saw an important increase in their budget and staff, they did not acquire additional supranational competences. The EASO's responsibilities remained limited to assisting and coordinating Member State authorities in the implementation of EU asylum rules. It can promote, but not enforce, uniform asylum decisions across the Union. The Commission also proposed to grant supranational competences to Frontex, such as the right to return rejected migrants and to deploy guards to EU Member States' borders without the consent of the government. These proposals were rejected by both the Council and the European Parliament. Instead, Member States reintroduced internal border controls.

In the end, the refugee crisis resulted in a (partial) suspension of the Schengen regime, rather than an adaptation of its fundamental rules. Instead of focusing on fixing the shortcomings of the system, EU Member States focused their efforts on preventing migrants from reaching EU borders in the first place. Ultimately, rather than leading to further European integration, this crisis led to renationalisation.

3.2.3 Explaining These Differences

Both the Eurozone and Schengen crises have increased transnational interdependence, yet to different degrees. During the Eurozone crisis, governments had to deal with powerful non-state actors, such as banks and other financial institutions. Governments were not only heavily indebted to domestic banks, but they were also responsible for saving them. Additionally, interdependence was not merely national. The crisis also increased the Eurozone's transnational market interdependence and brought together countries with opposing growth strategies. Germany and the North of the EU pursued an export-led growth strategy based on wage restraint, productivity and competitiveness, while the south pursued a demand-led growth strategy based on fiscal expansion and wage inflation.[67] As a result of this interdependence, financial markets saw southern Member States as safe countries due to their Eurozone membership. As a result, the North's balance-of-payment surpluses generated important financial flows to the south and the threat of sovereign default in the south thus left northern banks heavily exposed.

[66] Rittberger et al. (2017).

[67] Hall (2012), pp. 355, 358–359.

Throughout the Eurozone crisis, financial market actors compelled governments to act. The surplus countries had an incentive to avoid bailing out the deficit ones while debtor countries wanted to delay austerity measures. However, the growing mistrust and disengagement of financial markets, evidenced by rising interest rates on government bonds, forced both sides to cooperate reluctantly and take the necessary steps to prevent the disintegration of the Eurozone.[68] Financial market actors were therefore able to push Member States into further integration because exit costs were prohibitively high. Abandoning the euro would have resulted in sovereign default, a likely breakdown of the monetary and financial systems, hyperinflation, and isolation from external capital. The cumulative loss of GDP resulting from an exit of southern countries such as Greece, Italy, Portugal, and Spain from the Eurozone would be 69% for Germany and 154% for France.[69] In comparison, bailout costs and risks looked small.

By contrast, in the Schengen crisis, governments were confronted by weaker transnational actors. The pressure that refugees could put on national governments came from international human rights obligations under the UN Refugee Convention and informal moral commitments. These pressures were initially created by news and media images of refugees drowning in the Mediterranean. When public support waned as a result of the surge in migrant inflows, governments were able to either block or divert the flow of migrants by instituting border controls, erecting fences, or assisting their crossing. Whereas the most affected Member States in the Eurozone crisis were unable to avoid sovereign default, even vulnerable countries along the Balkan migration route were able to keep the situation under control without international assistance or cooperation.

Eventually, the burden on southern countries like Greece intensified. Unlike the Eurozone crisis where Member States feared risks of contagion if Greece were to collapse, there was no comparable incentive to support Greece in the Schengen crisis. This was due to the important difference in breakdown costs in both crises. According to the most pessimistic scenarii produced by studies published during the Schengen crisis, the annual costs of a 'no Schengen' Europe would not have exceeded 0.2% of GDP.[70]

In the absence of a strong common interest in cooperation, the bargaining structure of the Schengen crisis was different from the one in the Eurozone crisis. Member States did not feel compelled to alleviate the burden felt by frontline and destination countries. This situation contrasted with the chicken game situation of the Eurozone crisis in which even the least impacted countries would have suffered greatly had the regime collapsed.[71]

---

[68] Schimmelfennig (2015), pp. 185–187.

[69] https://www.bertelsmann-stiftung.de/fileadmin/files/BSt/Presse/imported/downloads/xcms_bst_dms_36656__2.pdf.

[70] https://www.bertelsmann-stiftung.de/fileadmin/files/BSt/Publikationen/GrauePublikationen/NW_Departure_from_Schengen.pdf.

[71] Rittberger et al. (2017).

3.3 What Does This Mean for Harmonisation?

Jean Monnet, one of the founding fathers of European integration said that he had 'always believed that Europe would be built through crises, and that it would be the sum of their solutions.'[72] Monnet attributed crisis-induced integration effects to a combination of self-interest, practical restrictions, and institutional autonomy. In response to the Community's first crisis in the 1960s, he wrote that 'intergovernmental discord, human ill-temper, and material confusion' could not derail the momentum of European integration. '[S]elf-interest, in moments of crisis, made up for any lack of European team-spirit.'[73] Furthermore, 'people only accept change when they are faced with necessity, and only recognize necessity when a crisis is upon them.'[74]

As illustrated above, crises have had different impacts on European integration. Similarly, crises have had different impacts on legal harmonisation. While states tend to prioritise state-centric solutions during times of crisis, they can also reveal the impotence of nation-states to find adequate solutions to protect their citizens in an integrated EU.[75] The COVID-19 crisis is a good example of this dilemma as countries' emergency responses to the pandemic clearly uncovered this tension between a continuous phenomenon of global interdependence on the one hand, and a preference for domestic governance on the other hand. This dichotomy was particularly acute in the EU at the onset of the pandemic where Member States preferred national solutions over harmonised, multilateral ones and devised national emergency solutions to tackle the sweeping effects of the crisis.[76]

During 'good weather' periods, legal harmonisation is easier to develop because European policies are established under lesser time constraints and domestic political timelines—such as electoral cycles—are known at European level too. This allows the European institutions to strategically plan the development of harmonisation policies in advance, through white or green papers or the Commission's work programmes. The implementation of these policies is also foreseeable and veto points can be anticipated. However, crises are precipitating events which shake the status quo and allow new issues to permeate the European agenda, prompting policymaking practices to change. Scholars speak of a kind of 'crisification'[77] of policymaking. While during peaceful times, traditional policymaking practices rely on extensive analyses of a particular issue and extended phases of consultation with stakeholders, a process akin to thoughtful problem solving in which arguments and perspectives are considered and debated,[78] crises

---

[72] Monnet (1978), p. 417.

[73] Ibid, p. 469.

[74] Ibid, p. 109.

[75] Barrett (2007), pp. 5–7.

[76] See Ghio et al. (2021).

[77] Rhinard (2019), p. 2.

[78] Joerges and Neyer (2006).

lead to a change in the policymaking actors, abbreviated decision-making procedures and 'new narratives of the raison d'être of European integration.'[79]

First, the pace of policymaking shifts to a logic of urgency, rather than bargaining or deliberation. Decisions must be made quickly and involve real choices with important practical consequences; 'they affect core values and interests of communities and the cost of decisions can be very high in socially, politically, economically and in human terms.'[80] As Boin and colleagues note, 'crisis decision-making situations are more likely than non-crisis situations to contain genuine dilemmas that can be resolved only through trade-off choices, or "tragic choices", where all the options open to the decision maker entail net losses.'[81]

Second, policymaking actors change in times of crisis. While during peaceful times, all institutions, as well as the Member States, are involved in policymaking and legislative initiatives, it is predominantly the European Commission that manages most of the crisis tools. It engages in the early warning task as part of the 70 or so early warning and rapid alert systems it maintains; it reports to networks of national actors outside the EU's institutional structure; and it liaises closely with the designated crisis experts in the Council to identify available options. In specific types of crises, certain kinds of experts are preferred by the European Commission[82] and the Council. For example, during the Eurozone crisis, the Council only involved epistemic communities.[83]

Therefore, the crisification of policymaking leads to new forms of networks and special arrangements for decision-making, and ushers in new participation patterns which depart from traditional decision-making methods and actors in the EU. Special crisis procedures shortcut politics and rely mostly on experts for crisis assessments.[84] Generally, when a crisis strikes, the Council rises in influence;[85] the Commission enjoys a boost of executive privileges;[86] new organisations emerge;[87] and the European Parliament takes a back seat.[88]

The issue with the crisification of policymaking is that European citizens increasingly:

> reject the texts handed down for their approval by political elites and so the texts are then converted into legally binding instruments through means that carefully avoid those voters [...] So deepens the lack of understanding; so grows popular resentment to an authoritarian sense of "we know best". And in the Eurozone, which shares a similar narrative of evading

[79] Rhinard (2019).

[80] Ibid., p. 11.

[81] Boin et al. (2016), pp. 43–44.

[82] Gronvall (2001).

[83] Kamkhaji and Radaelli (2017).

[84] Boin et al. (2013).

[85] Rhinard (2019), p. 627.

[86] Boin et al. (2016).

[87] Bickerton et al. (2014).

[88] Ripoll-Servent (2017).

> popular explanation let alone approval, the "we know best" claim is demonstrably not convincing anyway to many Europeans. An EU which is imposed on the peoples of Europe contains the seeds of its own destruction.[89]

Issues around the meaning, scope, and role of harmonisation have indeed pervaded political debates on the nature of the EU, its modes of governance, and respect for the Member States' national preferences and interests. Harmonisation has thus increasingly found itself at the heart of political controversies and is regularly trotted out in Eurosceptic discourse as the enemy of national sovereignty and cultural values. This situation has been exacerbated in times of crisis which have traditionally been associated with increased rejection of further European integration. With a broader rejection of the EU comes a narrower rejection of European harmonisation, and vice-versa.

4 Conclusion

While over the last 50 years, the EU has suffered a number of low points and setbacks—only to emerge somewhat fitter and stronger afterwards, attitudes towards, and opinions on, specific aspects of European integration give an ambivalent picture. National support towards the European project has recently stabilised, yet a significant proportion of the European population still believes that the EU is headed in the wrong direction. What current crises reveal is that the process of European integration generally, and the tool that is legal harmonisation more specifically, are increasingly contested. The polycrisis faced by the EU over the last decade or so has called into question the foundational basis on which the EU has built its integration agenda, including its harmonisation efforts.

As mentioned above, legal harmonisation has been confronted with several stressors over the years, such as the protection of national sovereignty and legal cultures, as well as an overall rise in Euroscepticism, prioritising state-centric solutions to common issues. The EU institutions are thus under greater pressure to adapt the harmonisation measures they draft to overcome these challenges. Discussions around the scope, desirability and feasibility of harmonisation are particularly relevant at a time when European integration seems to have lost some of its shine and the EU is experiencing some integrational panic. Platsas asks whether this is 'the right time for one to engage oneself with another legal harmonisation discussion?'[90]

The answer is yes, undoubtedly. No crisis should be wasted and now is exactly the time to rethink harmonisation. Crises are open decision-making situations. In the context of integration and harmonisation, they present a manifest threat and a perceived significant probability of disintegration but may also trigger reform activities. Therefore, crises and the tensions they generate are an opportunity to

---

[89] Weatherill (2016), p. 418.

[90] Platsas (2017), p. viii.

rethink the concept of legal harmonisation and the role of the European institutions in this process. After all, the word 'crisis' itself in Chinese is composed of two symbols: 'danger' and 'opportunity.' A crisis, therefore, is an opportunity, a 'moment of truth.'[91]

References

Armour J (2005) Who should make corporate law: EC Legislation versus Regulatory Competition. European Corporate Governance Institute Law Paper 54/2005

Barrett S (2007) Why cooperate? The incentive to supply global public goods. Oxford University Press, Oxford

Bebchuk L (1992) Federalism and the corporation: the desirable limits on state competition in corporate law. Harv Law Rev 105:1435–1510

Bickerton C et al (2014) The new intergovernmentalism: European integration in the Post-Maastricht Era. J Common Mark Stud 53:703–722

Boin A et al (2013) The European Union as crisis manager: problems and prospects. Cambridge University Press, Cambridge

Boin A et al (2016) The politics of crisis management. Cambridge University Press, Cambridge

Chesterston G (2007) Orthodoxy. Barnes and Noble, New York

Collins R (2010) The fundamental Holmes. A free speech chronicle and reader. Selections from the opinions, books, articles, speeches, letters, and other writings by and about Oliver Wendell Holmes Jr. Cambridge University Press, Cambridge

Cotta M, Isernia P (2021) Introduction. The challenges to the European representation system – away from the "old normal"?'. In: Cotta M, Isernia P (eds) The EU through multiple crises. Representation and cohesion dilemmas for a "sui generis" polity. Routledge, London, pp 1–19

Davis Cross M, Ma X (2015) EU crises and integrational panic: the role of the media. J Eur Public Policy 22:1053–1070

Deakin S (1999) Two types of regulatory competition: competitive federalism versus reflexive harmonisation. A law and economics perspective on Centros. Cambridge Yearb Eur Legal Stud 2:231–260

Deakin S (2000) Regulatory competition versus Harmonisation in European company law. University of Cambridge ESRC Centre for Business Research Working Paper n. 163

Debomy D (2015) The EU, despite everything? European Public Opinion in the Face of the Crisis (2005–2015). Notre Europe, Paris

Dedek H (2011) Law as culture/rights as culture: Some historical thoughts on the "Western" legal tradition. Paper Presented at the Conference on European Legal Culture, University of Oxford (16 December 2011)

Enriques L, Gelter M (2006) Regulatory competition in European company law and creditor protection. Eur Bus Org Law Rev 7:417–453

Friedman L (1989) Law, lawyers and popular culture. Yale Law J 98:1579–1606

Genschel P, Jachtenfuchs M (2014) Introduction: beyond market regulation. Analysing the European integration of core state powers. In: Genschel P, Jachtenfuchs M (eds) Beyond the regulatory polity? The European integration of core state powers. Oxford University Press, Oxford, pp 1–23

Ghio E (2022) Redefining harmonisation. Lessons from EU insolvency law. Edward Elgar Publishing, Cheltenham

[91] van Middelaar (2014).

Ghio E et al (2021) Harmonising insolvency law in the EU: new thoughts on old ideas in the wake of the COVID-19 pandemic. Int Insolv Rev 30:427–459
Gronvall J (2001) Mad cow disease: the role of experts and European crisis management. In: Rosenthal U et al (eds) Managing crises: threats, dilemmas, opportunities. Charles C. Thomas, Springfield, pp 155–175
Hall P (2012) The economics and politics of the Euro crisis. German Polit 21:355–371
Halpern S, Johnson P (2014) Harmonising copyright law and dealing with dissonance: Aaframework for US and EU law. Edward Elgar Publishing, Cheltenham
Herzfeld M (2005) Cultural intimacy: social poetics in the nation-state. Routledge, New York
Higgins R (1999) International law in a changing international system. Cambridge Law J 58:78–95
Hobbes T (1651) Leviathan. Penguin, United Kingdom
Hooghe L, Marks G (2008) A postfunctionalist theory of European integration: from permissive consensus to constraining dissensus. Br J Polit Sci 39:1–23
Joerges C, Neyer J (2006) Deliberative supranationalism revisited. European University Institute Law Working Paper No. 2006/20
Johnson B (2020) European Union (Future Relationship) Bill. Hansard (30 December 2020)
Kahn-Freund O (1974) On uses and misuses of comparative law. Mod Law Rev 37:1 27
Kamkhaji J, Radaelli C (2017) Crisis, learning and policy change in the European Union. J Eur Public Policy 27:714–734
La Porta R et al (2008) The economic consequences of legal origins. J Econ Liter 46:285–332
Legrand P (1996) European legal systems are not converging. Int Comp Law Q 45:52–81
Legrand P (2002) On the unbrearable localness of the law: academic fallacies and unseasonable observations. Eur Rev Priv Law 61–76
Legrand P (2003a) The impossibility of legal transplants. Maastricht J 4:111–124
Legrand P (2003b) The same and the different. In: Legrand P, Munday R (eds) Comparative legal studies: traditions and transitions. Cambridge University Press, Cambridge, pp 240–311
Liebowitz S, Margolis S (1995) Path dependence, lock-in and history. J Law, Econ Org 11:205–226
Lord Denning (1990) Introduction to the European Court of Justice: Judges or policy makers? Bruges Groupe, London
McCormack G (2011) Secured credit and the harmonisation of law: the UNCITRAL experience. Edward Elgar, Cheltenham
McCormack G (2021) International organisations and the search for global insolvency standards. In: Omar P, Gant J (eds) Research handbook on corporate restructuring. Edward Elgar Publishing, Cheltenham, pp 17–39
Monnet J (1978) Memoirs. William Collins, London
Montesquieu C (1949) The spirit of the laws. Hafner Press, New York
Parsons C, Matthijs M (2015) European integration past, present, and future: moving forward through crisis? In: Matthijs M, Blyth M (eds) The future of the euro. Oxford University Press, Oxford, pp 210–232
Platsas A (2017) The harmonisation of national legal systems. Strategic models and factors. Edward Elgar Publishing, Cheltenham
Posner R (2000) Path-dependency, pragmatism and critique of history in adjudication and legal scholarship. Univ Chicago Law Rev 67:573–606
Rhinard M (2019) The crisification of policy-making in the European Union. J Common Mark Stud 55:616–633
Richardson J (2000) Sovereignty: EU experience and EU policy. Chicago J Int Law 1:323–326
Ripoll-Servent A (2017) The European parliament. Palgrave Macmillan, London
Rittberger B et al (2017) Explaining uneven integration trajectories: a comparison of the euro crisis and the refugee crisis. EUSA conference paper
Romano R (1993) The genius of american corporate law. AEI Press, Washington
Romano R (1998) Competition for state corporate law. In: Newman P (ed) The New Palgrave dictionary of economics and the law. Macmillan Reference Limited, London, pp 364–370
Sabine G (1961) A history of political theory. Rinehart and Winston, New York

Schimmelfennig F (2015) Liberal intergovernmentalism and the Euro area crisis. J Eur Public Policy 22:177–195
Schimmelfennig F (2018) European integration (theory) in times of crisis. A comparison of the euro and Schengen crises. J Eur Public Policy 25:969–989
Schmitter P (1970) A revised theory of regional integration. Int Org 24:836–868
Sefton-Green R (2012) French and English Crypto-nationalism and European private law: an exercise in sentiment and reason. Eur Rev Contr Law 8:260–276
Sewell W Jr (1996) Three temporalities: Toward an eventful sociology. In: McDonald T (ed) The historic turn in the human sciences. University of Michigan Press, Michigan, pp 245–280
Smits J (2007) Law making in the European Union: on globalization and contract law in divergent legal cultures. Louisiana Law Rev 67:1181–1203
Steinmeier F-W (2017) Speech at the Formal sitting of the European Parliament, 4 April 2017 (Strasbourg), https://www.bundespraesident.de/SharedDocs/Reden/EN/Frank-Walter-Steinmeier/Reden/2017/04/170404-Strasbourg.html?nn=9042654
Stephan P (1999) The futility of unification and harmonization in international commercial law. Virginia J Int Law 39:743–798
Teubner G (1998) Legal irritants: good faith in British Law or how unifying law ends up in new divergencies. Mod Law Rev 61:11–32
Tiebout C (1956) A pure theory of local public expenditures. J Polit Econ 64:416–424
Twinning W (2000) Comparative law and legal theory: the country and Western tradition. In: Edge I (ed) Comparative law in global perspective. Transnational Publishers, New York, pp 21–76
Van den Bergh R (2002) Forced harmonisation of contract law in Europe: not to be continued. In: Grundmann S, Stuyck J (eds) An Academic Green Paper on European contract law. Kluwer Law International, New York, pp 245–264
van Middelaar L (2014) The crises in the Eurozone and Ukraine have heralded the "return of politics" to European integration. LSE European Politics and Policy Blog (21 May 2014), https://blogs.lse.ac.uk/europpblog/2014/05/21/the-crises-in-the-eurozone-and-ukraine-have-heralded-the-return-of-politics-to-european-integration/
Von Bar C (2002) From principles to codification: Prospects for European private law. Columbia J Eur Law 8:379–388
von Savigny F (2013) Vom Beruf unserer Zeit für Gesetzgebung und Rechtswissenschaft. Old Verlag, Germany
Weatherill S (2004) Why object to the harmonization of private law by the EC? Eur Rev Priv Law 12:633–660
Weatherill S (2016) Law and values in the European Union. Oxford University Press, Oxford
Webber D (2019) European disintegration? The politics of crisis in the European Union. Red Globe Press, London

Emilie Ghio is a lecturer in Corporate and Insolvency Law at the University of Edinburgh, Scotland, United Kingdom.

International Judicial Cooperation in Times of Crisis

Ricardo Perlingeiro

1 Introduction

This chapter focuses on global crises that give rise to conflicts that cross borders and, therefore, call on states to improve their international cooperation administrative and judicial toolbox in civil and criminal matters, to ensure that the law is applied, and rights are protected, in cross-border areas.

In crisis situations, there is a noticeable tendency for national and international authorities and agencies to mobilise their combined forces in order to overcome the new challenges that arise. Therefore, it is interesting to find out how the attitudes adopted in such contexts affect international judicial cooperation measures and what the effects of such mobilisation are on the national jurisdictions involved.

In this context, the author addresses the concepts of *approximation* and *convergence*, typical of legal harmonisation, as well as uniformity and divergence among national jurisdictions with respect to international judicial cooperation based on the analysis of three global crises: the financial crisis of the late 2000s; the 2015 European migration crisis and; the multifaceted crisis caused by the COVID-19 pandemic.

This study determines whether the increasing use of the mechanisms of international judicial cooperation in civil and criminal matters resulting from the global crises are promoting harmonisation, uniformity, or divergence among national jurisdictions.

For the review, the author wishes to thank Camila Pavi Garcia Rosa, a graduate law student at Fluminense Federal University and intern at the Federal Regional Court of the 2nd Region.

R. Perlingeiro (✉)
Fluminense Federal University, Niterói, Brazil

Birmingham City University, Birmingham, UK
e-mail: ricardoperlingeiro@id.uff.br

E. Ghio, R. Perlingeiro (eds.), *Are Legal Systems Converging or Diverging?*,
https://doi.org/10.1007/978-3-031-38180-5_15

2 Understanding Contemporary International Judicial Cooperation

This chapter discusses international cooperation as a practice between courts and administrative bodies of different states,[1] with the objective of enhancing the effectiveness of public powers that, due to the transnational nature of the interests involved, need to go beyond the borders of a single state.

To understand the scope of the expression 'international judicial cooperation' as used in this chapter, the concept of 'public powers' should be understood to mean the adjudicative powers intended for the protection of rights typical of the judiciary and assigned to certain administrative authorities. The concept of public powers of the administrative authorities includes the executive powers of law enforcement as well as police powers of supervision and control and powers of criminal persecution.

Examples of areas of international judicial cooperation in civil, commercial, administrative and criminal matters include communications and service of process; exchange of information about documents and proceedings; evidence-taking; joint criminal investigation between states; recognition and implementation of foreign decisions; cases of cross-border insolvency of companies and financial institutions; judicial measures of interim relief; and extradition.[2]

3 To What Extent Is International Judicial Cooperation Facilitated by the Harmonisation or Uniformity of Norms Among Jurisdictions?

For Emilie Ghio, 'harmonisation' is an umbrella term encompassing a variety of different regulatory mechanisms, including approximation (a top-down approach moving from the supranational level down to the national level) and convergence (a bottom-up phenomenon, whereby a state voluntarily borrows certain standards, principles, and rules from other jurisdictions, without abandoning all of its own national concepts. It is important to note that neither convergence nor approximation necessarily results in legal uniformity but rather, aim at achieving increased legal similarity.[3]

[1] On the concept of international judicial cooperation, see in general Caponi (2011) and Grinover et al. (2009), pp. 9–48.

[2] See Grinover et al. (2009), pp. 9–48.

[3] This interpretation is based on the etymological and literal meanings of the terms. See Boodman (1991), p. 699. See also the definition of 'harmonisation' in the Cambridge Dictionary ('the act of making different people, plans, situations, etc. suitable for each other' and 'the act of making systems or laws the same or similar in different companies, countries, etc. so that they can work together more easily.'); see the definition of 'approximation' in the Merriam-Webster's Dictionary ('a process of articulation, conjugation' that results in o'ne thing that is similar to another thing,

In this context, harmonisation among national jurisdictions in matters of international judicial cooperation can be analysed from two different perspectives. First, the topic can be examined from the point of view of the substantive aspects of cooperation, that is to say, the content of the measures of cooperation, and secondly from the standpoint of the procedural aspects of the measures of cooperation.[4]

International judicial cooperation makes it possible for powers, duties, rights and obligations instituted under the norms of one jurisdiction to be effective in another national jurisdiction. Thus, the recognition by one state of foreign judicial decisions and claims related to rights that are provided for only in another state, not involving convergence among jurisdictions, may help lay the groundwork for future convergence by familiarising one state with the laws, rights, obligations and duties of other states.

However, regarding international judicial cooperation procedures, it is possible to identify convergence, uniformity, or approximation among national jurisdictions, according to the national, international, or supranational nature of the normative sources of the cooperation procedures.

It should be pointed out that international judicial cooperation procedures enshrined in national norms are guided by legal values and principles that form part of fundamental human duties.[5] One state, by cooperating with another, will be promoting the fundamental rights enshrined in its own constitution, even if the foreign rights and decisions do not fully coincide with its own laws.

This being the case, international judicial cooperation is a *prima facie* duty to be honored by states, and refusing to cooperate must be an exceptional, proportional measure based on the need to respect certain limits imposed by the international public policy (*ordre public*) of the state asked to cooperate.[6]

However, what motivates or limits international judicial cooperation is the fundamental legal values and principles that depend on a *convergent interpretation* among cooperating states.[7] Convergence is essential in international judicial cooperation when based on norms of national origin.

Indeed, unless states apply the common principles that guide international judicial cooperation in a convergent manner, such cooperation will have little chance of being realised when based solely on national norms. Model laws on this topic, such

without being exactly the same thing'); see the definition of 'convergence' in the Cambridge Dictionary ('the fact that two or more things, ideas, etc. become similar or come together'). See also Ghio (2022), Chapter 6.

[4] See Kerameus (2003), pp. 443–451. See also Hazard Junior (2003), p. 437 and Van Rhee (2018), pp. 15–34.

[5] See Kinsch (2017), pp. 880–886.

[6] See Childress III (2017), pp. 1051–1056. See also Dolinger et al. (2023).

[7] See Liakopoulos (2019), pp. 150–193.

as the UNCITRAL Model Law on Cross-Border Insolvency[8] and the Model Code of Interjurisdictional Cooperation for Ibero-America,[9] strengthen the mission of convergence among national legal systems of international judicial cooperation. Similarly, non-binding recommendations and guidelines are developed by international and supranational bodies play the role of promoting legal convergence.

Without such convergence, the alternative is to go back to the origins of international judicial cooperation and promote express reciprocity, in other words, international judicial cooperation conditional on a specific pre-existing treaty among states who intend to collaborate with one another.

These days, there are countless bilateral and even multilateral treaties in this subject area, as shown by the conventions of Mercosul, Interamerican Specialized Conferences on Private International Law, the Hague Conference on Private International Law (HCCH) and the United Nations Organization (UN).

Where the cooperation procedures are based on a treaty, the objective is not convergence or approximation but rather *uniformisation* among the jurisdictions of the cooperating states.

Finally, within the European Union (EU), Regulation 1215/2012 on Jurisdiction and the Recognition and Enforcement of Judgments in Civil and Commercial Matters[10] and Regulation 848/2015 on Insolvency Proceedings[11] are examples of supranational rules concerning procedures for international judicial cooperation.

As states commit to such regulations, they will tend to incorporate European procedural rules of international judicial cooperation into the norms of their own jurisdictions. This is typically a phenomenon of *approximation* among jurisdictions.

4 Examples of How Crises Intensify International Judicial Cooperation

4.1 The Financial Crisis of The Late 2000s

The global financial crisis of the late 2000s revealed a lack of such legal instruments as are necessary for states to promote a coordinated action regarding the procedures of transnational insolvency of financial institutions. Additionally, it should be noted that in any case, it is not a good option to apply the rules of transnational insolvency of companies to financial institutions, although such procedures may be the only viable alternative at the time.

---

[8] UNCITRAL (2014).

[9] Grinover et al. (2009), pp. 9–48.

[10] European Commission, Regulation (EU) 1215/2012 of The European Parliament and of The Council on jurisdiction and the recognition and enforcement of judgments in civil and commercial matters (recast) (2012).

[11] European Commission, Regulation (EU) 2015/848 of the European Parliament and of the Council on insolvency proceedings (2015).

Directive 2014/59/EU of the European Parliament and of the Council of 15 May 2014, which promotes the approximation among jurisdictions with respect to the transnational insolvency of financial institutions was a clear consequence of the global financial crisis of the late 2000s, that resulted from recognising the need for 'a regime to provide the authorities with a credible toolkit in order to [. . .] prevent the destabilization of the financial markets and to minimize the costs for the taxpayers.' That is why the European Commission pointed out the following:

> The financial crisis highlighted the need for better regulation and supervision of the financial sector. It is the reason why the European Commission has since 2010 proposed nearly 30 sets of rules to ensure all financial actors, products and markets are appropriately regulated and efficiently supervised. These rules are the basic framework for all 28 Member States of the EU and underpin a properly functioning single market for financial services. When the financial crisis spread to Europe in 2008, we had 27 different regulatory systems for banks in place, largely based on national rules and national rescue measures, although some limited European minimum rules and coordination mechanisms already existed. The pre-crisis framework was incapable of responding to the financial crisis, in particular its systemic nature. There were for example no tools in place to deal with the collapse of large cross-border banks.[12]

With the advent of the global financial crisis, international organisations conducted studies on the convergence among national jurisdictions regarding the norms governing the insolvency of financial institutions. Such organisations included the Basel Committee on Banking Supervision III,[13] the Financial Stability Council,[14] the United Nations Commission on International Trade Law [15] and the International Monetary Fund (IMF).[16]

The Basel III Committee reinforced the pre-existing Principles for the Supervision of Banks' Foreign Establishments,[17] implementing, in addition, parameters of international accountability for supervision of bank branches and subsidiaries, especially through cross-border cooperation and information-sharing (Recommendation 7).

In this scenario, considering the fact that effective coordination on cross-border solutions may be complicated if the countries follow different approaches to crisis

[12] European Commission, Memo: A comprehensive EU response to the financial crisis: a strong financial framework for Europe and a banking union for the eurozone, 10 July 2013.

[13] Basel Committee on Banking Supervision, Report and recommendations of the cross-border bank resolution group. Basel, Switzerland: Bank for International Settlements (2010).

[14] Financial Stability Board, Key attributes of effective resolution regimes for financial institutions (2011).

[15] United Nations Commission on International Trade Law (UNCITRAL), Working Group V (Insolvency Law), 44th session, Vienna, 16–20 December 2013. Recent developments concerning the global and regional initiatives regarding the insolvency of large and complex financial institutions.

[16] International Monetary Fund (2010) Resolution of cross-border banks — A proposed framework for enhanced coordination. Policy papers 63:1–35.

[17] Basel Committee on Banking Supervision, Principles for the Supervision of Banks' Foreign Establishments (1983).

management—the effects of which may be exacerbated by procedural and legislative differences in insolvency—the Committee set out the following in Recommendation 3:

> national authorities should seek **convergence of national resolution tools and measures** toward those identified in Recommendations 1 [*Effective national resolution powers*] and 2 [*Frameworks for a coordinated resolution of financial groups*] **in order to facilitate the coordinated resolution of financial institutions active in multiple jurisdictions**. The management and resolution of failing financial institutions remains a domestic competence. The global nature of many financial institutions requires close cooperation among national authorities. Having similar tools at the national level, as set out in Recommendations 1 and 2, and similar early intervention thresholds may facilitate coordinated solutions across borders. The CBRG [*Cross-Border Resolution Group*] suggests that national authorities and international groups pursue and monitor developments toward the convergence in these legal frameworks.[18]

In addition, the Committee set out the following in Recommendation 4:

> Cross-border effects of national resolution measures to promote better coordination among national authorities in cross-border resolutions, national authorities should consider the development of procedures to facilitate the mutual recognition of crisis management and resolution proceedings and/or measures.

The Committee subsequently developed *Principles for Sound Liquidity Risk Management and Supervision,*[19] in order to make banks more resilient in the event of possible interruptions and structural lags in liquidity flow. The new principles are based on a 'fundamental review of good liquidity risk management practices in banking organizations', emphasising the importance of effective cooperation between supervisors and stakeholders, i.e. accurate tests of cross-border asset liquidation cycles, communication among public authorities to facilitate cooperation in connection with liquidity risk supervision and management; communication procedures and policies concerning a financial authority's decision to impose or ease restrictions on cross-border movements of assets/guarantees.[20]

The Financial Stability Board (FSB) is an international body created in order to monitor and make recommendations on the global financial system, with the aim of promoting financial stability -, recognised the existing agreement among the public authorities as to the merits of establishing the *Legal Entity Identifier* (LEI) system as a 'uniform global system' of financial entity identification:[21]

> The FSB considers that a legal form of foundation or body of equivalent legal form would provide a catalyst for such international and cross-sectional cooperation and coordination,

---

[18] Basel Committee on Banking Supervision, Report and recommendations of the cross-border bank resolution group. Basel, Switzerland: Bank for International Settlements (2010).

[19] Basel Committee on Banking Supervision, The Basel Committee's response to the financial crisis: report to the G20 (2010).

[20] Basel Committee on Banking Supervision, Principles for Sound Liquidity Risk Management and Supervision. Draft or Consultation (2008).

[21] The LEI developed into the subsequent creation of the *Global Legal Entity Identifier Foundation* (GLEIF).

> where the best ideas applicable for the global LEI system can be utilized, drawing on the experience of various experts from either finance or other sectors who have experience in the design and successful implementation of entity identification systems.[22]

Thirty-five recommendations were established for the purposes of strengthening 'principles and commitments specifying and defining a global structure and governance' to be applied on the international and local levels; supporting the implementation of common standards, in view of effective resolution of systemically important financial institutions.[23]

The LEI system, promoting convergence among jurisdictions, specifically for the purpose of financial transactions, and is applicable exclusively to legal-entity financial intermediaries, such as entities that are connected with capital structures or under the purview of financial regulators, including investment vehicles and exchange-traded funds.[24] Thus, the LEI system should also be able to function in the event of insolvency and bankruptcy of financial institutions through the identification and application of rules and procedures that must be followed in such a case (Recommendation 30).[25]

The global financial crisis also induced UNCITRAL to subsequently work on the consolidation of the resulting measures suitable. In its 42nd session in November 2012, it reported that:

> The fast-moving global financial crisis that started in August 2007 illustrated that many of the inadequacies of the frameworks and tools available to address the insolvency of banks and other financial institutions and particularly for managing cross-border impact that had been identified in the 1998 study still existed.(. . .) The impact of the 2007 crisis led to calls by the G203 and others for regulators and relevant authorities to strengthen, as a matter of priority, cooperation on crisis prevention, management and resolution and to review resolution regimes and insolvency laws in the light of the recent experience to ensure they permitted an orderly resolution of large, complex, cross-border financial institutions.[26]

---

[22] FSB, A Global Legal Entity Identifier for Financial Markets (2012).

[23] FSB, Consultative Document. Effective Resolution of Systemically Important Financial Institutions: Recommendations and Timelines (2011).

[24] 'Recommendation 8 SCOPE OF COVERAGE - Examples of eligible legal entities include, without limitation: all financial intermediaries; banks and finance companies; all entities that issue equity, debt or other securities for other capital structures; all entities listed on an exchange; all entities that trade stock or debt; investment vehicles, including mutual funds, pension funds and alternative investment vehicles constituted as corporate entities or collective investment agreements (including umbrella funds as well as funds under an umbrella structure, hedge funds, private equities, etc.); all entities under the purview of a financial regulator and their affiliates, subsidiaries and holding companies; and counterparties to financial transactions.'

[25] 'Recommendation 30 – CONTINGENCY ARRANGEMENTS [. . .] The system should also be able to function in the event of insolvency and bankruptcy of a component, through the identification and application of rules and procedures that must be followed in such a case.'

[26] UNCITRAL, *Insolvency Law Insolvency of large and complex financial institutions*. (A/CN.9/WG.V/WP.109). Note by the Secretariat. Forty-second session. Vienna, 26–30 November 2012.

In this context, UNCITRAL, when promoting convergence among jurisdictions, recognised the authoritative resolutions issued by the FSB in order to endow the national legal systems with the authority and capacity to implement resolutions from other jurisdictions and to render them enforceable through legal structures,[27] as was emphasised by the IMF publication *Resolution of Cross-Border Banks - a proposed framework for enhanced coordination,*[28] the provisions of which include, for example, legislative amendments for coordination among jurisdictions and an institutional apparatus capable of implementing international solutions.[29]

Moreover, it is important to point out that the conclusions expressed on this topic by international organisations are leading to new guidelines for contemporary international judicial cooperation in general, and not just for the transnational insolvency of financial institutions.

In fact, it is an extraordinary advance for contemporary international judicial cooperation to admit that techniques involving the mutual recognition of foreign administrative and judicial decisions around the world are essential, as admitted by Basel Committee Recommendation 4 on Banking Supervision, instead of the current view that mutual recognition is a privilege of States that have previously signed treaties with each other or that belong to certain communities such as the EU.

4.2 The 2015 European Migrant Crisis

The migration crisis experienced in Europe in 2015 was considered the most serious migration challenge since World War II. 1.25 million requests for asylum were received in the EU, in addition to illegal border crossings and episodes with fatal outcomes[30]—such as the notorious case of Alan Kurdi, in Turkey. Even though the European continent is one of the world's main destinations of migrants, the above-mentioned crisis revealed the vulnerabilities in the European migration system.

---

[27] 'The FSB proposed that each jurisdiction should have a designated resolution authority with legal and institutional capacities to implement resolution powers and measures [. . .] The legal framework should give effect to foreign resolution measures, either by way of mutual recognition or by taking measures that support and are consistent with the measures taken by the foreign home resolution authority.'; 'Processes should be established to give effect to foreign resolution measures, such as by way of mutual recognition, and mechanisms to protect the confidentiality of shared information should be developed.'

[28] IMF, Resolution of Cross-Border Banks—A Proposed Framework for Enhanced Coordination. Prepared by the Legal and Monetary and Capital Markets Departments (2010).

[29] 'Amendment of laws at national level to require national authorities to coordinate resolution efforts with their counterparts in other jurisdictions to the maximum extent possible, consistent with the interests of creditors and domestic financial stability'; 'institutional capacity to enable swift action across borders to implement an international solution.'

[30] See Migration in Europe, News European Parliament, 30.06.2017, https://www.europarl.europa.eu/news/en/headlines/society/20170629STO78632/migration-in-europe.

One of the main concerns brought to light by the crisis are the activities of cross-border smugglers, which have gained notoriety, especially since such smuggling was observed in 90% of the cases involving illegal migration.[31] It favours the practice of other criminal activities, as well, such as bribery/corruption and human trafficking, along with rape, kidnapping, robbery and extortion.[32] Similarly, smuggling conflicts with fundamental human rights,[33] the violation of which increases the vulnerability of migrants and refugees.

In this scenario, the European Parliament was urged to reassess its transnational policies, for example, by recognising the need for 'strong cooperation within the EU, as well as with non-EU countries of origin and transit, strategic partners, international organizations, and civil society'[34] in order to put a stop to smuggling and other criminal activities. To that end existing guidelines have been intensified, new directives have been being planned and dialogue between states has been encouraged."[35]

As an initial example, in May 2015, the European Commission published its *European Agenda on Migration* [36] as a quick response to the migration crisis and the human tragedy, in which it recommended 'to work[] in partnership with non-EU countries in order to manage migration in advance'; 'to reinforce the existing frameworks of cooperation'; 'to address the root causes by cooperating on development and humanitarian aid' and, finally, affirming that it should be the EU's model of action in future crises.

For the first time in the history of the EU, the role of the Commission as a policymaker was reduced to providing for the equality of the Member States on the Council.[37] Nevertheless, the *Agenda* also laid down new steps towards reforming the Common European Asylum System (CEAS) through packages of proposals, capable of improving directly applicable regulations, simplifying, clarifying and streamlining procedures and disparities among policies of the Member States, with greater convergence of the forms of protection.[38]

[31] European Commission, *Communication From the Commission to The European Parliament, The Council, The European Economic and Social Committee and The Committee of The Regions.* A renewed EU action plan against migrant smuggling (2021–2025). Brussels, 2021.

[32] UNODC, *Global Study on Smuggling of Migrants 2018.* United Nations publication, Sales No. E.18.IV.9.

[33] Universal Declaration of Human Rights, Art. 14: Everyone has the right to seek and to enjoy in other countries asylum from persecution. This right may not be invoked in the case of prosecutions genuinely arising from non-political crimes or from acts contrary to the purposes and principles of the United Nations.

[34] European Commission, A Renewed EU Action Plan Against Migrant Smuggling (2021–2025) – COM(2021) 591 (2021).

[35] See Butler (2018), pp. 277–310, and Alter and Zhang (2022), pp. 17–33.

[36] European Commission, A European Agenda on Migration COM(2015)240 (2015).

[37] Majone (2005), pp. 43–63.

[38] European Parliament, Policy of Asylum. Fact Sheets on the European Union (2021).

In the following year, the Commission of Civil Liberties, Justice and Internal Affairs of the European Parliament offered proposals for a regulation establishing a common procedure of international protection in the EU[39] and a regulation establishing the Union Resettlement Framework, and also amending the Regulation of the Asylum, Migration and Integration Fund (No. 516/2014),[40] premised on the following:

> (1-a) Resettlement is a well-established act of **solidarity with refugee-hosting countries** based on **humanitarian needs**. Resettlement consists of the selection of third-country nationals and stateless persons in need of international protection in a state in which they have sought protection and their transfer from that state and admission to another state with a view to granting them international protection and providing them with a durable solution. Resettlement has three interrelated and complementary functions: it is a tool for protection, it is a durable solution and it is a **responsibility-sharing mechanism**.

Solidarity and humanitarian motives gave rise to Regulation (EU) 2019/818 of the European Parliament and Council of 2019[41] establishing a framework of interoperability among EU information systems in the field of police and judicial cooperation, asylum and migration. Along the same lines, the UN General Assembly adopted, in 2018, the Global Compact on Refugees, as an expression of the international community's political will and ambition to strengthen cooperation.[42]

Regarding the aforementioned responsibility-sharing, the proposal for a *New Pact on Migration and Asylum* 2020, designed to integrate all the perspectives 'in a careful balance', increasing the procedural paths of cooperation—like Eurodac,[43] now represents a crucial instrument for cross-border cooperation on biometric data and offers immediate operational support.[44]

Such considerations are not restricted to the EU; they also extend to non-EU states.[45] In 2018, the International Organization for Migration drafted a document[46] designed to establish guiding principles and cooperative structures with the objective

---

[39] Report on the proposal for a regulation of the European Parliament and of the Council establishing a common procedure for international protection in the Union and repealing Directive 2013/32/EU (COM(2016)0467 – C8-0321/2016 – 2016/0224(COD)).

[40] Report on the proposal for a regulation of the European Parliament and of the Council establishing a Union Resettlement Framework and amending Regulation (EU) No. 516/2014 of the European Parliament and the Council (COM(2016)0468 – C8-0325/2016 – 2016/0225(COD)).

[41] Art. 5 - Non-discrimination and fundamental rights: (. . .) Respect for human dignity and integrity, including respect of the right to privacy and protection of personal data, should be fully ensured.

[42] United Nations, *Global Compact on Refugees* (A/RES/73/151). New York, 2018.

[43] Regulation (EU) n° 603/2013 of The European Parliament and of The Council. 26 June 2013.

[44] European Parliament, 5 Promoting Our European Way of Life. Legislative Train 05.2022.

[45] See in general Gammeltoft-Hansen (2018), pp. 373–395.

[46] Global Compact for Safe, Orderly and Regular Migration, 2018—Objective 23: Strengthen international cooperation and global partnerships for safe, orderly and regular migration. We commit to support each other in the realization of the objectives and commitments laid out in this Global Compact through enhanced international cooperation, a revitalized global partnership, and in the spirit of solidarity, reaffirming the centrality of a comprehensive and integrated approach [. . .]. See Carlier et al. (2020), p. 37.

of 'strengthening international cooperation and global partnerships for safe, orderly and regular migration.' Within the United Nations, the concept has taken shape around migration governance, considered as follows:

> A process in which the combined framework of legal norms and organizational structures regulate and shape how States act in response to international migration, addressing rights and responsibilities and promoting cooperation within and among countries.[47]

The OAS and OECD have also paid attention to Mediterranean migration issues, especially by jointly publishing the Third Report of the Continuous Reporting System on International Migration in the Americas (SICREMI), an initiative aimed at contributing to the promotion and development of public policies for facilitation, cooperation, institutional reinforcement and information access related to migration.[48]

The North Atlantic Treaty Organization (NATO) also made a positive contribution to the migration crisis by launching Operation 'Sea Guardian', in collaboration with the Operation Sophia—an EU initiative to reduce human trafficking in the Mediterranean through 'information sharing, logistical support and implementation of UN Security Council Resolution 2357',[49] depending maritime cooperation on the operational and tactical levels.

Multinational partnerships, networks, and structures likely to ensure cross-border and interdisciplinary collaboration and the various forms of international cooperation[50] emerged from the European crisis as a way to obviate the need to confront such crises in the future. This shows that it has been understood on the international level that the response should be made through schemes of voluntary coordination and cooperation among the relevant actors[51] independently from the existing multilateral treaties.

In the specific case of this migration crisis, in which supranational and international organisations led the mobilisation in favour of international judicial cooperation, there is an observable tendency towards convergence among the jurisdictions of European countries.

---

[47] UN(OHCHR), Principles and Guidelines, supported by practical guidance, on the human rights protection of migrants in vulnerable situations. (A/HRC/33/67) (2018).

[48] OAS, International Migration in the Americas: Third Report of the Continuous Reporting System on International Migration in the Americas (SICREMI) (2015).

[49] NATO (2018) Operation Sea Guardian, https://www.nato.int/cps/en/natohq/topics_136233.htm.

[50] IOM, Migration and the United Nations Post-2015 Development Agenda (2015).

[51] UN, Committee for Development Policy, *Strengthening International Cooperation for the Post 2015 Era* (2013).

4.3 *The Multifaceted Crisis Caused by The COVID-19 Pandemic*

The multifaceted crisis caused by the COVID-19 pandemic is a fine example of the important role to be performed by international administrative and judicial cooperation in the various spheres of public and private law.[52] According to the HCCH's Permanent Office (Secretariat):[53]

> [. . .] With international borders closed and containment measures in place, cross-border movement of people and goods is subject to unprecedented restrictions. In many jurisdictions, children and families remain stranded. Access to government services remains limited. Legal procedures have been delayed or suspended. Flows of goods have been reduced or restricted and businesses left unable to fulfil contractual obligations. However, even as we witness a surge in the use of technology to assist in these uncertain times, the fact remains that questions of private international law abound. Various HCCH Conventions and their supporting documentation provide valuable assistance as we navigate this crisis together and adjust to the new reality in which we find ourselves – a reality which will undoubtedly continue to have an impact on our everyday lives long after COVID-19.

International organisations that promote convergence among systems of international judicial cooperation, such as the Hague Conference on International Private Law, the United Nations and the EU, are developing studies, principles and guidelines intended to uniformise the interpretation and application of new measures of international judicial cooperation in the context of the COVID-19 Pandemic.

In that context, the HCCH developed the 'Pandemic COVID-19 Toolkit', including topics [54] related to international matters of child and family protection, child abduction and protection, child support and family maintenance and international abduction; as well as international judicial cooperation, resolution of conflicts and litigation related to apostilles (authentication of public documents), service of documents, evidence-taking, and international commercial contracts.

This Guide to Good Practice promotes long-distance mediation where in-person mediation is not practicable;[55] direct cross-border communications among courts in

[52] On the various implications of the Covid 19 Pandemic in international law, see Hathaway et al. (2021), pp. 151–244. See also Kaufman (2021), p. 421.

[53] Hague Conference on Private International Law (2020) HCCH Covid-19 Toolkit: The Hague Conference on Private International Law – HCCH, Netherlands p. 1.

[54] Ibid., p. 2.

[55] 'Mediation - This Guide to Good Practice promotes good practices in mediation and other processes to resolve international family disputes which fall within the scope of the 1980 Child Abduction Convention, in particular, the possibility to arrange long-distance mediation where in-person mediation is not practicable, a highly relevant alternative in the current context of physical distancing and travel restrictions.'

matters of child protection and family law;[56] as well as establishing new guidelines on international adoption.[57]

Regarding the authentication of documents, on the other hand, *e-Apostilles* have been implemented: a digital application that provides certification, and thus recognition, of public documents thanks to remote channels and information sharing, facilitating apostille processes.

Moreover, the Toolkit discusses evidence-taking via remote technology, reinforcing practices already provided for in the *Service Convention* and *Evidence Convention* and by holding the inaugural event *HCCH a|Bridged - Edition 2019.* With respect to the collection of evidence and proof, utilisation of such technologies for the transmission and execution of requests is encouraged, in accordance with the national legislation of the countries involved.[58]

Finally, as far as international contracts are concerned, the Toolkit recommends recognising the contractual choice of forum despite any allegations that the contract is invalid by reason of non-performance due to the crisis.[59] In its discussion of the recognition and enforcement of judgements given by a court designated in an Exclusive Choice of Court Agreement,[60] considering that such judgments are enforceable even if formed exclusively by digital channels, in compliance with the principles of non- discrimination and equivalency of digital communications and technological neutrality.

Besides that, the same conclusion was reached in the report on the meeting on the Impact of the Coronavirus Disease (COVID-19) on 'International Cooperation in Criminal Matters: A one-year overview' held in Vienna, on 25 and 26 March 2021, by the Conference of the Parties to the United Nations Convention against Transnational Organized Crime.

---

[56] 'Cross-Border Communications between Judges - As under normal circumstances, members of the International Hague Network of Judges can undertake direct judicial communications in the context of the HCCH 1980 Child Abduction and 1996 Child Protection Conventions, or in relation to other child protection or family law matters.'

[57] 'Intercountry Adoption - Where an adoption decision has already been issued by a competent authority, in due form and respecting all safeguards and relevant procedures, in the current circumstances it is possible that certain administrative procedures (in particular those relating to travel documents) remain to be completed. In these unique cases, both Central Authorities could consider exceptionally allowing the child to travel together with the adoptive parents to the receiving State.'

[58] 'Under the Service and Evidence Conventions, the use of technology is encouraged in both the transmission and execution of requests, where appropriate and subject to domestic law requirements.'

[59] 'For disputes that occurred because of the pandemic or other crises (e.g. non-delivery of goods or late payment), the exclusive choice of court agreements would not automatically be invalidated solely on the basis that the contract itself is not valid (Art. 3(d)). The severability of the choice of court agreements helps to ensure the effectiveness of that choice even in times of uncertainty.'

[60] 'Recognition and Enforcement of Judgments given by a Court designated in an Exclusive Choice of Court Agreement.'

> The panelist referred to the impact of the COVID-19 pandemic on the transformation of the modus operandi of organized criminal groups. He stressed that the pandemic had resulted in a significant increase in crimes such as trafficking in fake and counterfeit medical products, corruption, drug trafficking and cybercrime. In addition, he noted that one sector of judicial cooperation that had been affected by the pandemic, in particular by flight cancellations and other limitations resulting from it, was that of the surrender of persons sought in extradition proceedings, as well as proceedings relating to the execution of European arrest warrants. He highlighted that, in general, the feasibility of any transfer by air needed to be assessed on a case-by-case basis and often depended on ad hoc flights and the practical arrangements in place.[61]

Based on the above conclusions, recommendations were drawn up at the UN Conference against Transnational Organized Crime, on 8 April 2021,[62] including topics such as the seizure and sharing of evidence among Member States via digital channels; the use of videoconferencing for mutual judicial assistance; the electronic transmission of requests for international cooperation; utilisation and acceptance foreign electronic signatures.

Within the EU, in connection with the use of digital technologies, the European Commission initiated the process to create a norm intended to make international judicial cooperation in cross-borders proceedings in the EU more efficient and reliable in dealing with crises such as the COVID-19 pandemic. In the opinion of the European Commission:

> the considerable impact on the functioning of national justice systems has also adversely affected EU cross-border judicial cooperation, leading in many cases to delays and obstacles to access to justice for individuals and businesses alike. (. . .) has thus underlined the need to strengthen the resilience of the justice system across the EU. It has also stressed the importance to further cooperate with its international partners and promote best practices also in this policy area.[63]

Cross-border judicial cooperation progressed as the pandemic spread, leading to the development and adoption, in December 2021, of the proposal for a Regulation on the digitalisation of judicial cooperation and access to justice in cross-border civil, commercial and criminal matters.[64] In fact, self-isolation and travel restrictions have undermined conventional face-to-face legal services in court and accelerated the implementation of remote audiovisual communication processes worldwide.

---

[61] United Nations, Conference of the Parties to the United Nations Convention against Transnational Organized Crime. Report on the meeting of the Working Group on International Cooperation held in Vienna on 25 and 26 March 2021. p. 6.

[62] United Nations, Conference of the Parties to the United Nations Convention against Transnational Organized Crime. (CTOC/COP/WG.3/2021/3). April, 2021.

[63] European Commission, Digitalization of justice in the European Union. A toolbox of opportunities. COM(2020) 710 final (2020).

[64] European Commission, Proposal for a Regulation Of The European Parliament and of The Council on the digitalization of judicial cooperation and access to justice in cross-border civil, commercial and criminal matters, and amending certain acts in the field of judicial cooperation. COM(2021) 759 final (2021).

Doubts about the practicability of digital communications in a safe and reliable manner with high availability have become a major concern in connection with the democratic parameters pursued by the EU, from subjects such as judicial recognition of documents on to effective access to justice. As a result, digital international judicial cooperation proceedings are no longer the exception but have become the rule.

Consequently, the question of cybersecurity and the related challenges was raised in light of the rapid changeover of daily activities from the real environment to a virtual environment and the difficulties arising from that transition. The European Parliament, published the Resolution on the EU's Cybersecurity Strategy for the Digital Decade,[65] based on the following considerations

> whereas the COVID-19 crisis has further exposed cyber-vulnerabilities in some critical sectors, particularly in healthcare, and the associated measures of teleworking and social distancing have increased our dependency on digital technologies and connectivity, while cyber-attacks and cyber-crime, including espionage and sabotage, as well as the entering and manipulation of ICT systems, structures and networks by means of malicious and unlawful installation, are increasing in number and sophistication across Europe;

The above-cited Resolution highlights cooperation among the bodies of the EU and the Member States as a key factor in facilitating information sharing and enhancing cyber trust. Moreover, a proposal has been received to harmonise national laws with respect to (digitalised) consumer and supply chains in order to avoid ambiguity and fragmentation of the single market.

On the other hand, concern has been expressed within the Organization of American States (OAS) about the situation of migrants and refugees faced with the coronavirus pandemic, especially Venezuelans, with regard to the host countries. The OAS has established cooperation strategies for accreditation of university degrees and documents in the host countries, aiming at non-discriminatory regularisation processes corresponding to the employment and residence permits they need in the country of destination.[66]

In the framework of the Organization for Economic Cooperation and Development (OECD), the relevant topics have been addressed through workshops aimed at discussing how to facilitate access to data and information sharing between

[65] European Parliament, Resolution on the EU's Cybersecurity Strategy for the Digital Decade. (2021/2568(RSP)) (2021).

[66] 'Promote mechanisms of cooperation for the accreditation of university degrees for Venezuelan migrants and refugees, with special focus on health professionals.'; 'Promote mechanisms for the regularization of migrants and refugees so that they can access and participate in the formal economy.'; 'Streamline the processes for the regularization of the migration status of Venezuelan migrants and refugees, so as to facilitate their social integration.'; 'Process complaints about the violation of due process filed by migrants and refugees deprived of their liberty, with a special focus on minors.'. OEA, Propuestas para Mejorar la Situación de los Migrantes y Refugiados Venezolanos en el Marco del Covid-19 [Proposals to Improve the Situation of Venezuelan Migrants and Refugees in the framework of COVID-19], June 2020.

jurisdictions[67] -with a special focus on personal data protection and privacy issues related to COVID-19. The debate fostered by the OECD was especially important because it promoted cooperation in the tracking and processing of data among public authorities, especially biometric and geographical data.[68]

In parallel, regulations have also established in the field of aviation to deal with COVID-19. Taking into consideration the 'sharp drop in air traffic' and the resulting cancellation of services by air carriers, the European Parliament and Council, by means of Regulation (EU) 2020/459, assigned powers to the European Commission to adopt delegated acts[69] after consulting with experts appointed by each EU Member State, facilitating the receipt of documents and granting access to Commission meetings.[70]

The Resolution of 19 June 2020 (2020/2649(RSP)), which originated in the same context, clearly promotes convergence as follows:

> Enhanced solidarity and coordination in the EU tourism sector
>
> 20. Highlights the importance of moving towards a genuine European tourism policy that will significantly contribute to enhancing the competitiveness of the Union in this sector, **promoting cooperation between Member States and regions** (...) importance of **avoiding overregulation within the single marke**t for tourism services, **with the objective of removing and preventing regulatory contradictions and duplications, by ensuring better coordination of policies and legislation** affecting the tourism sector;
>
> 23. Highlights **the importance of enhanced cooperation between EU, national, regional and local authorities** and all relevant stakeholders (...) including the UN Sustainable Development Goals, (...) in coordination with Parliament and the Member States, which includes measures to be applied and observed by all Member States, industries and tourists;[71]

Thus, the International Air Transport Association (IATA), by setting guidelines for airline procedures, developing reference standards and regulations[72] which have been carried over to the national policy of various countries,[73] has invested in developing technology for data monitoring and mutual recognition of documents

[67] OECD, Online Workshop on Addressing the Data Governance and Privacy Challenges in the Fight against COVID-19. with the support of the Global Privacy Assembly (GPA), 15 April 2020.

[68] OECD, Tracking and tracing COVID: Protecting privacy and data while using apps and biometrics. Tackling Coronavirus (COVID-19). Contributing to a Global Effort. April, 2020.

[69] 'Delegated acts are non-legislative acts adopted by the European Commission that serve to amend or supplement the non-essential elements of the legislation; used, typically, when legislative acts — including their Annexes — have to be (regularly) adapted to take account of technical and scientific progress.' EUR-Lex. Glossary of Summaries, https://bit.ly/3xVLfEj .

[70] European Parliament and the Council, Regulation (EU) 2020/459 Amending Council Regulation (EEC) No 95/93 on Common Rules for the Allocation of Slots at Community Airports (2020).

[71] European Parliament, Tourism and Transport in 2020 and Beyond. Resolution of 19 June 2020 (2020/2649(RSP)).

[72] See NS21 airport slot returns WASB guidance; Guidance for ground handling during and post COVID-19; Resolution on the Reopening of International Borders.

[73] IATA, From Restart to Recovery. A Blueprint for Simplifying Air Travel (2021).

related to immunisation (e.g., *digital COVID certificate*), verification of protocols and credentials and document authentication—on the national and international levels—'enhancing security through integration with digital identity management, being used by border control authorities.'[74]

Finally, the International Civil Aviation Organization (ICAO), a specialised agency of the United Nations, has reinforced its intention, as a result of the consequences of the COVID directives, to 'harmonize air transport structures and define strategies for the development of a robust and economically viable global civil aviation system' by proactively promoting cooperation, collaboration and coordination of strategic approaches.[75]

The outlined proposal was based on the recognition and validation of documents by the border control authorities, especially in view of identification management, implementing the 'proof of identity' app (tracing, linkage and verification of the authenticity of the relevant documents); thanks to globally interoperable issuance and control processes and protocols.[76]

The coronavirus pandemic therefore fostered the development of instruments tending to promote approximation among national jurisdictions, such as the Regulation digitalization of judicial cooperation and access to justice in cross-border civil, commercial and criminal matters and the Resolutions of the European Parliament on the EU's Strategy for Cybersecurity and on Tourism and Transport in 2020 and beyond, as well as *convergence* jurisdictions, such as the Covid-19 Toolkit, the recommendations of the United Nations Convention against Transnational Organized Crime, and the strategies of data monitoring and mutual recognition of documents adopted by the OAS, IATA and OECD.

---

[74] 'Governments need to accept digital COVID-19 test and vaccine certificates in their dedicated traveler portal. Where this is not feasible, they must accept digital COVID-19 test and vaccine certificates at the border.' IATA, Digital Processes for Testing & Vaccines Critical for Restart (2021).

[75] 'Evidence of identity – credible evidence of identity, involving the tracing, linkage and verification of identity against breeder documents to ensure the authenticity of identity; Document issuance and control – processes and protocols for document issuance by appropriate authorities to authorized holders, and controls to prevent theft, tampering and loss; Inspection systems and tools – inspection systems and tools for the efficient and secure reading and verification; Interoperable applications – globally interoperable applications and protocols.'

[76] 'Evidence of identity – credible evidence of identity, involving the tracing, linkage and verification of identity against breeder documents to ensure the authenticity of identity; Document issuance and control – processes and protocols for document issuance by appropriate authorities to authorized holders, and controls to prevent theft, tampering and loss; Inspection systems and tools – inspection systems and tools for the efficient and secure reading and verification; Interoperable applications – globally interoperable applications and protocols.'

5 Final Considerations

The global financial crisis of the late 2000s, the European migration crisis of 2015, and the multifaceted crisis caused by the COVID-19 pandemic drove international and supranational entities to present binding regulations and directives, studies and recommendations capable of harmonising national jurisdictions, promoting approximation and convergence among them regarding the procedures of the cooperation measures that were imposed by reason of the new configurations of cross-borders conflicts.

In fact, the international community's efforts to reach a consensus on new measures of international judicial cooperation attest to the importance of its role in dealing with crises. International judicial cooperation has been playing a leading role in resolving conflicts driven by the global crises. Moreover, the standards and general principles of international judicial cooperation have evolved to an incredible extent, rendering it more effective.

References

Alter N, Zhang R (2022) European migration crisis: policy analysis of the frontier countries. Int J Law Ethics Technol:17–33

Boodman M (1991) The myth of harmonization of laws. Am J Comp Law 39:699–724

Butler G (2018) Legal responses to the European Union's migration crisis. San Diego Int Law J 19(2):277–310

Caponi R (2011) Judicial cooperation in the european legal culture: terminology and conceptual framework. Paper presented to workshop on Judicial Cooperation in the Area of Fundamental Rights

Carlier J-Y, Crepeau F, Purkey A (2020) From the 2015 European "migration crisis" to the 2018 global compact for migration: a political transition short on legal standards. McGill J Sustain Dev Law 16(1):34–81

Childress DE III (2017) Jurisdiction, limits under international law. In: Encyclopedia of private international law. Edward Elgar Publishing, Northampton, pp 1051–1056

Dolinger J, Greco L, Perlingeiro R, Miranda N (2023) Limites à jurisdição estrangeira (Limits on Foreign Jurisdiction). In: XI REUNIÃO TEMÁTICA DO GPEJ. Faculdade de Direito da UFF. Niterói, 03 de março de 2004. https://ssrn.com/abstract=2672441

Gammeltoft-Hansen T (2018) International cooperation on migration control: towards a research agenda for refugee law. Eur J Migr Law 20(4):373–395

Ghio E (2022) Redefining harmonisation. Lessons from EU insolvency Law. Edward Elgar Publishing Limited, UK

Grinover AP, Perlingeiro R et al (2009) Model Code of Interjurisdictional Cooperation for Ibero-America. Revista da Escola de Magistratura Regional Federal 11:9–48

Hague Conference on Private International Law (2020) HCCH COVID-19 Toolkit: The Hague Conference on Private International Law – HCCH, Netherlands, https://assets.hcch.net/docs/538fa32a-3fc8-4aba-8871-7a1175c0868d.pdf

Hathaway OA, Lim PJ, Phillips-Robins A, Stevens M (2021) The COVID-19 pandemic and international law. Cornell Int Law J 54:151–244

Hazard Junior GC (2003) International civil procedure and transnational civil procedure: the impact of regional economic integration - an overview. Uniforme Law Rev 8:437

Kaufman D (2021) Covid-19 rights & responsibilities: judicial & legislative responses to the covid-19 pandemic. Univ New Hampshire Law Rev 19:421

Kerameus KD (2003) Some reflections on procedural harmonisation: reasons and scope. Uniforme Law Rev 8(1–2):443–451

Kinsch P (2017) Human rights and private international law. In: Encyclopedia of private international law. Edward Elgar, Cheltenham, UK, pp 880–886

Liakopoulos D (2019) Integration and cooperation of international and European private law according charter of fundamental rights of European Union. Cuadernos de Derecho Transnacional 11:150–193

Majone G (2005) The community method. In: Dilemmas of European Integration. Oxford University Press, Oxford, pp 43–63

United Nations Commission on International Trade Law (UNCITRAL) (2014) Model law on cross-border insolvency with guide to enactment and interpretation, 1997. United Nations Publication, New York. https://uncitral.un.org/sites/uncitral.un.org/files/media-documents/uncitral/en/1997-model-law-insol-2013-guide-enactment-and.pdf

Van Rhee CH (2018) Civil procedure beyond national borders. Access to Justice in Eastern Europe, pp 15–34

Ricardo Perlingeiro is a professor of international and public law at Fluminense Federal University, Brazil.

The Influence of Binding Private International Instruments on Domestic Laws in Times of Crisis

Bruno Zeller

1 Introduction

The purpose of this chapter is to investigate whether the influence of private international laws is why national legal systems have converged on cross border issues, and whether previous divergences have created a crisis. This chapter will specifically look at the Vienna Sales Convention ('CISG') and, where appropriate, the New York Convention on the Enforcement of Arbitral Award ('New York Convention'). It will also refer to pertinent features of the Cape Town Convention.

This chapter discusses whether international instruments have harmonised the law on certain topics, achieving solutions potentially applied universally, and achieved convergence, as opposed to the application of domestic laws in transnational commerce. It is undeniable that the introduction and ratification of transnational law instruments in any legal system is a prime mover in positioning domestic legal systems into the new legal transnational landscape.

To put it differently, have domestic courts applied international instruments pursuant to the intention of the drafters? Have they done so despite the fact that, as some argue, 'the aims and objectives of the CISG have been defeated by the intrusion of domestic laws of different contracting states in the interpretation of the provisions of this Convention?'[1] At the outset, it has to be recognised that the CISG (and many other conventions) has not envisaged total convergence. Still, due to the political nature of conventions, divergence has been built-in where issues were purposefully left out of the convention. Hence the issue is to detect where divergence

[1] Nwafor et al. (2018), p. 156.

B. Zeller (✉)
University of Western Australia, Crawley, WA, Australia
e-mail: bruno.zeller@uwa.edu.au

E. Ghio, R. Perlingeiro (eds.), *Are Legal Systems Converging or Diverging?*,
https://doi.org/10.1007/978-3-031-38180-5_16

is necessary and where it is not. To that end, Article 7 of the CISG is of assistance. Article 7(1) notes that:

> [i]n the interpretation of this Convention, regard is to be had to its international character and to the need to promote uniformity in its application and the observance of good faith in international trade.

It should be noted that convergence is not only left to international instruments; domestic courts can also promote legal convergence over time. A very good example is the demise in common law of the privity rule in shipping, which has been universally replaced by allowing a person who is not a party to a contract to derive the benefits of the contract which is in line with commercial reality and in addition converges with civil law.[2]

An important point which needs to be considered is that, unlike with domestic legislation, the authors and the audience of conventions are not the same. International texts are created for an international community. As the text is a compromise between representatives of member states,—a diplomatic conference—they are not the authors. The author in the CISG is revealed in the preamble of the Convention, which asserts that 'the State Parties to this Convention [. . .] have agreed as follows [. . .]'[3] As Professor Kastely noted, because of the ratification process, 'the audience is composed, in turn, of all states who may consider joining the Convention and all business-people, lawyers, courts, and arbiters concerned with the activity of international trade.'[4] It follows, therefore, that the legal meanings of the provisions in the CISG are to be constructed just the same as any other statute. Professor Chiasoni suggests that:

> it is the output of a typically multi-stage, reflexive, holistic and re-interpretative process; the construction involves the use of an interpretive code [. . .] together with a set of interpretive resources an depends ultimately on each interpreter's cooperative attitude towards the text, the issuing authority, and the legal order as a whole, where the interpreter's attitude may in turn be, and usually is, the effect of the endorsement of some legal ideology.[5]

Linking Chiasoni's observation to Kastely, the emphasis is on the fact that the audience must always be aware of the author and hence the interpretive mandate which the authors embedded within the legal instrument.

The New York Convention, on the other hand, did not insert a preamble. Therefore, it can only be implied that the audience and the authors are in effect identical to the CISG. This is because the feature of any convention is the ratification process, which brings a state into a particular rhetorical community.

Therefore, the question at the heart of this chapter is 'where is the convergence, and what is the crisis which is the impetus of the drafting of conventions – or has the convention in time contributed to a crisis?' The answer to legal convergence is the

---

[2] See Zeller and Moens (2020).

[3] UN DOC A/CONF/97/19, 1489 UNTS 3 (adopted 1 January 1988), Preamble ('CISG').

[4] Kastely (1988), p. 595.

[5] Chiassoni (2019), p. 75.

fact that nations have ratified the convention and hence, have joined the rhetorical community of international law. Ratification obviously only takes place if a nation state can see the advantage in convergence unlike, for example, the United Kingdom (UK) and India in the case of the CISG. Nicholas noted that it should be left to the audience to decide whether 'the commercial world prefers the familiar certainties of English law or the Utopian and unpredictable ideals of Conventions.'[6] The question is whether England and India have understood the reasons for convergence or whether the 'home paddock' is too familiar and therefore, inward-looking attitudes are persistent. An interesting parallel issue in the case of the CISG is that the audience (users of the convention) have a choice to leave the rhetorical community of the CISG if they chose to contractually exclude it pursuant to Article 6. They then remain within the domestic audience by opting out of the CISG and relying on the domestic conflict of laws rules governing their international trade.

Commercial law by nature is not prone to what can be commonly called a 'crisis' such as the global financial crisis of the late 2000s and the COVID-19 pandemic, even though any crisis has some minimal effect on transnational commercial law. This is so as the allocation of risk in the drafting of contracts is the main aim of commercial instruments. Once an unexpected crisis changes the legal landscape, it is the aim of commercial instruments such as the CISG to overcome the problems. As an example, the effects of COVID-19 can be resolved via Article 79[7] which states that:

> A party is not liable for a failure to perform any of his obligations if he proves that the failure was due to an impediment beyond his control and that he could not reasonably be expected to have taken the impediment into account at the time of the conclusion of the contract or to have avoided or overcome it or its consequence.

The CISG, in Article 79, 'clarifies under which circumstances the remedy of damages is excluded which is reinforced in article 79(5) but it does not indicate that the contract has come to an end even if this non-performance is of a lasting nature.'[8] In effect, both parties are still contractually bound to the bargain. However, the CISG also makes it clear that 'the law should not be used to resolve issues which could have been avoided by a diligent party in allocating the risk which is foreseeable to one of the parties. In effect any risk can be allocated such as force majeure clauses in construction contracts.'[9]

Arguably it is the nature of commercial law to assist in resolving disputes which are the result of an economic crisis but only within the boundaries set by the legal instruments.

However, the problem is that transnational law is confronted by problems of inconsistencies and a divergence of legal solutions compared to commercial reality. Hence, the word 'crisis' in this chapter is used to elicit and investigate problems of

---

[6]Nicholas (1993), Conference paper on file with author.

[7]See Zeller (2022), pp. 601 et seq.

[8]Ibid, p. 601.

[9]Ibid, p. 618.

the law having diverged from solutions proposed by the convention. Therefore, it follows that a crisis must be viewed from different angles. The first question is: 'does the international instrument contribute to the resolution of a crisis?' The second question is: 'has a crisis been created by domestic courts by their less-than-uniform application, contrary to the international drafters' intentions?'

In short, in relation to the first question and as noted above, the driving force in the creation of a convention is to unify the law on certain topics in cases of international trade. This is the case as the initiators of international instruments—namely UNCITRAL and UNIDROIT—have realised that the drafting of a 'common law' is not achievable. This has been demonstrated by the fact that attempts by European scholars to devise the Common European Contract Law (CESL)[10] and earlier the Principles of European Contract Law (PECL)[11] have failed and the volumes are now collecting dust. A creation of a unified international common laws fails because such an attempt cannot overcome political or social divergences and hence it is correctly noted that:

> [it] is not only useless, but dangerous to extend attempts or harmonisation into fields in which legal differences reflect differences in political or social organisation or in cultural or social mores.[12]

As noted above, commercial law has never been prone to crisis as the law in each jurisdiction serving its audience has functioned well. Inconsistencies of outcomes only arise if the parties in a dispute are from two different jurisdictions. In these cases, the conflict of laws in the jurisdiction chosen by the plaintiff will decide the applicable governing law. As conflict rules are not uniform in all legal systems, 'forum shopping' ensues. Hence the 'crisis'—namely the lack of coherence and consistency in international disputes—is on display.

This potential conflict was the impetus for Rabel to advocate, in 1935, that international contract law would overcome the inconsistencies of decisions between legal systems and thus achieve a convergence of outcomes. Of course, the development of transnational laws must be placed in the context of internationalisation and globalisation. It is sufficient for the purpose of this discussion to point to the fact that globalisation and internationalisation are not the same. In brief, internationalisation is understood to refer to a cooperation of national actors beyond the nation state.[13] Delbruck, in 2001, noted in relation to globalisation that:

> [i]t is a multifaceted phenomenon that escapes easy definition [. . .] It is sufficient to observe that it is in the present stage of development of the international system that globalisation has been fully recognised as a specific feature of international relations, which impact the political, economic, ecological, social and cultural life of societies around the globe in an unprecedented manner. [14]

---

[10]See Berlinguer and Lehne (2019).

[11]See Commission on European Contract Law (2000).

[12]Capeletti (1978), p. 164.

[13]Delbruck (2001), p. 13.

[14]Ibid, p. 14.

Not surprisingly, the drafting of international law was a result of a 'de-nationalisation' of commercial law. It fitted into the trend of globalisation and attempted to converge transnational law and diminish the influence of national laws in transnational commerce.

However, as soon as four years later, John Ralston Saul wrote about the collapse of globalism.[15] He argued that globalisation was flawed from the beginning as it relied on an overstatement of free trade and technology and the superiority of rational management systems.[16] It has now given way to 'negative nationalism', which is 'a belief in the positive tension of uncertainty and the central importance of choice.'[17] Importantly, the argument is that nationalism is on the rise because 'the transnational technocracies have abandoned or half abandoned a whole series of areas that require too much hands-on attention to interest them.'[18]

Certainly, signs of nationalism are observable—and it is also true to argue that in law, the rate of drafting conventions and model laws has slowed significantly. The question is whether the transnational endeavour to facilitate trade is suffering the same fate as globalism or whether the areas where a common 'international' code is of relevance and assistance is saturated. There are certain signs that the approach to conventions has changed, as seen in the development of the Cape Town Convention.

If follows that two distinct periods of time must be investigated. Section 2 will investigate whether, at the time of inception of transnational law instruments, legal convergence took place. The importance of such an investigation lies in the fact that history sometimes is forgotten and the lessons we can learn from it are overlooked. The second point, to be examined in Sect. 3, is whether the wane of globalisation has led to a rise in nationalism and divergence (due to the inability of courts to uniformly apply the law) or whether transnational laws have endured. Section 4 concludes the arguments.

2 The Inception of Transnational Laws

2.1 The Vienna Sales Convention (CISG)

The claim that unified laws were an essential part of transnational trade started by Ernst Rabel in 1935 with a draft set of sales laws.[19] In 1978, real progress was achieved, specifically because:

> [t]he General Assembly of the United Nations, having considered chapter 11 of the report of the United Nations Commission on International Trade Law on the work of its eleventh

[15] Saul (2005).

[16] Ibid, p. 32.

[17] Ibid, p. 271.

[18] Ibid, p. 276.

[19] Rabel (1935), p. 1.

> session in 1978, which contained a draft Convention on Contracts for the International Sale of Goods, decided, by resolution 33/93 of 16 December1978, that an international conference of plenipotentiaries should be convened in 1980.[20]

Eventually, the final draft accepted by the Diplomatic Conference of 62 States was the CISG. Importantly it was not a drafting of 'new laws' but rather, as Koetz argued, a creation of 'general principles' which were the foundation for harmonisation or unification of international laws.[21] As general principles are the foundation of the CISG, the problem of divergent views of State representatives has been overcome. In effect, an autonomous contract has ceased to be an academic debate—it became an economic and legal reality. In essence, transnational sales laws are to be understood as a convergence of legal principles common to most domestic legal systems. As Amissah noted, the importance of drafting transnational laws is premised:

> [b]y a study not of contract law, but rather of contract practice [which] is the key to understanding the economic properties of contracting that are necessary to work out sensible uniform laws for commercial practices.[22]

The question is, therefore, 'what is the difference between contract practices and contract law?' Arguably, contract law is tied to a particular domestic system—hence a convention based on contract law would not contribute to convergence. Rather, the instrument would be ineffectual and would contribute to a 'crisis' expressed as a rejection of the transnational law such as CESL and PECL. On this issue, Honnold posed the question:

> [c]an clear, predictable international law be made from the divergent rules of dozens of domestic legal systems, rules built with local idioms for which there are no equivalent terms in other languages.[23]

His answer (unsurprisingly) was no, as only transplantation is possible – as has been seen where Turkey transplanted the Swiss Law of Obligation into their domestic system. This shows that the crisis of an inadequate contract law had been overcome by transplantation. It is obvious that transplantation, and the drafting of international laws, are divergent as conventions are not attempting to unify legal outcomes in a legal system but are 'seeking to substitute one law for the many legal systems that now govern this area.'[24]

Contract practices, on the other hand, look beyond the legal system and the law in general. Hence, contract practices are common elements which transcend borders. It can therefore be argued that a transnational law will only be accepted by States if the contract practices are expressed in such a way as to converge and enrich a legal system, and uniformly address cross-border issues. Contract law, on the other hand,

[20] Final Act of the United Nations Conference on Contracts for the International Sale of Goods (1980), para. 1.

[21] Koetz (1970), p. 672.

[22] Amissah (1997), p. 13.

[23] Honnold (1992), p. 11.

[24] Kastely (1988), p. 576.

is inward-looking and unconcerned with transnational issues. With the use of contract practices, the authors seek to establish 'a rhetorical community in which its readers first assent to the language and values of the text itself, and then use the language and values to inform their relations with one another.'[25] It follows that contract law and contract practices address different rhetorical communities. It is up to the users and interpreters of the law to understand which system it is in which they operate, and hence, choose the corresponding rhetorical community which the particular law addresses. Kastely, borrowing from Plato, describes the art of rhetoric—which 'may be described as the art of rendering an indeterminate situation determinate for the purpose of action [and hence] the study of law comes to focus on the ways in which legal discourse forms understandings of ourselves and our communities.'[26] One explanation is that it appears that the difference between contract laws and contract practices has been understood—specifically, that contract practices are a multi-cultural compromise as only general ideas and practices have been borrowed.

A preliminary conclusion is that a crisis in cross-border sales laws has been overcome. The CISG is a refinement on the application of laws when cross-border sales take place. It avoids the application of domestic laws which—depending on the choice of law rule—can lead to 'forum-shopping'. Hence, divergent results are the outcome. As Kastely has observed, the CISG 'is a rhetorical text, contemplating and creating an international rhetorical community.'[27] As such, convergence has been achieved and a 'crisis' in the application of a diverse domestic law can be avoided.

2.2 The New York Convention on the Enforcement of Arbitral Award (New York Convention)

The New York Convention, coming into force in 1958, preceded the CISG. The question is whether the purpose of its inception was founded on different reasons. The New York Convention was established as a result of dissatisfaction with the Geneva Protocol on Arbitration Clauses of 1923 and the Geneva Convention on the Execution of Foreign Arbitral Awards of 1927, both drafted by the League of Nations. Unlike the CISG, the impetus of change came from a private organisation—namely, the International Chamber of Commerce (ICC), which presented a draft convention to UNCITRAL in 1953. Despite its initial success, the 1927 Geneva Convention focused on 'the enforcement of only those awards that are strictly in accordance with the rules of procedure laid down in the law of the country where the arbitration took place—consequently, national awards only.'[28] In effect, it was the

[25] Ibid, p. 577.

[26] Ibid, p. 578.

[27] Ibid, p. 585.

[28] See International Chamber of Commerce (1998), p. 2.

shortcoming or crisis in the enforcement of awards which prompted the ICC to argue in 1951 that there could be no progress without full recognition of the conception of international awards.[29] In brief, the ICC noted:

> the fact that an award settling a dispute arising in connection with this agreement will produce its effects in different countries, makes it essential that it should be enforced in all these countries in the same way. The development of international trade depends on this.[30]

The crisis (or inconsistency in legislation) has been recognised, and the convention has been changed in order to achieve harmonisation in transnational enforcement of awards. As of March 2021, 168 States have ratified the New York Convention, indicating that harmonisation and convergence have been achieved. Additionally, as the New York Convention aims to be a complete statement of law on a narrow topic, the 'homeward trend' has not been an issue. As noted by the ICC, Article V is possibly the most controversial as it allows States to refuse recognition or enforcement of awards if the place of enforcement is different to the seat of the arbitration. The most contentious issue was the question of what constitutes a public policy, but recent decisions—especially in India—have moved towards convergence. Thus, arguably, harmonisation of international decisions has been achieved.

3 After Globalisation: Has the Dream Been Realised?

It is true that nationalism is on the rise—a phenomenon perhaps most noticeable in the United States (US). Additionally, the 'rush' of commercial conventions by UNCITRAL and UNIDROIT has passed, having taken place between 1958 and 1980. The purpose of international conventions in a globalised world is summed up best by the preamble of the CISG, indicating that the objectives were the 'establishment of a New International Economic Order' and 'the removal of legal barriers in international trade.'[31]

The question whether the usefulness of 'traditional' Conventions has passed cannot be accurately assessed. But arguably as the world has changed and globalisation (according to Ralston) has collapsed, a new order will come to the fore. To that end, the Cape Town Convention is of importance. It 'is unique because its invention was driven by industry rather than by government.'[32] Goode explained the purpose and scope of the Convention as follows:

> [i]n essence the Convention, with its Protocols, is designed to overcome the problem of obtaining secure and readily enforceable rights in aircraft objects, railway rolling stock and space assets which by their nature have no fixed location, and in the case of space assets are not on earth at all. The problem [to be resolved] is [...] the widely differing approaches of

[29] Ibid.

[30] Ibid, p. 8.

[31] CISG, Preamble.

[32] Chye (2016), p. 23.

> legal systems to security and title reservation rights, engendering uncertainty among intending financiers as to the efficacy of their rights.[33]

The novel approach was the adoption of a two-instrumented structure, specifically 'a Convention that would not be equipment-specific and a separate, and controlling, Protocol for each category of equipment covered by the Convention, namely helicopters, airframes and aircraft engines, railway rolling stock and space assets.'[34] This structure allowed for an expansion in secured transactions to other industry-specific assets, such as the later inclusion of the Mining, Agricultural and Construction Equipment (MAC) protocol.

In effect, ratification of the Convention is the cornerstone, and each state only needs to adopt the relevant protocol. This approach makes the Cape Town Convention unique and arguably ground-breaking. In essence, it is not a global general convention like the CISG, but instead is drafted to account for the needs of specific industries. With an understanding of where the industries of the protocols are predominantly situated, one might even argue that national interests are driving the new-age conventions. Therefore, convergence on discrete issues ought to be observable and alternative diversion on non-harmonised issues ought to be still prevalent.

That said, the drafting of international legislation as discussed above is one thing, but the interpretation and application of international law is another issue.

3.1 Issues of Interpretation and Application

As noted above, international trade law has overcome the 'crisis' of diverse judgments in international commerce by giving an option of replacing the application of domestic laws. As there are no international courts (as such), the application of the conventions is left to domestic courts. This has created a problem, or 'crisis', due to the inability of some courts to overcome the homeward trend, leading to diversion of judgments. In any case, the intentions of authors must be understood in order to correctly apply international law. These intentions may be explained within the law itself, but may also be understood through the overall purpose and scope of the instrument.

Of course, the interpretation of any legal text attracts never-ending debate. The issue is that the law is expressed through the use of words and in most cases only takes on meaning within a given social context. Richard Rorty put it elegantly stating that '[w]ords gain their fluctuating meanings from the fluctuating contexts in which people put them.'[35] The context is not only the current situation to be resolved, but also whether the text upon which courts rely is statute or common law. This distinction is important as the authors of the law are not the same (the source of

[33] Goode (2002), p. 4.

[34] Ibid, p. 1.

[35] Rorty (2004).

statutes usually being parliament, while the common law is made by judges). Additionally, with the author of transnational laws being a diplomatic conference, this adds another layer of interpretive methodologies. Even in 1961, the House of Lords in *Scruttons Ltd v Midland Silicones Ltd* observed that 'it would be deplorable if the nations should, after protracted negotiations, reach agreement [...] and that their several courts should then disagree as to the meaning of what they appeared to agree upon.'[36] Arguably, this observation did not resonate in all courts.

The difficulty is that courts need to interpret conventions autonomously. Conventions make this clear in different ways. The New York Convention has not included such a mandate, choosing to exclude an interpretative article—instead, it is implied in the act that legal instruments must be consistent in their application. The drafters of CISG, on the other hand, have included an interpretive article, Article 7, which states that 'regard is to be had to its international character and to the need to promote uniformity in its application and the observance of good faith in international trade.'[37] Courts therefore need to 'transcend [their] domestic perspective and become a different court that is no longer influenced by the law of its own nation state.'[38] Put differently, the CISG must be interpreted autonomously rather than nationalistically. This is the foundation or underlying principle of all international instruments which do not 'want to identify [themselves] with any legal system, because [they] want to conjugate with all.'[39]

A problem here with the CISG is—as it is built on legal principles and is a political document resulting from the participation of states—compromises had to be included. This means that the way in which the law is expressed is the result of compromise.[40] However, despite the compromise, a nationalistic interpretation is not justified under the mandate of Article 7. Andersen highlighted that '[e]xamples of divergences in the [interpretation and thus] application of nearly all the provisions of the CISG abound.[41]

Ferrari also commented that:

> a closer look at some decisions allows one to state that a "homeward trend' is discernible, at least by some courts. This trend is deplorable because it promotes parochialism and, thus, defeats the very purpose of the CISG, namely the creation of a uniform sales law aimed at the creation of legal certainty and 'the removal of legal barriers in international trade". In effect, the homeward trend deprives the collective signatories of the predictability and reliability of law which the CISG was meant to create.[42]

Cross has falsely suggested that due to Article 6 (which allows parties to opt out of the CISG), 'the propensity of US courts to interpret the Convention in light of

---

[36] *Scruttons Ltd. v Midland Silicones Ltd.* [1962] AC 446, p. 471.

[37] CISG, Article 7(1).

[38] Murray (1998), p. 367.

[39] Benedetti (1989), p. 9.

[40] Blair (2011), pp. 278–279.

[41] Andersen (2005), p. 162.

[42] Ferrari (2017a), p. 247.

domestic legal traditions may ameliorate the tendency of US parties to opt out of the CISG.'[43] The point is that either the CISG is applied or it is not, as otherwise the CISG, from functioning as a neutral law and its interpretation, may thus favour one of the parties.[44] However an important point needs to be understood: the CISG is not a complete law (that is, not a 'code') on the sale of goods. It expressly lets issues upon which consensus could be reached during the drafting process to domestic law. It is understandable that the drafters preferred to exclude these 'deal-breakers' than fail altogether in the creation of the convention.

This is exactly the problem Article 7 is aiming to overcome by mandating that the CISG be interpreted autonomously. It is therefore unhelpful (and based on common law practices) to argue that depending on the court making a decision, a different 'weight ought to be accorded to it.'[45] Unless a court interprets the CISG autonomously, it will fail in its understanding of the convention.

Despite diverse judgments, it is arguable that the crisis in interpretation is most prominent in 'hard cases'- that is, where provisions are vague. Dworkin suggested that:

> "hard cases" exist primarily for two reasons: "[s]tatutes and common law rules are often vague and must be interpreted before they can be applied to novel cases. Some cases, moreover, raise issues so novel that they cannot be decided even by stretching or reinterpreting existing rules.[46]

Gillet and Scott paint a very sceptical picture by arguing that:

> [i]n the case of the CISG, the lack of meaningful uniformity is exacerbated by the failure to create interpretive mechanisms that, over time, might have given substantive content to the vague default standards. The upshot is a treaty whose provisions are likely to become less and less useful as time goes on. Indeed, we predict that CISG ultimately will lose out in competition with alternative legal regimes.[47]

The above is wrong for two reasons. Firstly, the CISG will not be rewritten; otherwise, two instruments would be 'in circulation', akin to a crisis in application. Secondly, there is no appetite to devise a new contract or sales law. This is shown by the results of European efforts, which—as mentioned earlier—have not proven fruitful as they are based on contract law instead of contract practices with 'warts and all.' Instead, what is important is that those interpreting the CISG must be mindful of the potential pitfalls or crises, and hence minimise this problem to the best of their abilities. Whatever has been argued by commentators, the future of the CISG does not hinge on tribunals reaching uniform interpretations. The importance is that the divergence is recognised, steps are taken to minimise this divergence, and the overall outcome will be convergence.

---

[43] Halverson Cross (2007), p. 138.

[44] Ferrari (2017a), p. 248.

[45] Lazerow (2019), p. 374.

[46] Dworkin (1975), p. 1058.

[47] Gillette and Scott (2005), p. 485.

Divergence has several sources. The first is the homeward trend. The second is the effect of authentic languages. The third cause is the narrow reading of Article 7. Each of the divergences will be discussed separately. However, it is fitting to close this section by answering the question of Lazerow, who asked 'what is so great about uniformity?'[48] The simple answer is it will reduce non-uniformity as demanded by Article 7(1).

3.2 The Homeward Trend Defined

The most unsatisfactory explanation for divergence in interpretation is that it is the result of a tendency of interpreters to project domestic law into the provisions of the Convention. As Honnold predicted, the problem is 'the tendency to think that the words we see are merely trying, in their awkward way, to state the domestic rule we know so well.'[49]

In some instances, the CISG does impose a recourse to domestic laws by not mandating an outcome; however, this does not equate to a homeward trend as it is within the mandate of the convention. This is—as already noted above—the case where representatives of states objected to the inclusion of solutions into the CISG which were termed 'domestic sacred cows.' This is true, for instance, with respect to the expression 'private international law' (PIL) employed by the CISG.[50] The Tribunale di Padova explained the issue very well. First, they rejected the homeward trend, stating that:

> from a substantive point of view, it is necessary that the contract be one for the sale of goods which, however, the Convention does not define. Nevertheless, the lack of an express definition should not lead one to resort to a domestic definition, such as that to be found in Article 1470 of the [Italian] Civil Code. In effect, the Convention's concept of "contract for the sale of goods" has to be interpreted, as have the majority of concepts (such as that of "place of business", "habitual residence", "goods") [. . .] autonomously, i.e. without resort to concepts characteristic of any particular legal system.[51]

Secondly, in relation to PIL, the court commented that any interpretation must correspond to the one of the fora, being the only authority to define this term given that the CISG left its meaning open.[52]

At the same time, it is also wrong to argue that 'it can hardly be denied that the focus on the domestic laws interpretations of validity will not necessarily lead to a coherent and streamlined interpretation of art 4 CISG's validity rule.'[53] As the

[48] Lazerow (2019), p. 379.

[49] Honnold (1988), p. 208.

[50] Ferrari (2017a), p. 250.

[51] https://cisg-online.org/files/cases/6891/translationFile/967_36265745.pdf.

[52] Ibid.

[53] Nwafor et al. (2018), p. 157.

validity of a contract is left to domestic laws, a coherent and streamlined approach has never been intended. Harmonisation is only an issue once a domestic system judges a contract valid and the CISG becomes the governing law, but then does not apply the CISG and remains within the 'domestic paddock.' Schroeter correctly observed that in general, the risk inherent in Article 4 is overstated and as validity is excluded, the CISG cannot be the source of the very rule which is meant to control it.[54]

A classic example of the homeward trend can be observed in the Australian case of *Playcorp Pty Ltd v Taiyo Kogyo Limited*.[55] Here, the CISG was applicable, but in essence ignored. The parties were from Australia and Japan. Astonishingly, the defence argued that the CISG did not apply, in total ignorance of Article 1. The lack of understanding of the CISG was demonstrated by the argument that:

> [i]t was not suggested that there was any material difference or inconsistency between the provisions of art 35 and s 19(a) and (b) [of the Sale of Goods Act] and because of that and the way the case was conducted, it is unnecessary to consider whether there is. Counsel proceeded on the basis that there was no material difference or inconsistency.[56]

In addition, the court relied exclusively on domestic case law for guidance—in contravention of Article 7 of the CISG.

3.3 The Outward Trend

Ferrari has discerned another trend which he labelled an 'outward trend.[57] It equally contributed to the crisis which was the result of the inability of commentators and courts to understand the mandate of Article 7 and look within the four corners rule for an answer.

A 2008 Spanish Supreme court's[58] decision explains the outward trend well. The issue was a fundamental breach of Article 25. As the concept of fundamental breach is unknown in Spanish law, the court found it necessary to revert to the common law since the principle was known well in common law, as opposed to an autonomous interpretation pursuant to the CISG. This is not an isolated case. The Court of Appeal of Koblenz had to decide which measures are reasonable in relation to mitigate losses pursuant to Article 77 CISG. The court stated that:

> the standard for the appropriate conduct pursuant to Article 77, first sentence, CISG is [...] the conduct of a "reasonable person" [...] The plaintiff was required to take all such measures to mitigate the loss, which were reasonable in the sense of Article 77 CISG in the circumstances. The standard of a reasonable person, which originates in the English and

[54] Schroeter (2014), p. 98.

[55] [2003] VSC 108.

[56] *Playcorp*, [235].

[57] Ferrari (2017b), p. 57.

[58] https://cisg-online.org/search-for-cases?caseId=7559.

> Anglo-American Common Law, is referred to in numerous provisions of the UN Sales Convention (f.i. in Art. 8(2) and Art. 25 CISG) and counts among the Convention's general principles . . . Reference must be made to the conduct of a prudent person who is in the same situation as the concerned party [. . .] In case the contracting party exercises a profession or a commercial activity, reference must be made to the skills of a member of the profession to which it belongs (Art. 8(2) and Art. 25 CISG: "reasonable person of the same kind" [. . .]). Since the legal concept of the "reasonable man" is not used in this form in continental European law, the Court considers it essential to resort to principles established in the English and Anglo-American law.[59]

The obvious divergence is that despite recognising the relevant parts of the convention, the court moved outside the CISG to find an answer totally ignoring the mandate of Article 7(1) namely an autonomous interpretation relying on CISG jurisprudence and academic writing. The court 'equated the absence of a comparable concept in its own domestic law with the absence of a similar concept in all other continental European legal systems.'[60]

It needs to be noted, though, that courts have generally avoided either the homeward or outward trend by taking note of Article 7(1). However, some countries—specifically Australia—have succumbed to the homeward trend in the majority of CISG cases due to applying precedent of faulty decisions, hence perpetuating the mistake.

3.4 *The Effect of Language*

An additional issue which can contribute to diversion is the fact that the CISG has six official languages: Arabic, English, French, Spanish, Russian and Chinese. Lazerow argued that uniformity is unlikely not only due to the different languages but also because decisions are not readily available.[61] Arguably the second argument in relation to decisions is not very valid as scholars in many countries will inevitably discuss a decision which is in breach of Article 7. Additionally, to overcome this issue, any counsel or judge unfamiliar with a language merely needs to look at a decision in a familiar language to compare the outcome. On this issue, Andersen asserted that:

> [c]ertainly, most practical barriers to the use of foreign sources are now all but removed. Efficient access to multi-jurisdictional sources is now facilitated by the internet, where CISG databases can easily be found, along with full text translations of CISG cases. So there is today no good basis for claiming that it is too difficult to find or translate foreign CISG cases.[62]

---

[59] Oberlandesgericht Koblenz, 24 February 2011, https://cisg-online.org/search-for-cases?caseId=8217.

[60] Ferrari (2017a), p. 253.

[61] Lazerow (2019), p. 370.

[62] Andersen (2009), p. 53.

The problem of finding cases is now reduced for all transnational laws. In fact, the New York Convention (having been written only in English) still requires an international search for relevant case law in diverse areas such as public policy issues. Moreover, in domestic law, there are universally important unresolved issues such as the validity of penalty clauses. As an example England, Australia, and Singapore have not converged on this issue despite referring to the same precedents. James Perillo has observed aptly that 'nowhere in the law of contracts has the clash of common law and civil law seemed as irreconcilable as in the treatment of penalty clauses.'[63]

As far as the issue of language is concerned, the fact that courts rely on their own language is also a problem of a homeward trend. This is specially so as linguistic nuances will also play a role in CISG interpretations. This is only so if the contested word has a different meaning in an official language compared to the language used in the court. Whatever the argument is, the Swiss Federal court got it right by arguing that German is not an official language hence it follows that a translation had to be used. The court ruled that in these cases, only the original text is authentic and that the English text first and the French one second need to be consulted. The justification was that at the conference, English and French were the official languages, and all debates were conducted in English.[64]

In this particular case before the court, the issue was the translation of Article 39, and in particular, the phrase 'specifying the nature of the lack of conformity.' After engaging in a linguistic analysis of the French and English text compared with the German translation (*genau bezeichnet*) the court concluded that the original languages posed a lesser threshold in defining the breach of the contract as the word 'genau' equates to 'exactly' and not to 'the nature of the lack of conformity.' As another example of this issue, Kruisinga highlighted that Article 35(3) of the (unofficial) Dutch version of the CISG has a similar issue, whereby the phrase 'could not have been unaware' in translation required the buyer to erroneously perform a pre-contractual inspection.[65]

3.5 *Reading of Article 7*

As Article 7 is the cornerstone on which the interpretation, and hence application, of the CISG is based, it is important to briefly discuss the views of Blair, who argues that commentators have made a flawed assumption in narrowly reading Article 7. Blair stated that 'this narrow reading recognizes only a binary distinction between vague provisions involving gaps in coverage of the CISG-so called "internal

[63] Perillo (1994), p. 313.

[64] CISG-online 840 (*Used textile cleaning machine case*) (2003), https://cisg-online.org/files/cases/6766/fullTextFile/840_19602533.pdf Relying on Witz (2000).

[65] See Kruisinga (2004), pp. 53 et seq.

gaps"—and vague provisions involving matters outside of the coverage of the CISG-so called "external gaps."'[66] There is no debate that external gaps need to be filled by the otherwise governing law. In essence, Blair contends that a 'critical distinction in internal gap cases between CISG provisions that are intentionally vague—"open-textured standards"—and provisions that are vague because of drafting imperfections'[67] has not been vigorously debated.

Arguably, this has not been considered to be a problem as sophisticated parties regularly include, and even negotiate over, vague terms in their contracts such as 'best effort', 'reasonableness', or even 'good faith'.[68] As the CISG included open-textured standards and will not be revised, vague terms are here to stay. It is difficult to argue that 'gain[s] from having the default set comprised of open-textured standards might be eroded if CISG defaults framed as standards were slowly transformed into rules through application of the autonomous method of interpretation.'[69] This is because open textured terms are necessary as they only take on life within a given factual scenario. As an example, Article 39 notes that a lack of conformity must be communicated to the seller *within a reasonable time*. On this provision, The District Court of Flensburg noted that:

> [i]n order to estimate the adherence to the duty of giving notice within a reasonable period of time pursuant to Art. 39(1) CISG, one must consider the specific circumstances of the specific case. In the first place, it is important whether the goods are perishable or durable. The former often require a notification within a few hours or at latest within a few days.[70]

The fact that reasonable time is an open term has been recognised by courts such as the District Court of Florida, commenting that:

> Article 39 does not define "reasonable time;" however, neither Party provided the Court with the date that the matter was filed or heard by the Supreme Court of Peru. Reading the Complaint in light most favorable to the Plaintiff, it is plausible that Defendants had notice of the lack of conformity by nature of the proceedings in Peru.[71]

The factual approach is best illustrated by a US case where the goods concerned were lingerie, which is not perishable. The court noted that 'because the alleged breach (late delivery) would have been apparent on the date of Native's receipt of the goods, if not earlier, the one year delay plainly was unreasonable.'[72]

---

[66] Blair (2011), p. 272.

[67] Ibid, p. 273.

[68] See generally Scott and Triantis (2005), p. 190.

[69] Blair (2011), p. 303.

[70] Faculty of Law, University of Basel (2021) Search for cases: Live Sheep Case (CISG-online number 619). CISG-online, https://cisg-online.org/search-for-cases?caseId=6577.

[71] *GO Traders S.A. v. International Textile Mills, LLC et al.*, US District Court for the Southern District of Florida, https://cisg-online.org/search-for-cases?caseId=10124.

[72] *Shantou Real Lingerie Manufacturing Co., Ltd. v. Native Group Int'l, Ltd.*, US District Court for the Southern District of New York, 14cv10246-FM.

The conclusion which must be reached is that open-ended standards have been applied within the factual scenario. The question of autonomous interpretation is not an issue, and logically, no resort to domestic laws is observable.

However, it must be said that Blair reaches a correct conclusion by identifying two issues where uniformity of outcomes is not an appropriate goal-situation: where 'a CISG default provision was cast by the drafters of the Convention as an open-textured standard and situations in which the parties have modified a CISG.'[73] He is also correct in stating that 'the methodological uniformity called for in Article 7, combined with a proper regard for the structure of the Convention and its robust emphasis on freedom of contract, compels the conclusion that case-by-case differences in the interpretations of some provisions of the CISG are not only inevitable but may be necessary.'[74]

The conclusion in relation to the reading of Article 7 as proposed by Blair is that any argument as to convergence must be read in light of the general principles embedded within the CISG and not simply on a textual approach. Diversion is always an issue, but the law relies upon facts as much as on the law to reach correct decisions.

4 Conclusion

This chapter has demonstrated that international instruments have played an important part in the convergence process in international trade. The effects and limitations of domestic laws have been removed as far as possible—hence uniform outcomes are possible. However, at the same time, especially instruments which are not a complete statement of law such as the CISG have also created a crisis in the proper application of the transnational laws. The issue of the 'homeward trend' has been a problem due to the inability of courts to understand the mandate of Article 7 (the interpretive article), and also the challenges of diverse languages have been a problem.

Some of the reasons that may ultimately favour these trends under the CISG are intrinsic to the CISG and, therefore, cannot be corrected, as it is unlikely that the CISG will ever be revised to amend the current situation.[75] Correction is only achievable if courts and the legal profession as a whole understand the mandate of Article 7 and its status as the cornerstone of the CISG. The blueprint to a correct interpretation of Article 7 can be found in a New Zealand decision where the court observed that:

> [t]he requirement imposed by Article 7(1) namely to have regard "to the international character of the convention and to the need to promote uniformity in application" is

[73] Blair (2011), p. 319.

[74] Ibid.

[75] Ferrari (2017a), p. 257.

> generally accepted as establishing what has been called a principle of autonomous interpretation. That means the Convention must be applied and interpreted exclusively on its own terms, having regard to the principles of the Convention and Convention-related decisions in overseas jurisdictions. Recourse to domestic case law is to be avoided.[76]

However, the issue of convergence (rather than divergence) is dominant; both the academic literature and judicial observations point to this trend. For example, in a set of lectures given in 2010, Lord Bingham of Cornhill observed that '[j]udicial horizons have widened and are widening.'[77] Additionally, Yuval Shany observed that 'a certain quantitative and qualitative change, with more international law [being] applied by more national courts in a more consequential (and less parochial) way.'[78]

Conseiller Guy Canivet, formerly president of the French *Cour de Cassation* and now a member of the Conseil Constitutionnel, concurs:

> [c]itizens and judges [. . .] are less and less prone to accept that situations which raise the same issues of fact will yield different results because of the difference in the rules of law to be applied [. . .] There is a trend, one might even say a strong demand, that compatible solutions are reached, regardless of the difference in the underlying applicable rules of law.'[79]

Therefore, the conclusion is that the crisis of diversion of application in the CISG due to language and homeward trend is diminishing as the horizons of the legal fraternity are widening.

References

Amissah R (1997) The Autonomous Contract, reflecting the borderless electronic-commercial environment in contracting. Electronic Handel – rettslige aspector, Oslo

Andersen C (2009) The global jurisconsultorium of the CISG revisited. V J Int Comm Law Arb 13: 43–70

Andersen CB (2005) The uniform international sales law and the global Jurisconsultorium. J Law Commer 24:159–179

Benedetti G (1989) Commento all'art: 4 della Convenzione di Vienna sui contratti di vneidta internazionale di beni mobile. Nuove Leggi Civili Commentate 9:9

Berlinguer L, Lehne K-H (2019) Legislative Train Schedule: Connected Digital Single Market. https://www.europarl.europa.eu/legislative-train/theme-connected-digital-single-market/file-common-european-sales-law

Bingham T (2010) Widening horizons: the influence of comparative law and international law on domestic law. Cambridge University Press, New York

Blair HA (2011) Hard cases under the convention on the international sale of goods: a proposed taxonomy of interpretive challenges. Duke J Comp Int Law 21:269–320

[76] https://cisg-online.org/files/cases/8131/fullTextFile/2215_60673455.pdf.

[77] Bingham (2010), p. 3.

[78] Shany (2009), p. 2. Quoted in Roberts (2011).

[79] Kirby (2005), p. 2: '[J]udges of municipal courts in this century will assume an important function in making the principles of international law a reality throughout the world.'

Capeletti M (ed) (1978) New perspectives for a common law of Europe. Bruylant, Belgium
Chiassoni P (2019) Interpretation without truth, a realistic inquiry. Springer, Switzerland
Chye E (2016) The cape town convention – the Australian experience and views from the classroom. Univ West Aust Law Rev 40(2):23–40
Commission on European Contract Law (2000) Principles of European Contract Law, Parts I and II. Commission on European Contract Law (2000) Principles of European Contract Law, Parts I and II
Convention on the Recognition and Enforcement of Foreign Arbitral Awards (New York, 1958) (the "New York Convention"). United Nations Commission on International Trade Law, https://uncitral.un.org/en/texts/arbitration/conventions/foreign_arbitral_awards
Delbruck J (2001) Structural changes in the international systems and its legal order: international law in the era of globalisation. Swiss Rev Int Euro Law 1:13–17
Dworkin R (1975) Hard cases. Harv Law Rev 88(6):1057–1109
Ferrari F (2017a) Autonomous interpretation versus homeward trend versus outward trend in CISG case law. Unif Law Rev 22(1):244–257
Ferrari F (2017b) Heimwarts- und Auswartstreben in der Rechtsprechung zum UN-Kaufrecht. In: Blaurock U, Maultzsch F (eds) Einheitliches Kaufrecht und Vereinheitlichung der Rechtsanwendung. Nomos, Germany, pp 47–94
Final Act of the United Nations Conference on Contracts for the International Sale of Goods (1980) UN Doc A.CONF.97/18 (10 March-11 April 1980). United Nations Digital Library, https://digitallibrary.un.org/record/160584
Gillette CP, Scott RE (2005) The political economy of international sales law. Int Rev Law Econ 25(3):446–486
Goode R (2002) The cape town convention on international interests in mobile equipment: a driving force for international asset-based financing. Unif Law Rev 7(1):3–15
Halverson Cross K (2007) Parol evidence under the CISG: the "Homeward Trend" reconsidered'. Ohio St Law J 68:133–160
Honnold J (1988) The sales convention in action – uniform international words: uniform application? J Law Commer 8:207–212
Honnold JO (1992) Goals of Unification. In: Uniform Commercial Law in the Twenty-First Century: Proceedings of the Congress of the United Nations Commission on International Trade Law (New York, 18-22 May 1992). United Nations, New York, pp 11–13
International Chamber of Commerce (1998) The ICC International Court of Arbitration Bulletin Vol. 9/No.1 – Fr, https://library.iccwbo.org/dr-bulletins.htm
Kastely AH (1988) Unification and community: a rhetorical analysis of the United Nations sales convention. Northwest J Int Law Bus 8(3):574–622
Kirby M (2005) International law: the impact on national constitutions (Seventh Annual Grotius Lecture). Proceedings of the Annual Meeting (Am Soc Int Law Proc) 99:1–21
Koetz H (1970) Allgemeine Rechtesgrundsatze als Ersatzrecht. Rabels Zeitschrift für ausländisches und internationales Privatrecht 34:663–678
Kruisinga SA (2004) (Non-)Conformity in the 1980 UN Convention on the inter-national sale of goods: a uniform concept? Intersentia, Cambridge
Lazerow H (2019) Uniform interpretation of CISG. Int Lawyer 52(3):369–391
Murray J (1998) The neglect of CISG: a workable solution. J Law Commer 17(2):365–379
Nicholas B (1993) The United Kingdom and the Vienna sales convention: another case of splendid isolation?. UNCITRAL Law Library, https://unov.tind.io/record/5555
Nwafor N, Ajibo C, Lloyd C (2018) Reimagining transnational validity under the CISG: A gateway to "homeward trend" interpretations. JITLP 17(3):156–168
Perillo J (1994) UNIDROIT principles of international commercial contracts: the black letter text and a review. Fordham Law Rev 63(2):281–344
Rabel E (1935) Der Entwurf eines einheitlichen Kaufgesetzes. Rabels Zeitschrift für ausländisches und internationales Privatrecht 9:1–79

Roberts A (2011) Comparative international law? The role of National Courts in International Law. Int Comp Law Q 60(1):57–92
Rorty R (2004) The Spirit of France's Great Revolutionary Lives On. Times Higher Education (Nov. 12, 2004), https://www.timeshighereducation.com/features/the-spirit-of-frances-great-revolutionary-lives-on/192401.article
Saul JR (2005) The collapse of globalism and the reinvention of the world. Penguin, Canada
Schroeter UG (2014) The validity of international sales contracts: irrelevance of the 'validity exception' in Article 4 Vienna Sales Convention and a novel approach to determining the Convention's scope. In: Schwenzer I, Spagnolo L (eds) Boundaries and intersections: the 5th Annual MAA Schlechtriem CISG conference. Eleven International Publishing, The Hague, pp 95–117
Scott RE, Triantis GG (2005) Incomplete contracts and the theory of contract design. Case W Res Law Rev 56(1):187–201
Shany Y (2009) National Courts as International Actors: Jurisdictional Implications. Hebrew University International Law Research Paper No. 22-08, https://papers.ssrn.com/sol3/papers.cfm?abstract_id=1292056&download=yes
UNIDROIT International Institute for the Unification of Private Law. MAC Protocol – Overview (2019). https://www.unidroit.org/mac-protocol-overview
United Nations Commission on International Trade Law. Texts and Status. https://uncitral.un.org/en/texts
United Nations Convention on Contracts for the International Sale of Goods, UN DOC A/CONF/97/19, 1489 UNTS 3 (adopted 1 January 1988)
Zeller B (2022) COVID -19 and Article 79 – a revisit. In: Benatti F, Garcia Long S, Viglione F (eds) The transnational sales contract. Wolters Kluwer, pp 601–618
Zeller B, Moens G (2020) The Himalaya Clause. Connor Court Publishing, Redland Bay

Bruno Zeller is a professor in transnational commercial law at the University of Western Australia, Australia.

The Role of Soft Law in Times of Crises

J. C. A. van Dam

1 Introduction

In times of crisis, swift action is often needed to effectively respond to the (unprecedented) challenges and problems that present themselves. Characterised by features of informality, non-binding governance instruments are 'fast, flexible and easy to issue.'[1] Therefore, at least at first sight, they constitute a perfect response to take the swift and urgent action that is needed in times of crisis.

The popularity of such instruments, often referred to as 'soft law' in the literature, came to the fore during the COVID-19 pandemic. In the European Union (EU), numerous soft law measures were issued to address and counteract the consequences of the health crisis.[2] 'Soft governance' played an important role during the pandemic not only at the EU supranational level, but also at the level of individual Member States.[3] Yet, literature also reveals regulatory differences in the way governments responded to the crisis. Authors have found that in some countries—such as Denmark, Finland, Iceland and Norway—soft law played a pivotal role, with numerous soft law instruments being issued to tackle the crisis.[4] In other countries, such as Greece and Germany, soft law has played a lesser, sometimes even insignificant, role as a regulatory tool during the crisis.[5] Thus, the literature presents a varied picture

[1] Ştefan (2020), p. 663.

[2] Ibid. See also Eliantonio et al. (2021a).

[3] Eliantonio et al. (2021b); Boschetti and Poli (2021).

[4] Eliantonio et al. (2021b), p. 3.

[5] Ibid.

J. C. A. van Dam (✉)
Dutch Council of State and Department of Constitutional and Administrative Law at Leiden University, Leiden, The Netherlands
e-mail: j.c.a.van.dam@law.leidenuniv.nl

E. Ghio, R. Perlingeiro (eds.), *Are Legal Systems Converging or Diverging?*,
https://doi.org/10.1007/978-3-031-38180-5_17

and suggests that the role of 'pandemic soft law' is likely to be shaped by national legal culture and practice.[6]

Aiming to contribute to the research on the role that soft law plays during crises, and in particular during the COVID-19 crisis, this chapter predominantly explores the role of soft law in the Netherlands. As a decentralised unitary state, where soft law can play a role in coordinating and aligning different levels of government,[7] and a country where one category of soft law has been given a legal basis (in the form of so-called *policy rules*),[8] The Netherlands makes for an interesting case study, raising a series of questions: has there been room for soft, non-legally binding, instruments in the Dutch response to the COVID-19 pandemic? If so, what were the benefits of soft law in addressing the COVID-19 crisis? Were these potential benefits fulfilled, or did undesired side-effects or risks arise? And what lessons can be learned from the use of soft law for the future?

This chapter examines these questions and finds that soft instruments were used in The Netherlands to address the COVID-19 crisis. The informal rules and guidance took the form of *inter alia* 'guidelines', 'policy rules', 'questions and answers', 'dialogues' and 'template regulations.' These non-legally binding instruments have been issued with the intention of providing clarity and assistance to the municipalities in implementing the corona measures (discussed below), as well as to enable a more coordinated and coherent implementation of the legally binding corona measures. The analysis shows that, in practice, the provision of guidance and support allows for dialogue, (better) alignment, and convergence between municipalities and safety regions.[9]

However, the chapter also argues that the use of soft instruments risks de facto limiting the room for differentiation and tailored decision-making at the regional or local level—objectives that are central to the Dutch approach in addressing crises. What is more, the COVID-19 soft law measures also have (input) legitimacy drawbacks, with some measures mostly emanating from discussions with *private* parties.

The chapter is structured as follows. Section 2 outlines the 'hard' response to COVID-19, introducing the decentralised emergency regulations during the first phase of the crisis and the Temporary COVID-19 Act in the second phase of the crisis. Section 3 introduces the main 'soft law categories' in the Netherlands, followed by an overview of the COVID-19 soft laws that have been issued to address the pandemic in the Netherlands in Section 4. Section 5 reflects on the legal status of COVID-19 soft law, its converging effects, as well as the potential side-effects and legitimacy drawbacks. Section 6 provides the conclusion.

---

[6] Boschetti and Poli (2021), p. 51; Eliantonio et al. (2021b), p. 3.

[7] See Sect. 5.3.

[8] See Sect. 3.1.

[9] The safety regions are decentralised bodies that are committed to ensuring the safety of the inhabitants and that are responsible for facilitating regional cooperation in times of crisis and disasters.

2 A Hard Response to COVID-19: From Decentralised Emergency Regulations to the Temporary Corona Act

2.1 *Decentralised Emergency Regulations*

Initially, in March 2020, the Dutch response to address the pandemic consisted of the adoption of decentralised emergency regulations. These legally binding corona measures were issued at the level of the 25 'safety regions'—decentralised bodies that are committed to ensuring the safety of the inhabitants and responsible for facilitating regional cooperation in times of crisis and disasters.[10] These emergency regulations provided the necessary, yet far-reaching measures, such as the prohibition of public gatherings, the closure of cafés and restaurants and a 1.5-metre social distancing rule.[11]

This decentralised approach allowed, at least in principle, for a regional and differentiated approach that could take into account regional circumstances, while making decisions as close to the citizens impacted as possible.[12] Nonetheless, the room for regional differentiation remained limited, as the emergency regulations had to give effect to a legally binding instruction (*bindende aanwijzing*) from the Minister of Health directed at the Chairs of the safety regions.[13] Subsequently, the Safety Council -an umbrella organisation which represents the 25 safety regions—issued so-called non-legally binding 'model emergency regulations', from which it was possible to deviate within the boundaries set by the Minister's binding instructions. These model emergency regulations were, as discussed below,[14] the first soft law measures that accompanied the legally binding corona measures.

This initial decentralised response to address the crisis with emergency regulations adopted by the safety regions has been heavily criticised for lacking a firm democratic basis, whilst also severely limiting fundamental rights.[15] In this respect, it is pointed out that the emergency regulations were adopted by the Chairs of the safety regions[16] without the (direct) involvement or control of a democratically elected body such as, for instance, the municipal councils.[17] Instead, the legal competence of the Chairs of the safety regions to enact emergency regulations, laid down in the Public Health Act, is aimed at enabling swift action to address

[10] Article 39 of the safety regions Act (*Wet Veiligheidsregio's*).

[11] Broeksteeg (2020).

[12] Van Blommestein (2021), Sect. 2.

[13] Article 7 of the Public Health Act (*Wet publieke gezondheid*).

[14] See Sect. 4.1.

[15] Wierenga (2020); Wierenga et al. (2020), p. 1317.

[16] Article 39 of the safety regions Act and Article 176 of the Municipalities Act (*Gemeentewet*).

[17] Wierenga (2020), p. 239; Wierenga et al. (2020), p. 1317.

crises effectively.[18] In the words of Julicher and Vetzo, the Dutch response to the COVID-19 pandemic was an 'executive-led, decentralised response'.[19]

2.2 The Temporary Corona Act

In the summer of 2020, the Dutch Government presented a first draft of the Temporary Corona Act (TCA) to the House of Representatives. The first draft of the TCA was extensively debated in Parliament and significantly amended afterwards, with the final act only being adopted in December 2020. The explanatory memorandum to the legislative proposal explained that this act aimed to give the binding corona measures a more 'solid foundation', to enhance their democratic legitimacy, and to replace the emergency regulations.[20] At the same time, the aim of a strengthened democratic involvement had to be reconciled with the necessity to act effectively, as well as the need to leave room for flexibility and differentiation in addressing the crisis.

To this end, the TCA provided for the adoption of Ministerial Regulations that 'may contain far-reaching corona measures.'[21] The Ministerial Regulations needed to be approved by the House of Representatives (*de Tweede Kamer*).[22] However, for these Ministerial Regulations to be adopted, no prior approval from the Senate (*de Eerste Kamer*) was needed. While the explanatory memorandum took a different view, stating that the TCA had struck an 'optimal balance' between democratic legitimacy and the need for swift action and flexibility,[23] concerns were nonetheless raised about the democratic credentials of the corona measures laid down in Ministerial Regulations.[24]

The aim of the TCA was to strengthen the democratic credentials of the corona measures, while also bringing about a shift in the allocation of responsibilities. In the first phase of the crisis, the Chairs of the security regions were put in charge of tackling the crisis by means of decentralised emergency regulations.[25] The TCA, instead, strengthened the responsibilities and the role of the 355 Dutch municipalities and, in particular, of mayors, who became responsible for the implementation and enforcement of the corona measures laid down in the TCA and Ministerial regulations. They could grant licenses, designate places where specific corona measures were in place, give instructions or orders and take sanctioning measures

---

[18] See *Kamerstukken II* 2019/20, 35526, 3, p. 3. See also Van Blommestein (2021), Sect. 2.

[19] Julicher and Vetzo (2021).

[20] *Kamerstukken II* 2019/20, 35526, 3, p. 2.

[21] Ibid, p. 7.

[22] Article 58c of the Public Health Act (*Wet publieke gezondheid*).

[23] *Kamerstukken II* 2019/20, 35526, 3, p. 7.

[24] See for instance Julicher and Vetzo (2021).

[25] Safety Regions Act, Article 39.

if needed. With this decentralised implementation approach, the TCA aimed to leave room for differentiation as well as tailored decision-making at the local level.[26]

The TCA was a temporary legislative act and while it was extended four times, it expired on 1 June 2022. Therefore, the restrictive corona measures are currently no longer in force. The Minister of Health has announced that a legislative proposal for permanently allowing for the adoption of pandemic measures will be presented in due time.

Nevertheless, it is relevant to explore what role soft law instruments have played in relation to the legislative framework that, until recently, has governed the corona measures, as this provides insights into the role that soft measures can play during times of crisis. Furthermore, future legislation might again be complemented with soft law measures. It is therefore apt to draw lessons from earlier regulatory experiences in how to address crises

3 Soft Law in The Netherlands

As in any other legal system, the phenomenon of pseudo-legislation, or 'soft law' is common in Dutch administrative law and practice. For a long time, administrative authorities in the Netherlands have issued administrative rules to exercise their administrative discretion granted by the legislator.[27] One type of administrative soft law, the so-called 'policy rules', has even been given a basis in the Dutch General Administrative Law Act (GALA). While most of the debate in Dutch scholarship and practice has concentrated on this peculiar legal construction, policy rules are certainly not the only type of soft law that can be found in the Dutch legal order. Other (more) informal instruments feature in the Dutch regulatory landscape as well. Hence, the concept of 'soft law' can be understood in a broad manner, namely as non-legally binding rules or guidance on how to use an administrative decision-making power.[28] This chapter uses the terms soft law and guidance (documents) interchangeably, referring to the same non-legally binding rules that fall under this umbrella definition.[29]

This section discusses the three main categories of administrative soft law that feature in the Dutch legal order: (i) 'policy rules'; (ii) 'informal policy rules' and; (iii) 'guidelines'.[30] This overview will help to categorise and understand the peculiarities of the COVID-19 soft law measures that were issued during the crisis.

---

[26] *Kamerstukken II* 2019/20, 35526, 3, p. 8; Article 58e of the Public Health Act (*Wet publieke gezondheid*).

[27] Bröring (2019), p. 168.

[28] Ibid., p. 175.

[29] Van Dam (2020), pp. 23–24.

[30] Bröring and Geertjes (2013), Sect. 2.1.

3.1 Policy Rules (Beleidsregels)

The first category of soft law instruments consists of 'policy rules.' Policy rules are decision-making rules issued by administrative authorities that indicate how they will exercise the discretionary powers conferred on them by the legislator. Article 1:3 GALA defines a policy rule as 'an order, not being a generally binding regulation, which lays down a general rule for weighing interests, determining facts or interpreting legislative provisions in the exercise of a power of an administrative authority.' GALA also provides the general legal basis for administrative authorities to issue policy rules when exercising an administrative competence conferred upon it by the legislator.[31]

An important characteristic of Dutch policy rules is that they are not legally binding, making them soft law and distinguishing them from 'hard law', or legally binding legislative acts. However, Dutch policy rules exert a 'self-binding effect' on the issuing authorities, which follows from Article 4:84 GALA, which states that the administrative authority shall act in accordance with the policy rule 'unless, due to special circumstances, the consequences for one or more parties would be out of proportion to the purposes of a policy rule'.

GALA does not prescribe what form policy rules should take and thus, policy rules can take various forms and shapes such as 'policy notes, circulars and even letters.'[32] This follows from their adoption process, which remains highly informal. The only requirement set in GALA is that policy rules should be published; other than that, there are no specific procedural requirements that regulate the adoption of this type of soft law.

3.2 Informal Decision-Making Rules

The second type of administrative soft law consists of 'informal decision-making rules' issued by an administrative authority to exercise its discretionary powers. One of the main characteristics of these decision-making rules is that they do *not* qualify as policy rules, for instance for the reason that the rules have not been published.[33] Informal decision-making rules can take the form of internal instructions laid down in, for example, internal instructions, protocols, handbooks, framework documents, technical guidance or even in algorithms. Furthermore, this broad category also

[31] Article 4:81(1) GALA states: 'An administrative authority may establish policy rules in respect of a power conferred to it, which is exercised under its responsibility or which has been delegated by it'.

[32] *Kamerstukken II* 1993/1994, 23700, 3, p. 107.

[33] Bröring (2019), p. 170.

encompasses (unwritten or implicit) 'lines of conduct' that are derived from established decision-making practices.

Even when not taking the form of a policy rule, lines of conduct (based on informal decision-making documents or established practices) still generate a self-binding effect for the administrative authority. This self-binding effect is a 'mediated binding effect'[34] as it arises though the application of general principles of law such as the principle of equal treatment and the principle of legitimate expectations. Nonetheless, this binding effect is considered less strong than the binding effect of policy rules provided for in Article 4:84 GALA.[35]

3.3 Guidelines (Richtsnoeren)

The third type of soft law that features in the Dutch regulatory landscape are the so-called *richtsnoeren* or 'guidelines' that—contrary to Dutch policy rules—do not have a legal basis in the Dutch GALA.[36] *Richtsnoeren* are issued by a different authority or organisation than the authority that uses the guidelines to exercise its administrative discretionary power. In other words, Dutch policy rules are issued by the authority itself to exercise its administrative discretion, whereas *richtsnoeren* are 'alien', in the sense that they are issued by another authority than the competent authority. Guidelines are issued, for instance, by the Association of Dutch Municipalities (an umbrella organisation through which Dutch municipalities cooperate) with the aim of assisting municipal authorities in implementing and enforcing national legislation. Guidelines may also have a highly technical character when issued by expert organisations. Examples of such 'expert guidelines' *(deskundigenrichtlijnen)* are the guidelines issued by the National Institute for Health and the Environment (RIVM). Those guidelines that are issued by experts have a binding effect on their addressees, which derives from the principle of care as well as the duty to provide reasons for decisions. They can be described as a 'comply or explain' obligation. Deviation from expert guidelines is permitted, provided that the departure from the guidelines is adequately reasoned and well explained. Nonetheless, the binding effect of *policy* guidelines that address discretionary powers is considered to be weaker,[37] or even 'legally non-existent.'[38]

[34]Compare Ştefan (2013), p. 182.

[35]Bröring and Geertjes (2013), p. 6.

[36]Bröring (1993).

[37]Ibid, p. 489.

[38]Bröring and Geertjes (2013), p. 6; Bröring (1993), p. 483.

4 Soft Law During the COVID-19 Crisis

As outlined in Sect. 2, the initial response to address the pandemic in the Netherlands consisted of the adoption of hard, binding measures that first took the shape of decentralised emergency regulations, subsequently codified in the Temporary Corona Act. Complementary to this legal framework, soft law measures were issued as well. In fact, informal instruments have mushroomed throughout the crisis, serving as a tool to assist, as well as to align and coordinate, the actions of the local authorities.

This section gives an overview of the soft law instruments that have been issued during the COVID-19 crisis. It addresses soft law measures during the first phase of the crisis when the corona measures were laid down in binding emergency regulations, and subsequently reflects on the second phase of the crisis, when soft law measures complemented the Temporary Corona Act. The aim is to give some general insights into how soft rules can play a role that is complementary to the 'hard response' to address crises. This section also briefly reflects on soft law instruments issued during another crisis, i.e. the refugee crisis, showing that the COVID-19 soft law instruments are not a unique phenomenon.

4.1 *Model Emergency Regulations Issued by the Safety Council*

During the first phase of the COVID-19 crisis, soft regulation played an important role in aligning the content of the legally binding emergency regulations issued by the Chairs of the safety regions. As already discussed in Sect. 2, within the boundaries of the binding instructions given by the Minister of Health, the Chairs of the safety regions were given broad discretion to decide on the content of these emergency regulations and hence, on the corona measures being taken.

As also noted in Sect. 2, in order to give guidance and support to the safety regions, the Safety Council enacted so-called 'model emergency regulations.' Remarkably, even though these model emergency regulations lack legally binding force, in practice the model emergency regulations have considerable harmonising effects. Research conducted by Boogaard et al. shows that the emergency regulations issued by the Chairs of the safety regions largely 'copy' the templates issued by the Safety Council.[39] Only exceptionally do the emergency regulations depart from the model regulations and *if* amendments are made, this is coordinated by the safety regions.[40] Hence, the non-legally binding model regulations play an important role in aligning the legally binding rules issued by the safety regions. What is more, an

[39] Becker et al. (2020).

[40] Ibid.

'Interpretative Committee', composed of public officials, was created to answer interpretative questions by the safety regions on the provisions in the template regulations.[41]

To conclude, in the first phase of the crisis, the non-legally binding regulatory templates and a mechanism of informal questions and answers exerted strong harmonising effects on the decentralised and legally binding emergency regulations issued by the 25 safety regions.

4.2 Guidance on the Implementation and Enforcement of the Temporary Corona Act

When the Temporary Corona Act entered into force in December 2020, Dutch municipalities faced a new situation. Indeed, with the entry into force of this Act, the municipalities became the central actors in implementing and enforcing the rules that were laid down in this act and the accompanying Ministerial Regulations. In this changed regulatory landscape, with corona measures laid down in legally binding rules, soft rules and (other) guidance documents came to the fore again. This time, guidance and assistance was provided mostly by the Dutch Association of Municipalities. As will be shown, the COVID-19 guidance documents issued in this second phase of the crisis are numerous and take various forms.[42]

The main aim of COVID-19 guidance documents is twofold. First, the documents seek to provide assistance to the municipalities with respect to the implementation and enforcement of the Temporary Corona Act.[43] Second, the COVID-19 guidance documents aim to ensure a certain consistency and uniformity in the way in which Dutch municipalities implement the Temporary Corona Act. For instance, the policy framework for municipalities explains that 'consistency with respect to the interpretation and use of measures to address the crisis and accordingly more clarity with regard to the administrative actions are needed.'[44] The document also states that '[t]he aim is to find a fine balance between the necessary regional coordination and the use of competences within the political-administrative context at the local level'.[45]

The remaining part of this section gives a general overview of the various forms of COVID-19 guidance documents that aim to support effective and coordinated

---

[41] Insights on (the existence of) this Interpretative Committee were shared during interviews with chairs of the safety regions that were conducted by prof. Geerten Boogaard and mr. Roel Becker (Department of Constitutional and Administrative Law, Leiden University). I would like to thank Geerten and Roel for sharing their insights and research findings with me.

[42] See for an overview of the guidance documents issued by the Dutch Association of Municipalities: https://vng.nl/artikelen/tijdelijke-wet-maatregelen-covid-19.

[43] See for instance the Handreiking Tijdelijke wet maatregelen COVID-19 voor gemeenten. VNG, Pels Rijcken & Droogleever Fortuijn, June 2021, p. 6.

[44] Voorbeeld-beleidskader Twm voor burgemeesters. VNG, 20 November 2020, p. 1.

[45] Ibid, p. 1.

action with a view to implementing the corona measures laid down in legally binding rules.

4.2.1 The 'COVID-19 Guide' on the Implementation of the TCA for Mayors

The main guidance document that provided support to the municipalities in their task to implement and enforce the rules laid down in the TCA and Ministerial Regulations, is the *Handreiking Tijdelijke wet maatregelen COVID-19 voor gemeenten* ('COVID-19 Guide'). The first thing to note is that the COVID-19 Guide was issued by the Dutch Association of Municipalities in collaboration with Pels Rijcken & Droogleever Fortuijn, a Dutch law firm and the State's Advocate.[46] Not surprisingly, as further discussed below, this raises questions concerning the democratic credentials of this act.

With over a hundred pages, the COVID-19 Guide was a voluminous document. It gave an extensive overview of the rules and responsibilities of the Dutch municipalities under the 'new' legal framework. This overview had a highly explanatory character, summarising and explaining the legal framework and the methodology that it follows. Nonetheless, the guide also gave (interpretative) guidance on the elements to be taken into account when taking decisions on the granting of licenses (such as, for instance, the guidelines on the granting of licenses for events under Article 58i of the Public Health Act).[47] Finally, the *Handreiking* included 'formats' for administrative decisions, which gave practical advice on the points that should be addressed in decisions for granting licenses, decisions on administrative penalties or decisions imposing a burden under penalty.[48]

4.2.2 A Model 'Policy Framework' for Mayors and Chairs of the Safety Regions

In addition to the *Handreiking* discussed above, the Dutch Association of Municipalities issued a guidance document outlining a so-called 'model-policy framework' (*voorbeeld-beleidskader*) for all 355 mayors.[49] The introduction to the policy framework stressed the importance of coordination and alignment between different municipalities, as this is expected to lead to more consistency and clarity as regards the measures that are taken during the crisis.[50] Hence, this policy framework

[46] See: https://www.pelsrijcken.nl/en/about-us/state-advocate-nations-attorney.

[47] Handreiking Tijdelijke wet maatregelen COVID-19 voor gemeenten. Pels Rijcken & Droogleever Fortuijn, June 2021, p. 22.

[48] Ibid, pp. 81–94.

[49] Voorbeeld-beleidskader Twm voor burgemeesters. VNG, 20 November 2020.

[50] Ibid, p. 1.

explained the competences that mayors have under the TCA, gave guidance as to the policy decisions that could or needed to be made, and outlined to what extent the regulations provided room for differentiation (*maatwerk*).

A 'model-policy framework' was drafted by the Safety Council, this time addressing the Chairs of the safety regions.[51] The document explained that even though competences shifted to the municipalities, the Chairs of the Security Regions still played an important coordinating role in implementing the TCA.[52] The policy framework gave an overview of the responsibilities the Chairs of the safety regions still have after the entry into force of the TCA. For instance, the Chairs of the safety regions remained responsible for providing information to the Minister of Health and communication concerning the pandemic to the public.[53] In general, the document stressed the importance of coordination between the different relevant actors, i.e. minister, safety regions and municipalities, and included a list of matters to be coordinated regionally.[54]

4.2.3 A 'Legal Helpdesk', Questions and Answers and Dialogues

In addition to the guidance documents discussed above, the Association of Municipalities also provided guidance and support to the municipalities in other, even more informal ways. These initiatives involved a 'legal helpdesk', an overview of 'questions and answers' as well as 'Dialogues in times of corona'.[55]

First, the legal helpdesk is a support mechanism designed by the Dutch Association of Municipalities and the Ministry of the Interior. As part of this support mechanism, the Association of Municipalities, ministries, and other organisations share their knowledge and expertise with the aim of assisting the municipalities. Members of the Municipal Councils and municipal officials were invited to ask questions concerning the implementation of the TCA. Still today, even though the TCA has expired, municipal officials are invited to contact the helpdesk in order to ask their legal questions related to COVID-19.[56]

[51] Beleidskader Tijdelijke wet maatregelen COVID-19 voorzitters veiligheidsregio. Veiligheidsberaad, VNG, 2021.

[52] This coordination takes place in the context of the regional policy team that continues to exist under the TCA on the basis of article 39 of the safety regions Act. See on the role of the safety regions after the TCA entered into force Van Blommestein (2021), Sect. 4.

[53] As follows from article 58s of the Public Health Act; see Beleidskader Tijdelijke wet maatregelen COVID-19 voorzitters veiligheidsregio. Veiligheidsberaad, VNG, 2021, p. 4.

[54] Beleidskader Tijdelijke wet maatregelen COVID-19 voorzitters veiligheidsregio. Veiligheidsberaad, VNG, 2021, p. 9, 10.

[55] See https://vng.nl/artikelen/tijdelijke-wet-maatregelen-covid-19.

[56] See https://vng.nl/rubrieken/coronavirus-covid-19.

Second, the website of the Association of Municipalities provided a list with 'questions and answers' related to the implementation of the TCA as well as the Ministerial regulations.[57] Questions and answers addressed, for instance, the competences of the mayors and Chairs of the safety regions as well as the role played by the municipal councils. The website also included questions and answers related to the Ministerial Regulations that complement the TCA. These questions and answers related to the Ministerial Regulations have since been deleted from the website as the Ministerial Regulations have expired.[58]

Third, the Association of Municipalities launched the so-called 'dialogues in times of Corona', which provide support to the municipalities in implementing and enforcing the TCA. The dialogues took place in the form of online conferences and workshops during which officials and experts provided information on the TCA, as well as on the responsibilities of the municipal authorities and safety regions under this Act. During the first edition of the corona dialogues, in November 2020, insights were shared by officials working for responsible ministries, the authors of the abovementioned COVID-19 Guide, as well as officials working for the Dutch Association of municipalities. Several other editions have followed, the most recent concentrating on 'post-corona recovery plans.'[59]

4.2.4 Action Frameworks Issued by Mayors

COVID-19 soft law not only took the form of guidance issued by the Association of Municipalities, but also assisted the mayors and municipalities in their implementing tasks. Mayors themselves issued the typical Dutch 'policy rules' in order to make clear how they intended to use their discretionary powers granted by the corona measures. Indeed, as explained above, in the Netherlands, mayors were largely responsible for the enforcement of the legally binding corona measures laid down in the TCA and the Ministerial Regulations. The competence to issue policy rules followed from the general legal basis laid down in Article 4:81 GALA.[60] Several mayors of Dutch municipalities issued policy rules, most of them titled 'action framework' (*handelingskader*).[61]

---

[57] The questions and answers can still be found at the website of the Dutch Association of Municipalities. See https://vng.nl/artikelen/vragen-en-antwoorden-tijdelijke-wet-maatregelen-covid-19 and https://vng.nl/artikelen/vragen-en-antwoorden-uitvoering-tijdelijke-regeling-maatregelen-covid-19.

[58] See Sect. 2.2.

[59] See https://vng.nl/artikelen/vng-dialoog-in-coronatijd.

[60] See above Sect. 3.1. The possibility to issue policy rules also is explicitly referred to in the explanatory memorandum to the Temporary Corona Act See *Kamerstukken II* 2019/20, 35526, 3, p. 25.

[61] An overview can be found at the governmental website that provides an overview of 'local legislation and regulations', see https://lokaleregelgeving.overheid.nl/.

The *Handelingskader Tijdelijke wet maatregelen Covid-19* issued by Aboutaleb, the mayor of the city of Rotterdam, provided a good example. This *Handelingskader* outlined and explained how the mayor intends to use his competences to enforce the COVID-19 legislation laid down in the TCA and Ministerial Regulations.[62] Remarkably, the introductory statement to this action framework largely resembled the introduction statement of the action frameworks issued by other municipalities near Rotterdam. Hence, it seemed some alignment occurred between the policy rules issued by those municipalities. Whether and to what extent the mayors (of other regions) aligned the content of the policy rules requires further (empirical) research.

4.3 Beyond COVID-19: Soft Law and the Refugee Crisis

The COVID-19 crisis is not the only crisis in the Netherlands where soft law measures have played a role. The refugee crisis is another recent example where soft law measures have been issued. In May 2022, the Dutch Association of Municipalities, responsible ministries, and other partners issued a guide for the reception of Ukrainian refugees by Dutch municipalities,[63] as well as a guide for individuals hosting Ukrainian refugees.[64] Together with the Central Agency for the Reception of Asylum Seekers, the Association of Municipalities also issued a guide for the reception of asylum refugees in general, again addressing the Dutch municipalities.[65]

Similar to several of the COVID-19 instruments, the guides addressed to the Dutch municipalities which concern the reception of refugees fall in the category of 'guidelines' (*richtsnoeren*), revealing that in this field as well, soft law documents play a role between different levels of governance. In this context, it is relevant to note that the reception of refugees is expected to become more and more decentralised. A legislative proposal is being prepared rendering the municipalities responsible for hosting refugees and introducing the possibility of giving binding instructions to the municipalities to receive (a certain number of) refugees.[66] What role (if any) soft law will play under this new allocation of responsibilities remains to be seen.

---

[62] Handelingskader Tijdelijke wet maatregelen COVID-19, Rotterdam, 23 February 2022.

[63] Handreiking Gemeentelijke Opvang Oekraïners, version 3.0. Rijksoverheid, 20 May 2022.

[64] Handreiking Particuliere Opvang Oekraïners (POO), version 3.0. Rijksoverheid, 24 June 2022.

[65] Handreiking Proces tot realisatie opvanglocatie asielzoekers. VNG, 2021.

[66] Wetsvoorstel dwang asielzoekers vóór de zomer af. Binnenlands Bestuur, 15 April 2022, https://www.binnenlandsbestuur.nl/sociaal/wet-gedwongen-asielopvang-dichterbij.

5 Analysis

The previous sections revealed that in the Netherlands, non-binding instruments featured alongside 'hard', legally binding measures to address the pandemic. 'Model emergency regulations' and informal Q&A mechanisms guided the content of the emergency regulations adopted by the Chairs of the safety regions during the first phase of the crisis. At a later stage, when the corona measures were given a legal basis in the TCA, guidance documents in various forms were issued to provide assistance to the municipalities and safety Regions. Dutch mayors issued policy rules that explained how they intended to use their discretionary powers.

The first observation that can be made based on the above overview is the large variety of the soft law instruments that were issued. The instruments are labelled under various names such as 'guides', 'model-regulations', 'policy frameworks', 'action frameworks', 'questions and answer' and 'dialogues.' This calls into question the legal status and effects of these documents. Do these documents have a binding effect on their addressees and/or on the issuing authorities? And what can be said about the legitimacy of those documents?

A second observation is that the aim of the guidelines (*richtsnoeren*) issued during the crisis was twofold.[67] First, they sought to provide guidance and assistance to the Chairs of the safety regions (in particular during the first phase of the crisis) and to the municipalities and mayors (during the second phase of the crisis) as to the implementation and enforcement of the legally binding corona instructions and measures. Second, the COVID-19 soft law instruments also sought to align, and harmonise, the design and implementation of the corona measures—first at the level of the safety regions, and later at the level of the municipalities. Here, the question arises whether these instruments have fulfilled these objectives in practice, and/or what this means for their role and function in the regulatory landscape governing the corona crisis.

This final section analyses the COVID-19 soft law instruments against these questions. It first looks at the legal status of the COVID-19 soft law documents, addresses legitimacy questions, and subsequently investigates whether the instruments have had a harmonising effect, and if so, to what extent, on the way in which the pandemic has been addressed.

5.1 The Legal Status of COVID-19 Soft Law

5.1.1 Mostly 'Guidelines' (Richtsnoeren)

The overview of the various non-legally binding documents that were issued during the pandemic shows that most of them were issued by another organisation than the authority that was competent to adopt or to implement the binding corona measures.

[67] As also mentioned in the introduction of Sect. 2.

Those COVID-19 documents issued by the Dutch Association of Municipalities and the Safety Council fall under the category of what are called 'guidelines' or *richtsnoeren*—the third category of Dutch administrative soft law. Indeed, a key characteristic of 'guidelines' is that they are issued by another authority or organisation than the authority to whom the guidelines are addressed. As explained above, 'guidelines' lack legally binding force, yet judicial practice and scholarship has recognised that they might exert binding effects through the principles of care and the duty to provide reasons for decisions. These binding effects vary according to the type of guidelines. Binding effects of guidelines that concern the use of 'discretionary' competences or policy choices are generally considered to be 'weak', or 'legally non-existent'. In contrast, strong 'comply or explain'-like binding effects arise in the case of expert guidelines.[68]

The guidelines issued during the pandemic sought to steer the policy and discretionary decisions of the safety regions and municipalities, and therefore fall under this latter subcategory of guidelines having a weak binding effect on their addressees. The 'model emergency regulations'[69] issued by the Safety Council in the first phase of the crisis provided policy guidance on how the safety regions could use their discretionary rulemaking powers to issue emergency regulations. During the second phase of the crisis, when the TCA entered into force, the model policy framework[70] issued by the Association of municipalities gave general policy guidance to the municipalities. The COVID-19 Guide[71] (*Handreiking*) addressed the discretionary powers of the municipalities to enforce the legally binding COVID-19 legislation. In this second phase of the crisis, the Safety Council also issued policy guidance[72] ('model-policy framework') addressing the Chairs of the safety regions.

Hence, at least from a legal perspective, the COVID-19 guidelines issued during the pandemic did not exert a strong legal binding effect vis-à-vis the municipalities and safety regions. Nevertheless, ensuring consistency and convergence has been a 'power of argument'[73] which may have led the municipalities and safety regions to follow the policy framework and guidance in practice.[74]

5.1.2 What About More Informal Support Mechanisms?

In addition to the policy framework *(beleidskader)* and the COVID-19 Guide (*Handreiking*), the Association of Municipalities also issued (even) more informal COVID-19 guidance documents. Indeed, 'questions and answers', a legal helpdesk,

[68] See Sect. 2.

[69] See Sect. 4.1.

[70] See Sect. 4.2.2

[71] See Sect. 4.2.1

[72] See Sect. 4.2.2.

[73] Bröring (1993), pp. 483; 489.

[74] See Sects. 5.3 and 5.4.

online dialogues and workshops were created in order to support the municipalities and mayors in their task to implement and enforce the legally binding corona measures. Even though these support mechanisms addressed the municipalities, they cannot automatically be considered to fall under the categories of 'guidelines'. Indeed, a key characteristic of *richtsnoeren* is that they seek to structure or 'influence' the way in which the competent authority uses its administrative competences.[75] Insofar as these informal mechanisms only provide information on the applicable corona measures or on the allocation of responsibilities under the TCA, the documents do not meet this requirement.

Another COVID-19 support mechanism was the provision of advice in the form of individual answers to the questions raised by Dutch officials (in the context of the 'legal helpdesk' for instance). Neither these questions, nor the answers to these questions, have been published online (as far as the author knows) and therefore, they cannot be considered to be 'general rules' which, however, is central to the definition of *richtsnoeren.*[76] Thus, it seems that under Dutch administrative law, these informal mechanisms do not fall under the scope of 'guidelines' either. Consequently, these guidelines are not likely to have a binding legal effect on Dutch municipalities.

5.1.3 Policy Rules

The most 'formalised' forms of COVID-19 soft law are the policy rules issued by mayors, spelling out how they intended to use the (discretionary) administrative powers to implement and enforce the corona measures laid down in the Temporary Corona Act and Ministerial Regulations. Policy rules are regulated by the legal framework that governs the issuance and use of policy rules in the Dutch GALA. This means that the COVID-19 policy rules have a self-binding effect on the mayors and that deviation is possible only if this is required in light of special circumstances.

5.2 *COVID-19 Soft Law: Low Levels of Democratic Legitimacy?*

The COVID-19 soft law instruments show a differentiated picture. Not only did they take different forms and shapes; they were also issued by different actors. COVID-19 soft law instruments have been issued by the Safety Council and by the Dutch Association of Municipalities, while the principal COVID-19 guide has been drafted in collaboration with a Dutch Law firm. Policy rules have been issued by Dutch mayors. The issuing of these non-binding documents does not follow a standardised

---

[75] Bröring (1993), pp. 92; 483.

[76] Ibid, pp. 94; 483.

process. Instead, as is often the case for soft law documents, the issuing process is largely unregulated and hence characterised by informality.[77] What does this imply for the democratic (input) legitimacy of these documents?[78] To what extent have democratically elected institutions been involved in the issuing of such documents; And/or was the general public (citizens) consulted about draft versions of the documents?

Let us start with the 'model emergency regulations' issued by the Safety Council in the early stages of the crisis. The Safety Council represents, as said above, the 25 safety regions and is composed of the 25 'Chairs' of the safety regions.[79] The Chair is generally the mayor of one of the largest municipalities of the safety Region.[80] The Safety Council is considered to be a form of 'extended' local governance (*verlengd lokaal bestuur*).[81] However, this does not mean that the non-legally binding model emergency regulations issued by the Safety Council were enacted following a democratically legitimised procedure. In contrast, democratic involvement prior to the adoption of these regulations is limited; while the content of the model emergency regulations was coordinated by the responsible Minister,[82] there was no direct involvement of a democratically elected institution (such as the municipal councils) or of citizens of the safety regions. This only adds to the already weak democratic legitimacy of the legally binding 'emergency regulations' adopted by the safety regions. Indeed, as discussed, the model emergency regulations (that largely copied non-binding model emergency regulations) have been criticised for their lack of democratic legitimacy.[83]

What about the guidance issued by the Dutch Association of Municipalities to assist the mayors and municipalities in implementing the TCA? The board of the Association of Municipalities is composed of mayors, aldermen and councillors, and is supported by several committees. However, there are no signs (as far as the author has found) that the municipal councils (the democratically elected bodies of Dutch Municipalities) were directly involved in the adoption of the COVID-19 guidance instruments issued by the Association of Municipalities.[84] Hence, the issuing process of guidance given to the municipalities during the COVID-19 pandemic is not characterised by high levels of democratic legitimacy. In this respect, most remarkable is the COVID-19 Guide that was drafted in collaboration with the private law

[77] See on the 'features of informality' of EU guidance documents Van Dam (2020), pp. 33–41.

[78] See on the concept of input legitimacy, Scharpf (1999), p. 7.

[79] See Sect. 2.1.

[80] They are elected by the general board of the safety regions which is composed of all mayors from the municipalities that belong to that safety region.

[81] As states the website of the safety regions: https://www.veiligheidsberaad.nl/over-het-veiligheidsberaad/#:~:text=De%20veiligheidsregio's%20zijn%20verantwoordelijk%20voor,zijn%20verantwoordelijk%20voor%20hun%20veiligheidsregio.

[82] As follows from: https://www.veiligheidsberaad.nl/2020/03/17/landelijke-model-noodverordening-voor-de-veiligheidsregios/.

[83] See Sect. 2.1.

[84] Compare Bröring (1993), p. 487.

firm Pels Rijcken. While the COVID-19 Guide is perhaps the most important guidance document advising mayors on how to use their enforcement powers and how to implement the TCA, the law firm does not have any democratic credentials. This low democratic legitimacy needs to be stressed and questioned.

The policy rules issued by the Dutch mayors (the more formalised form of COVID-19 soft law) find their origins in the discretionary powers granted by legislation, in this case the TCA. As said above, the competence to issue policy rules was given a legal basis in the Dutch GALA.[85] Nonetheless, the issuing process of policy rules does not require the involvement of electoral bodies (such as the municipal council) or citizens. A quick look at the COVID-19 policy rules issued by the mayors also does not reveal traces of such involvement or consultation. Thus, the issuing of COVID-19 soft law rules is not directly subject to democratic scrutiny. So saying, the legislation granting discretionary powers (in this case the TCA and Ministerial Regulations) that form the basis for the adoption of the policy rules was adopted following a legislative process – which in any case does to a certain extent endow these rules with democratic legitimacy.[86]

From the above, it follows that the COVID-19 soft law rules score rather poorly when it comes to democratic (input) legitimacy. In this respect, the COVID-19 soft law issued during the pandemic in The Netherlands is neither unique nor exceptional. Low levels of democratic legitimacy are often pointed out when it comes to the issuing of soft law rules—not only at the national level, but also at the EU and international level. For instance, the various EU soft law measures that were issued to tackle the COVID-19 crisis have been firmly criticised for their low democratic credentials. Eliantonio and Ştefan show that these EU soft law documents were issued without involvement of the European Parliament and 'with minimal and unsystematic consultation with stakeholders, national authorities and scientific bodies.'[87] The authors argue for stakeholder consultation and involvement of the European Parliament within short deadlines so as to improve the democratic credentials of EU soft law issued in times of crises.[88]

Would a similar solution work for the COVID-19 soft law instruments that were issued in the Netherlands? Would it be desirable that electoral bodies such as municipal councils and the public or stakeholders be consulted prior to the issuing process of the COVID-19 guidelines? From a democratic legitimacy perspective only, the answer to these questions is 'yes'. Yet, the answers to these questions require further thought and study. Indeed, such procedural requirements, even if short deadlines are applied, might lead to a longer and more cumbersome issuing

[85] See Sect. 3.1.

[86] Yet the democratic legitimacy of the TCA and Ministerial Regulations is also subject to criticism and discussion, as has been briefly pointed out in Sect. 2.2.

[87] Eliantonio and Ştefan (2021), p. 173.

[88] Ibid.

process, detracting from their flexible character, needed for a swift response to changing circumstances and developments requiring urgent action.[89]

In this respect, it should also be kept in mind that the most important function of soft COVID-19 measures is related to their output legitimacy.[90] Soft law documents largely derive their legitimacy from their 'problem solving' character and efficiency gains, which are particularly useful in times of crisis.[91]

5.3 *Coordination and Harmonisation: The Promises of COVID-19 Soft Law*

The main rationale behind the issuing of the COVID-19 soft law instruments was to facilitate a more consistent, harmonised, and coherent implementation of the legally binding corona measures between the Dutch safety regions and the Dutch municipalities. The fulfilment of these objectives are important for these documents to be effective and legitimate 'governance instruments' (and related to the output legitimacy referred to above in Sect. 4.2).

Current research indicates that the soft law instruments issued during the COVID-19 crisis might certainly shape the way in which municipalities implement and enforce the legally binding corona measures. The study conducted by Boogaard et al. shows that the 'model regulations' issued by the Safety Council served as a basis for the emergency regulations issued by the Chairs of the safety regions.[92] Deviations from the Model Regulations are found to be exceptional and often coordinated between the Chairs of the safety regions.[93] A possible reason for the alignment of the safety regions' regulatory practices is the potential 'waterbed effect' that arises when differences exist between municipalities in the way activities are being enforced or licensed.[94] Activities then concentrate in the municipalities or places that are most 'lenient' when it comes to licensing and/or enforcing corona measures. Van den Berg and Mireau note, for instance, that when 'Brabant went into a kind of voluntary lockdown in March [2020], bars in Nijmegen were filled with Brabant residents'.[95] These differences then give incentives for further alignment and coordination.

Whether the guidelines issued by the Dutch Association of Municipalities (during the second phase of the crisis) have had a similar steering effect on practices of the

[89] See on this 'regulatory conundrum' Van Dam (2020), pp. 7; 8; Eliantonio and Ştefan (2021), pp. 173–175.

[90] Scharpf (1999), pp. 10–11.

[91] Compare Boschetti and Poli (2021), p. 24.

[92] Becker et al. (2020).

[93] Ibid.

[94] Van den Berg et al. (2021), p. 4.

[95] Van den Berg and Mierau (2020).

municipalities requires further (empirical) research. There is, nonetheless, good reason to believe that the municipalities also aligned their implementing and enforcement policies in light of the COVID-19 guidelines. Not only was following these guidelines giving practical and policy advice to the municipalities the 'easiest thing to do', it also prevented the potential 'waterbed effect' in the event differences arise.

From the above, it follows that 'soft rules' and informal mechanisms play an important role in harmonising and aligning the decentralised implementation of the legally binding corona rules. Furthermore, these informal mechanisms facilitate a dialogue and coordination between the responsible authorities: the municipalities, the Chairs of safety regions, and the responsible minister. A pivotal role in promoting informal coordination and alignment is played by the Dutch Association of Municipalities. This umbrella organisation has not been granted an official function in implementing the TCA, yet in practice, plays an important coordinating role by issuing guidelines on how the municipalities could use *their* competences to implement and enforce the binding rules.

Hence, a soft regulatory network has been set up that operates alongside, or in the shadows of, the legally binding rules, and which echoes so-called forms of 'network based governance'.[96] In the literature, it has been argued that a network-based approach is needed for a successful and effective response to the crisis.[97] It seems that the issuing of COVID-19 guidance is key to such an approach where within the formal allocation of responsibilities, guidance and dialogue enable coordination and alignment.

5.4 Differentiation and Tailored Decision-Making at Risk?

COVID-19 soft law promoting coordination and harmonisation also has some disadvantages. Indeed, striving for uniformity in implementing and enforcement practices could mean that local authorities are less inclined to make tailored decisions that take into account the local circumstances. The room for differentiation that is provided for in the TCA and the Ministerial Regulations might not be utilised by the municipalities in practice. This is at odds with the 'decentralised implementation approach' that lies at the heart of the TCA. Indeed, by empowering municipalities (and mayors in particular) to enforce and implement the TCA, the room for differentiation and tailored decision-making is one of the key objectives of the TCA. This is also made clear in the explanatory memorandum to this Act.[98] The effect of too much uniformity and harmonisation between the municipal practices is also at odds with the concept of decentralised autonomy, a (constitutional) principle[99] that is

---

[96] See e.g. Van Blommestein (2021).

[97] Ibid.

[98] *Kamerstukken II* 2019/20, 35526, 3, p. 8.

[99] See on this principle for instance Esser and Boogaard (2020).

foundational to the Dutch legal order as a decentralised unity state. Hence, the various COVID-19 soft law measures that assist municipalities and safety regions on how to implement the corona measures, might lead to a less diversified approach in addressing the crisis, de facto leaving less room for municipal autonomy.

This leads to the (preliminary) conclusion that in the Netherlands, COVID-19 soft law has had an important function in promoting a coordinated and aligned implementation of the legally binding COVID-19 measures. At the same time, striving for harmonisation needs to be balanced against the objectives of tailored decision-making and differentiation, as well as the (constitutional) principle of decentralised autonomy. Otherwise, the room for tailored decision-making and differentiation provided by the TCA and Ministerial Regulations risk becoming an illusion in practice.

Thus, when soft law measures are issued to address future crises in the Netherlands, the challenge lies in drawing a fine line between harmonisation and differentiation, leaving sufficient room for municipal autonomy in implementing and enforcing the legally binding measures.

6 Conclusion

Aiming to contribute to research on the role of soft law in times of crisis, this chapter studied the role of soft law during the COVID-19 pandemic in the Netherlands. It finds that COVID-19 soft law indeed played an important role complementary to legally binding COVID-19 regulations. During the first phase of the crisis, non-legally binding model emergency regulations were used as templates for the (binding) regulations issued by the Dutch safety regions. During the second phase of the crisis (from December 2020 onwards), the COVID-19 guidance documents—in various forms—assisted municipalities in implementing the Temporary Corona Act, an act Parliament.

The analysis of the COVID-19 soft law rules shows that the role of these documents needs to be seen against the Dutch regulatory and constitutional context. The role of COVID-19 soft law is shaped by the fact that the Netherlands is a decentralised unitary state while in the legal context, typical forms of soft law—such as the guidelines (*richtsnoeren*) and policy rules (*beleidsregels*)—are part of the Dutch regulatory landscape. The analysis shows that the COVID-19 soft law rules' main objective was to assist the safety regions and municipalities in taking the required (implementing and regulatory) measures, in order to promote consistency and coherence in the way the crisis was being addressed. However, striving for consistency and harmonisation might come at the detriment of the room for differentiation and tailored decision-making that is provided for in the TCA, and which is central to the decentralised implementation approach.

This potential side-effect is not the only drawback of the issuing of COVID-19 rules. The legal status and binding effects of the so-called 'guidelines' (*richtsnoeren*) on their addresses might not always be crystal clear, potentially leading to (legal) uncertainty for their addresses (the mayors) and the public. The issuing of COVID-19 soft law rules also has low democratic credentials. This is especially so for the COVID-19 Guide that was issued by the Dutch Association of Municipalities in collaboration with a law firm. The stronger the regulatory effects of these soft law documents become in practice, the more this low democratic legitimacy becomes problematic. At the same time, it should be kept in mind that the major advantage of soft rules is that they can be swiftly issued and revised, without the need for cumbersome issuing processes.

What future lessons can be drawn from this 'Dutch case' of COVID-19 soft law? Studying COVID-19 soft law in The Netherlands has shown that, complementary to hard law rules, soft law can be an effective instrument to bring about a more effective, consistent and harmonised response to the crisis, especially when regional and local authorities are involved. However, soft law is not flawless; it comes with some disadvantages or undesired side effects. In light of the absence of clear regulatory principles or rules governing the issuing and use of those instruments—and in particular of Dutch 'guidelines' (*richtsnoeren*)—it is all the more important that the actors that issue these documents are aware of the downsides of soft regulation and do their best to limit these downsides as much as possible. For instance, municipal councils could be consulted on draft versions of guidelines issued by the Association of Municipalities (elevating democratic credentials) and the documents (and hence drafters) should stress the importance of making use of the room for differentiation provided by regulations. Perhaps, in the future, a more principled approach towards the issuing and use of soft law, especially the highly unregulated soft law category of 'guidelines', could further improve these forms of soft governance.[100] Such meta-regulation of (Dutch) soft law, and *richtsnoeren* in particular, requires further study and research.

References

Becker R et al (2020) Mate van juridische differentiatie door veiligheidsregio's. Corona Papers, 21 December 2020, https://coronapapers.nl/nieuws-1/nieuws/mate-van-juridische-differentiatie-door-veiligheidsregio-s

Beleidskader Tijdelijke wet maatregelen COVID-19 voorzitters veiligheidsregio. Veiligheidsberaad, VNG, 2021., https://vng.nl/sites/default/files/2020-11/voorbeeldbeleidskader-tijdelijke-wet-maatregelen-covid-19-voorzitters-veiligheidsregio.pdf

Boschetti B, Poli MD (2021) A comparative study on soft law: lessons from the COVID-19 Pandemic. Cambridge Yearb Eur Legal Stud 23:20–53

Broeksteeg H (2020) Voorschriften met gebreken. In: Heringa AW, Schinkelshoek J (eds) Coronacratie. Rechtsstaat en democratie in tijden van crisis een eerste balans. Montesquieu Instituut, The Hague, pp 41–50

Bröring HE (1993) Richtlijnen. Over de juridische betekenis van circulaires, leidraden, aanbevelingen, brochures, plannen. Kluwer, Deventer

[100] Van Dam (2020), pp. 277–282; Van Dam (2021).

Bröring HE (2019) Bestuursrechtelijke soft law: tien opmerkingen. In: Barkhuysen T et al (eds) 25 jaar Awb - In eenheid en verscheidenheid. Wolters Kluwer, Deventer, pp 167–179
Bröring HE, Geertjes GJA (2013) Bestuursrechtelijke soft law in Nederland, Duitsland en Engeland. Nederlands Tijdschrift voor Bestuursrecht 2013:74–87
Eliantonio M, Ştefan O (2021) The elusive legitimacy of EU soft law: an analysis of consultation and participation in the process of adopting COVID-19 soft law in the EU. Eur J Risk Regul 12: 159–175
Eliantonio M, Korkea-Aho E, Ştefan O (2021a) Introduction. In: Eliantonio M, Korkea-Aho E, Ştefan O (eds) EU Soft Law in the member states. Theoretical findings and empirical evidence. Hart Publishing, Oxford, pp 1–18
Eliantonio M, Korkea-Aho E, Vaughan S (2021b) EJRR Special Issue Editorial: COVID-19 and soft law: is soft law pandemic-proof? Eur J Risk Regul 12:1–6
Esser J, Boogaard G (2020) 25 kapiteins, 1 vloot. Differentiatie, deconcentratie en decentralisatie in de Covid-19 noodverordeningen. Nederlands Juristenblad 2020:1644–1651
Handreiking Gemeentelijke Opvang Oekraïners, version 3.0. Rijksoverheid, 20 May 2022. https://www.rijksoverheid.nl/onderwerpen/opvang-vluchtelingen-uit-oekraine/documenten/publicaties/2022/03/13/handreiking-gemeentelijke-opvang-oekrainers
Handreiking Particuliere Opvang Oekraïners (POO), version 3.0. Rijksoverheid, 24 June 2022. https://www.rijksoverheid.nl/documenten/publicaties/2022/04/15/handreiking-particuliere-opvang-oekrainers-poo
Handreiking Proces tot realisatie opvanglocatie asielzoekers. VNG, 2021. https://vng.nl/publicaties/handreiking-proces-tot-realisatie-opvanglocatie-asielzoekers
Handreiking Tijdelijke wet maatregelen COVID-19 voor gemeenten. VNG, Pels Rijcken & Droogleever Fortuijn, June 2021. vng-handreiking-tijdelijke-wet-maatregelen-covid-19.pdf
Julicher M, Vetzo M (2021) COVID-19 in the Netherlands: of Changing Tides and Constitutional Constants. Verfassungsblog, 22 April 2021, https://verfassungsblog.de/covid-19-in-the-netherlands-of-changing-tides-and-constitutional-constants/
Scharpf F (1999) Governing in Europe: effective and democratic. Oxford University Press, Oxford
Ştefan O (2013) Soft law in court: competition law, state aid, and the Court of Justice of the European Union. Wolters Kluwer, Alphen aan den Rijn
Ştefan O (2020) COVID-19 soft law: voluminous, effective, legitimate? A research agenda. European Papers 5:663–670. https://www.europeanpapers.eu/en/europeanforum/covid-19-soft-law-voluminous-effective-legitimate
Van Blommestein W (2021) Coronacrisisbeheersing: ervaringen uit de praktijkNederlands Tijdschrift voor Bestuursrecht 174:391–398
Van Dam JCA (2020) Guidance documents of the European Commission in the Dutch legal order (dissertation). Leiden University, Meijers-reeks nr. MI-337
Van Dam JCA (2021) De voorstellen voor een Europese Awb als inspiratiebron voor een beginsel-gestuurde doorwerking voor Europese guidance. Nederlands Tijdschrift voor Bestuursrecht 2021:338–342
Van den Berg C, Mierau J (2020) Regionaal maatwerk, maar hoe dan?. Aletta Jacobs School of Public Health, 03 November 2020, https://www.rug.nl/aletta/blog/regionaal-maatwerk-maar-hoe-dan-03-11-2020
Van den Berg C, Dreef S, Clemens S (2021) Regionaal bestuur tijdens de coronacrisis. Corona Papers, 21 December 2020, pp 1–4
Voorbeeld-beleidskader Twm voor burgemeesters. VNG, 20 November 2020. https://vng.nl/artikelen/tijdelijke-wet-maatregelen-covid-19#beleidskader
Wetsvoorstel dwang asielzoekers vóór de zomer af. Binnenlands Bestuur, 15 April 2022. https://www.binnenlandsbestuur.nl/sociaal/wet-gedwongen-asielopvang-dichterbij
Wierenga AJ (2020) Noodverordeningen in coronacrisis despotisch van aardRechtsgeleerdheid Magazijn Themis 2020:238–240
Wierenga AJ, Schilder J, Brouwer J (2020) Aanpak coronacrisis niet houdbaar. Nederlands Juristenblad 2020:1317

Clara Van Dam is a legal advisor at the Council of State of the Netherlands (*Raad van State*) and guest staff member at the Department of Constitutional and Administrative Law at Leiden University, the Netherlands. Any views and opinions expressed in this article are solely those of the author. They do not represent the views of the Council of State.

Part V
Concluding Comments

Conclusion: Are Legal Systems Converging or Diverging?

Emilie Ghio

Discussions around the phenomena of legal convergence and divergence have been discussed vigorously in the legal literature. Decades later, the debate over whether legal systems are converging or diverging is still ongoing. Studies in convergence or divergence have traditionally adopted a purely thematic approach, i.e. comparatively studying whether one area of law is converging across countries[1] or a common law versus civil law dichotomy.[2] However, nowadays, national legal systems do not exist in isolation from one another; they interact and conduct a 'legal dialogue', which support their improvement, development, and overall change. Therefore, it is impossible to truly determine whether legal convergence is happening without conducting a cross-legal disciplines study.

At a time when the world seems to be in a state of disintegration following several successive crises, one may question the timeliness of discussions around convergence. Jean Monnet famously wrote that 'people only accept change when they are faced with necessity, and only recognize necessity when a crisis is upon them [. . .]'[3] It is true that the world is in shambles. Circling back to the discussion presented in the introduction, the number of crises in the last two decades has been at an all-times high, while their nature has been extremely varied, ranging from economic crises to global pandemics.

The chapters of this books have analysed how specific areas of law have evolved over the last 20 years in selected jurisdictions, with a view to determining whether, on the whole, legal systems are actually converging in times of crisis. As explained

[1] Naude (2019); Siems (2008); van Niekerk (2002); Mullineux (2007); Robertson and Tilbury (2016); Goanta (2016).

[2] Mattei and Pres (2008); Nottage (2001).

[3] Monnet (1978), p. 109.

E. Ghio (✉)
University of Edinburgh, Edinburgh, UK
e-mail: Emilie.Ghio@ed.ac.uk

E. Ghio, R. Perlingeiro (eds.), *Are Legal Systems Converging or Diverging?*,
https://doi.org/10.1007/978-3-031-38180-5_18

in the chapter entitled "Terminology", legal convergence aims to apply similar legal responses to similar facts or situations (in the case of this book, crises), irrespective of the place in which they occur or of the domestic elements involved. In ordinary language, 'convergence' is commonly defined as '[the] fact that two or more things, ideas, etc. become similar or come together'[4] and in evolutionary theory, as the 'independent development of similar traits or features in unrelated species or lineages.'[5] Therefore, convergence is the process by which legal systems become *more similar*. Convergence is a spontaneous phenomenon, whereby states borrow standards, principles, and rules from other jurisdictions or supranational/international entities and organisations without necessarily abandoning their own. 'Legislators look at the neighboring cooking pots, taste different dishes, and select what suits them best.'[6] Convergence is a process of legal emulation, of gradual adaptation of states to each other's legislation, rules, and standards. It is an organic process which leads to the conscious—or more rarely, unconscious—agreement among individual states of what constitutes best practices. 'In practical terms, the legal point of convergence might be nothing more than the meeting of minds on a given legal matter, which is followed by political agreement and legal implementation.'[7] Convergence is usually the result of the fact that states are faced with the same problems and therefore, opt for the same solutions. As David Nelken has pointed out, '[b]orrowing other peoples' law is just a method of speeding up the process of finding legal solutions to similar problems—a process being encouraged all the more by the pressures towards convergence brought about by globalisation.'[8]

This is particularly true in times of crisis, as 'global crises require global solutions'[9] and because national strategies are not always enough or adequate. As discussed in chapter "Terminology", a crisis is an unexpected, abrupt shock, which compels political and legal actors to take a new set of decisions with a sense of urgency. In other words, a crisis is a situation which cannot be resolved with existing rules or tools, and which leads to a legal change. Therefore, crises challenge countries' legal systems and prompted some institutional responses to tackle perceived shortcomings in specific legal fields. As highlighted in the Introduction of this book, the crises witnessed by the world over the last two decades have highlighted two paradoxical tendencies:

(i) increased cooperation and a natural phenomenon of legal convergence as States find common solutions to common problems; or
(ii) a preference for state-centric solutions, which prioritise domestic interests, a rejection of supranational standards and harmonisation efforts and a protection

[4]Definition of 'convergence' in the Cambridge Dictionary (2021).

[5]Definition of 'convergence' in the Merriam-Webster Dictionary (2021).

[6]Mistelis (2000), p. 1069.

[7]Platsas (2017), pp. 8–9.

[8]Nelken (2002), p. 27.

[9]Lomborg (2004).

of domestic sovereignty, possibly leading to a phenomenon of legal disintegration.

The authors in this book have attempted to determine which tendency has been more prominent over the last 20 years. The position can be summarised as follows:

Area of law	Country	Convergence	Divergence
Bankruptcy	United States		x[a]
Labour law	United Kingdom	x	
Consumer law	Ghana	x	
Family law	Chile	x	
Contract law	Germany	x[b]	
Environmental law	China	x	
Healthcare law	Denmark		x
Immigration law	Russia	x	
Social rights	Australia	x[c]	

[a]While US bankruptcy law may not have converged with foreign laws or international standards, many jurisdictions around the world have mirrored its approach to rescue, especially by adopting rescue mechanisms copying chapter "Healthcare Law in Denmark"
[b]It should be noted that while German contract law has significantly converged with EU supranational standard, this phenomenon of convergence has not been the result of crises
[c]However, it should be noted that in the absence of systematic protection of social rights in Australia, their regulation follows a patchwork approach. In times of crisis, while the position is uneven and depends on each individual right, Beth Gaze (chapter "Social Rights in Australia") suggests that convergence is prevailing

The analyses provided in the chapters of this book seem to point to the fact that overall, in times of crisis, legal systems tend to converge, rather than diverge. This supports Alan Watson's polemical claim that legal transplants are not only the most common method of legal development, but should also be considered 'socially easy'. Watson defined social ease as: 'whatever opposition there might be from the bar or legislator, it remains true that legal rules move easily and are accepted into the system without too great difficulty.'[10]

The discussions in this book also reveal that while convergence is happening, it takes place in different ways. There can be convergence of legal systems on a top-down (contract law in Germany) basis, and on a bottom-up basis (environmental law in China); at a regional level (contract law in Germany) and at a global level (family law in Chile). Convergence can be substantive (social rights in Australia) and procedural (immigration law in Russia).

The chapters in this book also reveal that, over the last two decades, there have been two prevailing factors behind this phenomenon of legal convergence. First, legal convergence is primarily the result of acculturation, driven by the desire of individuals to fit in with a reference group of modern states.[11] International

[10]Watson (1974), pp. 95–96.

[11]Goodman and Jinks (2005), pp. 983–998; Goodman and Jinks (2013).

interactions generate a convergence of legal preferences which, in turn, leads to legal convergence (or institutional isomorphism in the words of Ryan Goodman and Derek Jinks.[12] Second, another factor of legal convergence is rooted in the premise that legal rules will drift towards efficiency over time. According to John Merryman and colleagues, there is often a unique optimal solution to a legal problem.[13] Therefore, countries will naturally converge towards the same rule when faced with the same legal problem, which is often the case in times of crisis. In the comparative law literature, this process is referred to as natural convergence. 'Different legal systems will give the same or very similar solutions, even as to detail, to the same problems of life, despite the great differences in their historical development, conceptual structure, and style of operations.'[14]

What, then, of Pierre Legrand's claim that 'legal systems are not converging'? Antonios Platsas[15] rightly points out that:

> Legrand [. . .] seemed to have committed the mistake of looking for a perfect world of legal convergence in a world of imperfection in human affairs. Practically, Legrand was advocating perfect convergence: a utopia. Such a utopia will never exist [. . .] Thus, perfect harmonization of legal systems is a utopia [. . .] As such, Legrand might be wrong in inferring that the apparent lack of perfect [convergence] of [. . .] legal systems constitutes an impossibility for the whole of the convergence exercise between legal systems.[16]

In times of crisis, legal systems certainly seem to be converging towards the adoption of similar rules, standards, and solutions. Therefore, it is our argument that crises are, in fact, a vector for convergence.

References

Cambridge Dictionary (2021)

Goanta C (2016) Convergence in European consumer sales law. Intersentia, Cambridge

Goodman R, Jinks D (2005) International law and state socialization: conceptual, empirical, and normative challenges. Duke Law J 54:983–998

Goodman R, Jinks D (2013) Socializing states: promoting human rights through international law. Oxford University Press, Oxford

Lomborg B (ed) (2004) Global crises, global solutions. Cambridge University Press, Cambridge

Mattei U, Pres L (2008) Civil law and common law: toward Convergence? In: Caldeira G et al (eds) The Oxford handbook of law and politics. Oxford University Press, Oxford, pp 267–280

Merriam-Webster Dictionary (2021)

Merryman J et al (1994) The civil law tradition: Europe, Latin America and East Asia. Michie Company, Charlottesville

---

[12] Ibid.

[13] Merryman et al. (1994).

[14] Zweigert and Kötz (1998), p. 39.

[15] See also chapter "The Concept of Legal Convergence".

[16] Platsas (2017), p. 16.

Mistelis L (2000) Regulatory aspects: Globalization, harmonization, legal transplants, and law reform – some fundamental observations. Int Lawyer 34:1055–1069
Monnet J (1978) Memoirs. Doubleday, Garden City
Mullineux A (2007) Financial sector convergence and corporate governance. J Financ Regul Compl 15:8–19
Naude T (2019) Fragmentation versus convergence of consumer law within one legal system and across legal systems: an African perspective. J Consum Policy 43:11–33
Nelken D (2002) Legal transplants and beyond: of disciplines and metaphors. In: Harding A, Örücü E (eds) Comparative law in the 21st century. Kluwer Law International, London, pp 19–27
Nottage L (2001) Comment on civil law and common law: two different paths leading to the same goal. Victoria Univ Wellington Law Rev 32:843–852
Platsas A (2017) The harmonisation of national legal systems. Strategic models and factors. Edward Elgar Publishing, Cheltenham
Robertson A, Tilbury M (2016) The common law of obligations. Divergence and Unity. Hart Publishing, Oxford
Siems M (2008) Convergence in shareholder law. Cambridge University Press, Cambridge
Van Niekerk G (2002) The convergence of legal systems in Southern Africa. Comp Int Law J South Afr 35:308–318
Watson A (1974) Legal transplants: an approach to comparative law. Scottish Academic Press, Edinburgh
Zweigert K, Kötz H (1998) An introduction to comparative law. Oxford University Press, Oxford

Emilie Ghio is a lecturer in Corporate and Insolvency Law at the University of Edinburgh, Scotland, United Kingdom.

The manufacturer's authorised representative in the EU is Springer Nature Customer Service Centre GmbH, Europaplatz 3, 69115 Heidelberg, Germany. If you have any concerns regarding our products, please contact ProductSafety@springernature.com

Printed and bound by CPI Group (UK) Ltd, Croydon, CR0 4YY
28/09/2026
02224070-0011